THE GRAND SCAM

THE GRAND SCAM

HOW BARRY TANNENBAUM CONNED SOUTH AFRICA'S BUSINESS ELITE

ROB ROSE

Published by Zebra Press
an imprint of Random House Struik (Pty) Ltd
Reg. No. 1966/003153/07
Wembley Square, First Floor, Solan Road, Gardens, Cape Town, 8001
PO Box 1144, Cape Town, 8000, South Africa

www.zebrapress.co.za

First published 2013

1 3 5 7 9 10 8 6 4 2

PUBLISHER: Marlene Fryer
MANAGING EDITOR: Robert Plummer
EDITOR: Mark Ronan
PROOFREADER: Bronwen Leak
COVER DESIGNER: Georgia Demertzis
TEXT DESIGNER: Jacques Kaiser
TYPESETTER: Monique Cleghorn
INDEXER: Sanet le Roux

Set in 10.5 pt on 13.5 pt Minion

Printed and bound by Logo Print

ISBN 978 1 77022 621 0 (print)
ISBN 978 1 77022 622 7 (ePub)
ISBN 978 1 77022 623 4 (PDF)

Contents

Preface

The story of Barry Tannenbaum isn't a new one. It is a record on repeat that has played out in forgotten corners of the country through the 'vrotmelk' scandal in the 1960s, the Krion scam in the early 1990s, the Miracle 2000 fraud a few years later, and the Brett Kebble swindle during the early years of this century.

How an innocuous former advertising salesman in his early forties, described as a 'great human being', managed to dupe South Africa's cleverest and most financially savvy out of so much money makes it perhaps the most audacious of all South Africa's cons.

I realised a few years back, after I'd worked as a journalist for a while at publications like *Business Day*, the *Financial Mail* and the *Sunday Times*, that this country has so many spectacular stories to which few other countries could lay claim. These stories often make sensational headlines for a few months then flame out into a series of scrappy ill-informed updates, anorexic in detail and insight. Institutional memory fades quickly, and before you know it it's the same thing all over again in a new dress, ten years later. As if it has never happened before.

But I realised that the Tannenbaum story, labyrinthine in its development and intriguing in its peculiar detail, was one of those that demanded to be set to paper as a narrative, told from front to back so that, next time it happens, we'll know that this time it isn't different. The Americans, with a rich history of narrative journalism, do this well. At last count, there were more than ten books on Bernie Madoff, deconstructing that country's biggest fraud and tabulating the lessons from it. Yet on Tannenbaum, who fleeced South Africans with a fearful symmetry to Madoff, we have nothing.

My goal, based on the new information I found out in the past year, was to provide a recipe book for how a Ponzi scheme is brewed, as well as provide insight into what personal demons would lead someone to do this.

I first happened upon the story as any journalist would, a tip-off back in May 2009, and I wrote about it extensively at the time. But drawing together the strands into a cohesive narrative wasn't easy. Many investors didn't want to speak about it, understandably, as it had rudely embarrassed them. To the fifty or so investors who did have the courage to confront their own painful past on-the-record, as well as the members of Barry's family, the investigators, lawyers, bankers and public officials, thank you for helping tell a story that should prove instructive to the country.

Distilling the details, personal stories and numerous documents onto the pages you're now reading was a grind, not least because whole sections of my house were commandeered and promptly buried underneath about 200 lever arch files of court documents, transcripts and bank statements. It demanded endless patience from my wife Janice, not least because when I started writing, my son Jamie was three months old. Ten months later, he's had his first birthday and he's tripped over many of those files while learning to walk. Simply thanking my family for their indulgence doesn't come close to cutting it.

Many other people helped too: my editors Robert Plummer and Mark Ronan must have torn out their hair as they saw yet another email land in their inbox with yet more final, last-last-minute changes. And I can still taste the first chocolate I got as a 'reward' for writing the first chapter of this book in Paige Williams's Nieman writing class at Harvard, where I learnt a lot about telling the true story. Hopefully, this is a true story that will resonate beyond simply Barry Tannenbaum.

ROB ROSE
OCTOBER 2013

Abbreviations

AFU: Assest Forfeiture Unit
ANC: African National Congress
APIs: active pharmaceutical ingredients
ARVs: antiretrovirals
BEE: black economic empowerment
Didata: Dimension Data
DTC: Depository Trust Company
ENS: Edward Nathan Sonnenbergs
FNB: First National Bank
ICT: Imperial Crown Trading
IRBA: Independent Regulatory Board for Auditors
IRS: Internal Revenue Service
JSE: Johannesburg Stock Exchange
JTA: Jewish Telegraphic Agency
MCC: Medicines Control Council
NPA: National Prosecuting Authority
PwC: PricewaterhouseCoopers
RMB: Rand Merchant Bank
SAPI: South African Pharmacists in Industry
SARS: South African Revenue Service
SEC: Securities and Exchange Commission
UN: United Nations
WHO: World Health Organization

Prologue

'Are you sitting down?' asked the voice on the end of the line. 'I've got the story of your life.'

Journalists are told that a lot. Usually it's a whopping exaggeration. Usually it's just the story of the caller's life. Perhaps good enough for a 400-word page-nine filler. With a big picture. If you're lucky.

But this time, the caller was Warren Goldblatt, a five-foot-eight investigative veteran who runs his own 'intelligence company', Specialised Security Group. The first time you see him, you're struck by his resemblance to the box-shaped children's character Mr Strong. Goldblatt, who operates out of an innocuous office park in the industrial area of Marlboro, has a mystique about him.

The rumour, whispered behind lowered fingers in some circles, was that Goldblatt's company was a Mossad front. But then, an equally prominent rumour was that he assisted al-Qaeda cells in South Africa, so you took your water-cooler chatter with a taste of salt.

What was true was that Goldblatt got sharp intelligence. Thanks to an extensive network of informants in government departments you didn't even know existed, Goldblatt would drop several facts into any casual conversation, each of which could easily be the subject of a Pulitzer Prize–winning investigation. If you had the tentacles to confirm the spectacular tales, that is.

But Goldblatt had come in for some serious heat in the previous four years for supposedly using illegal tactics to spy on his targets. It was scary stuff: stories emerged in the press detailing how, for not much more than R100, he could get you a copy of someone's bank accounts or their telephone records. Illegal, sure, but then everyone was doing it. Goldblatt denied it. 'I'm not Rockefeller, I'm the other fella,' was a favourite line he trotted out, as if to suggest that had he broken the rules, he would be a lot richer.

It was Goldblatt who called me out of the blue with the story of my life. 'You might want to see what you can find about someone called Barry Tannenbaum,' he said. 'And a lawyer called Dean Rees.'

I hadn't heard of either. Goldblatt said I'd know about them soon enough. He added that we needed to meet. 'I've got a library for you,' he told me. We planned to meet a few days later, with his client – one of the 'investors'.

Two hours later, I got another call, from a lawyer I knew. A reliable source of scandal, but as jumpy as a colt. 'I've got the story of your life,' he told me. 'We need to talk.' There was a big meeting the following week at law firm Routledge Modise, he said, about this massive investment scheme that had gone bust. 'Stands to embarrass the whole country, big CEOs who lost out. Looks like it's a scam,' he assured me. 'I'll call you later with details,' he said, 'but don't tell anyone, it's a big secret.' Then he hung up.

I was intrigued. But this Barry Tannenbaum was nowhere to be found: anonymous on the internet, absent from all the databases I could lay my hands on. The only thing Barry Tannenbaum had done until that point, it seemed, was to work at Times Media – the media conglomerate that owns the *Sunday Times* and *Business Day* newspapers – during the late 1990s, peddling advertisements. Then he'd disappeared.

A week later, I snuck into the Routledge Modise meeting, and was struck by the similarities with the Bernie Madoff scandal in the US, which was just unravelling. As with Madoff, hundreds of people thronged into the law firm's auditorium, as confused as each other by the presence of the others in the room.

The story was remarkable. This Barry Tannenbaum, it turned out, was the mastermind of South Africa's largest scam, its most audacious raid on the pockets of South Africa's rich, and the most embarrassing episode in the careers of the well-heeled executives who had parked their SUVs outside Routledge Modise.

Straight after that meeting, I called Barry Tannenbaum on his cellphone in Australia. He answered immediately, and wasn't shaken by my call in the least. After I introduced myself as a journalist from the *Financial Mail*, he said, 'Oh, yes. Do you know I worked there? For your company?'

Faced with a journalist posing awkward questions and dropping words like 'fraud' and 'Ponzi scheme', this Barry Tannenbaum just wanted to reminisce.

Taken aback by Barry's nonchalance – even if it was a pretence – I figured it best to put my questions down in an email. Perhaps it would help him realise the gravity of the situation – after all, *he* hadn't spoken to the investors, spitting flames and darkly threatening a trip to Sydney to 'sort him out'.

I wrote a breezy enough email: 'Like I said on the phone, I really want to present your side of the story accurately, so that the full truth emerges. Some of the investors I spoke to believe you're the bad guy in all this, who sold them a line, and pocketed the proceeds. So I wanted to give you the forum to tell people what happened.' I included twelve questions, one of which was: 'There was much talk this morning that criminal charges would be laid, and attempts would be made to have you extradited back to South Africa. Would you return back to South Africa to deal with this matter voluntarily?'

Barry replied immediately: 'Thanks, Rob, email received, and I will work on it over the weekend. Have a good day. Kind regards, Barry.'

Two days later, he hadn't responded, so I pressed him for a reply. After midnight on Sunday, Barry wrote: 'Hi, Rob, sorry to have missed your call. Been very busy this side, as you can imagine. I will get to responding to your email tomorrow. When is the deadline? Thanks and regards, Barry.'

I replied, saying my deadline was the next day, Monday, imploring him to please reply and explain what had happened, lest we unfairly brand him as a con artist.

'Thanks, Rob, will make sure I do,' Barry replied in an email from his Black-Berry. 'What time in SA will you need it? Do you know of any other papers or publications that are covering the story? Thanks, Barry.'

He seemed relaxed, but again, it was long after midnight in Australia.

Over the next two days, he deflected my pestering. On Monday morning, he wrote: 'Hi, Rob. Thanks, all going very well. Been in meetings all day with very important guys. Will try you later. Looks like I am winning the race! Will call you later … Barry.'

Later that day, he emailed again: 'I am still very busy here, and looks like it will go on all night. In the meantime, all I can say is that I deny the truth of the aspersions that have been levelled against me and the fanciful allegations that are being made. I will come back to you in due course with more detailed responses. I would still very much like to use you as my forum. I am sure you can understand that what I am doing at the moment is very important in providing evidence to support my innocence. I will be in touch soon. Thanks and kind regards, Barry.'

Time was exceptionally tight. The *Financial Mail* magazine was being laid out, the 3 000 words I'd written that would break the story were being edited and the cover picture was being crafted. The only picture available anywhere was one of Barry Tannenbaum donating a Torah to a Chabad house in KwaZulu-Natal: the Torah had to be airbrushed out. The words on the cover read 'SA's Madoff?'.

Still Barry dodged my calls and ignored the emails asking him for some explanation. At about 9 p.m., he sent another email, again saying he would try to call later.

At 11 p.m. Australian time, Barry said he was 'still stuck in meetings. Going to be a long one.' He said: 'I will only be able to respond to your questions once I have finished my investigations. I am not sure who the responsible parties are, but intend finding out.' He added, as he had all week: 'I will still try give you a call later.' He signed the email 'many thanks'.

The dice had been thrown. All journalists have the fear, the cold-sweat paraly-sis, as soon as the button has been pushed, and their story is spirited along the cable to the printers, and then into the distribution trucks, and then onto the shelves: What if I have it wrong? What if I've overlooked something, some reasonable explanation? What if it was a legitimate business, not some Madoff-style Ponzi scheme?

You don't sleep that night, as if closing your eyes would somehow halt the printing presses from causing the damage that you *know* the story will.

Wednesday morning, a person called Darryl Ackerman called. 'I'm Barry's lawyer,' he said. 'I understand you've been saying all kinds of things about my client which aren't true.' The story had been printed, but wouldn't be on the shelves until midday, so Ackerman didn't know it was too late to stop anything. I told him. 'Well, if it's too late, it's too late. We'll deal with it as we must,' Ackerman said. He put down the phone.

The *Financial Mail* is usually delivered to some newsagents by about midday on Wednesday, and by that evening it had sold out. Investigative magazine *Noseweek* had clearly been tipped off too, because as soon as the editor, Martin Welz, had heard about the *Financial Mail* story late on Wednesday, he called around town, trying to get a copy. Welz immediately appeared on Radio 702, seeking to break the story. To the public, of course, it means nothing if a story emerges at midday in a magazine or 6 p.m. on a radio show. But to journalists like me and Welz, such competitive anxieties are fundamental to how well we do our jobs.

Within hours, the internet had lit up as searches for 'Barry Tannenbaum' flooded Google. The story of Barry's 'investment scheme' was intriguing: son of a pharmaceutical empire and using the Madoff template to siphon cash from South Africa's elite. It made for easy telling. As the daily newspapers flashed Barry's Torah-donation photo across its front pages, new details drip-fed through to the public, reinforcing the narrative.

Four years later, the story of *how* he did it is well known, as are the headline flashes of *who* he did it to. But what wasn't known, what hadn't properly been answered, was *why* he did it. What drives a man to betray his impressive family legacy, his community, his friends?

Why would Barry Tannenbaum, a portly, unobtrusive man in his late forties – he appears as indistinct as anyone else you'd pass by in a neighbourhood hardware store – construct a complex, darkly insidious fraud, complete with a sophisticated series of forged invoices and bank statements?

In the four years since the news articles first appeared, new facts and details have emerged that throw a sensational light on what Barry Deon Tannenbaum was doing in the death hours between midnight and 4 a.m. in his Sydney house, and why he was doing it.

This is that story.

1

White knuckles

'It looks like we've all been caught in a gigantic Ponzi scheme.'
— Lawyer Dean Rees to 'investors' (June 2009)

The Johannesburg winter had dug in its claws, but that wasn't why Dean Rees's hands were trembling when the thirty-nine-year-old lawyer stood up to face the mob of shell-shocked millionaires.

You could argue that it would not be entirely legitimate to describe an elite of 200 collared and primped professionals, sausaged elbow to elbow, into the genteel surroundings of a law firm's auditorium, as a 'mob'.

Nor, strictly speaking, were all of them millionaires – especially now, at any rate.

But then, legitimacy wasn't exactly enjoying much currency at that moment. Legitimacy had flown out the window a long time ago.

Pale and startled, Rees stood at the front of the auditorium clutching a folder of papers, as tightly as a poker player does his cards. Glowing under the unrelenting downlights, he didn't open the folder to glance at the papers as he began to speak.

The investors facing him that cold Thursday morning in June 2009 were taking up every inch of the cavernous auditorium, either seated in the chairs randomly scattered near the front, propped against the nearest pillar or wall, or jostling for standing space at the rear.

Almost exclusively white, about half were older than sixty, which made it more difficult to discern the ripples of concern on their foreheads from general weathering. Many of them appeared furtive, as ill at ease as Rees, glancing round the room skittishly without recognition in their eyes.

When he spoke, Rees said he knew how concerned 'all of us are' with finding out what had happened to the money. Rees said he was 'doing his best' to figure out what had happened and that he was 'as shocked as anyone by all this'.[1]

Rees said he'd only figured out there was a problem a few weeks before when angry investors had confronted him about why they hadn't been paid, as promised. He'd contacted Barry, but hadn't got a straight answer. This was the first mention of Barry, the supposed kingpin, the man at the centre of the drama.

Rees said he had then contacted Aspen Pharmacare to find out why it, one of South Africa's two largest pharmaceutical firms, hadn't paid the R140 million it supposedly owed Barry for pharmaceutical supplies. (Technically, that R140 million wasn't owed to Barry Tannenbaum. Rather, it was owed to Frankel Chemicals, the company in which these investors believed they had put their cash. Incorrectly believed, it turned out.)

Rees then opened the folder for the first time. He extracted a single piece of paper, which was dated 19 May and signed by Aspen's senior executive Bert Marais, and began to read: '... as of the date of this letter, there are no monies due and payable to Frankel Chemicals by Aspen Pharmacare ... the signature on the [invoice] is false, together with the company letterhead.'

Rees put the letter down. 'The invoice was forged,' he told the audience. 'They don't owe Frankel any money.'

Rees told the audience that he'd then gone to Frankel Chemicals, where someone called Arlene Tannenbaum had apparently 'shocked' him when she extracted the company's accounts, which showed debts of only R2 million to investors. This from a company that had taken more than R3.7 billion in 'investments' from people in the room. This from a company whose glossy brochures boasted that it was making R6 billion in annual sales.

Rees paused. The audience remained mute, staring at him. The penny clearly hadn't dropped entirely, so he punched in the bottom line.

'It appears it was a Ponzi scheme,' he said. 'It looks like we've all been caught in a gigantic Ponzi scheme.'

Still no one shifted position. It was as if he was talking about someone else, someone else's money. They waited for Rees to continue, to reveal some punchline. This wasn't what they wanted to hear.

While it was clear from looking around that many of the people in the room were old, wealthy and Jewish, there were exceptions.

Uraj Tewary, a thirty-two-year-old call-centre administrator from Johannesburg, was watching quietly from the back, ruing his decision to plough R800 000 (roughly $80 000) – including his wife's entire pension after she had lost her job – into Barry's scheme.

'My wife is due to have a baby any day now, and I don't have money to pay the doctor,' he said later, after the meeting had finished. As if someone had a solution for him.

Allon Rock, a professional tennis coach in his early forties, was even worse off. Rock had cashed in his investments, taken out a second mortgage on his house and ploughed everything into this 'get-poor-quick' scheme. 'I've got an extra bond, a daughter that needs orthodontic treatments,' he said later that day.

The common thread was that all of them had assumed they were part of

Barry's coveted inner circle, a group of less than fifty people for whom he had drawn back the curtain and shared the secrets of his fantastic investment elixir.

Unfortunately, Barry had emigrated to Australia two years before. According to the lawyer, Dean Rees, Barry wasn't likely to come back either. Instead, for months already, Barry had been relying on his two agents in South Africa to handle the investments and repayments. These agents were a disagreeable, fast-talking, Lamborghini-obsessed lawyer named Darryl Leigh and a flashy attorney with a patchy legal career named Dean Rees – the man who was now addressing them.

Having unveiled the forged invoice, Rees said he'd confronted Barry. Barry had then apparently admitted that certain invoices were indeed 'fake'. Barry hadn't said why he'd done this, but it seemed pretty clear to Rees. Barry, it appeared, was a very bad guy, and it wasn't clear to what extent his business had ever been real.

Rees stopped speaking and invited questions. Initially, no one spoke, as if fearing being identified, as if doing so would somehow compromise the odds of clawing back any of the cash they'd given to Barry to invest for them.

Then, Mervyn Serebro, the once celebrated CEO of supermarket chain OK Bazaars, stepped up to the confessional. Serebro said he felt violated. He described how members of his family had sold their houses and invested that cash with Barry. 'What must they do now?' he asked.

Warren Drue, a brash, spiky-haired mergers-and-acquisitions lawyer from Routledge Modise, the law firm where the meeting was taking place, said Serebro's family weren't alone in losing their shirt. 'We've all been devastated ... it appears there was no fundamental business, so the money we've invested must be gone.'

Though the tightly wound Rees was the main act of the day, it was Drue who was really running the meeting, based on the fact that his firm was hosting it. It was Drue who had kicked off events by introducing Rees, before sitting down directly in front of him, as if to provide protection were someone to lose it and attack him.

But the angrier elements in the audience did not speak up, remaining menacingly silent instead, stewing on thoughts of culpability and vengeance. For them, the perpetrator was no longer 'Barry', the affable Santa Claus 'incapable of hurting a fly', as someone later described him.

Instead, they could only spit out his surname: Tannenbaum.

* * *

On that Thursday, 4 June 2009, the name Barry Tannenbaum wouldn't have netted a single entry on Google, let alone a flicker of recognition at any one of Joburg's affluent society dinner parties that would take place that weekend.

Of course, some of the city's wealthiest citizens, its corporate elite, who lived behind twenty-foot walls with round-the-clock security guards in the city's old-money northern suburbs, had known Barry for years. Based on this, they had unwisely trusted him with truckloads of their money. But most wouldn't have admitted it publicly, either before or after he was exposed.

Perhaps the most respected of Tannenbaum's victims was Norman Lowenthal, a bespectacled seventy-one-year-old former stockbroker, businessman and serial director. Along with his accountant son, Howard, Lowenthal was instantly recognisable as a proper blue-blooded member of Joburg's corporate aristocracy.

For three years until 2000, Lowenthal had chaired the Johannesburg Stock Exchange, Africa's largest stock exchange and ranked the eighteenth-largest in the world. With $1 trillion worth of listed stock, the JSE is the epicentre of Africa's financial world.

Appropriately, the JSE's glass-encased headquarters bobs in the centre of a sea of glistening skyscrapers in Sandton, a suburb ten kilometres from central Johannesburg, which is moated by a constantly flowing river of Mercedes-Benz sedans. It is dubbed, with equal measures of scorn, envy and awe, 'Africa's richest mile'.

It wasn't always like that. A century ago, when gold prospectors shook off mining dust before entering the overtraded taverns on Harrison Street in central Johannesburg, companies jostled for position in the coveted city centre. But as inner-city crime soared and cufflinked drivers were hauled out of their BMWs at gunpoint, companies fled north, up the see-sawing Oxford Road, to Sandton, where the security guards at least bothered to create the illusion that they were in control.

It was Lowenthal who relocated the JSE from the city centre to what he called the 'new financial centre' of Sandton in 1999. 'We are joining the migration from the Johannesburg city centre where conditions have deteriorated and made it difficult to recruit staff,' he said at the time.

Lowenthal was street smart, and should have known a bit about investment. So why would he plough millions into an investment scheme that promised returns in some cases of beyond 219 per cent a year? Especially with Tannenbaum, whom he barely knew?

How could Lowenthal's son, Howard, an accountant who ran a stockbroking firm selling bona fide investment schemes all day long, have thought that Tannenbaum ran a legitimate business, with such stratospheric investment returns?

Later that week, Howard Lowenthal tried to answer these questions, as much for himself as for others asking. 'We were told Frankel Chemicals was a high-margin business,' he said. 'There are many lending businesses charging 5 per cent interest a month, and so it seemed we were being paid a similar return for bridging finance. At the time, I thought being paid interest of 12 per cent over three months was high, but not entirely unfeasible.'[2]

If you annualise that 12 per cent, it comes to 48 per cent over the course of a single year. Far higher than you'd get in most legitimate businesses, of course, but still less than the 219 per cent that Tannenbaum was offering to some investors. If you had invested R1 000 under that scenario in January, you'd expect to get back R3 190 just after Christmas.

For two weeks after the story broke, the country was gripped in a curious cocktail of voyeurism and *Schadenfreude*, as more names of high-profile victims – the very cream of Joburg's financial society – tumbled out.

Sean Summers was the first high-profile victim to publicly acknowledge he'd been suckered. 'Yes, I was a participant,' he said, before joking, 'but unlike with food extortion, we appear to know who the perpetrators are in this case.' (Pick n Pay, one of South Africa's largest supermarket chains, which Summers headed until 2007, had been hit a few years earlier by an extortionist threatening to poison food in the stores unless the company paid him.)

Summers, it later became clear, had lost R19 million through his dalliance with Tannenbaum.

As CEO of Pick n Pay (market value: R17 billion), Summers had been roundly lauded as 'a visionary', 'an exemplary leader' and one of corporate South Africa's brightest lights. Summers himself cultivated this image. 'If you're not taking risks, having fun, you're in the wrong business,' he told the *Financial Mail* magazine in 2005. 'If this was just about the money, I'd be working overseas like some of our sports stars. But this is about commitment to a company and a country.'[3]

If Summers had considered Barry Tannenbaum's investment scheme a risk worth taking, well, who else shouldn't?

There were some who refused to speak, or to acknowledge their involvement at all. And the way that corporate big shots who were involved handled their 'outing' spoke volumes about their character.

Take Jeremy Ord, the chairman of South Africa's largest home-grown technology company, Dimension Data. Rumours of Ord's involvement rippled around Joburg, but when asked directly, Ord denied it emphatically, claiming that it had happened to 'some of his friends'.[4]

Well, it turned out that this wasn't the whole truth. Emails, spreadsheets and documents later confirmed that, yes, Ord had invested big with Tannenbaum. Only after being directly confronted did Ord eventually admit his involvement. For Ord, perhaps the biggest lesson of the Tannenbaum debacle was that perhaps it would have been better to use the words 'no comment'.

Tom Lawless, the gruff former CEO of South Africa's Bond Exchange, which trades more than R1.5 trillion a year in government and company bonds, also attended the Routledge Modise meeting.[5] Lawless had been sitting mute towards the back of the auditorium, but he must have wished he'd been wearing a large hat as well. When contacted later that day to be asked if he had invested, Lawless snapped back: 'How do you know that?' When it was pointed out that he had filled out the list of names and telephone numbers at the meeting, he relented. 'Well, it's quite a painful thing for me, to be honest,' he said. 'I don't want to discuss it.'

This was another point about the Tannenbaum scheme. Privacy was high priority, privacy was *essential*, for this well-to-do clan. Being known as stupid, reckless or just plain unlucky for having been trapped in a Ponzi scheme wouldn't have charmed investors in Dimension Data, for example. (A year after the event, after the Tannenbaum scheme had hit prime-time television news as far away as Australia and the UK, one of the wealthier investors confided to a friend: 'If someone else calls me stupid, I'll pop him one.')

For many investors, any hint that the media were aware of this swindle would have driven them into hiding. They certainly wouldn't have attended the meeting at Routledge Modise, or revealed their exposure to the scam. Notice of this gathering was meant to remain secret.

On 2 June, two days before the meeting, Rees had sent a two-page letter to some of the investors. 'Dear participant,' it read, 'the writer's status as chief operating officer and general power of attorney were revoked yesterday. The commencement of the audit yesterday by Deloitte and Touche was not allowed.'

Rees detailed how he had discovered various problems, including that 'purchase orders placed on Frankel are forgeries'.

The letter concluded: 'The writer recommends that a general meeting of all investors be held at 09h00 on Thursday 4 June 2009, where a full briefing will occur. This will take place at Routledge Modise Eversheds ... please call Patrick on 011 519 9000 to confirm attendance.'

Not all the investors who eventually attended the meeting got Rees's notice. But they heard soon enough, as it was whispered along a grapevine that hadn't existed until the previous few weeks. So they simply pitched up.

Had they known that their anguished revelations in the auditorium would be recorded, or that they would be attending the unmasking of South Africa's grandest scam, they would probably have thought twice about coming at all.

* * *

For Dean Rees, the mood in the auditorium that Thursday morning swiftly darkened as the questions from the investors gained pace.

During his speech, Rees had offered to 'investigate' what had happened to their cash. He asked for a 'mandate to get to the bottom of this'. An incoherent rumble crept through the audience. Eyebrows narrowed. Then someone stood up: 'I don't think Dean is the man to do that,' challenged Ian Levitt, a lawyer known to love a good tussle and a good scandal. Levitt was often written off by those he crossed as simply an ambulance-chasing lawyer, but this would be to diminish his prowess for sniffing out the bad guys.

'I wrote to Dean three months ago, saying that the pharmaceutical companies don't unilaterally extend credit terms [like Tannenbaum suggested]. I didn't get a response,' said Levitt.

Warren Goldblatt, dressed in black and wearing an earpiece, had been standing ominously at the back of the auditorium with his client. He spoke up now, echoing Levitt's sentiment. 'I don't think Dean is in a position to spearhead this on behalf of investors either,' he said.

Then Goldblatt directly challenged Rees: 'You emphatically informed us that you had successfully concluded two trades in Hong Kong and the funds would be available shortly … what has happened to these funds?'

Some in the audience nodded, others grumbled their ascent with Goldblatt's sentiment. Rees didn't answer.

Immediately, Warren Drue stood up, turned to face the crowd and held his hands up, a traffic warden trying to redirect the flow. 'Now, this is not a thing about Mr Rees,' he said. 'Dean came forward as a white knight.'

There were a number of dismissive snorts. An elderly man near the back, who also didn't identify himself, added derisively: 'A white knight? He's the one who took my money.'

Why, Goldblatt continued, would anyone allow Rees to 'investigate' what had happened to the cash when he was part of it, when he had earned millions in 'commission' by acting as an agent for the scheme.

Rees protested: 'Why would I fly back here if I was part of it?'

But Drue again killed the discussion. 'We don't need to be blaming people now,' he said. 'We need to find a strategy to track down the money, and Dean is doing his best to help.'

(A year before, Rees had relocated, along with his wife, Dominique, to Switzerland. At the time, he was perhaps the only man in South Africa who described himself as 'commuting' between the two countries, 8 400 kilometres apart.)

Rees backtracked, saying that even if he wasn't involved in any committee, he thought that investors urgently needed to form a group to investigate. Drue suggested the investors write down their names and contact details, and he would 'coordinate' this committee. Clearly, some people weren't happy with Rees having *any* further involvement, but this seemed a workable compromise, initially at any rate. Foxes and henhouses were mentioned in the same breath as the name 'Rees'.

After nearly three hours, the meeting just sort of ended without punctuation, as many of the investors began drifting towards the back of the auditorium to write down their names. Rees was still standing at the front, the survivor of what could have been a far worse assault. He had been smiling, his shoulders noticeably less taut than when he'd begun speaking, but he blanched when he saw a business card that read 'journalist'.

'I'll help you whatever way I can,' he said. 'It's terrible. Really. We couldn't have known.'

* * *

News of the meeting, or of the Tannenbaum Ponzi scheme, wouldn't break publicly for another week. Even then, it would take months for the identities of various investors to emerge. Many of the largest investors have yet to be publicly identified.

Some of them could not stand the embarrassment of Joburg society knowing they had being trapped in such a wretched scheme, knowing that their fêted investment skills had so thoroughly deserted them and they would be accused of indulging in nothing more complicated than raw greed.

For others, it was far worse: the mystique they had built up of having a special power, a magical ability to read the investment markets, to decode the lousy stocks from the winners, had been exposed as a convenient myth. After years devoted to darkened boardrooms, ratifying minutes and reinforcing this myth, some of Tannenbaum's investors could not stomach seeing themselves naked.

So how did it work exactly?

All the investors were wooed with a similar refrain, passed along by word of mouth from those in the know – from someone who had by chance happened to find out about this fantastic opportunity from 'Barry', and mentioned it to someone else.

This 'Barry' would then be implored to expand his 'select club' by just one more person, to allow just one more investor into his 'investment scheme', a scheme run through Frankel Chemicals, an anonymous company with a pleasingly generic name located incongruously in the wealthy residential suburb of Bedfordview.

Reluctantly, 'Barry' would agree. But just as a favour, just this one time, and just because he so loved 'helping' members of the community, just because he was such a nice guy that he wanted to share his good fortune.

And no one must know that the rules were broken to accommodate you. Like children who had stumbled on a magical Easter egg tree, these participants were warned to jealously guard this knowledge. Tell too many people about this secret investment club, and the magic would vanish.

So, to arrive at the crowded auditorium of a Sandton law firm and find out your secret club extended into the hundreds, filled with people also granted admission 'as a special favour', was enough to make you feel 'violated and stupid'.

For this magic Easter egg tree to remain a potent fable for investors, Tannenbaum needed a plausible 'unique investment advantage' that you wouldn't find elsewhere in the world. Something *believable* that could plausibly explain why investors would be paid returns that were hundreds of times more than they would get from any bank or investment elsewhere.

Tannenbaum found this plausibility in HIV/AIDS, a blistering epidemic in a country with the highest infection rate in the world.

In South Africa, HIV/AIDS has been alarmingly, chaotically, out of control. In South Africa, in the age group between the ages of fifteen and forty-nine, 17.3 per cent are estimated to be HIV-positive. By 2011 the United Nations (UN) estimated that 5.6 million South Africans had been infected, and the virus was still spreading at a time when other countries were getting a grip on curbing this beast, if not defeating it outright.[6]

Partly, this impotence was thanks to a lost decade of health management, in which hocus-pocus snake-oil remedies had been proposed as a solution for HIV/AIDS by South Africa's dotty former health minister, Manto Tshabalala-Msimang – a former physician whose grasp on reality in the last few years before her death had receded almost as sharply as her fondness for an odd drink had increased.

Tshabalala-Msimang was derisively called 'Dr Beetroot' for advocating AIDS remedies including garlic and herbs, rather than AIDS drugs 'with unknown side effects' – an attack on antiretroviral drugs, which she characterised as 'toxic'.[7]

Infamously, at the global 2006 International AIDS conference in Toronto, South Africa's exhibition showcased garlic, lemon and beetroot, rather than antiretrovirals. This infuriated the UN's ambassador to Africa for AIDS, Stephen Lewis, who closed the Toronto conference with a blistering attack on South Africa's government, calling it 'obtuse, dilatory and negligent'.[8]

Lewis said South Africa was 'the only country in Africa whose government continues to propound theories more worthy of a lunatic fringe than of a concerned and compassionate state'.[9]

Tshabalala-Msimang responded in a way that was characteristic of her tone-deaf stubbornness: 'We haven't shocked the world, we have told the truth … I don't mind being called Dr Beetroot.'[10]

Playing politics is all very well. But the upshot of this bureaucratic numbskullery was that South Africa had precious few regulations governing the production of antiretroviral drugs. As far as the government was concerned, at least during Dr Beetroot's tenure, these drugs were a sordid poison anyway. The thinking was, you can have all the rules you want for the production of arsenic, but at the end of the day, you're still making arsenic.

Enter Barry Tannenbaum.

In an audit report he signed for Frankel Chemicals, Tannenbaum described his business as that of 'pharmaceutical components'. A description boring enough to cause most people to nod and look away.

The way it worked – well, the way he said it worked, at any rate – was that you, as an investor, would 'finance' the purchase of small components that would ultimately go into making AIDS drugs. These raw materials from countries like India and China, known as active pharmaceutical ingredients, or APIs for short, would be used to make the drugs.

That investor would be 'lending' the cash to Barry's company, Frankel Chemicals, so he could buy the APIs. Then, drug companies, like Aspen Pharmacare or Novartis' generic drugs unit Sandoz, would 'buy' these APIs from Frankel Chemicals, and combine them to make the drugs you would see in a pharmacy and ultimately buy off the shelf.

The theory was that Tannenbaum would then take the money paid him by Aspen or Sandoz and repay the investors a 'return', while keeping a small portion for himself, as an 'intermediary fee'.

Usually, the investors would be asked to stump up cash for a 'consignment' lasting between ten and twelve weeks. Theoretically, they would then be 'repaid with interest' within a few weeks.

But because the money on offer was so mouthwatering, investors would often 'roll over' their investment, allowing Tannenbaum to keep the money to be used for future investments. You could of course take your profit, or even part of it, but given the immense profits on offer to those who rolled over, most did.

There were a few holes in this business plan, however.

The first yawning chasm was this: why didn't Tannenbaum just go to a bank and take out a loan to finance the purchase of these drugs? Then, not only would he be able to keep all the immense profits he was supposedly making, but it would also be less hassle than managing a sprawling network of investors, all with different accounts. After all, what proper businessman likes giving away money to other people that he could keep for himself?

Tannenbaum's answer was that the banks were too full of red tape. Pharmaceutical deals need to be done quickly, on the fly. And he just couldn't wait around while one bureaucrat filled out papers and faxed them to another bureaucrat two floors up, and then waited a week for the funds. It was easier to get short-term finance from individuals.

And as for the super-profits, well, that is just the nature of pharmaceutical firms – they are just that ridiculously profitable. Or so he claimed.

When pressed for evidence of these orders, Tannenbaum would provide letters or invoices from 'clients'. For example, one letter he produced was from drug multinational Pfizer, signed by Bindert K. Vriesema, its vice president for Europe, Middle East and Africa, on 7 March 2008.

It read: 'I, the undersigned ... hereby declare that Frankel Chemicals, PO Box 75804, Garden View 2047, South Africa, are our sole distributors for our active pharmaceutical ingredients in South Africa, and this since March 1994. Our main contact with Frankel Chemicals is Mr Barry Tannenbaum, sales and marketing director.'

He would also produce 'invoices' for immense amounts of money, from Aspen Pharmacare, from Sandoz-Novartis, casual evidence of the river of cash flowing to Tannenbaum and, by extension, his investors.

As it turned out, many of these invoices were blunt forgeries. In some cases, these companies did have some business dealings with Frankel Chemicals. But nothing of the magnitude described in the invoices, nothing running into the hundreds of millions, as Tannenbaum would have the investors believe.

Then there were the heavy secrecy clauses, the almost obsessive requirement that not a word should be breathed to anyone. Ever. About anything.

One investment contract sent to a surgeon, Julius Preddy, in exchange for a R66 245 investment, reads: 'You will not disclose your investment, any documentation in your possession or any details with regard to the financed party/ parties to any third parties, without the prior written consent of the financed party and who, in their sole and absolute discretion, can withhold [that consent].'

Spies have been recruited with less onerous restrictions.

Preddy was to be repaid a 16 per cent return on that R66 245 in only nine weeks. So, within weeks, he could transform R66 245 into R76 844. In this case, as in so many, it was Rees who had drawn up the contract and sent it to Preddy.

But for a Ponzi scheme, it was exactly the design needed: absolute secrecy, a unique investment advantage you could sell, agents on the ground to spread the word covertly. And a queue of people who cannot believe their luck, and think they are one of the chosen few.

Sipping coffee outside Routledge Modise's auditorium after the June meeting, one Johannesburg businessman (who would not give his name) mournfully recounted how he had blown his family's savings against his better judgement. 'Up until last week, my head was telling me it would never work, but my heart was saying "please let it work",' he said. 'I invested first two years ago, and in the end, I had R3.2 million invested with him after two years, even going so far as to selling part of my business to raise the cash. Now I feel stupid.'

Howard Lowenthal describes the way the scheme was sold to him: 'Essentially, Barry borrowed money from me to buy these medical components which he then on-sold, and he'd pay me a return. So, I'd deposit R1 million into his RMB

Private Bank account for a twelve-week term, and he'd send me two post-dated cheques – one for R1 million for the capital, and R160 000 in interest.'

The cheques were meant to act as security: had Tannenbaum not repaid the money, the investor could then simply cash the cheques. (It didn't work out quite like that, as you might imagine.)

When the twelve weeks were up, Darryl Leigh (who, like Rees, was acting as Tannenbaum's agent) would call Lowenthal and ask him if he wanted to 'roll over' the investment. 'I would agree because the interest I'd earn on it [by rolling it over] was about 15 per cent for the two months, which is very good. It worked well for two years, but towards the end of April, there were cash-flow issues and he asked us to wait before cashing [the cheques],' he says.

Some investors got out in time. They opted not to roll over their investments and took the cash. They were the lucky ones.

Lowenthal says, 'When I got to the meeting … I was astounded: it looked like we'd all been caught in a local Madoff scheme.'

* * *

Though no one explicitly mentioned Bernard Madoff's twenty-year Ponzi scheme in the US at the meeting, it was an implied presence. And the similarities were eerie, especially since the two schemes were operating in tandem on two different continents, and would blow up at roughly the same time.

Madoff, like Tannenbaum, was seen as a pillar of the Jewish community, and wealthy Jewish investors were the core market for the scheme. Madoff, like Tannenbaum, had begrudgingly 'allowed' investors to place their money with him, to join the select club.

Both would turn out to be the largest investment scams in their respective countries. In Madoff's case, about $65 billion was said to be involved. In Tannenbaum's case, the initial estimates were around R2 billion, but this later escalated to nearly R12 billion – easily the largest scam to hit a continent that has seen its fair share of con men.[11]

Madoff, a former chairman of the NASDAQ stock exchange in the US, had run into trouble towards the end of 2008, when he realised he couldn't repay his investors. On 9 December 2008, he confessed to his family that his business was 'a big lie' and 'basically, a giant Ponzi scheme'.[12]

But the comparisons diverge after that.

Madoff was arrested on 11 December 2008, charged with eleven counts of fraud on 12 March 2009 and sentenced to 150 years in prison on 29 June (three weeks after the Tannenbaum meeting at the Sandton law firm).[13]

The thing is, rapid justice is just not South Africa's style. Especially when it comes to extraditing a mastermind residing in the upmarket suburb of St Ives in Sydney. The sharpest South African con men know how to string out a good prosecution for years – and, sometimes, decades.

Most notorious was the case of financial-services company Tigon, once the fortieth-largest South African company. The breadth and audacity of what happened in Tigon led financial journalist Deon Basson to dub the case 'South Africa's Enron'.[14]

In the real world, a tigon is the genetic mutation you get when a tiger mates with a lioness – a sterile mixture that says more about humans' desire to say 'we did it', rather than ask 'should we do it?' But in South Africa's financial world, Tigon became a catchphrase for how to run circles around an increasingly inept prosecutions service.

Tigon was led by a tall, white-quiffed and silver-tongued schemer named Gary Porritt. Nominally, Porritt and his business partner, Sue Bennett, ran a financial-services outfit and a telecoms company called Shawcell. But when the police came calling, they accused Porritt of simply running a crack fraud racket, inflating their assets through smart related-party deals that no one could see through.

Porritt and Bennett were hit with 3160 criminal charges ranging from racketeering and fraud to money laundering in a charge sheet that ran to 1385 pages. It's one thing to throw the book at someone, but quite another to risk crushing them with it.[15]

The thing is, the pair were arrested more than a decade ago. By 2013, Porritt and Bennett were no closer to going to trial than they were in 2002. Both are bailed and living in multimillion-rand houses. Prosecutors will chortle that Porritt and Bennett will die of old age before they hear a judge read their sentence.

To string it out for so long, you need some tricks up your sleeve. And Porritt and Bennett have long sleeves. Most recently, Porritt and Bennett filed papers in the Constitutional Court to get better-quality free 'legal aid' – money paid by government to hire lawyers – a service that is usually only given to the poorest South Africans. Close your eyes, and you can almost picture Gary Porritt popping his tongue firmly inside his cheek, before lodging his 'legal aid' papers.[16]

In a country whose legal system operates like this, you can imagine Tannenbaum has little fear of the courts. And that's before the small matter of extradition is even discussed.

Back at the Routledge Modise meeting, someone asked whether they couldn't just 'get him back' here, referring to Tannenbaum. Rees replied to the effect that extraditing Tannenbaum from Australia would be unlikely to succeed, mainly because of a previous ruling in Australia, conveniently enough, in which a court had rejected an extradition request from South Africa.

This was true. In what was a real *snotklap* for South Africa's correctional-services proficiency, the Australian Federal Court ruled in 2004 that Jacob de Bruyn could not be extradited to South Africa to face fraud charges because conditions in South African jails were so gruesome that De Bruyn was likely to contract HIV/AIDS. This, they ruled, would have amounted to 'cruel and unusual punishment'.[17]

This weakened the prospects of getting Tannenbaum back to South Africa: any fight to extradite him would inevitably be protracted. And even if it were a success, the Tigon disaster meant that any trial would likely take the better part of a decade.

But in June 2009, most investors weren't even convinced Tannenbaum was the bad guy – some believed that Rees himself was the mastermind instead. Or even Darryl Leigh.

As was the case with the Madoff tale, these investors just couldn't reconcile the image they carried of Barry the Philanthropist with the portrait painted at the meeting of Barry the Scheming Charlatan.

Wayne Gaddin, one of Tannenbaum's long-standing friends and an investor himself, says he just couldn't fathom that he was involved. 'Barry's a great human being. He lives in a modest home and he's so trusting: if you tell him it's raining outside, he won't even go to the window to check.'[8]

Many investors had a similar gut response. After a single meeting, usually breakfast or lunch, organised by Rees or Leigh, they felt they knew Barry. They felt they could trust him with their life savings.

The truth is, they didn't know him well at all. Few of them knew what really motivated him or about the dark places in his head where he retreated to after midnight. Many had the rough sketch. But when pressed, hardly any could recall details of his family life, his upbringing, or where he'd worked before. They knew he was 'related to' Harold Tannenbaum, the man somehow responsible for the formation of Adcock Ingram, one of South Africa's largest drug companies.

But they weren't really sure if Harold was his father, his grandfather, or some other distant relative. And what exactly had happened to the Tannenbaums' controlling interest in Adcock Ingram no one could say.

So who was this Barry Tannenbaum? How could this unknown man emerge from nowhere to cook up South Africa's biggest swindle?

2

Krugersdorp royalty

'Today, a search for the name Tannenbaum on the Adcock Ingram website doesn't return a single match.'

– Arnold Tannenbaum, lamenting how the family name vanished from the annals of the company they had founded

The story of how Barry Tannenbaum strung together the country's largest swindle winds back to the dusty mining town of Krugersdorp, about twenty kilometres west of Johannesburg.

Before the scheme popped in 2009, brochures had been handed to investors – with characteristic faux reluctance – which contained a fantastical, stylised version of Barry's heritage. Brochures long on grandiose claims, but short on truth.

'Through [Barry Tannenbaum's] knowledge, and reputation and history of the Tannenbaum name, Frankel Chemicals acquired new and more valuable agencies globally,' these brochures proudly trumpeted.

Frankel, the brochures suggested, was simply the latest incarnation of the long-standing Tannenbaum pharmaceutical dynasty. Barry was simply the dutiful heir stepping up to shepherd the business through another generation. Frankel Chemicals 'was founded in 1960 by Harold Tannenbaum', Barry's father, they said.

'Harold was one of the founding members of the biggest listed pharmaceutical manufacturing company in South Africa, namely Adcock Ingram, which was sold in 1980 to Tiger Oats, now known as Tiger Brands, and Harold was seconded to the board for three years.' (It was actually sold in 1978, two years before.)

It goes on: 'Harold then explored the possibilities of purchasing a company that would service Adcock with their APIs (active pharmaceutical ingredients) and other types of excipients that were utilised in the production of medicines.'

Liberally sprinkled with half-facts, it was largely a fairy tale. No doubt Barry *wanted* it to be true. It just wasn't.

The real story of Barry Tannenbaum, Adcock Ingram and Frankel Chemicals starts in Krugersdorp towards the end of the nineteenth century.

Back then, Krugersdorp was a bustling pioneer town, percolating with gold panners and prospectors, and traders flogging them whatever they needed to get through the day.

Visit Krugersdorp now, and you'll be struck by its tumbled-down factories, streets pockmarked by signs for Viagra miracle cures, and furniture retailers hawking easy credit terms for junk lounge suites, guaranteed to last only as long as the payment term. Every second store seems to be either flogging liquor or hiring out DVDs – anything to suck up the tedious hours after the night dust settles, between clocking out and clocking in.

On Ockerse Street, where the Tannenbaums' family fortunes were launched, you'll now find the furniture shops Lewis, Morkels and Barnetts, alongside Camdix – *'wapens en ammunisie'*, a store flogging bullets – each with its own three-foot posters. Once a frontier town, always a frontier town.

The unwelcoming Cue Tip Pub has an immense steel grate for an entrance, down the road from an Ekuphileni Muti Shop, selling superstition and body organs for all kinds of ailments. Next door is Akhalwaya's Fast Foods, providing greasy toasted-cheese sandwiches over lunchtime to the personnel of every fly-by-night driving school and cellphone shop hawking stolen electronics on the road.

You leave with the impression that when the mines stopped spluttering gold, everyone who could had left. Or might as well have left. You can imagine how someone would say, or do, anything to get out.

What the town's rotting centre masks, however, is a rich history that eloquently captures the texture of South Africa's messy clash of cultures, the brawling for resources, the boom and bust of its frontier towns, the desperate gulf between those who've made their fortunes and those who never will.

* * *

Until 1880, Krugersdorp was just farmland, populated by cows and dry-as-dust highveld grass that grew up past your thighs. Then it was called Paardekraal and was owned by Vaal Martiens Pretorius, a farmer who had inherited the land from his nephew, Andries, the former leader of the Boers.

This was the way it had been ever since Andries stopped in the old Transvaal region where Krugersdorp is based, after a 1600-kilometre journey that had begun in the Cape in 1837 when he and a group of fellow Afrikaners packed their pots, children and chickens into ox-wagons, and trekked north. These Voortrekkers were searching for a simple thing: a world ungoverned by the Union Jack.

At first, the British left them alone, and let them have their independent Boer republics, thanks largely to Andries's negotiations. But after 1850, when the Afrikaner settlers began reporting spectacularly rich gold finds towards Barberton and Pilgrim's Rest, the British began to take notice of what was happening over their shoulders up north. By the time diamonds were found in 1867 on the banks of the Vaal River, the British were sitting bolt upright.

So in 1877 they simply annexed the Transvaal. The Afrikaners were furious, and Paardekraal became the site of one of the first major Afrikaner insurgencies against the British when, in 1880, between 8 000 and 10 000 men gathered to pledge their support for a fight for an independent Transvaal – the original name for Africa's richest bloc, the region encompassing Johannesburg and Pretoria.[1]

At Paardekraal, the Afrikaners asked their God for divine assistance to defeat the British. Remarkably, the Boer forces prevailed at the Battle of Majuba on 27 February 1881 – a victory commemorated by the lonely Paardekraal monument that still stands in the centre of Krugersdorp. Built by the revered Boer leader Paul Kruger in 1891 in honour of that victory, which secured a free Transvaal – the Boer Zuid-Afrikaansche Republiek – the monument is one of the few testaments to the blood spilt on the site. The Boers had won the battle, but it was simply a minor skirmish in a war they would ultimately lose.[2]

In the meantime, news began filtering west from the mining settlement known as Johannesburg – then only six years old – of extraordinarily rich gold finds, said to be stemming from the Witwatersrand reef, which runs from east to west through Paardekraal. Within months, public gold diggings were taking place on Paardekraal and neighbouring farms.[3]

In 1887 Pretorius donated a large chunk of Paardekraal to the newly independent Transvaal government, asking that it be named Krugersdorp after his friend and the man who lent his name to the iconic gold coins.

The Second Anglo-Boer War, which broke out in 1899, changed things dramatically, as the British reasserted control of Krugersdorp. Pioneering the concept of concentration camps, the British rounded up groups of Afrikaners and corralled them into an area of Krugersdorp now known as Coronation Park.[4]

It was an epic migration, as more than 6 000 women and children were shifted into concentration camps. As one report puts it: 'Many of the inhabitants perished in the over-crowded, unsanitary and ill-organised camp. Water pollution was a major health hazard, as well as starvation and malnutrition. The general unsanitary condition of the camp with exceptionally severe epidemics of measles, pneumonia and dysentery contributed to the high number of deaths the camp experienced in October and November 1901.'[5]

It was a move that shattered the unspoken truce between the English and Afrikaners in Krugersdorp, an intervention that created a legacy of poverty that continues to this day. When the war eventually ended in 1902, the shattered Afrikaner prisoners returned to unfarmed land mutilated by three years of neglect and Britain's by-now infamous scorched-earth policy of setting fire to farms to cut off resources to Boer commandos in the field.

Visit Coronation Park now, and you'll be struck by the fact that it seems to be something of an eerie twenty-first-century 'concentration camp', economically speaking. Initially transformed into a picnic site for Krugersdorp's protected white middle class during the 1960s, Coronation Park is now a caravan park thronging with squatting jobless poor whites, embittered about affirmative action, embittered about having to repay the sins of apartheid.

As Reuters photojournalist Finbarr O'Reilly puts it:

It's home to some 400 white squatters living in cramped tents and caravans and sharing a single ablution block. Cats and dogs roam noisily through the camp, dodging heaps of rubbish, piles of scrap metal and abandoned car parts. Water is heated and food cooked on open camp fires. The local council cut electricity to the camp after failing to evict the white squatters.[6]

Park manager Hugo van Niekerk told O'Reilly: 'We won't get houses from this government. If we were black maybe yes, but we are white.'[7]

Coronation Park's residents evoke images of a dispossessed monarchy. They are unclear of the reasons for their seismic fall from power; their caravans are cluttered with remnants from a privileged past – photographs of plush weddings on rolling lawns, inherited trinkets obviously worth more in sentimental value than could be wrestled out of the tills of the pawnbrokers lining Krugersdorp's Main Reef Road.

These poor whites, unable to parlay their years of considerable advantage under apartheid into an economic cushion, remain trapped on the outskirts of Krugersdorp, trapped on the wrong side of history once more.

Not that they would have an inkling about how black South Africans were forced to live by law, not simply through circumstance and poor decisions, during Krugersdorp's boom years between 1940 and 1980.

Blacks who came to work on the mines around Krugersdorp, like Westrand Consolidated and Leopardsvlei, were corralled into two 'native settlements' nearby, Munsieville north-west of the town and Kagiso to the south-east.

They were standard townships of the time, no title deeds, running water from a single tap per street and rickety shacks housing far more people than they should have.

Gerald Buitendach, a former director of BOC Africa, which included gas company Afrox and Afrox Healthcare, lived a block away from Hymie Tannenbaum in the 1960s. Buitendach says Krugersdorp's residents were simply blind to how the other half of their society lived at the time.

'Every day you'd see hundreds of people walking into Krugersdorp from Munsieville about five kilometres away,' he says. 'Our family, the Tannenbaums, nobody tried to change anything, we just accepted that as the way it was, which is one regret I have.'

But it was just the way it was in South Africa back then – there was nothing to provoke anyone to slip out of their comfort zone, which a black slave class was institutionally mandated to make even cushier for the pampered white middle class.

A stone's throw away from Hymie Tannenbaum's house was the Krugersdorp fire station. Every night, at 9 p.m., the bell would sound. It was the signal that every black person had to be off the streets.

The Tannenbaums, Barry's forebears, were no different. Right from when the family arrived in town, a few years after the first 200 plots were auctioned off to form Krugersdorp, the Tannenbaums had other priorities, like establishing their presence amid a growing number of merchants. Soon enough, the name assumed a royal presence in the town.

* * *

How the Tannenbaums of Lithuania ended up in a dusty mining town on the other side of the world is one of the thousands of untold migration stories among the Jewish population of the late nineteenth century.

More than two million Jews fled Russia and its satellite states between 1880 and 1920, escaping the choke exerted by the country after Czar Alexander II was assassinated – for which the Jews were widely blamed. Laws were passed stopping Jews living in villages, and preventing secular schools from having more than 10 per cent Jews in their ranks. Newspapers were full of unbridled hostility towards them.

Unlikely as it may have seemed, South Africa was a big drawcard for Jews fleeing Europe, so much so that it became known as a 'colony of Lithuania'.[8]

Charles Tannenbaum had heard great things about the new colonies of Africa, with stories of diamond and gold finds drifting as far east as Lithuania and Belarus, on the western fringes of the Russian Empire. So he and his brother boarded a ship, and set sail for South Africa to lay the platform for a new life.

They followed distant relatives who had already made the trip to the Transvaal – a bone-dry land of endless veld where you were as likely to get slain by the Ndebele tribes as you were to get eaten by lions. But it had diamonds and it had gold.

Satisfied with the newly formed town of Krugersdorp, and the need for a new merchant class, Charles and his brother sent for their wives. The Tannenbaums arrived in 1890 and bought two properties barely 100 metres from each other in Roodepoort.[9]

The Tannenbaum settlers joined the battle for trading space in the new, thriving mining town, and opened a general store amid a glut of similar shops that were starting up at the time.

The other Russian Jews of Krugersdorp provided the Tannenbaums with a ready-made community, and steadily they slotted into life on the reef, along with their four sons, Hymie, Jack, Len and Archie.

It was Charles's eldest son, Hymie, who was to be the empire builder of the Tannenbaum pharmaceutical name, its Shaka Zulu, its Julius Caesar. Charles and his wife Tilly had ambitions for Hymie, so they arranged that he be apprenticed to a friend of theirs, Jack Blair, who ran a pharmacy in Krugersdorp. Blair had bought the pharmacy at 47 Ockerse Street from its founder, E.J. Adcock, who had started the business in 1890, but had retired.[10]

Running a pharmacy in the early days of the twentieth century was far more of a lick-and-spit magic trick than the sophisticated prepackaged business it is today, where precisely apportioned ingredients are flagged on a perfectly symmetrical box.

Back then, the average life expectancy on the Joburg highveld was forty-seven. The main causes of death in those days were pneumonia, flu, tuberculosis and diarrhoea, according to a publication put out by Adcock Ingram in 2010 to commemorate 120 years of trading. Large families were obligatory because you never could predict when chickenpox, scarlet fever, dysentery or measles would decimate your family labour force. According to the profile,

> the few doctors that have made the arduous trek to the Witwatersrand goldfields from the Cape or Kimberley have precious few medicines to choose from in their traditional black leather bags. These mainly comprise crude medications such as plant-based purgatives and intrinsically poisonous drugs, administered in quantities to hopefully kill the disease before killing the patient.[11]

A modern person walking into an early-twentieth-century pharmacy would be astounded by its resemblance to a snake-oil-peddling operation. On the shelves you would see a range of powders, mercury (for syphilis and ringworm) and colchicine for gout. If you'd been laid low by malaria, you could buy quinine from the pharmacy, or opt to take it the old-fashioned way, with three fingers of gin.

They seem primeval by today's standards, but back in 1900, these medications represented pulsating innovation compared to the crude medicines fashioned from mustard, opium and liquorice even further back in the mists of pharmaceutical time.

In the pioneer town that was early Krugersdorp, there was no dispute that any business promising to cure the frightening maladies of the highveld was guaranteed a thronging trade. So E.J. Adcock's owner, Jack Blair, didn't need too much persuading to take on young Hymie Tannenbaum.

Yellowed photographs of Hymie, in his later years when he'd begun to bald and grey, create the impression of a rough-featured gold trader, wedged uncomfortably into a three-piece suit by his wife, Polly, for the sake of the photographer, rather than a Breitling-studded Wall Street executive. Shorter and stouter than his brothers – Len, Jack and Archie – Hymie flexes for the camera with the regal pose of the family patriarch.

E.J. Adcock Pharmacy was only a stepping stone for the Tannenbaum clan, which is just as well, given how the Krugersdorp decay has grown like mould over the pharmacy's initial shopfront. Now at 47 Ockerse Street, you can still see the remains of the original sign, but it just reads 'Cocks Pharma'. The rest has been obliterated on the right by a handwritten sign for 'Rashid Cellular and Electronics', and on the left by a handwritten sign advertising 'Binding, Internet Cafe, Laminating and Stationery'.

Rashid's store sells every kind of tacky electronic knock-off you could imagine, perishing cellphone covers and second-hand TVs. Next to the sign for the internet café, there is a business that simultaneously operates as a hair salon and public phone shop.

You sense that any of these enterprises could vanish by tomorrow morning – either gone bust or gone to chase the cash all the way to Joburg – and could just as easily be replaced by another indistinguishable store under another handwritten banner, selling pretty much the same wares, hoping for a different result.

It says a lot about Krugersdorp today that Hymie Tannenbaum was able to launch an empire from a shopfront now adorned with the words 'Cocks Pharma'. It's a fittingly poignant metaphor for the town's decline.

* * *

Many of the pins holding up the story of how the Tannenbaums built Adcock Ingram emerge from Jack's son, Arnold, who has become something of a family historian. At the time of writing, in 2013, Arnold Tannenbaum is a jaunty eighty-five-year-old, lean with wispy white hair, and a face that echoes the genetics of his ancestors. Arnold Tannenbaum lives in elegant 'old-age apartments' in Bramley, east of Johannesburg, a stone's throw from his grandchildren, and barely five kilometres from the Hillbrow pharmacy that he spent so many years building.

Arnold dutifully followed his uncle, qualifying as a pharmacist at Durban Technikon in 1948, before slotting into the Tannenbaums' expanding empire. Although he slaved away at it for decades, the truth was the business world wasn't for him. He defines himself as a 'gentle' person, who escaped the sordid business of money in the late 1970s, dabbling in Scientology for years before escaping that cult.

But Arnold Tannenbaum's memory is incisive, and he committed much of it to paper for a report he wrote for the *SA Jewish Report* and *SA Pharmaceutical Journal* charting the family's rise, titled 'How the Tannenbaum brothers started Adcock Ingram'.[12]

Arnold writes of how Hymie, particularly, hated ostentation. 'He never wore a tie and usually did not bother with a jacket, preferring to work with rolled-up sleeves. Paradoxically, he was generous to a fault, but was typically quiet about his generosity, preferring to be an anonymous donor,' he says.[13]

The early Tannenbaums eschewed the glitzy adornments typical of made-good businessmen of the time. So rather than building gleaming offices to advertise his success in creating South Africa's largest pharmaceutical company, Hymie's office for most of his career was situated at the bottom of a lift shaft, under E.J. Adcock's pharmacy on Ockerse Street.

Gerald Buitendach was friendly with Hymie's son Charles, and spent many hours with the Tannenbaums. 'I remember Hymie as just an amazing person,' he says. 'He used to help us with our science homework in the basement of the office. He was the first person to show us how to separate water into hydrogen and oxygen using electrodes.'

And rather than paying for the sort of estate with cascading lawns tended by an army of foot servants, as was expected at a time when immense properties cost virtually nothing, Hymie lived in a small house at number 34 Burger Street. At the time, it was considered relatively plush.

'The thing I remember most are the most luxurious Persian carpets you've ever seen,' says Buitendach. 'I think it was only a three-bedroom house with only one bathroom, but it wasn't bad for the time. I remember the Tannenbaums as a classy, conservative family.'

That's where Hymie lived, and that's where he died. Look at 34 Burger Street now, the house where Adcock Ingram was effectively founded, and you get the impression that it hasn't had a lick of paint since he passed away. Green, spiked palisade fencing is crudely attached to a thigh-high cream wall. A green corrugated-iron roof squats on top of an unexceptional whitewashed house, which has clearly been the victim of a number of home-building projects over the years. An inflatable swimming pool has been plopped on the porch to take the sting out of the beating West Rand sun.

Not exactly the Michelangelo Hotel, where Barry would put himself up (at investors' expense) when he travelled to South Africa shortly before his investment scheme went pop.

Arnold continues: 'He also drove the smallest of Ford cars, the Anglia. He drove fast and collected so many speeding tickets on his way to visit his brothers in Johannesburg that he eventually realised it would be easier and cheaper to hire a driver. The new driver looked at the Anglia and refused point blank to drive it. Hymie was forced to buy the next car in the Ford range – a Zephyr.'

This says a lot about Hymie's instinctive eye for the margin, which allowed him to impress himself on the minor stage that was Krugersdorp. In the 1960s,

Krugersdorp was a thriving metropolitan centre. It had its own orchestra, one of the country's best schools, and roaring Jewish, Anglican and Catholic communities.

For Hymie's first trick, he lured his brothers into the pharmacy. Next, he negotiated with Blair to buy E.J. Adcock. 'Blair was quite elderly then,' says Arnold, 'and he had these dynamic young men pushing him to expand, expand, expand. So he decided to sell to them and let them do what they wanted to do.'

The next trick was the riskiest: using the cash they'd made in Krugersdorp, Hymie and his brothers set about buying – or where there was nothing to buy, building brick by brick – a connect-the-dots network of pharmacies along the gold reef, all the way from Johannesburg to Carletonville.

With the deft instinct of an emperor, Hymie figured the best way to keep a handle on his enterprise was to ship his brothers off to manage various corners of the empire. So 'Long Len' was sent to manage Ingrams Pharmacy – which he soon built into the largest pharmacy in the country – in a newly built cosmopolitan area called Hillbrow, north-east of Johannesburg. Jack was also sent to Hillbrow, but to Keatings Pharmacy on Pretorius Street, while the youngest brother, Archie, was to handle the distribution to all the stores.

Today Hillbrow is the pulsating, dripping heart of Joburg sleaze, the cesspit into which all Africa's narcotics seem to slope. High-rise slums, where up to thirty people share single studio flats, teeter grubbily next to hijacked buildings, where the lights haven't worked since the 1990s. In the movie *Jerusalema*, the seedy desperation is summed up by a Nigerian gangster who runs drugs and prostitutes from Hillbrow: 'Think of it as a free-enterprise zone.'

But when Arnold ran Keatings Pharmacy in the 1970s, it was almost Africa's Paris, its Jerusalem – outdoor cafés, restaurants, book stores, night clubs open till dawn. But what really defined Hillbrow was that the police were powerless there to enforce the Group Areas Act, the law intended to scissor blacks from whites. The ruling National Party's defeat in Hillbrow by-elections foreshadowed their inevitable capitulation in 1994.

This is how one former resident described Arnold Tannenbaum's Hillbrow:

When Joburg slept, Hillbrow used to wake up. It had the best nightlife in South Africa. And, yes, it broke the backbone of the Group Areas Act. Black and white people mingled and respected each other so well. I stayed at 1212 Highpoint – that was my first independent home from my parents. I would go the pharmacy at Highpoint at 9 p.m., and its doors would still be wide open. I would go to Fontana to buy chicken and rolls at 2 a.m. I used to dine at Porterhouse (my favourite was at the corner of Twist and Kotze streets), or alternatively at the Three Sisters restaurant. I used to take my girlfriend to the movies at

Nu Metro in Pretoria Street or Ster-Kinekor in Kotze Street. My Sunday afternoons were spent at Look & Listen (the very first one) at the corner of Pretoria and Claim, or further up at Hillbrow Records ... I used to go to Milky Lane to treat my sweetie to some ice cream. We used to enjoy cocktails at Karos Hotel, at the corner of Twist and Wolmarans streets ... The Summit Club or Moulin Rouge or Why Not were options for a night outing. Browsing books at Exclusive Books (their very first store) was so good. I can still smell the bread from Fournos confectionery (their first store) in Pretoria Street.[14]

Arnold has similar memories: 'Keatings was the busiest pharmacy in the country, and we were the first to stay open late in the evenings. We built Ingram's Corner – Adcock Ingram's first headquarters – right on that block, corner of Twist and Kotze streets. It was a great place to be then.'

Ingram's Corner still exists. Only thing is, where once it housed offices, it now houses betting shops and kite-flying 'business consultants'. During its heyday, Harry Lotzof, the renowned war photographer who took the pictures of Roosevelt, Churchill and Stalin at the Yalta Conference, had a studio at Ingram's Corner.[15]

If you drive through Hillbrow today, picking your way through the drug dealers, opportunistic street kids armed with spark plugs to break your windows if they spot something they want on the back seat, and prostitutes working in the middle of the day, you'll find a high-rise building on the corner of Twist and Kotze streets that still bears the inscription 'Ingram's Corner'. The entrance is now caged in two layers of steel doors, sandwiched between a market called Hyper Hillbrow, which advertises on its blacked-out windows that hawkers should buy from it to 'buy bulk and save', and the Affritude Hair Salon.

The hair salon, besides revealing in painstakingly handwritten print that it is 'small but mighty' and promising that 'you design your garment, it's our business to design your hair', also sells airtime for the three main cellphone networks, Vodacom, MTN and Cell C.

The pillars at the entrance to Ingram's Corner, already choked by an inch of dust, are buried under pamphlets for 'Prophet Andreus' and 'Special Fertility Doctor'.

On the top few floors of Ingram's Corner, there used to be the Brenthurst Clinic. Now, right from the seedy News Calypso bar on the first floor of the building, promising 'Live entertainment, restaurant, pool bar', to the top of the building, you'll find enterprises of increasingly dubious legality.

The symmetry between the sullying of the Tannenbaum name and the degeneration of their former headquarters is striking.

* * *

If Hymie had put in place the basic architecture for what would become known as Adcock Ingram, some moments of entrepreneurial brilliance provided it with products no one else was able to easily replicate.

The Johannesburg of the mid-1900s percolated heat, dust and desperation. The city is 1800 metres above sea level, and the highveld air as dry and inviting as a thorn bush in the Namib. Even the growing urban sprawl of Hillbrow hadn't tempered the environment. Long Len Tannenbaum describes in his notes how the family pharmacy business stumbled on something of a miracle cure for skin baked red and chapped by the Johannesburg air, all courtesy of a twenty-six-year-old German chemist on the run from Hitler. That product, known as Ingram's Camphor Cream, was soon on the shelf of every home in Johannesburg.

When Hans Rose arrived at Len's pharmacy pleading for work, Len said, 'Hans, look at my hands', volunteering digits that were chapped and bleeding, despite being covered in cream meant to prevent that. 'Can you give me soft hands?' he asked.[16]

'Yes, I can, if you will help me,' said Hans. 'Give me a note to the wholesalers Sive Bros. & Karnovsky, and ask them to supply me with my requirements. I have very little money and promise you that I shall pay back every penny.'

Early the next morning, Len recounted, 'little Hans, almost doubled over, came in carrying a huge black pot filled almost to the brim with a white glistening cream'. Len was uncertain, partly because the cream had no smell, but Hans promised to remedy this.

Long Len's mind was working at a rapid pace. 'In a drawer in the dispensary was a large quantity of red-and-white labels. Old man Ingram, long deceased, used to sell a liquid cream called Ingram's Camphor Cream, which had been off the market for many years,' he said.

'Camphor?' Hans responded. 'How terrible! It will never sell.'

But Len was insistent: 'Camphor it is, and nothing else.' At midday, Hans returned. The smell of camphor filled the air from a hundred yards or so. Long Len found a four-ounce jar, which he filled with the cream. The Ingram's Camphor Cream label fitted like a glove. The ready-made instructions described the usage of the cream. Long Len dabbed a large portion of cream into one hand and then massaged it in.

The cream was a huge hit, catching on after Len began sending it to nearby hospitals. Hans couldn't keep up with the demand, so eventually production had to be shifted to the Adcock factory in Krugersdorp.

Long Len describes how some time later, Hans Rose again walked into his pharmacy, having scored a job at a pharmaceutical company. 'In one hand he held a bunch of red roses, and in the other an envelope. "The roses are for your good wife and the envelope is for you."' Long Len accepted both gifts and wished him a very successful future. When he opened the envelope, he found that it contained the formula for Ingram's Camphor Cream and the method of manufacture. A short note said that Hans promised he would never use that formula again and wished them every success with the cream.

Ingram's Camphor Cream became an iconic South African brand. Despite being more of a herbal remedy, it was registered as a medicine in South Africa, which had the lucky effect of making it free from excise duty.

There were other similar breaks that helped launch Adcock Ingram.

In the 1930s, a Hungarian medical scientist, Dr Bondi Janovicks, had been sent to South Africa by a pharmaceutical company called Chinoin to help sell its products. It had been a dismal failure, and Janovicks was to be called back.

Arnold recalls: 'He was desperate not to go back. He said, "There'll be war, so there's no ways I'm going home. Let me stay here and help you manufacture medicines."'

This was quite a revolutionary concept back then. In the 1930s, most *serious* medicines were imported into the country – except for the most basic liquids, and hand-rolled pills and powders. There were no locally made injection drugs, for example, or anaesthetics, intravenous drips or capsules.

In return for not being sent home to Nazi-controlled Hungary, Janovicks said he'd establish all this for Adcock Ingram. Says Arnold:

> So my dad bought the house next door to Keatings in Hillbrow. Bondi and another Hungarian friend of his, Kuno Hoffer, set about experimenting in the kitchen of that house, making medicines. I was about ten years old, and I can tell you, to see these two white-coated chemists working in that kitchen, making the most ghastly smells, was something else. They used to go to abattoirs to collect pituitary glands, livers – you name it, they tried it.

In 1939, a year before Hungary joined Hitler's axis, Janovicks and Hoffer presented Jack Tannenbaum with the holy grail: a small box containing ampoules of ethyl chloride – the first time that an anaesthetic had been produced in South Africa.

The Hungarians weren't finished either. Soon they began growing penicillin, producing eyedrops and making tablets under their new laboratory name, Saphar.

Another deal that Jack did, which took incredible chutzpah at the time, was to clinch a distribution contract with Baxter Healthcare in the US, in 1947. Daryl Kronson, Adcock Ingram's former financial director, says:

> At the time, intravenous solutions were painstakingly shipped to South Africa. So Jack just pitched up at the Baxter Chicago headquarters, and asked

for the right to manufacture and distribute intravenous solutions in South Africa. It was an incredibly gutsy thing to do at the time, but two days later, Jack left Chicago with a handshake. That handshake became a five-page agreement, which, although amended several times since, still stands today.

South Africa became the first country to have such a distribution agreement – all thanks to the ballsiness of Jack Tannenbaum.

Adcock Ingram may have been born in a sweaty pharmacy in Ockerse Street, but it was no longer one-dimensional. Besides the gold nuggets of Ingram's Camphor Cream and the Saphar laboratory, Jack had strung together exclusive distribution deals with American pharmaceutical firms like Abbott, and G.D. Searle. And the company soon branched out into various other fields – for example, it launched Etkinds, the photographic store.

It seems an unfeasibly romantic notion to create, virtually overnight, a miracle cream that would become the cornerstone of the multinational pharmaceutical giant Adcock Ingram. Wedding that to the lucky breaks that led to Saphar's success, the tricky world of commerce may have seemed almost too easy.

The young Barry Tannenbaum would have heard these stories, no doubt embellished in the telling, many times. Perhaps to a young boy, they fuelled the naive notion that with a grand enough plan and enough audacity, there was easy money out there, just waiting to be corralled.

The difference, of course, was that Ingram's Camphor Cream *was* actually a real product. The laboratories *were* actually making medicine. Barry Tannenbaum's antiretroviral components were merely an idea, at first. Later, his plan became completely untethered from reality, becoming just a series of numbers in an Excel spreadsheet, representing whatever mythical returns somebody expected to get.

* * *

By the time Hymie Tannenbaum died in September 1970, the Tannenbaums pretty much *were* South Africa's pharmaceutical industry. By 1975 they boasted eight pharmaceutical chemists – the largest number in a single South African family. This empire included the four brothers – Hymie, Jack, Len and Archie – as well as Jack's son Arnold, Hymie's son Harold, and his cousins, Ivan, and Archie's son Stanley.

From a grimy shopfront in a Krugersdorp side street, Hymie had pioneered one of South Africa's great entrepreneurial success stories. In 1950 Adcock Ingram listed its shares on the Johannesburg Stock Exchange, becoming the first pharmaceutical company to sell its shares to the South African public.[17]

When he died, Hymie left behind two children, Harold and Charles, and a nursery of grandchildren, including Harold's three children, Michael, the four-year-old Barry and their younger sister, Jacqueline.

The obituary columns ran tributes to Hymie for days, fêting the passing of a Krugersdorp institution. The *Sunday Times*, two days after he died, dedicated no fewer than two columns – forty classified notices in total – from friends, family and business partners, mourning the loss.

'The passing of a great leader,' was the message posted by his brother Jack and Jack's wife, Sally. 'Deeply mourned, condolences to Tannenbaum family', read the message from Park Pharmacies, many miles away in Vanderbijlpark.

What Hymie didn't live to see was his family losing control of Adcock Ingram. In 1978 another iconic South African company, Tiger Oats, bought Adcock Ingram from the Tannenbaums. Arnold explains the decision to sell: 'Hymie was the big shot, and after he died, the new generation pretty much lost interest. I had been groomed to take over in a way, but I was never really keen on it. I was sort of a round peg in a square hole, so I wasn't going to do it.'

Politically, it was a tough time in the country's history, and there was concern that the country could descend into civil war. The Soweto riots of 1976, where young black children in the townships protested at having to learn Afrikaans at school, had shattered the illusion that there was any kind of sustainable future for the apartheid experiment. Overseas businessmen kept using terms like 'crime against humanity', and darkly muttering the word 'sanctions'.

'It was a good time to be out of South Africa,' says Arnold.

It was during these years that Krugersdorp began to splutter. The mines continued hauling metal out of the ground, but, in the era of giant diversified mining firms like Anglo American and Gencor, the head offices of many Krugersdorp companies shifted to Johannesburg. Companies that had started in the mining town now had their addresses on Jeppe Street and Diagonal Street.

For Adcock Ingram, the Tannenbaum era was also waning.

Jack stayed on as chairman of Adcock Ingram for a few years, and Lex Tannenbaum, Len's son, who became a lawyer, remained a director of the company until 1989. Lex headed the wholesale pharmaceutical business, and was one of the few Tannenbaums eager to continue with the business.

Daryl Kronson, Adcock Ingram's former financial director, says that 'Lex was a bright guy, but operating in a very difficult business, where there were tiny profit margins, and the pharmacies were lobbying for ever greater discounts'.[18]

Jack, by this stage pushing eighty, had scaled back his involvement but remained a revered figure, keeping an office for many years. Kronson remembers: 'Jack would always come out to present the long-service awards to people. And even though it was in the middle of the 1980s, Jack would present an award to the lowliest black factory worker in the company, and he'd know all about his family, that his kids were going to university, or whatever. He was that kind of guy.'

As for Arnold, he had long since drifted away from his birthright, and into the grabbing arms of the burgeoning cult of Scientology. At this point, Arnold's personal life story gets particularly interesting.

What many people don't know is that Scientology is deeply rooted in South Africa – the country might even have ended up as the global base for the newly formed movement, had the cards fallen in the wrong direction.

In September 1960, the cult's founder, L. Ron Hubbard, moved to Johannesburg and made his home on Linksfield Ridge, east of the city, in an immense open-plan double-storey box of a house with spectacular views stretching up to sixty kilometres. 'I'm very fond of Joburg,' Hubbard wrote. 'I have walked up your hills and my lips have turned blue and I have puffed from the rarefied air.'[19]

Morbidly, Hubbard's unsightly hilltop residence with egg-box windows and *circa* 1970s architecture behind iron bars is now deified as a Scientology Heritage Site. Tours are given of Hubbard's study, his leathered conference rooms, his zebra rugs, his tacky African art, and even his motion-picture camera that he used to film early 'Scientology sessions'. A bust of an open-mouthed Hubbard sits behind his desk among yellowed pictures of his African adventure – the same bust that has been copied and now sits in all Scientology churches worldwide.

The official PR for the heritage site explains Hubbard's African sojourn thus: 'The cold war was threatening to turn hot overnight. Searching for a safer base of operations for Scientology, L. Ron Hubbard set his sights on the southern hemisphere, particularly South Africa. He arrived in Johannesburg ... and took up residence high on Linksfield Ridge.'[20]

Here, Scientologists claim, Hubbard 'developed virtually every introductory line of our organisation, [including] advancing into the public phase of Scientology'. What Scientology would later become was fine-tuned, it seems, as Hubbard looked out over the Johannesburg skyline.

A video clip of the house on a Scientology website, enticing visitors, says 'his study stands just as it was when he drafted letters to South African ministers'. It's a nauseatingly sanitised version of Hubbard's South African trip, worthy of Barry Tannenbaum himself.

What Scientologists don't want you to know is exactly what was in those letters to the South African ministers. They've gone out of their way to airbrush Hubbard's craven fawning over the apartheid government and, specifically, his gushing praise for the father of the racist ideology, Dr Hendrik Verwoerd.

When Scientology fell foul of the South African government in the early 1970s, the Kotze Commission was set up to investigate the 'religion'. And in that commission, a raft of correspondence from Hubbard tumbled out.

In one letter to Verwoerd, Hubbard writes: 'May I state that you have conceived and created in the Johannesburg townships what is probably the most impressive and adequate resettlement in existence. Any criticism of it could only be engaged upon by scoundrels or madmen, and I know now your enemies to be both.'[21]

It was an unmediated, passionate endorsement of apartheid from Hubbard – but one that Scientologists have conveniently erased from their memories. Instead, the promotional video says that Hubbard 'authored a "one man, one vote" constitution for apartheid-shackled South Africa. He likewise presented a bill of rights and penal code for equality and justice.'

The joke since 1994 is that nobody ever voted for Verwoerd's National Party. You won't find many people admitting to it – and Hubbard's religion isn't about to concede any ground on this front either.

But ultimately, Hubbard's toadying didn't help: Scientology was banned for two decades after the Kotze Commission. Since its unbanning, Scientology has won over at least 15 000 South Africans – scoring an estimated R100 million a year from these acolytes.[22]

For years from the early 1960s, Arnold was a devout follower of Hubbard. 'I cannot describe how deliriously happy I was,' he says now. 'It was nothing less than a total high. I felt like I could see through everything, see the whole universe for what it was, see the beginning of all time. I was literally mad, and I thought I knew everything. Hell, I was a pain in the neck.'

Arnold even testified to the Kotze Commission in 1973, and the report records that 'the witness, Mr Tannenbaum, claims that his intelligence was increased' as a result of the religion's influence.

One story he told to the commission, as recorded in the Kotze report, is particularly fascinating:

Mr Tannenbaum desired to solve a problem relating to the disappearance of drugs in his pharmaceutical business and called upon Mr Van Niekerk, who was then conducting business under the style of 'industrial security agent'. By the use of a machine which resembled the E-meter [which Scientologists use to determine the truth] and a security check form, he singled out the alleged thieves – one of them committing suicide as a result. Mr Tannenbaum 'regarded this use of the instrument in question as an abuse of Scientology.[23]

The Kotze Commission saw this as evidence of Scientology's harmful effects, probably helping them decide to ban the religion for decades.

But Arnold suffered the embarrassment of being turfed out of the cult twice – events that provide a fascinating insight into the paranoia that governs the church's everyday operations:

Adcock's pharmacy, Keatings, was open late one night, and L. Ron Hubbard came in with a prescription to be filled. How could this be, when Scientologists aren't meant to get ill? So I went to the [church] and asked them, how is it that L. Ron Hubbard could be sick, when he's supposed to be an OT (Operating Thetan) that has moved beyond illness? He's not meant to get ill, so how could this be?

For his trouble, the church booted him out. Arnold Tannenbaum remained iced out for nearly a year, until the South African leadership changed. Then he was promptly booted out again, this time at a global Scientology conference in Copenhagen.

After that, he remained outside the tent. 'Immediately after I was kicked out, I was a mess,' he says. 'I had nothing else in my life, and literally didn't know what to do. Only now do I see how I was blinded by it all. And how they took everything from me.'

Financially and spiritually, Scientology tends to insert its proboscis and keep sucking until there's nothing left.

Arnold Tannenbaum escaped early enough and has no regrets. He does, however, want to correct the injustice he feels has been done to his family by the current leadership of Adcock Ingram, who have erased all mention of the family's role in the company's genesis.

'The name has been virtually obliterated from Adcock Ingram's history. There is no mention of the Tannenbaum name on the company website, for example, and they don't seem interested in correcting this. I wrote to one of the senior executives about this, and he replied rather sarcastically,' he says.

For a while, Adcock Ingram kept a 'Tannenbaum' room, with portraits of the four brothers hanging on the wall. But even that was demolished after a while. 'When they shipped the portrait of Jack back to me, it was all torn,' says Arnold.

Now, after Barry has dragged the family name into the murky world of pyramid schemes and financial fraud, you'd imagine he'd almost be grateful for that small mercy. You'd imagine that there'd be a lot of shaking of heads in the Adcock boardroom when someone mistakenly utters the name Tannenbaum.

Adcock Ingram now has fancy new headquarters at number 1 New Road, Midrand. Situated amid a rash of generic, knock-off faux-Tuscan townhouses, it's a million miles from the squalor of Hillbrow, where once it was based.

When you visit Adcock Ingram, its iconic medical products are emblazoned on thirty-foot-high signs propped up over its corporate windows – signs for headache tablet Panado, energy supplement Bioplus and probiotic Probiflora.

Inside, exhibits of early pharmaceutical tools – rustic-looking pestle and mortars, and pill-counting machines – sit alongside meeting rooms named after Adcock Ingram's best-selling products. This means that guileless marketing executives can schedule a meeting in the Corenza-C Room, for example, at the same time as number geeks debate figures in the Citro-Soda Room, the Bioplus Room or the Sabax Room.

There is no Tannenbaum Room.

For Arnold Tannenbaum, this tells him that his family's role in creating the country's largest pharmaceutical firm, now worth R12 billion and one of the 100 largest companies listed on the JSE, has been wiped clear, like so much dust off a windscreen.

'That's just not true,' says Dr Jonathan Louw, the CEO of Adcock Ingram, who has been working at the company for twelve years. 'We wrote to Arnold Tannenbaum, and told him this wasn't the case. If you walk into our boardroom right now, you'll still see a photograph of the four founders of the business, the Tannenbaum brothers.'[24]

He adds that this is some unusual testament to Adcock's history, dating back as it does more than four decades: 'I don't expect that when I go, they'll have a painting of me up on the wall.'

Dr Louw, more than you might think, appears to appreciate the heritage Barry's family left. But then, he is not your average pinstripe-and-abacus boss of a stock-exchange-listed titan. Most chief executives earn their corner spot by virtue of their ability to boost their company's goodwill numbers, slash the cost-to-income ratio and channel the marketing jargon at lifeless corporate presentations.

Louw's favourite book might be Malcolm Gladwell's pop-psychology work, *The Tipping Point*, and he might spend all his free time scuba diving, wine tasting or cycling, but he's not the corporate cliché you might expect. Not many CEOs, for example, can say that their first job was working as a medical officer for the Red Cross Children's Hospital.[25]

In 1993 Louw graduated with a medical degree from the University of Cape Town, then spent a stint working as an anaesthetist at London's St Mary's Hospital. In 1999 he returned to South Africa and quit medicine for business. First, he worked for AstraZeneca, but two years later took up the role of head of new business at the Tannenbaums' former company, Adcock Ingram. Louw says he understands the Tannenbaum family's anger over what Barry did. 'We were very disappointed that we were even vaguely associated with this mess,' he says. 'But for the Tannenbaum family, I can imagine they're even more hurt and disappointed. Especially since this is the sort of thing that will get more recognition than all the good things they've done by starting this company.'[26]

Not that Adcock Ingram has distinguished itself by climbing from strength to strength. Instead, Tiger Brands' conservative strategy for its pharmaceutical arm under Tiger's former CEO Nick Dennis meant that Adcock failed to make the smart moves, unlike Stephen Saad's Aspen, which branched into countries like Brazil.

'Aspen literally has stolen Adcock Ingram's breakfast,' says Kronson, who put together many of the deals that were vetoed by Tiger Brands' board. 'To me, it's galling: I grew up with Adcock Ingram as the number-one player around. But when they didn't want to go ahead with a deal to buy into Romania, I realised just how conservative they really were.'[27]

In 2008 Adcock Ingram was spun out of Tiger Brands, and relisted on the JSE as a separate company – minus some of its key consumer brands, like Ingram's Camphor Cream and Gill Shampoo, which Tiger managed to grab on the basis that they were consumer, not medical, products.

Nonetheless, the company founded by the Tannenbaums continues to more than eke out a living. A not inconsiderable living that made it R4.59 billion for its financial year to September 2012, hawking the staples of every South African medicine cabinet: Panado, Myprodol and Corenza-C. Of this, about R986 million was profit.

Arnold Tannenbaum is, predictably, ashamed of how Barry has sullied the family name. 'He has disgraced us. When I introduce myself now, people say, "Oh, Tannenbaum? Like Barry Tannenbaum?" He has blotted the name.'

He remembers meeting Barry a few times when the latter was a young boy: 'He was a lovely, wide-eyed curious bloke. To do what he's done, it's hard to believe he's not a sociopath.'

Famous people dubbed sociopaths include Bernie Madoff, Enron's Kenneth Lay, former Italian premier Silvio Berlusconi and cycling's Lance Armstrong. In South Africa, murdered mining boss Brett Kebble, the last corporate hotshot to be outed for spending hours in an office with a stick of glue and a pair of scissors, forging documents, would instantly qualify too.

Now in prison, Madoff sees a prison psychiatrist every week at his North Carolina Federal Correctional Institution in an effort to understand why he did what he did, what perverted the course of his life to such an extent.

'Everybody on the outside kept claiming I was a sociopath,' he told Steve Fishman, a journalist from the *New York* magazine, in a fascinating interview that shone a light into Madoff's misplaced anger at how he believed he'd been miscast as a villain by the outside world.[28]

'I asked her [the therapist], "Am I a sociopath?",' Madoff said. 'She said, "You're absolutely not a sociopath. You have morals, you have remorse."'

Madoff said to Fishman, triumphantly, 'I am a good person.' As if his therapist's response validated his tortured reasoning that he'd somehow been coerced by someone else into deceiving his investors – as if her view undid his wrong-doing.

It's an easy term to throw about, 'sociopath'. But it is indistinct from the term 'psychopath' to many people. If anything, the word 'sociopath' can seem like a lazy catch-all for defining somebody as bad, without interrogating their individual pathology.

University of New Mexico neuroscientist Dr Kent Kiehl wrote in a paper for *Scientific American Mind* that psychopaths are 'bereft of loyalties and passions, they wander through life, often straying into criminality on a whim – forgeries, thefts, assaults, even murders may be committed out of some trivial impulse'.[29]

If you believe Kiehl, then impulse control is a problem for them, as is guilt, remorse, or 'appropriate moral value judgments'. They are 'insensitive to social expectation', he says, and 'notoriously good at learning and exploiting the weakness of others'.[30]

Kiehl says people with this sort of antisocial disorder also have 'trouble shifting gears' when things are going wrong: 'Once fixed on a goal, psychopaths proceed as if they can't get off the train until it reaches the station.'

But whereas you could easily fit people like Charles Manson, Hitler and most serial killers into that mould, you wouldn't call them sociopaths, who are typically defined as reluctant to descend into physical violence.

In her book *The Sociopath Next Door*, former Harvard Medical School researcher Martha Stout paints those who can be defined as sociopaths as people lacking any form of conscience, whose sole game is to control events and people, and manipulate them.[31]

Stout describes sociopaths as people who lie for the sake of lying, who tell increasingly larger fibs to see what effect it has. More often than not, the one thing people remember about a sociopath is that they were 'so charming'.

The most desirable target of a sociopath is someone extremely loyal, of high character (because it is more rewarding to manipulate people who have made something of themselves, apparently) and who could help you improve your position in the world.

Sociopaths get bored extremely easily so they like to find things to fill their time. Like inventing games. Or gambling.

3

Big shoes, small steps

'The family were saints in Johannesburg. They were philanthropic, genteel, modest people.'
 – **A South African-born Jew living in Australia, to news agency JTA**

As the scion of what passed for royalty in Krugersdorp, Barry Tannenbaum was used to things coming easy as a child.

A charmingly innocent letter written by ten-year-old Barry to Sir Sebastian, a cat that was the face of the junior club of the *Sunday Times* newspaper, records the undemanding life led by white children in the easy days of the 1970s, the sunny-skies-and-Chevrolet era before sanctions against the apartheid government began to bite.

Young Barry, according to his letter, 'likes playing tennis, rugby and cricket, as well as swimming and listening to pop music'.

He seemed like any other young white boy in 1970s South Africa, where the biggest challenge was deciding whether to pick cricket or tennis for your after-noon activity, and which LPs of David Bowie, Fleetwood Mac or the Rolling Stones warranted purchase. Like all kids his age, he was oblivious to the politics that lay behind the presence of a squadron of maids and gardeners, tasked with picking up his cricket bats and tennis rackets.

Says one family member: 'Barry was literally the sweetest kid. So naive, such a great child. It's hard to understand what happened to him.'

Barry was the second of Harold Tannenbaum's four children – Michael, the oldest, then Barry, Jacqueline and Hylton. He was particularly close to Michael, who would later become the financial director of a London-based property company that until recently was listed on the London Stock Exchange, called Westcity plc.

(The relationship didn't work out particularly well for Michael, however, whom Barry conspired to suck into his Ponzi scheme. In the end, with Michael's fingerprints all over some of the main transactions, prosecutors took a keen inter-est in his role in putting together the elaborate con. Later it turned out that those fingerprints belonged to someone else, and that Michael's signature had been forged to make it look like he was involved. But then it's hard to put together a scam unless you take *some* liberties along the way.)

Hylton, Barry's younger brother, became a headline success as a film director, and most recently as the owner of a Cape Town–based production company. He is described as talented by advertising executives; his advertisements for fast-food company Steers, car company Kia and restaurant chain Cape Town Fish Market have won a number of awards.

Given the subtlety and panache with which Barry marketed Frankel Chemicals, it shows Hylton wasn't the only one in the family with a knack for advertising. Compared with his overachieving brothers, Michael and Hylton, Barry was already the flailing black sheep by the mid-2000s.

But in a macabre twist of notoriety, Barry will probably end up more famous than either of them.

* * *

Like Michael, Barry initially went to Krugersdorp High School, the largest and most well-respected institution on the west side of Johannesburg, until midway through high school.

Then, in the late 1970s, Harold and Avril Tannenbaum made a critical decision: they left Krugersdorp for Johannesburg following the exodus of Jack and Len towards the flashing glitz of the big city, leaving behind the increasingly dimming town where their family had made their fortune.

They moved into an enormous white house in Dunkeld, one of Joburg's poshest suburbs, next to Hyde Park at 60 Cradock Avenue. Barry and Hylton were sent to King David, a traditionally Jewish school in Victory Park, on the western flank of Johannesburg.

One of Barry's schoolmates at King David, who didn't want to be named, said he had the air of an entitled rich kid right from the start. 'The first thing I noticed about his parents is that they bought the biggest house they could find in the fanciest suburb. You could immediately see they were very conscious about their money, and needing to live a certain lifestyle.'

Sasfin Securities deputy chairman David Shapiro, who knew the Tannenbaum family well, says there was a certain mystique about them in those days:

> When I was a young accountant, I did my articles at Schwartz Fine, who were the auditors of Adcock Ingram. In those days, the Tannenbaums were royalty – they were highly respected and had a huge empire. There were certain high-level Jewish families of this calibre at that time, like the Lubners (who founded Plate Glass), the Frankels (Tiger Oats), the Blooms (Premier Milling) and the Rapps (Rapp and Maister). That was the quality of Tannenbaum's pedigree.[1]

Shapiro describes Harold Tannenbaum, Barry's father, as 'a large man, tall and very empowering'. He adds: 'Why [Barry] had to do what he did, well, I just don't know. There seems no obvious reason for him to do something like that.'

Arnold Tannenbaum also describes his cousin Harold as 'very sociable', a 'gentle sort of soul, who liked playing bridge and that sort of thing'.[2]

Daryl Kronson, Adcock Ingram's former financial director, says Harold was 'just a very nice guy, quiet, who reached a stage where he just wanted to do something else'.[3]

Barry arrived in Joburg overweight, but soon trimmed down and made sure he slotted in with the right crowd. Flippant, a smooth talker, and with an obvious craving for social acceptance, Barry soon wormed his way into the 'cool crowd'.

Says Barry's schoolmate: 'What I remember is that he was incredibly lazy, and very entitled at the same time. He tried to avoid the religious stuff at school pretty much.' This is surprising, given how Barry later became conspicuously devout, almost cravenly so.

And former teachers suggest Barry's academic credentials were not good. 'His marks weren't great,' says one.

Norman Lowenthal, the ex-head of the JSE, knew the family well – Hymie and Harold particularly, from the days of Adcock Ingram. They visited each other's houses, and both were considered part of Joburg's business elite. 'That family was gold. Just lovely, there really wasn't a bad thing you could say about them,' says Lowenthal, a view he held until he and his son, accountant Howard Lowenthal, were both lured into Barry's investment scheme, both losing, if not their shirts, then a good-sized strip off each sleeve.[4]

Howard Lowenthal agrees with his father about Barry: 'He was a laid-back guy back then. The sort of guy who was never going to do a day's work in his life.'

Sharon Green, the only Jewish teacher at Krugersdorp High School from the late 1970s, says the Tannenbaum name was particularly well known, which is why the Ponzi scandal ricocheted through the community. 'Everyone knows about it. Krugersdorp is a small place,' she says.[5]

John W. Hall, a deputy headmaster at the school in the 1980s, says the family had something of an impressive pedigree. 'There was a Tannenbaum bursary at the school, in accounting or something along those lines. Something that was put in place by old man Tannenbaum.'[6]

Despite displaying no obvious sign of academic brilliance, the desperation to emulate the family's renowned pharmaceutical credentials saw Barry enrol for a bachelor of science degree at Johannesburg's University of the Witwatersrand, from 1984 to 1987. But he never finished his studies at Wits. Despite that, the CV peddled to investors punts his studies prominently. It doesn't reveal that Barry dropped out.

Quite why he dropped out isn't clear. The bottom line, though, was that Barry's name didn't join the seven other members of the Tannenbaum family on the list of registered chemists.

If Barry had an almost pastoral childhood, this cocoon was crudely ripped apart in 1988, when he was summoned to serve in the South African Defence Force. This was a rite foisted on all white boys until 1993, whether they were willing or not, in an effort to protect the apartheid state.

The National Party made brutes out of many of South Africa's young white men. Conscripts were brainwashed into the notion of defending the apartheid state from the ANC and its 'terrorists' like Nelson Mandela, who, the administration claimed, were plotting increasingly macabre ways of slaughtering all whites and implementing communism – something of questionable claim anyway, as communist regimes were slowly breaking up at that time.

Boys, whose sole source of conflict came in the form of Saturday-afternoon rugby clashes against neighbouring schools, were trained and brainwashed, then sent into the townships to lay low any uprising. This at a time when black South Africans sensed the frailty in the tribalistic National Party, and were becoming more strident in their demands for democracy. Necklacing, the practice of throwing a burning tyre around the neck of people believed to be apartheid spies, was making gruesome front-page news in the *Wall Street Journal* and the *New York Times*.

In the late 1980s, any conscript forced into army duty was not only ill-prepared to understand the political dynamics, but was also at risk of ending up on the business end of a panga for a cause they couldn't comprehend.

Barry was called up two years after besieged president P.W. Botha had declared a 'state of emergency', which ended one year before Mandela was released from prison. The period coincided with unparalleled township violence.

Conscription made savages out of teenage boys. One boy called up to the army described how, in going into the townships to 'restore order', he simply became a brute: 'There is a tremendous sense of power in beating someone up. Even if you are the most put upon, dumb son of a bitch, you are still better than a [black person], and you can beat him up to prove it'. But then, it's easy to be a bully when you have an R4 assault rifle strapped to your side, and a group of equally naive boys egging you on.[7]

This shattered many of the boys. In 1986, for example, 326 of the conscripted white soldiers attempted suicide, and 18 succeeded. By contrast, only 116 died doing actual army business.

After leaving the army, Barry Tannenbaum then veered off course, eventually getting a job in the media industry.

'The best thing that could have happened to Barry would have been for his father to have stayed at Adcock Ingram, because then he could have easily got a job at the company,' says one of Barry's acquaintances from his early days. 'As it is, I heard he went from job to job for a while, then popped up selling ads for

Business Day. I remember thinking that was probably the right job for him. But I heard he was pretty useless at that too.'[8]

Ironically, Barry spent his formative commercial years working for the very media company that would haunt him in later years, splashing his picture on the front of magazines and newspapers, and portraying him as a villain of Madoff-esque proportions.

Photographs of a youthful Tannenbaum around that time are an antidote to those of the balding, middle-aged man with the ballooning midriff who donated the Torah to the Umhlanga Chabad. The twenty-six-year-old Tannenbaum was dark-haired and with purpose in his eyes, a determined business-like smile on his lips of the sort that was mandatory for the 'People on the move' columns of the day.

Barry spent two years at Times Media as an advertising executive, the company that owned the *Financial Mail*, *Business Day* and *Sunday Times* – papers in which his later exploits were given the full treatment.

'He was a phenomenal chap. He had all the charm in the world,' says Ian Tasman, a former colleague of Barry's at Times Media. 'I mean, I never thought he was a rocket scientist, but he was one of the boys. Just a great guy to be around, with a great sense of humour.'[9]

Tasman says that when he first saw the headlines, he just couldn't picture Barry Tannenbaum, the jolly guy who went for drinks with the advertising staff and who seemed to get on with everyone, as the mastermind of a multinational pyramid scheme running into billions of rands.

'I nearly fell off my chair,' he says. 'I thought, no, it's impossible. Which makes you wonder, who was really the brains behind it. Barry might have got the ball rolling, but I'm pretty sure someone else took it and ran with it.'

When Barry quit Times Media, he told people that he was going to work in his father's business, that an opportunity had presented itself. It was time to move on, he said.

But Barry didn't move straight into the family business. Instead, in 1992, he moved to Los Angeles, where he spent a year, before coming back home and getting engaged in December 1993 to Chareen Anstey, daughter of Teddy Anstey, a well-known, accomplished engineer with impeccable Jewish credentials.

'It was a very serious relationship,' says a member of the Jewish community who mixed in the same circles as Chareen and Barry, but who didn't want to be named. 'Her family was enormously wealthy. He probably liked that. Even at that age, you could see he craved wealth, money and stature.'

It remains unclear exactly why the relationship fell apart. But one story that emerged was that Chareen's father, Teddy, wasn't particularly keen on Barry. One way or another, the marriage was called off. (Chareen now lives in the US, and is married to someone else. She didn't respond to requests for comment.)

Barry moved on too; in 1999, he married Debbie Blou, a dress designer from Cape Town two years his junior, who had been working as a marketing consultant for a company called Markinor.

For their antenuptial contract, signed by both in January 1999, each had to record the value of their estate after debt. Barry signed that his was worth R150 000; hers was worth R100 000. Not exactly filthy rich.

The years between his stint in America and his reinvention as an imaginary pharmaceutical tycoon in the middle of the first decade of the 2000s remain sketchy. Friends say that while he did then take an interest in the family business, he was initially fairly invisible at Frankel Chemicals, where he began working in 1993.

In September 1999, Barry opened an account at Investec Bank. He described himself as a 'sales and marketing director' for Frankel, and put his monthly income at R30 000, which came to about R22 000 after tax.

The mortgage on his house at the time cost him about R3 500, and the repayments on his two cars – a BMW 323i and a Honda 150i – came to R2 000 per month. At the end of every month, Barry reckoned he had a surplus of about R9 000.

In June 2001, when Barry applied for a credit card at Standard Bank, he put his total monthly income at R28 500.

What is odd is that the numbers between his various bank applications and his declarations to the South African Revenue Service didn't tally.

For example, his tax assessment for 2002 put his total income at R143 363, claiming deductions of R88 333. This meant that because his taxable income was so low, at only R55 030, he could claim a credit from the taxman of R21 892.

His tax assessment for 2003 put his total income at R134 820. Yet, within two years, many millions would be sluicing through his accounts. It would represent one of the most rapid increases in wealth one could ever imagine.

It allowed the Tannenbaums to go from distinctly middle class to dizzyingly wealthy.

On 1 February 2007, Debbie Tannenbaum signed an offer to buy a ritzy town-house unit (530 square metres) in an upmarket complex in Morningside, Terra Promessa, Johannesburg, for R3.1 million. At the same time, Barry traded in his ageing car and splashed R780 000 on a BMW X5 4×4 and another R244 000 on a new Mini Cooper.

Barry appeared to have been cheating the taxman for years, and he wasn't about to stop, just because he'd got extra loot. For the 2009 tax year – a year in which literally billions went through his account – he estimated his taxable income at R1 002 132. He said the amount he owed SARS was a meagre R316 730. (As it later turned out, this was many times less than what he should have paid.)

Of course, you wouldn't know how non-existent Barry's business career really was from reading his CV, detailed in the brochures given to investors to illustrate his impressive pedigree and business acumen. Those brochures, passed from hand to hand, create an altogether different collage of Barry's business acumen and commercial experience.

That CV appears to take eye-popping liberties with events, dates and people, to promulgate the impression of a jet-setting entrepreneur sent off to learn the ways of the world before being recalled to the family business to put his extensive knowledge into practice.

The CV says: 'Eurochemicals, trading as Frankel Chemicals, was founded in 1960 by Harold Tannenbaum. Harold was one of the founding members of the biggest listed pharmaceutical manufacturing company in South Africa, namely Adcock Ingram, which was sold in 1980 to Tiger Oats, and Harold was seconded to the board for three years.'

When it comes to Barry's credentials, it says that after returning to South Africa from Los Angeles, 'Barry joined Frankel Chemicals and, in 1998, the Tannenbaums purchased Frankel Chemicals.'

Frankel Chemicals was the main vehicle for Tannenbaum's scheme. When investigators from the Hawks, the country's top criminal-investigating team in the South African Police Service, began investigating the Ponzi scheme, they billed their probe Project Frankel.

But the version of events palmed off on investors doesn't match the facts. Instead, official Companies Office records show that Eurochemicals was registered on 11 February 1983 by Barry's father Harold, who signed the original memorandum of incorporation – not 1960. While on that point, Harold doesn't appear to have even been on the board of Adcock Ingram – Jack was. And, as we've seen, Harold wasn't one of the founding members of Adcock Ingram either. Harold then resigned in February 1998, with the shares being transferred to Selwyn Kahanovitz.

It was a series of half-truths, peddled as fact. But what it does illustrate is Barry's grandiose vision of himself as the chip off the old block, the scion of a dynasty dating back to the day when Hymie Tannenbaum first walked into the pharmacy in Ockerse Street as a young man.

It was, of course, an elaborate fairy tale, a soap opera. More *Dallas*, *Dynasty* and *Egoli* than sobering reality.

Celebrity swindle:
The story of June Kraus

June Kraus is a break from the mould of the usual Tannenbaum victim. She isn't a lawyer; she isn't a highly paid executive; she isn't even an architect. In fact, Kraus, a Salzburg-trained opera singer, has never had what you might call a real job in her life.

Born in New York to parents who had escaped Hitler's concentration camps, she trained at the world-famous Juilliard School of Music in 1966, before being invited to take master classes in opera, concert and art songs in Austria's Alpine town of Salzburg, at the prestigious Mozarteum, nearly two centuries old.

Even among such august company, Kraus was precociously talented. In her first year as a professional at the Salzburg Opera House, she sang an astounding six leading roles – kicking off a European stint where she had thirty-three leading roles in musical productions, from Vienna to Verona.

In 1986, when she moved to South Africa – where she has performed for Nelson Mandela, among others – it was something of a cultural coup for the country. It was also, fatefully, where she met Dean Rees two decades later.

'I was one of the first sixty investors,' Kraus says, echoing a line that was peddled frequently to all Tannenbaum's victims.

Despite more than two decades in South Africa, Kraus's American east coast accent hasn't faded. She speaks purposely and warily, as if the scars of having been swindled once are still raw. Nor has her bitterness towards Tannenbaum diminished in the years since she was scammed.

'I met Dean Rees through a friend, who told me it was a fabulous investment,' she says. 'I had a meeting with Rees and Tannenbaum in 2007, who took me to the Design Quarter [near Fourways, north of Johannesburg] and bought me expensive champagne.'

As the French champagne flowed at the meeting, attended by more than fifty would-be investors, Kraus's immediate thoughts about Barry were unflattering. 'Tannenbaum had no personality,' she says. 'He was fat, dysmorphic, an unappetising person. He looked like a beanbag with tiny eyes, a tiny mouth, a small nose. He didn't smile, he had no charm, no expression. You wouldn't remember him if you passed him in Sandton City the next day.'

But Kraus says it wasn't Tannenbaum who convinced her: it was Rees. She is hardly any more complementary about Rees though, describing him bitterly as 'a slimy eel, a bit creepy, and a bit flashy with his cars'.

Nevertheless, the seduction tactic worked. Kraus took her entire inheritance of R6 million, and paid it into an overseas bank account in the tax shelter of the Isle of Man – a bank account belonging to Dean Rees.

The first year of investment, she says, worked out well. Statements arrived punctually, detailing exactly how her investment was rocketing.

Excited about what she was earning – at least what the statements claimed she was earning – Kraus then told her son, Daniel Kraus, about this sensational investment.

But Daniel, the founder of www.stockalert.co.za, a registered futures and currency dealer, and regular talking head on financial television shows on CNBC Africa and Summit Television, was immediately suspicious.

'He said to me, "Don't believe it: it's a Ponzi scheme." But to me, it sounded legal and above board, so I kept rolling my investment,' she says.

When you speak to Daniel Kraus, the first thing he says is that if he finds Barry Tannenbaum, he'll kill him. He's exaggerating, as you'd expect from a cocksure stock-market trader who trades in absolutes, but there's more than a fleck of steel in his voice when he says it.

'I told her from day one it was a scam, and two years later, it came out that it actually was,' says Daniel. 'I mean, I knew it was fishy, but I didn't think it was an *actual* Ponzi scheme.'

Daniel says the money that Tannenbaum took 'would have been our inheritance, but now it's all been pissed down the drain'.

When Daniel challenged his mother on this 'investment', June would always show him the 'statements' sent to her by Dean Rees as 'evidence' that it was legitimate.

'I couldn't believe how amateurish it looked,' he says. 'They were just PDF files with numbers. I'd say to her, "Mom, this isn't from a bank, it's not a bank-generated document. It's just a PDF – I could make this at home in ten minutes." She'd always reply, "No, no, here's the signature and everything".'

What made it 'extra fishy', he says, is that Rees had warned her repeatedly not to breathe a word to anyone about the scheme – supposedly because it was a 'niche investment for only six to ten people'. 'What legitimate business operates like that?' he asks.

By the time it went bust, June had every cent tied up with Tannenbaum. On paper, she was worth more than R11 million. In reality, she hadn't a shiny rand left.

'I ended up with zero,' says June today. 'My son had to give me R60 000 just so I could get through the year. I realised I needed to do something, so I started my own business, I started my own life.'

From being a wealthy, virtually retired singer who worked when she felt like it, a cash-strapped June Kraus hit the performance trail with purpose. First, she founded the June Kraus Performance Academy, to teach kids everything she knew around the parabola of performance singing, then hit the concert trail with vigour from mid-2009.

Daniel says that his mother still gets tearful about the episode, having squandered an inheritance that her parents had worked for after escaping from a concentration camp. 'I imagine that she'd rather not be working, but her business has become a huge success. A lot of those kids she teaches to sing idolise her, so in a way, I suppose some good has come of it,' he says.

That might be a bitter consolation, when your inheritance, built up over six decades, has been sucked away without a second thought by a sociopath living thousands of miles away. But it's something. Not everyone had a silver lining.

4

This time, they came for the Jews

'People are angry and embarrassed and disappointed that a Jewish person is alleged to have taken other people, including Jews, for a ride.'
                    – A South African-born Jew, living in Australia

When Barry was growing up in Krugersdorp, there were few hints that he would become public enemy number one in the Jewish community, constructing South Africa's largest con in the process. But then, many other ethnic and cultural groups in South Africa have had their day under the spotlight of various Ponzi schemes.

In the late 1990s, it was a group of poor Afrikaners from the industrial south of Johannesburg who got taken for a ride in a scheme known as Krion. This happened in an area known as the Vaal Triangle, fittingly evoking comparisons with the Bermuda Triangle, where planes and ships disappear.

In the Vaal Triangle, it is ambition, style and common sense that are nowhere to be found. It may only be thirty kilometres away from Johannesburg's over-priced malls, but the Vaal Triangle might as well be in the middle of the Karoo. When it comes to grunge and depression, it is South Africa's Birmingham or Oklahoma City.

It was here that Marietjie Prinsloo cooked up the pyramid scheme Krion, which sapped more than R1 billion from hundreds of people, mostly blue-collar workers from factories, shops and churches eager to believe in her scheme.

Krion was sold to Prinsloo's victims as an investment in 'micro-lending', supposedly getting people to invest in her scheme with cash (strictly cash, of course) that would be on-lent to the new black middle class. Investors would then supposedly be repaid from the mega-riches that would supposedly flow from the scheme. In all, 8 748 people invested that R1 billion in Krion, and R975 million of that was repaid to the investors, leaving a shortfall of about R600 million.[1]

Prinsloo was deified by her 'investors', at least when they were being paid out. She earned the moniker the Angel of Vanderbijl for how she'd supposedly 'saved' so many people, dragging them out of poverty.

Of course, this isn't what she did.

Judge Cynthia Prinsloo, who sentenced Marietjie Prinsloo to jail for twenty-five years, summed up the nature of this pyramid scheme adeptly: 'She knew in taking each investment that she could not pay the investors back, but [that] did not stop her. It, in fact, fired her up to take more investments so that she could keep her previous investors happy, so that they would, in turn, refer new investors to her.'[2]

This, the judge said, was 'good for her ego'.

Ego is the unspoken presence in these sorts of scams, it seems. Often, it turns out, the men or women who put together these schemes do not do it for the cash: they do it for the kudos of acceptance, often as an unintentional extension of what started as a real business. Often, it is the agents, or the vampires on the periphery, who really make the big bucks. For the mastermind, the money is just a means to an end.

That is not to say that these kingpins lead a life of austerity – Marietjie Prinsloo had bought big game farms in Limpopo, and even a helicopter. And Barry Tannenbaum certainly didn't skimp on his home comforts. It's just that these are almost fringe benefits of a larger game, a game in which the main goal is to keep the players on the pitch as long as possible.

In the end, in October 2010, Prinsloo was convicted of an astounding 118 409 charges, including the staples of fraud, theft, and breaking the Banks Act and the Prevention of Organised Crime Act. She remained free, however, pending her appeal.

Judge Prinsloo said that Krion was run through a 'banditry' that caused many, including the elderly, to lose all they had. 'Some investors lost everything, and they were down and out to such an extent they had to move in with their families or some, for months, had to eat with the dog,' the judge said.[3]

Prinsloo was not the only one to receive a prison sentence. It was a family business: her ex-husband, Burt, daughter, Yolande Lemstra, and niece, Izabel Engelbrecht, each got twelve years behind bars. Yolande's husband, Gerrit Lemstra, got a fifteen-year sentence, and Prinsloo's son, Cobus Pelser, got five years.

For the Vanderbijlpark community, Krion was catastrophic. Reporters from the South African Press Association tracked down a number of victims, and the stories of people who'd borrowed every cent they could to invest were sobering.[4]

One seventy-five-year-old man, when he heard he was about to lose his house, lay down on his bed and waited to die. Others had to move into empty garages or build makeshift shacks. Church groups began delivering food parcels.

An entity known as Mental Health Vaal Triangle reported that depression in that region shot up by 35 per cent, family violence and alcohol and drug use spiked, and car sales in the area halved after Krion fell apart.

It didn't help that under South Africa's draconian insolvency laws, the investors who'd already been ripped off then had to repay the liquidators of Krion more than the R130 million they'd been paid by the scheme – irrespective of whether they might have been net losers.

Theoretically, this R130 million should have been divided among all the investors at the end. In practice, however, lawyers and liquidators hoovered up a big chunk of it.

A decade and a half earlier, in 1984, there had been a similar scheme that ripped off poor Afrikaners, known as the Vrotmelk scandal. This was started by an Afrikaner, Adriaan Nieuwoudt, who placed advertisements telling people they could make a windfall by investing in a new milk-culture product.[5]

It worked like this: people would buy a dry powder for R30, which could apparently be cultivated as a 'milk culture' known as Kubus, which would then supposedly be sold as a miracle ingredient for cosmetics. Once the culture had been cultivated, the investor mailed batches of it back to the Kubus nursery for R10 a pop as the 'cultivated product', and the nursery supposedly sold it to cosmetics firms.

The only thing was, there were no cosmetics firms buying the cultures. Nieuwoudt and his lackeys simply took the culture samples mailed to him, ground them up and resold them to new investors – a classic Ponzi scheme. And he collected R140 million doing this.

The Cape Supreme Court declared it an illegal lottery, but this didn't stop a rash of copycat scams breaking out around the country.

For example, J.P. Botha, who lived in the small Transvaal town of Brits, did exactly the same thing, taking R30 million from the public. Back in 1984 – the era of Ronald Reagan, Margaret Thatcher and 'grand apartheid' – that was nothing to sneeze at. In 1989 Supreme Court judge Gustav Hoexter described his scheme as an immense fraud. '[J.P. Botha] knew that Trio Kulture would be able to meet its contractual obligations to buy the dried product produced by growers only for so long as new growers were recruited at a rate faster than that at which growers earlier recruited were able to produce the dried product.'[6]

Simple maths, the judge said, would have made it very clear to anyone 'of ordinary intelligence that the scheme was not a viable proposition, and that sooner or later it was doomed to failure'.

He continued: 'Why then, it may be asked, did the scheme attract so many investors? The probable answer is supplied by history, which teaches us that in the human breast, greed and gullibility are often partners. It is on these twin weaknesses that all confidence tricksters trade, and not a few flourish.'

A timeless sentiment that could just as easily be applied to the Tannenbaum case, two decades later.

If Krion and Kubus were schemes that swindled poor white Afrikaners, Miracle 2000 would do the same thing with poor black South Africans.

Miracle 2000 was started by Sibusiso 'Master' Radebe, yet another charismatic con man, who swindled poor black people in townships by offering investment returns of more than 1700 per cent a year.

Radebe, a former freedom fighter with the ANC's armed resistance movement, Umkhonto we Sizwe, during the days of apartheid, had turned *askari* – a derisive term for those who betrayed the movement and ended up working for the apartheid administration.[7]

Worse, Radebe worked for the apartheid security police at its most notorious assassination and 'counterinsurgency' unit based at the Vlakplaas farm just outside Pretoria, reporting to the man dubbed 'Prime Evil', Eugene de Kock. De Kock's unit kidnapped, tortured and murdered hundreds of people – crimes for which De Kock remains in prison.

After the demise of apartheid, Radebe started Miracle 2000 from a house in Spruitview, a poor black area on Johannesburg's East Rand, near Alberton. The scheme worked like this: investors paid R50 registration, then invested any amount over R300, and would get 200 per cent return after six weeks.[8]

It was an elixir of instant wealth for people starved of a living wage. People queued outside Radebe's Spruitview house, sometimes for days, eager to hand in their money and become millionaires, as Radebe vowed they would. During that time, Radebe got scores of expensive leather jackets, sixteen cars worth a total of R2 million, two houses paid for in cash and lots of friends. He even bought a luxury Mercedes-Benz for his pastor, it turned out.

The crowds defied description. Radebe's neighbours turned their houses into B&Bs to accommodate the mob; taxi drivers parked their vehicles outside the Spruitview house and charged people R15 per night for a seat to sleep on.[9]

The people were still queuing in mid-winter, July 2000, when Radebe was led out of the house by the crack Scorpions crime-fighting unit. More than R10 million in cash was seized that day by the police from Radebe's three premises.

Yet, as with Tannenbaum, some of the investors refused to believe Radebe was a crook, even after his arrest. The *Beeld* newspaper reported scenes of investors cheering him on during his court appearances, accusing the Scorpions of trying to kill black entrepreneurialism. One investor was quoted by the Independent Newspapers group as saying:

> Miracle 2000 is not a pyramid scheme. What Sibusiso has done is what we call black empowerment. None of the investors have complained about not getting their money back. The government failed to come up with a better way to fight poverty. Instead they are treating the man who has made a difference to so many people's lives as a criminal.[10]

In August, several hundred Miracle 2000 investors even held protests at the Union Buildings, the seat of the Presidency, holding placards reading: 'No Miracle, No Vote', imploring then president Thabo Mbeki to change the laws to allow Radebe's scheme to continue.

Despite Radebe's claims that he made no money, his wife paid his considerable R1 million bail in cash, money brought into the court building in briefcases.

To the profound disbelief of his investors, Radebe's lawyers struck a deal with the prosecutors, admitting guilt on two charges – breaking the Banks Act by illegally accepting deposits, and conducting a harmful business practice. Radebe said he 'wrongfully and unlawfully conducted a harmful business practice in that [he] accepted investments from at least 13 324 people, amounting to R36.3 million and offered them effective rates above commercially accepted returns by financial institutions'.[11]

Magistrate James van Wyk was quoted in the press as saying Miracle 2000 was the right name for Radebe's scheme, because 'nothing short of a miracle would have eventually stopped people from losing'.[12]

Bizarrely, Van Wyk ruled that Radebe need not serve a day in jail, sentencing him to a fine of R150 000 or three years in jail, while another three years' imprisonment was suspended. This when R5.3 million of the money that Miracle 2000 took was still missing.

Prosecutors appealed the light sentence. Finally, the Johannesburg High Court saw sense, and sent Radebe to jail for two years, with another four years suspended.[13]

What the Miracle 2000, Krion and Tannenbaum cases have in common is that the con artists placed themselves in the centre of the communities that they blithely stole from. Radebe lived in the Spruitview community, Prinsloo in Vanderbijlpark, and for Tannenbaum, it was the Jewish community who bore the brunt. The irony was that Tannenbaum was devoutly Jewish – and it was a body blow to the community he had spent years engaging with at synagogues, cultivating their credibility and friendship.

* * *

Barry was brought up in a devoutly Jewish household. An advert in the *Sunday Times* on 28 January 1979, in the bar mitzvah section, reads: 'Barry, son of Harold and Avril, will conduct portion of the Friday evening service and read Maftir and Haftorah on Saturday, February 3rd at the Krugersdorp Synagogue.'

The Tannenbaums had defined themselves as primarily Jewish from the outset. Ever since stepping off the boat from Europe, Charles and Tilly Tannenbaum had kept their religion as an unbending exoskeleton within the otherwise dynamic environment of dust and grinding labour that they found in South Africa.

Luckily for Charles and Tilly, they arrived as part of a mass exodus of Lithuanian Jews fleeing Russia's efforts to force them into ghettos, which provided solidarity. For example, 12 800 Jewish immigrants arrived in South Africa in 1893 – more than thirteen times the number of immigrants thirty years earlier in 1863.

Unlike many European states, which were steadily blocking the influx of Jews at the time, neither the Cape Colony nor the new Boer Transvaal Republic maintained restrictions against them. Those governments had bigger fish to fry than worrying about Jews – like keeping the black population off the land registers, while trying to lure them to the mines to do the really gritty work.

Partly thanks to this, the Tannenbaums found a thriving Jewish community, which had been steadily expanding since 1795 when the first Jews had stepped onto the Cape shore. Krugersdorp had become something of a desired destination for newly established Jews, following the lead of Abner Cohen, who had arrived in South Africa in 1881.

The *Jewish Chronicle* of 1898 says Cohen 'fell in with the Boers, learning their language and trading with them. On his way to Johannesburg in 1887, he pitched his tent on a great heap of stones seventeen miles to the west of the town, which became the site of the town of Krugersdorp. He was thus the first English settler in the town, and has done much towards its development.'[14]

Cohen chaired the Krugersdorp congregation, and was given two freehold sites for the Jewish community by President Paul Kruger.

The Tannenbaums became a pillar of this community. Though their sons, Hymie especially, were busy building their pharmaceutical empire, they still kept up their visits to the Krugersdorp synagogue, built in 1904. Hymie's brother Archie was made an honorary member of the South African Jewish Board of Deputies and, according to the *American Jewish Yearbook* of 1982, remained a 'prominent Zionist' in the Krugersdorp community.[15]

Barry too remained a devout Jew. Even when his cellphone was being assaulted with text messages asking 'where's my money', he continued to donate to Jewish causes and Jewish institutions.

Reports said that Tannenbaum had been a platinum member of the Chevrah Kadisha, the body that provides welfare for the needy. Looking through his bank accounts, amounts were clearly donated to welfare causes – but only a fraction of what was spent on other things.

In 2006 Barry, Debbie and his children were on holiday in the upmarket beach destination of Umhlanga on South Africa's KwaZulu-Natal north coast. During shul, they heard Rabbi Shlomo Wainer tell of how he needed a Torah for the new Umhlanga Chabad he hoped to launch.

Rabbi Wainer explains: 'I spoke about something along those lines in the service, and he came to me and said he'd do it. So I found a second-hand one, from one of the outlying communities that wasn't being used, and we restored it.'[16]

It was a big deal: each Torah is hand-inscribed and can take up to a year to complete. Wainer says the Torah cost about R70 000. Barry also donated cash over the years to the North Coast Chabad: his FNB account in July 2006 shows an international banking transfer worth R120 000, and the payment description says 'Chabad North Coast'.[17]

At the time, it was a large chunk of change for Tannenbaum, but the donation revealed much about his desperation to be respected in the way his grandfather had been. An inscription on the front of the Torah reads 'Dedicated in honour of our children'.

The pay-off happened on 18 June 2006, a few months after he began taking investors' money, supposedly for Frankel Chemicals. That was the day Barry officially donated the Sefer Torah scroll to launch the Umhlanga Chabad in an extravagant ceremony, captured in dozens of photographs by Wainer. The event made headlines as a procession of 200 community members paraded down Lagoon Drive, led by Tannenbaum holding the Torah while religious leaders held a chuppah over his head. A Zulu rickshaw driver whooped and danced in front of him. A police escort cleared the traffic.

One report on the Chabad website described the procession as 'Jew'bilant'. The Jewish-affairs website, Lubovich.com, reported the ceremony as follows:

> A strapping Zulu tribesman, garbed in sheepskins and colourful, woven cloaks, resplendent in his five-foot-tall headdress of cattle horns, feathers dyed blood-red and black, furs and studded mosaics led the parade in honour of the new Torah. Leaping as he strode along the route, the Zulu, and his two-wheeled rickshaw cart, added a dash of local colour to the procession.[18]

Pictures showed a clearly elated Tannenbaum, dressed in grey trousers and an open-necked striped shirt, beaming alongside his wife, Debbie, who was cloaking half her face under oversize aviator sunglasses.

'It felt like my bar mitzvah again,' Tannenbaum told reporters at the event. As he watched his two children ride in a rickshaw, he told them 'a high has hit my heart'.[19]

Perhaps the sort of high that you'd want to replicate, derived from the level of approbation for helping out others. The sort of admiration you'd need to feel again, even if 'helping out' some people meant that others ended up holding the shortest of straws.

In Umhlanga, the donation conferred a certain prestige on Barry and Debbie. It unlocked doors to wealthy business people who spent their holidays in the coastal town, and Barry would relentlessly hit them to invest in his scheme.

Under Deborah's name, the Tannenbaums bought a 176-square-metre unit at number 301 Oyster Schelles in Umhlanga Rocks, one of the most exclusive holiday complexes in an already pricey area. (Debbie had no idea how this transfer actually happened, no idea who paid for it, or where the money had come from. She just signed the forms, she said.)

Bought in 2007 for R3.1 million, they sold it for R4.2 million when they left for Australia. The complex was secluded behind Umhlanga's boutique hotel, the Oyster Box, and has a sprawling balcony from where you can see whales and dolphins, and enjoy views of one of the best beaches that South Africa's east coast has to offer.

Tannenbaum said he had spent most of his holidays in Umhlanga since he was a schoolboy. He said he preferred Umhlanga to Joburg, where walking to the synagogue 'can be dangerous'. 'Umhlanga is a nice haven. You feel safe,' he said.[20]

* * *

'It was a second-hand Torah,' spits a certain Johannesburg-based lawyer, embittered after spending months fighting to recover his money. 'But at the time, it seemed to underline his credentials, and give him more credibility in the community.'

Warren Drue, the lawyer who organised that infamous meeting at Routledge Modise, said he'd known Tannenbaum since university, and he'd been 'quite active' in South Africa's Jewish community. However, Drue says that the Torah was donated 'probably with our money'.

The implication was that the Torah was bought with money pumped into Barry's scheme by his investors. What raises red flags about this is the identity of the other two donors of the Torah alongside Barry and Debbie: Wayne and Melanie Gaddin.

Gaddin, a good friend of Tannenbaum, had also invested his money with Barry and still defined him as a 'great human being', even after it became clear that investors had been swindled.

What this shows, even at this early stage, is that Barry was already sucking in his friends, parlaying cash that probably didn't belong to him, in order to gain influence.

'The roots of that family were what many people were influenced by,' says Mervyn Serebro, the ex-CEO of OK Bazaars and himself a devout Jew. 'They were very integrated in the community, and the Adcock Ingram story was even more reason [for investing with him].'[21]

Serebro himself invested in the scheme and, when it was going well, fatefully encouraged his family to join up. The tale of how his cousin, David Serebro, lost his shirt as a result of this is a template for how many others were suckered.

After the scandal broke, there was a lot of concern within Wainer's Chabad about what to do with the Torah: should they give it away, keep it, hide it? A committee, including lawyers, spent hours poring over the options.

Eventually, they decided to keep the Torah. 'The decision was that the Torah will remain where it is [and] will not be returned to anybody,' says somebody with intimate knowledge of what went on in that committee. 'The decision was the culmination of discussion and research into what Jewish law required.'

Rabbi Wainer says this was the right decision. 'You can't say one thing has to do with the other,' he says. 'It doesn't bother me. It bothers me what he *did*. But whatever funds [he is alleged to have stolen], and I know it's millions and millions, this is R70 000 – a drop in the ocean.'[22]

Wainer says he understands the reality is that Barry's scheme ripped people off, but says, 'I didn't believe it.' He says this in a way that makes you think he still doesn't believe it, that it will soon emerge that there was some other, unexplained third force directing events. Perhaps Leigh or Rees. 'I found him to be friendly, obliging, very sincere. Everybody did,' he said.

In an odd twist, Wainer's pictures of Barry donating the Torah in 2006 were initially the only recent pictures of Tannenbaum anywhere. The first article that broke the news in the *Financial Mail* used Wainer's photo of Tannenbaum hugging the Torah close to his face.

The *Financial Mail*'s art department had scoured the internet, but could only find one source of pictures of Barry – the photos from the Torah donation ceremony. Sensitive not to anger the Jewish community, the editors took the decision to cut out the Torah, and blur Barry's face. It created a ghoulish, macabre effect: a sepia-tinged picture of Barry staring intently off camera with a half-formed self-satisfied smile curling at the side of his lips.

The *South African Jewish Report* said that while most media 'had the good sense to edit the Torah out of the picture' – so as not to make a 'blatant connection with his Jewishness' – one newspaper later wasn't quite so scrupulous, and had to publish an apology.[23]

'People came from around the world for those pictures,' says Wainer. 'They wanted to buy the photographs. They wanted exclusive rights to them, I suppose. But I said I can't do that. I can't sell somebody.'

* * *

After the bubble popped, the Jewish community would turn on Barry Tannenbaum with a focused, malevolent rage. Many of them had lost big, especially the poorer of them.

Perhaps unsurprisingly, the richest of Tannenbaum's investors – the likes of Jawmend Rossi, Jeremy Ord and Arnold Sharp – came out fine. Some even made a profit.

Part of the anger from the Jewish community stemmed from the fact that Tannenbaum's actions had the potential to reinforce some really nasty stereotypes.

The *South African Jewish Report* in July 2009 said the 'coincidental Jewishness' of both Madoff and Tannenbaum was 'an aspect frequently noted privately, but mostly skirted around in general society out of politeness or fear of being labelled anti-Semitic'. The newspaper continued: 'The saga has in some quarters raised the spectre of strengthening negative stereotypes of Jews as cunning "Shylocks" – the money-grabbing Jewish usurer with ill-gotten banknotes pouring out of his pockets. Jews have many enemies who will try to exploit such events to foster hatred towards them – and often, by extension, Israel.' [24]

Jonathan Ossher from Uitenhage wrote in the same newspaper that the Tannenbaum case 'did little to further our image in the world community, especially given the nasty historical prejudices about Jews indulging in sharp practices'. [25]

It might seem paranoid, but, unfortunately, it isn't.

Neo-Nazi website Stormfront, one of those sites inhabited and run by trolls from West Palm Beach in Florida, immediately seized on the Tannenbaum Ponzi scheme, posting articles about it and opining, with characteristic bumbling, that it came 'hot on the heels of Modoff [sic]'. [26]

Stormfront is the sort of hate website you'd expect to be produced by pre-1994 apartheid nationalists. In reality, it is run by Don Black, a former grand wizard of the Klu Klux Klan, who now identifies himself with America's Republican Party. Nowadays, in a democratic era, South Africa's hate-speech jurisdiction would soon see Stormfront shut down. But America seems to have a higher tolerance for brute prejudice.

To people with room-temperature IQs, like Black, the Tannenbaum case would always be used as validation of their perverse beliefs. But then, to those sorts of people, global warming is a scam, the earth is about to clock its 6 000th birthday and Fox News is fair and balanced.

Nonetheless, if you imagined that Tannenbaum would be loudly excoriated for what he'd done within the community, you'd be mistaken. If you imagined that his wrongdoings would be debated publicly, you'd be wrong. Outwardly, the Jewish community pretty much pursed their lips, as if daring to mention the name Tannenbaum would somehow conjure him into their living rooms. But behind closed doors, it was another matter, as the Tannenbaum story was debated at length over Friday-night Shabbat dinners.

Rabbi Mendel Lipskar, who runs South Africa's Lubavitch Foundation, says Tannenbaum's donation of the Torah was a 'non-issue then and remains a non-issue now'. He refused to comment on the effect of the Tannenbaum scheme on the wider Jewish fraternity. [27]

David Shapiro, a veteran investment analyst, now deputy chairman of Sasfin Securities, says he is surprised by how outwardly quiet the Jewish community in particular remained over this scam:

It was a very big thing – and some very big names were involved. There may be two reasons for it, I think. First, just the sheer embarrassment of being caught in something like this, it just exposes how dumb and how greedy some people are. Secondly, in some cases at least, it seems like not everyone declared what they were doing, so not all the money was kosher.[28]

Shapiro should know, as Sasfin Securities is the new incarnation of a company called Frankel Pollak, a brokerage firm whose origins go back to the early 1890s but which nearly crumbled amid an acutely embarrassing stock-market scandal in the early 1990s, now spoken of only in hushed tones as the Greg Blank affair.

Along with the Brett Kebble story, the Greg Blank saga is perhaps the best-known scandal to have hit the JSE. More than twenty years later, every member of Joburg's investment community knows the name Greg Blank, even if they don't know what he did.

Blank, a charismatic rough-hewn stock trader from a relatively poor family, whose father had been sequestrated for unpaid debts, worked for Frankel Pollak in the late 1980s.

As a stockbroking wunderkind, Blank had clocked an unheard-of annual commission at the time exceeding R1.5 million a year, developing a taste for the high life, as detailed in Rex Gibson's book *Prisoner of Power*. This meant a Ferrari 328 GTS, a BMW 535i, a Harley-Davidson motorbike, an art collection worth more than R1.3 million, including paintings by Marc Chagall and Joan Miró, not to mention a fortune invested in racehorses – one of his deeper passions.[29]

But Blank became the symbol of corporate malfeasance after being sucked into a 'front-running' scam that ended his career.

'Front-running' is a complicated business, but in a nutshell, Blank was part of a secret investment club of certain traders, including three from Old Mutual, who kept hidden share-trading accounts. They would buy certain stocks for their personal accounts and then get their companies – like Old Mutual – to place 'buy orders' for those shares, driving up the price. The club would then sell their shares, and make a princely profit.

Blank was arrested late one Sunday night in March 1991, and despite a plea bargain that he thought would save him from serving a day in jail, he was slapped with an eight-year sentence from Judge Tom Cloete, who brushed aside his entreaties with the words 'the accused deserves to go to prison'.

In the end, Blank served two years in Krugersdorp Prison. It might have been a reduced term, but it still wasn't a picnic: 'I saw two people stabbed in my first week,' he told the UK *Independent* newspaper. But at least in those days fraudsters actually *saw* the inside of a jail cell.[30]

Having paid his debt to society, Blank is now a day-trader (for his own account) and owner of 100 racehorses. ('Really, I work to support the horses,' he jokes.) It could have been worse for Blank: a man called David Schapiro (not to be confused with the Sasfin deputy chairman) was one of the three Old Mutual traders accused of running the scam, and he ended up hanging himself in a Cape Town prison over the affair.

The other David Shapiro says: 'What many people didn't know was that Greg was close to a lot of top businessmen, including people in the Jewish community at the time. And the speculation was that he was helping them find creative ways to take money out of the country, at a time when exchange controls were quite strict. Again, the Jewish community closed ranks, and this wasn't discussed.'[31]

The theory was that what Blank was doing for them was creating a series of shady transactions: they'd 'sell' shares they owned to a foreign company, say in London, then buy those shares back a few days later for a lower price. The 'profit' would stay in London, neatly sidestepping exchange controls. The upshot was that you'd move your money offshore, even though there was no change in your actual assets.

Just like the Tannenbaum case, this isn't something you'd want to advertise. And just like the Tannenbaum case, it's the kind of thing where, once exposed, you close the curtains and put the phone on silent, anything to make it go away.

'Among Blank's clients were a number of Jewish businessmen that I knew and, being part of the Jewish community, I was surprised by their support for Blank, despite his obvious transgressions,' says Shapiro.

He himself was never approached to invest with Tannenbaum. Nor did he even hear about the 'Tannenbaum option' until after it upended. Says Shapiro:

> You learn over the years, as my good friend Kokkie Kooyman says, to find out and distinguish the Kebbles from the Ruperts. Would I have entertained [investing in] such a scheme? Not on your life! I would have kicked them out of my office. I know that if I put my money into Standard Bank shares, or Sasol shares, I'll get a 4 per cent dividend. When somebody is offering you 20 per cent, 30 per cent, you know there's no ways it'll happen legitimately.[32]

The fact is that many people struggle to make that distinction. Brett Kebble was a charming con man. Johann Rupert, steward of the Anton Rupert empire, built on companies like British American Tobacco and Richemont, is equally charming but completely above board. The trick is to interrogate the business. Even then, Tannenbaum put up a convincing case – backed up by forged documents. Some people were smart enough to just say no, to realise that 200 per cent profit a year wasn't forthcoming unless a few corners were being cut.

'Why would you as an investment professional do that? Unless, of course, it's just greed,' says Shapiro.

In Australia, the reaction was equally outraged.

'The family were saints in Johannesburg. They were philanthropic, genteel, modest people,' one South African-born Jew living in Sydney told news service JTA, the Jewish Telegraphic Agency. 'People are angry and embarrassed and disappointed that a Jewish person is alleged to have taken other people, including Jews, for a ride.'[33]

Once in Australia, Tannenbaum continued to lead a devout existence. He sent his children to a Jewish school, and joined the Kehillat Masada, an orthodox synagogue in St Ives, Sydney, close to where they lived.

It seems that Barry kept himself to himself there. Cecil Zinn, president of the synagogue, says, 'I didn't know Barry Tannenbaum at all. I was the president, and he came as a member. I wouldn't recognise him.'[34]

5

The dry run

'Stay with me, and we'll make you rich.'
– **Darryl Leigh to Sarah West (November 2009)**

Ripping people off with a backstory of investing in pharmaceuticals isn't as hard as it may appear. Most people wouldn't know their APIs from their NSAIDs (which are simply non-steroidal, anti-inflammatory drugs). Throw in the Tannenbaum name, and the recipe would be lip-smacking enough for Christmas lunch.

What few people know is that the Ponzi scheme that sucked more than R10 billion from the public wasn't Tannenbaum's first 'investment scheme' built on shaky premises. There was an earlier, cruder scheme that had fired briefly before flaming out entirely. This goes some way to explain what Barry did during his wilderness years.

Pyramid schemes often start small. In many cases, they even start out legit. In the case of Krion, Marietjie Prinsloo started it off as a small money-lending business from her house. By the time it collapsed, R1.2 billion was involved.

For Barry Tannenbaum, in 2004 it was all about furniture. Getting people to invest in a cross-border furniture scheme is a lot trickier than it is with pharmaceuticals. After all, people *know* furniture. You can't bluff them that there is some hidden market for tables and chairs that will somehow pay you north of 200 per cent a year.

In itself, Barry's furniture scheme might be considered a failure. But in terms of a dry run for the bigger swindle the following year, it was a colossal success.

Crucially, it identified his 'runners' – the foot soldiers that would make the Frankel pharmaceutical scheme happen. Through the furniture scheme, Tannenbaum was able to anoint his main general, a man with some powerful connections in Johannesburg's slippery legal world, a lawyer called Darryl Leigh.

Over the course of four years, Leigh, a man of no great repute in the legal or business world, clocked himself a profit of at least R114 million through his association with Barry Tannenbaum. Now, people ask, where did all the money go? A good place to start looking is in the wallet of Darryl Leigh.

* * *

Three months before Tannenbaum's Ponzi scheme was unmasked, Leigh, a white-haired bruiser of a man in his early sixties, got a taste of the media blitz to come.

At about 4.30 in the afternoon on a sleepy Sunday in March 2009, a gruesome and bizarre road accident claimed the life of Jan Embro, the fifty-three-year-old head of the South African division of Swedish multinational Ericsson.

Embro, a Swedish-born engineer, had bounced around the world – Malaysia, Saudi Arabia and Lebanon – before settling in South Africa in 2001. Though a curling, crackling pocket of energy, he seemed thoughtful, responsible. But Embro was a racing enthusiast, and the proud owner of a custom-built Ultima GTR, a flame-red supercar whose British manufacturers boast that it is the 'quickest accelerating and decelerating supercar of all time'. That's no idle boast: the car lapped the Dunsfold Aerodrome circuit near London in one minute 9.9 seconds in a test organised by Jeremy Clarkson's TV programme, *Top Gear*. This broke the record set by Formula One icon Michael Schumacher of one minute 10.7 seconds.

And you don't buy the Ultima GTR to have people think that their car can take you. Even if their car is a Lamborghini Murciélago LP640 roadster.

Quite how lawyer Darryl Leigh, whose smattering of second-rate work experience, including working for the Development Bank of Southern Africa as a legal advisor, had managed to afford the silver Lamborghini LP640 would only become clear to the South African public in the following months.

But in the months before the accident, Leigh had been parading the Lamborghini to everyone he met. He wasn't about to retreat into the shadows now, just because someone had a car that was even faster, or which they *claimed* was faster.

Reports said it appeared that Leigh and Embro decided to race each other down William Nicol, a dual-lane road with a speed limit of 100 kilometres an hour, which runs from the upmarket suburb of Hyde Park, past Sandton and Bryanston, and out to the nouveau riche suburbs of Fourways.

With traffic lights every few kilometres, the road winds past churches, schools and shopping centres – hardly the ideal location for two supercars to be revving their egos against each other.

Someone who knows Leigh well says that the lawyer didn't know Embro at all before the incident. 'This guy came up to Leigh and revved, [eager] for a race. Darryl took it on. The guy aced him and disappeared. Then he returned for the next round and lost control. It was childish.'

Police spokeswoman Edna Mamonyane described to Afrikaans newspaper *Beeld* in March 2009 how Embro lost control of the Ultima GTR 'when he couldn't get past the Lamborghini'.[1]

'It burst through a fence, rolled, came to a standstill in the veld and burst into flames,' she said.

One eyewitness was almost sliced apart by the shrapnel flying through the air that splintered off Embro's car.

One woman who saw the accident along with her three-year-old daughter tried to extinguish the flames using her small fire extinguisher, but it wasn't up to the job. Embro burnt to death inside his car.

Medical group Netcare sent an ambulance, but it was too late for Embro. 'Paramedics found the car lying on its roof,' said Netcare's Nick Dollman in a statement. 'Tragically, it was on fire and paramedics could not get near the wreck due to the heat.'

Dollman says an eyewitness claimed that Embro's Ultima had actually collided with Leigh's Lamborghini 'before losing control and leaving the road'. Others say Leigh played no role in Embro's crash, and there was no collision.

Leigh, however, wasn't injured, and refused medical attention.

Pictures of the crash attest to the horror: Embro's car, completely charred, with all identifying marks scorched off, and the tyre rubber gone, had been cindered down to below hip-height. The red bonnet with the headlight casings lay severed from the rest of the frame, and parts of the car's body were trapped inside the two-metre fence it had ripped through after leaving the road.

Leigh's silver Lamborghini was shown parked at the scene, glinting menacingly in the afternoon sun, in front of a billboard for the Yellow Pages with a picture of a light aircraft and text in the bottom right-hand corner, which read, 'Flying Lessons?'

Though Mamonyane said a case of culpable homicide was being investigated, nothing ever happened to Leigh.

That horror crash in Sandton in March 2009 – three months before Leigh was unmasked as Tannenbaum's bag man – provided profound insight into Leigh's character. Having made good almost at the end of his career, Leigh was determined that people should know about his freshly made millions. Damn the laws. Colleagues of his said simply, 'that's Darryl': a braggart and a bully, with not much respect for the law he is professionally mandated to implement.

One person on a motoring chat room put it best: 'People with too much money and absolutely no respect for other road users. I am a major petrol head, but if you want to play with these babies, at least have the balls to go and do it on a racetrack.'[2]

* * *

Until 2006 Leigh was arguably a nobody. Though trained as a lawyer, he had bumbled from company to company without making a particular mark anywhere.

He described himself to friends as a 'banking attorney', but while it is true that he had worked in Nedbank's corporate finance division at one stage, he doesn't seem to have had a wealth of banking work. After he left Nedbank, Leigh went to work for the government-owned Development Bank of Southern Africa. Then he quit, devoting himself full time to being filthy rich and thoroughly dislikeable.

In the years before the Ponzi scheme, Leigh had led a comfortable life, but was hardly what you'd call wealthy. Initially, he lived in Birdhaven, a suburb next to the Wanderers cricket ground, in a property he bought for R244 000 in 1996.

His salary at the time was, if anything, shy of what most other lawyers in Joburg's corporate world brought home. His tax returns in 2002, for example, showed that he only earned R226 503. In 2003 he declared R278 057 in earnings, which shot up to R351 656 in 2004, then dropped to R335 851 in 2005. This was equivalent to the salary of a mid-level professional – far less than most lawyers of his generation earned.[3]

But then Leigh's luck turned, thanks to his former neighbour, a man called Barry Tannenbaum.

In about 2000, Leigh was living in the same complex as Tannenbaum, in a cluster-housing complex in a boomed-off cul-de-sac near Sandton called, pretentiously, Le Mistral. 'They got on well together,' says one person who knew them well at the time. 'Barry and Darryl sat on the residents' committee of the complex together. Darryl was a difficult man, so he was often kicked off the committee.' Tannenbaum lived at 18 Le Mistral, Leigh opposite.

Darryl Leigh was a hard case. Few of his neighbours liked him because he was one of those people who was an inflexible stickler for the rules in the way that reminded you of a customs official, or some other petty bureaucrat, of a tin-pot country.

He'd raise all manner of havoc if, for example, one of the residents parked in the wrong spot. 'Most people thought he was an asshole, and he was,' says that same person. 'But the thing is, Darryl is very particular about rules, about things being in their place. He wasn't asking anyone to do what he wouldn't.'

Even before he'd made money, many people saw Leigh as a truculent, testy individual, not averse to using whatever little power he had to demean others. The sort of man who would complain about his food at a restaurant, just to see the waiters scramble.

Neither Barry's property nor Darryl's was particularly cheap.

It was Morningside, after all – a suburb overgrown with townhouse complexes, stuffed with stock traders, executives, lawyers and accountants. Close enough to Sandton to access clients.

Tasha Rossen, an estate agent who used to work for one of South Africa's largest realtors, Pam Golding, knows Leigh better than most. She was there right at the genesis of the Ponzi scheme – and ended up as one of the unlucky investors too.[4]

Uniquely, she knew all of the main protagonists separately. She'd met Barry in April 2002 when she brokered the sale of his Le Mistral property, netting R900 000 for him. And in 2001, she hired Rees to defend her after her ex-husband took her to court to get his child maintenance reduced.

But it was her meeting with Darryl, back in October 2000, that changed her life.

She recalls: 'A colleague who had concluded the rental agreement for Darryl at Le Mistral asked me to please phone him as he was looking for investment properties in the Sandton area. She said I must please look after him as he'd complained about Pam Golding's service.'

Her first impressions weren't flattering. He seemed rude. But in Rossen, Leigh found someone who gave it back to him. She diligently avoided him, despite the fact that he was a potential customer. 'It was the height of the property boom,' she says today. 'I was selling lots of property, I didn't need his rudeness.'

Instead, Leigh sought her out, visiting her show houses, wooing her, despite the fact that, at fifty, he was fifteen years her senior. Voluptuous, with striking eyes and high cheekbones, Rossen was a looker. Leigh clearly knew it.

She was emerging from a nasty divorce, and they drifted together. 'A lot of people never saw it, but Darryl was a lot of fun,' she says. 'He had a great sense of humour and could be very supportive. Most people never saw that side, unfortunately.'

Some people didn't think Darryl *had* a redeeming side. Soon after she got together with Darryl, Rossen asked one of her colleagues at Pam Golding, Sarah West, if she knew him. She did: she'd rented out some properties to him, but found him rude and unlikeable.

'I do. He's an arsehole,' she replied.

'Oh,' Tasha said. 'Well I'm going out with him'.

When he was young, Darryl was, contrary to all expectations, quite the charmer. Rossen says she'd been told how, in his youth, Darryl was 'one of the boys, a good looking, charming young man who got all the girls'.

'When I met Darryl, he was so funny, and had a brilliant sense of humour,' she says. 'He was difficult and wanted things done in a specific way, but he wasn't a big loudmouth show-off, just good fun.'

But then, everything changed for everyone.

'One day, in August 2004, Darryl came to me, wanting an opinion on an investment opportunity. He said: "Barry spoke to me. He says he's got this consortium that is importing furniture through his brother, who works at a big London property company. He says his father-in-law pulled out of one deal, and if we can put in a short-term loan of R300 000, we can make R90 000 in three months".'

That would be a 30 per cent return for a three-month investment – 120 per cent if you annualise it.

What is particularly intriguing is that Barry's first steps into soliciting invest-ments from Darryl revolved around furniture – not AIDS drugs, as he would later become most famous for.

The way Barry explained it to Leigh was that his brother, Michael, then a director of a company called Westcity plc, was buying up dilapidated properties in London, fixing them up, and selling them to rich investors. Those properties needed to be furnished, and there was a margin to be made by buying cheaper South African furniture and flicking it on to Westcity for a chunky profit.

Rossen recounts Barry's explanation: 'A certain amount of business was allo-cated to different people – he called them tribes – which were small consortiums financing the furniture. Barry claimed he ran one of these consortiums for his brother. Barry claimed that his father-in-law had pulled out, so he was short of the R300 000.'

Darryl, however, wasn't keen to do it. He was nervous and needed convincing.

Rossen recalls: 'He asked me, and I said to him, what do you have to lose? It's a lot of money you can make very quickly. The worst that can happen is you lose the R300 000.'

So, Leigh bit. He transferred the R300 000 – a fairly large amount of cash for him at the time. A few weeks later, almost against his expectations, Barry trans-ferred R390 000 back to him. Leigh even had a heart: he gave that entire R90 000 profit to Rossen, who had been struggling to pay her kids' school fees.

Another 'opportunity' came up with Barry, so Leigh did it again, and it worked again. He was just like every other investor who got sucked into the scheme: at first, it seems implausible, but after you've seen the magic work the first time, you start to believe.

Years later, the police investigating this case would attest to Rossen's version of events, that Leigh first began doing business with Barry in 2004.

Colonel Piet Senekal, an investigator with the Hawks priority crimes unit, spells out in an affidavit how the business relationship was formed:

Tannenbaum originally approached Leigh to assist with trade finance for the export of furniture to the United Kingdom. Leigh made substantial returns from Tannenbaum in this regard. Leigh eventually abandoned his day job as a legal advisor with the Development Bank of SA to manage 229 investors who he induced to participate in the Frankel scheme.[5]

The money brought Leigh and Tannenbaum closer. In February 2006, Leigh added Barry as a third trustee to his Darryl Leigh Trust, an account that appears to have held his property assets, like the Le Mistral townhouse.[6]

Leigh and Tannenbaum then registered a property company together, Tann Leigh Properties.[7] The plan was to buy a house in Sea Point for Darryl's father using Tann Leigh, which both Barry and Darryl could later use as a holiday home. The two were now in cahoots. Barry had found his fence, his patsy, the man who would allow him to deny culpability.

Leigh's bank balance rocketed almost immediately. During 2006, Leigh told the taxman, he had earned R4 139 891 – more than ten times what he'd earned the previous year.[8]

But how much he subsequently scored from the scheme wasn't immediately disclosed. Johann van Loggerenberg, the head of enforcement at the South African Revenue Service (SARS), said that by 2009, Leigh had not filed tax returns for 2007 and 2008.

As the circumstances around Embro's fiery demise would suggest, Leigh apparently wasn't averse to breaking the odd rule. Van Loggerenberg said: 'The Darryl Leigh Trust should be a registered taxpayer. According to the SARS income tax system, I can confirm that the trust is not registered for income tax.'[9]

If Van Loggerenberg is right, it seems Leigh may have been dodging tax on that trust for a good sixteen years before the taxman even found out. So much for not getting away with it.

This doesn't accord with Rossen's view of Leigh, however. 'The irony of this whole thing is that Darryl is one of the most honest people you'll ever meet,' she says. 'He has his other faults, but he's meticulous, and doesn't break the law. I can tell you now, if he ever thought it was illegal, he never would have put a cent into it.'

According to Rossen, Darryl even spoke to his tax consultants about Tannenbaum's scheme, and they both declared it above board and legitimate. ·

You might be forgiven for thinking. 'Well, Rossen would say that, wouldn't she?' But she broke up finally with Darryl Leigh back in 2007 – nearly two years before the Routledge Modise meeting, which effectively exposed the scheme as fraud. She has little incentive to lie.

'It was a very tempestuous relationship. We broke up a number of times,' says Rossen.

But they drifted back together various times, until, in late 2007, Rossen called it quits for the final time after a bust-up at Heathrow Airport – two years before the bubble eventually burst.

'The whole thing had changed him. He became unbearably arrogant. I just couldn't take it any more, so I said no thanks,' she says.

Before he met Tannenbaum, Leigh drove a five-year-old BMW. The money changed him, as he blew cash on smart cars and expensive houses – and then, stupidly, bragged about it.

Keith van der Spuy, a former Investec banker who worked at Nedbank when Leigh was a legal advisor there, says he went from leading what appeared to be a 'relatively modest' life to that of an exceptionally wealthy man. 'He said he'd bought a house for R22 million in Camps Bay, Cape Town, an apartment for R16 million in Clifton, Cape Town, and expensive sports cars, such as Lamborghinis.'

Although those numbers weren't quite right, property records confirm that very quickly after making his first investment, Leigh did go on a spending spree.

First, he bought a house at the top of the hill in Cape Town's picture-postcard luxury neighbourhood of Camps Bay for R3.57 million. He splashed down R500 000 in cash as a deposit immediately for a townhouse at 8 Woodhead Drive, overlooking the Atlantic Ocean. (It is notable that while Standard Bank gave him a R3 million bond, his deposit was more than he had declared as his earnings for the entire previous year.)

He then set about overhauling the Woodhead Drive townhouse, spending months at a time in Cape Town.

There, he bought the apartment in the Sea Point suburb for his father through Tann Leigh, a sale organised by two Cape Town lawyers and property developers, Richard Goudvis and Craig Delport.

How is it that you're able to buy all these properties, they asked. Leigh told them, and they were obviously impressed. By the end of 2008, Goudvis and Delport would be representing a number of investors in Cape Town.

Darryl also bought a 1520-square-metre house for his daughter, Laura, on Medburn Road in Cape Town, under the shadow of Lion's Head. He parted with R8.8 million cash for the house in November 2007.

Leigh was barely any more discreet in Joburg. There, he bought a 1700-square-metre house at 4 Carol Ann Road, Morningside, for R8 million, and the house opposite, number 5, for R6.5 million. He took no bond on either.

Barry's money had begun washing through Darryl's accounts.

* * *

Barry had thrown out the hook, but he couldn't appear too eager. One day, he dropped it into a conversation with Darryl, as if by chance, that he was funding these 'trade finance deals' through Sasfin, a niche Johannesburg lender – but the bank was treating this as short-term finance and demanding interest of 35 per cent.

Rossen recalls: 'So, Darryl said to Barry, well, rather than paying the bank, why don't we get together a consortium to invest in your business? It makes more sense.'

You can imagine Barry's faux reluctance at the suggestion, his staged 'well there's an idea I'd never thought of'.

Darryl's original group for the furniture investments was small. Rossen was part of it, but so too were Darryl's old friends like John Miller, Rob Lowdon, Rossen's mate Andrew Armstrong, and others he'd only recently met, like former OK Bazaars boss Mervyn Serebro. 'Darryl did not want any more people,' says Rossen.

Soon, however, Leigh's investors ballooned beyond the original fifteen, partly a result of people steeling themselves to ask how he was suddenly swimming in money. He let slip, and soon they were coming along for the ride. Friends he met at the racetrack, his ex-wife Sharon Haarhoff, people who saw him pitching up at their houses in his Lamborghini – everyone wanted a piece of it. The virus spread.

Initially, for every deal Barry would provide a post-dated cheque (which could, theoretically, be cashed should any deal go south), as well as a written 'acknowledgement of debt'. After a while, investors stopped asking for the acknowledgment of debt.

Chris Leppan, like Leigh a lawyer who wasn't practising, ran driver training programmes for Lamborghini. Darryl had casually mentioned his 'investment consortium' a number of times to Leppan, and asked him to join. 'It sounded as if one needed to invest several million. As this was well beyond my reach, I never took the matter further,' he says. 'I discovered that certain other friends of mine in the Lamborghini fraternity had invested in the consortium, and were pleased with their investment.'

Leppan soon jumped at the bait. 'But before we invested, we met with Leigh to satisfy ourselves. We met in January [2008] at Leigh's townhouse in Rivonia, from where he ran the consortium.'[10]

As it was seemingly all above board, and recognising the names of other Joburg businessmen on the list, Leppan dived in, and so did his wife, a lawyer – with disastrous results.

Leigh was useless with technology – ironic, given his penchant for expensive Italian-designed engines. Even his friends jokingly referred to him as 'BC' – Before Computers. So whereas Dean Rees at least typed out 'investor letters' setting out the terms and conditions of their investment, Leigh never did this. Instead, he had a series of what appear to be laughably amateurish handwritten notes, with different amounts owed to various investors scrawled on them.

This deterred some. Keith van der Spuy, his former colleague at Nedbank, took up Leigh's invitation to invest in the Tannenbaum scheme, but chose to do this via Dean Rees. He says that 'Rees's administrative processes were more sophisticated than those of Leigh', and Rees also gave him formal documents.[11]

Others didn't mind Leigh's archaic style. Howard Lowenthal, for example, says, 'I didn't need anything from him. I had all the records of my investments, everything, on my computer.'

At this point, Leigh might as well have been using banknotes to wallpaper the outside of his house, so blatant had the scheme become.

Sarah West, Tasha Rossen's friend at Pam Golding, was retrenched in March 2007. She asked Rossen if the scheme was a safe bet. 'Sarah, all I can say is that I've received payment on time, every time. If you want to know more, speak to Darryl,' Rossen told her.

So West met Leigh for lunch at the fancy Hyde Park Shopping Centre, close to where she lived. Leigh sketched the broad outline of the scheme, making much of Barry's heritage and knowledge of the medical industry.

'According to Darryl,' says West, 'the one side of the business was to use the funds to purchase furniture in South Africa, and send it over to the UK where Barry and his family had apartments they rented out. The other side of the business was apparently to use the funds to purchase raw materials for the manufacturing of generic and antiretroviral drugs.'

She asked Darryl if any documents needed to be signed. 'According to him, it wasn't necessary,' she says now. Instead, Darryl said Barry would provide postdated cheques to the investors, dated just after each deal. That way, if Barry didn't repay, they could simply cash the cheque.

'Because I knew Darryl very well, I had no reason not to believe him, and I was convinced that this would be a legitimate business transaction,' says West.

A few weeks later, on 10 May 2007, Darryl called Sarah. It turned out there *was* a deal going down soon. All she had to do was put down cash and, seven and a half weeks later, she'd get her money back plus 12 per cent interest.

Darryl told her to deposit her cash into Barry's private bank account at Rand Merchant Bank, an investment bank owned by FirstRand. Sarah followed the instructions, unconcerned that if you annualised that return, it would amount to an epic 82 per cent.

The very next day, she rushed to the nearby Craighall branch of First National Bank and deposited R400 000 – R300 000 for herself and R100 000 for her mother.

She was due to get her money back on 2 July, but before that even happened, Leigh called her with a new deal. So West plugged in another R300 000 and her mother put in a further R200 000.

When the time came to get paid, Leigh called West with an offer to 'roll over' her capital. She was firmly hooked.

Sarah says Darryl 'screened potential investors very carefully'.

In November 2008, Darryl invited Sarah to meet the *man* himself for breakfast, Barry Tannenbaum.

She arrived at the Wedge Shopping Centre, a chic and proudly snobbish centre in Morningside, north of Sandton. It's the sort of shopping centre that can afford to support shops selling specialist maternity wear and yoga studios, alongside the middle-class food shops like Woolworths and Food Lover's Market.

At the breakfast meeting with a handful of potential investors, Barry explained his business: 'He said he did not go to conventional banks as they were not happy to give cash upfront for purchasing pharmaceutical raw materials. They preferred to use guarantees, and countries like India and China, where he bought most of his materials, only worked with cash.'

Barry, philanthropist to the last, wasn't going to work with banks that were so inflexible. No, instead, he told Sarah, he 'wanted to help people' as they had helped him build the business. He liked to help others, he said.

West was impressed. 'After this meeting, I spoke to Barry and Darryl Leigh, and told them I had sold my house, and wondered if it was a good idea to invest the money with them. I was assured by both that this was "not a good option – it was the *only* option".'

Darryl told her: 'Stay with me, and we'll make you rich.'

She did just that, plugging in every last cent. By March 2009, Sarah and her mother's initial small investment was worth, on paper, a staggering R3.8 million.

Sarah wasn't working. With that kind of cash rolling in, she didn't have to. Instead, she devoted herself full time to managing her investment portfolio. 'I would sit and work out projections, look at the spreadsheets,' she says.

Then, red lights began to flash.

'On 5 March 2009, I received [a] call from Darryl Leigh, to say Barry's mother was ill, and so the deal maturing this day would be rolled into the deal [maturing] on 12 March.'

One of Sarah's friends raised his eyebrows at this. 'This is supposed to be an international businessman trading in high stakes,' he told her. 'Yet what kind of a business defaults on payments just because the CEO's mother is sick?'

Still convinced that it was the real deal, Sarah asked to cash out her mother's portion – R840 000 – just in case, content for the other R3 million to be rolled over again.

However, she was let down. 'I called Darryl and asked him what was going on. He told me to phone Barry directly. So I called Barry in Australia and he told me there'd been a few problems with the banks, but not to worry.'

Despite Tannenbaum's assurances, the bells in Sarah's head were ringing almost non-stop by this stage. She was calling Leigh often to find out when she could get her money. 'Darryl, I just need to cash out my mother's investment now. What's going on?' she asked in one call.

Leigh shot back: 'Sarah, pull in your neck.'

There was no option but to wait, white-knuckled, and hope it would all work out. A few weeks later, Darryl called her back. 'He told me, Barry's done a dirty on him. Barry's been lying to him. Then I realised,' she says.

Having sold her house and lost more than R450 000 to Tannenbaum, West was forced to move out of the ultra-fashionable Hyde Park district. 'I'm renting now,' she says. 'I can't afford to buy a new property, thanks to Mr Tannenbaum.'

Sarah's mother, having lost half of her retirement savings, is now living in an old-age home. Some of her friends, who invested in the scheme through her, blame her for what happened.

'At the height of it all,' West recalls, 'I was speaking about it with a friend of mine, trying to reason it out. She told me, "Most of the big businessmen, the Sean Summers and the like, they usually have one lucky break in their lives. Sarah, this is our lucky break."'

Only, it wasn't so lucky after all. She didn't get a cent.

* * *

Many of those who knew Leigh described him as rude and objectionable, so why did people invest with him?

'Well, he was rude and I thought he was a pig,' says West. 'But he seemed honourable. He did what he said he'd do, so I didn't think he'd break an agreement.'[12]

Leppan said that when the wheels began to fall off, and he contacted Leigh, he became 'aggressive and unhelpful'.

Another lawyer, who shares the sentiments about Leigh's abrasive nature, paints a picture of a spoilt bully who had all the personal charm of Richard Nixon. 'This is the kind of guy he was: Darryl lived in a townhouse complex, and one day, there was a car parked in his way so he couldn't get his car out. Rather than going to ask the neighbour to move the car, Darryl just sat in his car with his hand on the horn. That was Darryl.'

Ian Irvine-Fortescue, an entrepreneur who ended up investing with Barry, described how many years before, Leigh had arrived at his house on his Ducati motorbike, which he fawned over. 'My daughter, who was quite small at that stage, came out and was fascinated by the motorbike and put her hand out to touch it. Darryl turned around and growled at her, "If you touch the bike, I'll kill you." She ran away crying.'[13]

Irvine-Fortescue recalls another nasty incident when his driver, Dan, went to Leigh's townhouse to collect some post-dated cheques (from Barry). Leigh was very particular about things being done in a certain way, so as not to unnecessarily disturb the order of his world.

Normally, you'd have to ring a bell to be let into Leigh's complex through the formidable security gates. But that day, the gate was open, so Dan simply drove in.

Leigh freaked when Dan 'mysteriously' appeared, and allegedly threatened the poor driver before sending him packing, chequeless.

'Dan popped his head into my office when he got back to explain why he hadn't got the cheques. He told me, "No boss, eish, that man! He's very dangerous. I'm not going there again, please boss, next time send Enos."'

But Rossen says the people now eager to savage Leigh's character were nowhere to be found back then when they were making a killing on Barry's scheme.

'Human nature amazes me,' she says. 'All these people now maligning Darryl, pointing out his abusive and bullying behaviour and his personality shortcomings were ever-so accommodating to those traits when they were making a good profit. They licked his arse, inviting him out to dinner, for drinks at clubs, joining him on holidays, and buying his cars.'[14]

The extreme toadying fed his ego. 'I was the only one who had the courage to tell him what I thought, when his behaviour became totally unacceptable,' she says.

Darryl's flash brought out the worst in Joburg society. Rossen recalls: 'I watched women try and pick [up] Darryl at traffic lights, at the shops – one mother was even encouraging her young daughter to talk to him in the parkade of the Sandton City parking garage. Money clearly is the aphrodisiac of the human species.'

She may no longer be his girlfriend, but she clearly feels some loyalty to Darryl. Perhaps it's a misplaced sense of guilt, since it was she who cajoled him into investing right in the beginning, when Darryl wasn't keen.

But then Rossen says she lost out too. 'People think I made money from this thing, and I can tell you, I didn't. In the beginning, in February 2005, I put in R300 000 I had in my own money, and I raised an extra R1-million bond on my house to invest.'

It worked, and she kept pumping in more, the greed feeding itself.

'It sounded suspicious at first, but you become comfortable with it,' she says. 'You get repaid a few times, and you're not as suspicious as before. I trusted Darryl.'

That is, until they broke up a few years later, in late 2007. Then, Leigh booted Rossen out of the scheme. He did the same thing to others with whom he had flaming rows – including, at one time, even his own daughter, Laura.

But Rossen was in no mood to take any more of Darryl's uphill. 'Fine,' she said, 'pay me out what I reinvested, and I'm gone.'

Then, something strange happened. It was the kind of thing that should have set off alarm bells.

'Out of the blue, Barry calls me,' says Rossen. 'He says, "I understand you're fighting with Darryl. It's a nasty situation, but you don't have to leave. Why don't you invest directly through me instead, rather than going through Darryl?"'

So she took up Barry's offer. Now, of course, she wishes she hadn't, as it soon became impossible to get her money out.

'In October 2008,' she says, 'Barry told me about this plan he had to do the same thing internationally, through the German company he was starting. So, I transferred R11 million to his Australian account. A few months later, it all went belly-up.'

On paper, it looked like Rossen made a fortune of more than R20 million. Barry paid her R42 million, of which she reinvested R22 million, she says. But add in legal costs, and the fact that she had to repay SARS and the trustees of Barry's estate, and Rossen says she actually lost.

Keith van der Spuy lost even more – and is in no mood to defend his former colleague: 'He was always full of himself and conceited. I was doing an MBA at the time, and he helped me with some legal parts on one of the projects. I tell you, by the time I'd finished it, he was strutting around as if the project was his brainchild. I generally gauge people by the way they treat secretaries and waiters. By that measure, Darryl was a complete arsehole.'

Van der Spuy says Leigh, a mid-level staffer who checked Nedbank Corporate's fancy structures or tax schemes for legal compliance, was just making a living – nothing more. 'We were paid peanuts back then. My salary was R211 000 a year. Darryl wasn't rich at all back then.'

After Darryl quit Nedbank, he took the job at the Development Bank, before hooking up with Tannenbaum. Then he called Van der Spuy and suggested he invest in the scheme. 'I said, "Listen, Darryl, it's a get-rich-quick scheme, it'll never work." But what happened is that, unbeknown to me, my missus put the money in.'

Van der Spuy had transferred R2 million into a Nedbank account for his son's benefit, then went on holiday to Bulgaria. But when he came back, he found that his wife had given it to Leigh to invest in Frankel. Van der Spuy decided that since it was already done, he wouldn't cause waves.

'It surprised me, because it worked. So I thought at the time, well let me put some more in, and then some more. It kept working, until it didn't. I still kick myself every day.'

In the end, Van der Spuy took a thrashing. He'd invested R54 million in Frankel, and though he had been paid out certain tranches of interest, he ended up with a net loss of R30 million.

It crippled him financially. 'I'm working my arse off right now,' he says. 'I went from being worth in excess of R100 million, to a situation where I'm now struggling to pay my kid's school fees, because of this thing.'

The schools may be private, but the fees aren't of the order of South Africa's most expensive colleges, the likes of Hilton and Michaelhouse, which top R150 000 a year. So Van der Spuy trades, develops and sells properties and shopping centres, bartering for what he can get. He's currently working in Letselele, in the creaking and corruptible north of the country, near Tzaneen, a task made even tougher because there's no reliable electricity connection. It's a state of being that he largely attributes to the disagreeable Darryl Leigh.

Darryl with money was far worse than Darryl without it. During the height of the scheme's success, Leigh even dragged his daughter Laura to court. In a private email exchange between Tannenbaum and Dean Rees, Barry marvels at this. 'I do know she is getting a summons today from her father. Can you ever think of suing [your own children]? Shows you what we are dealing with.'

Laura had invested in Barry's scheme through her father. But, according to Barry, Darryl had booted her out, and she was 'trying very desperately to regain her position and has contacted me directly'.

That email exchange provides rich insight, revealing as much about Darryl's character as it does about how little respect Barry clearly had for his own partner, the man who had launched his investment scheme.

The assessment of Leigh's brusque manner was one shared by journalists. 'You're obviously not hearing me: at this stage, I'm not saying anything,' was Leigh's first response when contacted by the *Financial Mail* in June 2009. He was no more cordial when contacted three years later, in late 2012: 'I'll go back to my earlier comment, which is no comment.'

'You're not family of mine, you're not a friend of mine: explain to me how speaking to you could be beneficial for me?'[15]

Say what you want about Darryl Leigh, but at least he's still in South Africa – even if not behind bars. That's more than you can say about Barry or Dean Rees.

* * *

Leigh might have been a detestable human being, but did he know it was a scam?

Rossen is adamant he couldn't have known – for a number of reasons. 'For one thing,' she says, 'don't you think that if he knew it was a Ponzi scheme, he would have invested money and been repaid in a company account rather than through his single Standard Bank account? If you look at the others, like Dean Rees, they all had many accounts.'

Secondly, Leigh, she claims, initially wasn't keen to invest at all. It was only because Rossen told him he had nothing to lose that he first invested. For a while, he was – or thought he was – Barry's only investor.

'Darryl was duped – first by Barry, then by his own greed, then by Dean,' she says.

'At the beginning, for many months, there were only fifteen investors at most,' she says. 'The thing is, we were being paid out our full capital, plus returns, and we could then choose to reinvest. People weren't just rolling it into new investments. So if it was a Ponzi, how could Barry have paid us all out?'

A good question. A Ponzi scheme would use new investors' cash to repay the existing investors. But if Leigh's consortium was repaid every cent, there were only two possible answers: either it was a legitimate investment, or Barry had other funders at the time, unbeknown to Leigh.

The paper trail makes it very clear that the first option can't be true. The furniture scheme was about as legitimate as an IOU from the tooth fairy.

Details that appear to confirm the theory that there were other investors before Leigh can be found in the mountains of court papers filed across South Africa and Australia since the scheme burst.

For example, the first 'acknowledgement of debt' was signed by Barry in favour of the Van Flyman Group in June 2004 for R200 000 – R100 000 of which was capital, the other half interest. By October 2004, unbeknown to Leigh, Barry was already borrowing large chunks of money from Jawmend Rossi Capital – a company owned by three seasoned businessmen, Jonathan Jawno, Roberto Rossi and Michael Mendelowitz. By March 2005, Barry was busy signing these same 'acknowledgements of debt' for Robert Lowdon.

The furniture deals required investors to suspend their disbelief that South African tables and chairs were so monumentally underpriced that it allowed for a margin of more than 120 per cent. Crucially, it also required Barry's brother, Michael, to be part of the scam, or to shut up when asked.

Perhaps that's why, by 2006, the furniture deals had begun slipping to the periphery. In their place, by 2008, was a wonder story about HIV/AIDS drugs.

But when Darryl Leigh first signed up as Barry's bagman, it was all about the furniture.

Documents prepared by the National Prosecuting Authority, in order to be sent to the high commissioner of Australia in December 2011 as part of a request for 'legal assistance' from that country, spell it out: 'Since approximately 2003, Tannenbaum solicited loans from various investors [and] from a number of hand-picked investors to finance the export of furniture to the United Kingdom where his brother, Michael Tannenbaum, is involved in property development.'[16]

The trick, of course, is to have people on the inside who can make such a deal happen. Or who you can *make people believe* can make it happen.

Cue Michael Tannenbaum, the man for Barry's plan.

After graduating from Krugersdorp High School, Michael had gone to Wits, where he studied accounting, breaking with the family tradition. After graduating, he joined Touche Ross & Co., the company that merged with Deloitte Haskins & Sells to become Deloitte & Touche, one of the big four global auditors.

In 1985, two years after Barry matriculated, Touche Ross & Co. transferred Michael Tannenbaum to their office in London. He then joined a property company called Capital and Counties, which was run by South African property wunderkind Michael Rapp.

Michael Rapp, now in his late seventies, has the accolade of being an esteemed aristocrat of South Africa's insular business environment, but he is also revered as nothing less than an omniscient King Midas of the property sector. Rapp was the brains behind creating Africa's most glamorous shopping mall – the icon to kitsch that is the bubbling Sandton City – when he worked for property company Liberty as Donny Gordon's right-hand man.

Sandton City was built in 1973, then just a mall among dust roads and horse trails. It was originally intended to be a residential development of twelve houses. As author Ken Romain puts it, 'the plans were changed dramatically as Michael Rapp rapidly grasped the importance of the site he had assembled on land adjoining the new town's city centre'.[17]

It was some giddy vision. Now Sandton is the financial centre of sub-Saharan Africa. Two of the continent's four biggest banks, the world's eighth-largest stock exchange and global banks like Citigroup and Standard Chartered jostle elbow to elbow in the two square kilometres around Sandton City.

Ira Rapp, Michael's son, has firmly grasped the family chalice. Since moving to London, Ira Rapp has started a chain of restaurants with a unit inside Harrods department store, and had a string of spectacular successes with Westcity, notably spearheading a £185-million plan to build and sell 456 penthouses around the Paddington Basin in west London. In 2001 the *Observer* described Rapp's plan to 'raise the standards in the way upmarket residential property is sold in this country' as 'among the most radical and expensive of recent property marketing campaigns'.[18]

All of the 456 apartments sold out within four months.

For Michael Tannenbaum, working with the Rapps was an easy choice: the family were wealthy, successful, Jewish South Africans stamping their family seal all over Europe's financial capital. Ira Rapp was Westcity's CEO and, like Mike, he knew a thing or two about being the chip off the old block in a commercial dynasty stretching back decades. And perhaps most importantly, Michael was joining at the right time. Westcity was just being launched by Ira with the plan to build residences for wealthy Londoners, so he would be part of creating something from scratch.

Dedicated, smart and methodical, Mike Tannenbaum rolled up his sleeves and became the Rapps' indispensable money man in London, the bean counter at the heart of Westcity. In 2006, Westcity was reverse-listed into a London Stock Exchange–listed company, with Michael as its financial director and company secretary. (Westcity delisted in 2010, but Michael remains the financial director.)

By contrast, his younger brother, Barry, had juggled as many jobs as he had had ideas, darting skittishly from semi-permanent posts to one harebrained scheme after another.

* * *

Barry's elder brother was the success story that Barry wanted to be. But in lieu of that, Mike Tannenbaum's success was something he could exploit to make money. A trail of emails sets out exactly how he did it, duping Darryl Leigh, Rossen and their consortium into ploughing cash into fake furniture deals.

The first email, dated 26 January 2005, was sent by Barry to Darryl Leigh, with the subject heading 'FW: GOOD NEWS'.

Though the printout of the email is poor quality, it is easy to make out that Barry writes that Darryl should read the forwarded 'email from my brother', attached in his message, saying things were 'looking good'.

Underneath is the message from Mike Tannenbaum (email address, miketan@ westcity.co.uk), sent on 25 January 2005 at 4.33 p.m., headed 'GOOD NEWS'. It reads:

Dear Poochman
I have arranged an extra quota for you for the next deal. We are currently on 1.2M and I am able to get this increased next time only to 2.8M. Please advise participation and once accepted we can't let them down. My split is the same the return for you entirely will be 30%. Dates have changed somewhat as they are anticipating [...] 4 containers this year. All cash must be in at the usual Nedbank account no later than March 10 and payout will be April 28. I am sure this ensure [*sic*] a good Pesach for you!
Also, the current deal is on it's [*sic*] way and going according to schedule. There is a further R250k available if you want at the same rate. [A colleague] needs his stake back. Can you do something? Let me know Thursday the latest. Anyway, boet all well this side. Folks are well and not driving me mad yet.
Keep it hanging
MT

Scrawled on that printed-out email are some handwritten notes that read: 'Allotmt: 2,800,000', with the amount divided between 'Barry, Darryl, Tasha, and John'.

From other emails, it is clear 'John' refers to John Miller – a long-term friend of Leigh's. 'Tasha' refers to Rossen.

A second email is dated 28 June 2005, when Barry wrote to Leigh about the furniture, attaching a message from his brother. It reads:

Hi Darryl,

Herewith email from Mike. I am in a meeting now to 12h00. I will call you to discuss thereafter.

Also, I mean to tell you that I think Rob's local deal is maturing soon, but we can roll it at the same terms. I will talk to you about this as well.

Have a good morning.

Warmest regards,

Barry

Presumably, 'Rob' refers to Rob Lowdon and Barry's email signature reads 'Frankel Chemicals'. Again, attached to that email was an email from Mike Tannenbaum (email address, miketan@westcity.co.uk) to Barry on 28 June 2005 at 08.51 a.m. The subject of the email was 'GOOD NEWS'. It reads:

Poochie –

As I mentioned to you on the phone this morning, I can get the following for you and the boys:

The current deal matures July 8. Steve and his team need some more furniture to complete Clock B [presumably Block B] in the Trussards. We are busy arranging an air freight shipment now to be sent second week July. I have convinced [my colleagues] that it is our turn this time, and we can fund this shipment. R3.5 Million is required immediately, but you can use the funds clearing next week. The length of the deal will last 4 weeks to August 12 2005. I can get a good return for you for this period at 35%. I need to know by the latest tomorrow morning.

The sea freight deal thereafter commences August 23 2005 and will run through to October 28 2005. The rate will be 30% and I have arranged a quota for you at R8.5 Million. I will try and do better for you but will only be able to let you know closer the time [sic]. The deal thereafter will commence around mid-November and will run to first week February. I will only know dates early August. As I have mentioned to you before, this is not evergreen and it seems as if we are now going to source the goods ex-Korea. However boetie, I am trying to involve us in the funding albeit offshore. I will let you know the finer details in time. Maybe you can use Silverside to do the funding?

Anyway, let me know as soon as you can about the R3.5 Million.

Are you guys coming for Rosh Hashanah?

Call me later when you can.

Love ya

MT

In a third email, on 29 August 2005, Barry writes to Darryl:

> Hi Darryl,
> Welcome back! Nice to have you home.
> To confirm in writing the current deal that has commenced today:
> Darryl Leigh   900,000
> John Miller   700,000
> The returns applicable as follows:
> Darryl Leigh 20% on 900,000 plus 10% on 700,000 therefore total capital
> is 1,150,000.
> John Miller 7.5% on 700,000, therefore total return plus capital is 752,500
> The Deal matures Monday 19 September 2005 and all the values mentioned
> above is in South African Rand.
> Many thanks and best regards,
> Barry Tannenbaum

What is interesting in this email is that it appears evident that Darryl is now earning a 10 per cent commission on the investors he is bringing to Barry, acquiring 10 per cent of the R700 000 invested by John Miller.

Darryl's commission structure is then reinforced by a fourth email, dated 13 September 2005, from Barry to Darryl, with the subject heading 'PROPOSED DEAL'. It reads:

> Hi Darryl,
> This is to confirm our conversation of today whereby I proposed a 'new' deal
> with regard [sic] Frankel funding
> VALUE   R3.1 Million
> COMMENCEMENT   26 September 2005
> MATURITY   7 November 2005
> The returns will be 25% wherein I will maintain 5% for the direct funding
> you do and for the balance of other investors we will share the difference
> from what you offer to them.
> Kindly confirm receipt of this email.
> Thanks and best regards,
> Barry Tannenbaum

It gets particularly interesting in the fifth email, sent on 26 October 2005 from Barry to Darryl. That message contains the first sign that Barry is now considering scrapping the furniture investments altogether to concentrate on the pharmaceutical business that would later make him infamous.

In that email, Barry writes to Darryl saying, 'I spoke to my brother and he has advised the following', detailing the 'next London deal', which apparently was due to start on 25 November. Discussing that London deal worth R20.25 million, he says 'the very good news as a result of the strengthening of the British pound against the South African rand is that we are able to get 35% for this deal!!! The bad news is that this appears to be the last deal for South Africa. It seems the potential suppliers in the East are promising good service.'

In the next point, Barry then plants the seed that, despite the disappearance of the furniture orders, the pharmaceutical business will more than make up for it. He writes:

I have taken orders in for next week, and should you want to make use of some quick Frankel deals, then R1.4 Million is required by Monday 31 October to Wednesday 16 November 2005 and a rate of 20% is offered. 10% for Frankel has been taken into account and so you have 20% less my 2.5% cut to work with. These funds are required on those dates as customer needs the stock for production before summer closure. Let me know.

In the sixth email, sent by Barry to Darryl on 7 November 2005, Tannenbaum shows that the new pharmaceutical business can deliver returns that were just as good as the furniture operation. In it, Barry gives a detailed breakdown of who is putting in what for twenty-two orders. He adds: 'I told you that I would make the extra R250k' and says he will get more 'for Cape Town for you.' It's not certain what this refers to – perhaps the down payment on the Camps Bay property?

Barry then adds: 'Also, the bank is waiting for my instruction for the Tasha instruction of R720,000.' He signs off: 'Thanks as always and for being a great mate over the past week. Your support through my trip made it almost successful. I am always there for you too. A bit of sentiment! Best regards, Barry.'

That string of emails provides acute insight into how Barry, with a watch-maker's attention to detail, carefully built the mechanics of his 'investment business' from at least 2004.

Quite how Tannenbaum was able to convince Leigh that he'd managed to happen on not one, but *two* industries where you can earn interest rates well past 100 per cent – opportunities that more experienced and smarter men hadn't found – required either a degree of gullibility from Leigh, or a defiant willingness not to interrogate the plan.

It's difficult to say which, particularly as neither Tannenbaum nor Leigh have yet spoken about the emails, which appear to have been printed from Leigh's email account.

* * *

At first blush, it seems Michael Tannenbaum was central to his brother's scheme – a willing accomplice. He was certainly in a position to assist with the furniture scheme: as financial director of Westcity, he could easily have placed the furniture in the upmarket residences that Westcity was building all around London.

The claim in the email that his colleagues at Westcity were also investors deepens the conspiracy. If anything, that sentence makes it appear that a high-profile property firm soon set to stamp its name up in lights on the London Stock Exchange was wholly immersed in a shady cross-border furniture-trading operation.

The only thing is, the reality isn't what it seems.

When shown the emails by the author, Michael Tannenbaum was profoundly alarmed: 'The emails relating to furniture transactions, purportedly from me, have been fabricated,' he said. 'The email address shown – which changes between emails – does not match any email address I use, or have used in the past.'

That is true. His official email address is mike@westcity.co.uk. Yet, in the various forged emails, it is first given as miket@westcity.com and then miketan@westcity.co.uk.

Why would any forger be so particularly sloppy? Especially considering that Michael Tannenbaum's email address isn't a state secret. And even if you'd been that careless the first time, why change it in the second email?

Email addresses aside, Michael said the entire furniture-investment scheme was news to him. 'I have never heard about these transactions before, much less been involved in them,' he said. He explains that 'it would make absolutely no commercial sense to import full furniture containers from South Africa and pay high interest rates and costs where we could finance these ourselves'. And, he adds, 'The monitoring surveyors, banks and shareholders would never have allowed it in any event.'

So who would have done this? Darryl Leigh is one candidate. But then, he appeared to be the target of this particular ruse, the man who was supposed to accept that these were real. Dean Rees, the lawyer who later addressed the June 2009 meeting of investors at Routledge Modise, is another candidate. But, tellingly, Rees only met Tannenbaum in 2006 – after those emails had been sent.

No, the most likely candidate is Barry himself. Not only does the phrasing in those emails echo the vernacular between the two brothers – Mike calling Barry 'poochie', for example – but the style is also similar in the forged emails and his own emails. For example, he uses capitalised 'M's to represent millions, which, although not definitive proof, is certainly an indicator.

When asked who he believed forged these emails and for what purpose, Mike Tannenbaum said, 'I don't want to speculate.' Which is probably just as well for fraternal relations. But behind closed doors Michael Tannenbaum was furious.

After he heard his name had been so abused to raise cash for these furniture investments, he called Barry in Australia. 'No, it was all Darryl Leigh …,' Barry started to claim, but Michael cut him short. Bullshit, he said, Darryl Leigh didn't know all these names, who these guys were in my office: you, Barry, knew who they were, only you could have written that email. Barry began apologising, saying sorry repeatedly. But Michael had had enough. Haven't you ruined our lives enough, he asked before hanging up.

Since then, Michael and Barry have not spoken. Barry's father, Harold, is the only common link, still speaking to both of them. It's an icy relationship that hasn't thawed.

* * *

This wasn't the only time that Mike Tannenbaum ended up on the wrong end of Barry's murky world of swirling investments and ambitious emailed promises. Later it emerged that Mike Tannenbaum's signatures were forged on yet more documents needed to suck cash from investors. But that tale, even more intricate than the furniture forgery, will emerge later in this story.

What is clear is that as 2005 drew to a close, Barry had realised the furniture investments were a dead end. You can only kid people for so long that the rand is reversing, and that companies are willing to pay 35 per cent more than they should for tables, chairs and couches.

This left only the active pharmaceutical ingredients. But having stress-tested the structure and method of the furniture investments, and having found people willing to bite, Barry knew this was a modus operandi that was easy to duplicate in the medical field. At least this was a world where Barry could profit from his heritage. Finally.

6

The scheme takes off

'Estelle, you don't have to worry about money. I'll always look after you.'
– Barry Tannenbaum to Estelle Wittenberg, an employee of
twenty-three years' service in his company, justifying
why he never set aside a pension for her

The thing about Barry Tannenbaum's pharmaceutical scam is that it wasn't always a scam. His Ponzi scheme started off legit; it used a legitimate company, Frankel Chemicals, at any rate.

Go to Frankel's headquarters now, at 1 Eastgate Lane, Bedfordview, and it's as if Barry Tannenbaum's pharmaceutical company never existed. Frankel used to be on the top floor of an anonymous office block behind the Eastgate Shopping Centre, about three kilometres from L. Ron Hubbard's 'heritage site'.

There are no signs indicating Frankel's existence. 'Who?' asks a security guard at the front of the office block. Then she raises her eyebrows, as recognition sparks in her eyes: 'Yes, there was something like that here. But it went away, many years ago.'

The name has been wiped from the sign boards, an apt illustration of just how transient existence is for smaller companies operating in lifeless office blocks, their lives snuffed out without sentiment at the first sign of a bounced rent cheque.

Where Frankel Chemicals used to operate, now there is a series of cookie-cutter offices: cream carpets, beige wallpaper, the smell of Jeyes Fluid and all with the individuality of Lego pieces. Financial consultants working for Discovery occupy one section, lawyers another.

Frankel was never quite what people imagined. But hardly anyone bothered to visit to check whether Tannenbaum's company was the sort of place likely to be turning over R500 million a year. The brochures sketched the picture of a bustling medical operation with a hive of pharma geeks slaving away at 1 Eastgate Lane in white coats, poring over drug charts, and ferrying test tubes and pipettes from one end to the other.

The reality, however, is that it was simply an admin office, an anonymous unit with boxes of files and paper next to Johannesburg's greasy Bruma Lake, a glop of water east of the city surrounded by Chinese clothing traders. The misconception is that Barry Tannenbaum's pharmaceutical business didn't exist at all – that it was just a brittle quilt of straw, with nothing behind it.

One Johannesburg businessman who pumped more than R5 million into the scheme says as much in his affidavit: 'I do not believe that there were any APIs imported or exported as I was told by Barry Tannenbaum. I believe that a misrepresentation was made to me in order to obtain money.'

But this isn't true. 'Of course they had a real business. Frankel Chemicals had been going on for a very long time,' says Estelle Wittenberg, a veteran employee at Frankel, who basically ran the office.[1]

Estelle, now touching her seventies, would know better than most what was real and what wasn't. Though she now lives in the treeless wasteland of the Free State near the Lesotho border, she worked for Tannenbaum's company for more than two decades. Estelle joined the company in March 1983, soon after she first divorced, fortuitously the year that Harold Tannenbaum bought it from its founder, Lothar Frankel.

Now retired, and keen to put 'this mess behind' her, Estelle channels the institutional knowledge of Frankel when she speaks – grandmotherly and omniscient – about the business she knew intimately for decades. The glue that held it all together while bosses, staff and suppliers came and went, Estelle saw it all. 'I'd been running that office from the time that Harold left for Australia,' she says. 'Even though everyone thought it was Barry who was running it, it was really me.'

And though some investors who were stung in 2008 might have believed Frankel was set up only days before, with prefabricated walls and a photocopier to roll off the forged documents, it had been grinding along for over four decades. The company first opened its doors in 1967, when Lothar Frankel started an anything-goes trading business with his wife, Aida, mostly focusing on leather goods. But soon after Frankel had hit on the idea of trading pharmaceuticals, Harold Tannenbaum pitched up with a cheque.

'[Harold] had built it into a very nice business,' says Estelle. After Harold bought Frankel, he set about building an API business, buying the raw ingredients for medicines and trading them with companies he knew and trusted. Adcock Ingram, for starters.

APIs were a relatively new phenomenon. But the desire to produce cheaper, generic drugs for emerging markets, in particular, fostered a market for suppliers who could source the cheapest ingredients. Initially, things were slow. Pharmaceutical firms had their own suppliers. Why go through a broker like Frankel if you can do the deal yourself? But Frankel tied up some deals that made it the exclusive agent for API firms in South Africa, which helped in the bargaining. The business wasn't on the scale of Adcock Ingram, which Harold's father, Hymie, had built, but it was growing steadily.

Then Barry joined his father at the company. 'Barry went to America for a few years, and when he got back, his father said, "Why don't you come work for me?" So he did,' explains Estelle. 'Then a few years later, Harold Tannenbaum sold the business to Selwyn Kahanovitz. Harold wanted to leave for Australia because his daughter, Jacqueline, was there.'

Selwyn and his father, Nehemiah Kahanovitz, were both registered directors of Frankel for a while.

After his father left, Barry had stayed on at Frankel, continuing to work as the sales manager for Selwyn Kahanovitz, until he managed to scrape together enough cash to buy them out. Barry bought 100 per cent of the Frankel Trust, which owned the business, from Selwyn Kahanovitz and immediately sold half to Kevin Kramer, a pharmacist in his late forties.

Though Kramer's name is on the company paperwork, and is widely credited with having helped Barry turbo-charge the business, Wittenberg says this wasn't the case. 'Kramer was never in charge. He was the accountant. He did have a share of the business, but Barry was managing it.'

Eventually, Tannenbaum bought out Kramer to gain full control of Frankel Chemicals. In 2008 Kramer went to Australia, following in the footsteps of Harold Tannenbaum, where he started a similar API business called Maxitrade. Barry later said he paid Kramer about R2 million for his shares – this at a time when the business was supposedly making billions.

Days after Barry Tannenbaum's name was splashed across the front pages of Australian newspapers, the *Sydney Morning Herald* tracked down Kramer to the Maxitrade offices in Dover Heights in Australia. 'I'm so shocked I can't tell you,' he told them. 'This has hurt so many people. I can tell you honestly that no money could have gone through that business. I would have been the first person to see it.'[2]

Kramer also attested to Barry's 'sterling' reputation among Joburg's elite, saying that 'in five years, I never saw anyone have a fight with him'.

The *Sydney Morning Herald* described Kramer as 'clearly distressed', saying he ended the interview so he could 'get some advice'.

Ironically, Kramer's Maxitrade does pretty much what Frankel did. His own company brochures mention Frankel, but conveniently erase any mention of Tannenbaum. Maxitrade's brochures state:

Initially founded in 1967 in Johannesburg by Lothar Frankel and Kevin Kramer, the then Eurochemicals (today trading as Frankel Chemicals) grew quickly to become a major player in supplying the pharmaceutical, veterinary and nutraceuticals market in South Africa and surrounding countries. They quickly established their initial target turnover of R40 m and continue to grow from strength to strength today.

Kramer explains that he moved to Australia after 'an incident stemming from the sometimes harsh reality' of day-to-day life in Johannesburg in 2008. After which he started Maxitrade, essentially replicating Frankel's business in Australia.

Barry used Kramer's name liberally, fully dragging him into the scheme. When investors would ask why Barry and not Frankel was 'borrowing' cash from them personally, he would explain that this was because Frankel was owned 50 per cent each by him and Kramer, and that 'Kevin had his own scheme'.

Kramer says this is 'just not true'. But he won't elaborate. Neither will he answer any questions, coming across as if petrified, scalded by the association.[3]

'Since I disposed of my shares in Eurochemicals and Asterix Pharma, I have had no association with Barry Tannenbaum,' he says. 'I have cooperated fully with the South African police and other authorities, and have no further comments.'

But even after Barry's name was the sole one on the letterhead, Frankel appears to have continued doing business straight. Initially.

Says Estelle: 'Frankel's suppliers were in Europe – Italy, Germany, France, Switzerland, the UK – and in America we had two suppliers, and in Israel. The API market was small, but because of the agency agreements we had, it made it a strong company.'[4]

Barry would justify taking investors' cash for short periods because, as his brochures stated, 'pharmaceutical manufacture is cyclical, and works on periods of between 8 and 15 weeks. These [sic] means that Frankel Chemicals are then committed to supplying their customers with regular shipments. Both suppliers and customers favour a reliable source.'

However, a fundamental misconception that drove his scam was that APIs are a cash extravaganza – that the market generates so much profit that returns in the order of 200 per cent a year are normal.

Wayne Gaddin, a close family friend of Tannenbaum and who had donated the Torah to the KwaZulu-Natal Chabad along with him, echoes this view: 'From what I'm aware, the margins in the pharmaceutical industry are monstrous, and everyone is making huge numbers. The market for APIs is growing hugely.'[5]

Not so, says Estelle Wittenberg. 'Very seldom would an agent ask for more than 10 per cent. And if the API was used for a government tender, then the profit margin is very low. You wanted your customer to get the tender, so you quoted on a 3 or 5 per cent handling fee,' she says.

Perhaps most significantly, Frankel didn't sell any APIs that could be used in the manufacture of drugs to treat HIV/AIDS (antiretrovirals). Not a single one.

'The APIs were used for drugs for various things: hypertension, heart disease. They were used in antibiotics, antihistamines, anything your doctor prescribes,' says Wittenberg. 'But we never bought APIs for AIDS drugs.'

Later on, this particular fact would become particularly relevant, considering that antiretrovirals were a key element used to sell the Ponzi scheme.

* * *

Barry first got serious about taking investments for the AIDS drugs in 2005. To do this, he needed a plausible story, some sort of brochure which tied together the narrative.

In July 2006, Barry wrote to a potential investor, Chris, saying, 'I would very much like you to participate in this next deal as the returns are good, and the time period is short. It would be a good start for me to welcome you on board.'[6]

Chris obviously needed some convincing, so Barry sent him an email setting out a fanciful version of his past:

> I have managed to put together a history of my family as well as a simple story in [sic] what we are currently doing to enjoy some nice returns. We are busy putting together a deal this week that will be used to fund the active [ingredients] of certain Anti-Retrovirals manufactured by Aspen Pharmacare in Port Elizabeth, and supplied to the World Health Organization for distribution in Africa.

Barry then pleads with Chris to keep whatever is discussed 'in extreme confidence' because 'certain information released could damage my business with some very well-known listed companies in South Africa, as well as damage my margins per deal'. He then liberally muddles fact with fantasy in a number of bullet points. 'My father, Harold, was one of the founding members of the biggest listed pharmaceutical manufacturing company in South Africa, namely Adcock Ingram. My family sold Adcock Ingram in 1980 to Tiger Oats, now known as Tiger Brands, and my father had to remain on the board for three years.'

(Arnold Tannenbaum describes this version of events as junk: 'Harold? He was a gentle sort of soul, and certainly wasn't one of the founders, and he was never the MD. He was basically in charge of the photographic section.')

Barry continues his potted family history: 'A milestone for the company was created when in 1998 my father retired to Australia, and I took the business over. I then identified the need in the industry for an ex-stock system for our "blue chip" customers. The company then experienced tremendous growth, and today more than 50% of the turnover is on stock procured for customers and held in our warehouse.'

But then he makes the bold, and according to Wittenberg incorrect, claim that drugs for HIV/AIDS had become one of the cornerstones of the Frankel business: 'Recently, Frankel Chemicals has been given the contract to procure the ARV (antiretroviral) ingredients for a very large manufacturer in South Africa. The business was awarded based on the good relations Frankel has with this customer, and also that the material is imported via a local company that is soon to be BEE-rated.'

Barry explains that for the HIV/AIDS drugs, Frankel places an order with a supplier in India whom it must first pay in full. Frankel then pays for the shipping, clearing and delivery of the drugs, and the customer then pays for the drugs within thirty days. Each deal, he says, has a duration of about ten weeks.

'Funding is required for the ARV deal mentioned above for Aspen Pharmacare, as well as other similar types [of] requirements by our customers in South Africa,' he writes. 'I have a very good relationship with all the procurement officers in these companies, as well as the CEOs of such companies.'

Barry then says that he has a 'personal – both business and friendship – relationship with the captains, namely Stephen Saad (CEO Aspen), Trevor Edwards (CEO Enaleni Pharmaceuticals) and Dr Jonathan Louw (MD Adcock Ingram)'.

This was a line that Tannenbaum trotted out often. Later, when he was living in Australia, he would jet into Johannesburg, and tell 'investors' that he was on a whistle-stop tour to visit his 'good friend' Stephen Saad and other well-known corporate hot shots. It turns out Barry was friends with them in the same way that rock icons are 'connected to their fans' – controversially, and probably not at all.

Saad, eager to put distance between Aspen and the Tannenbaum affair, denies the friendship emphatically, saying he 'had no personal relationship' with Tannenbaum.[7]

'Their main business with Aspen was to bring in a batch of chemicals and break it up, and supply Aspen and other local players,' he says. 'They were never in our antiretroviral supply chain, and provided documentation where they fraudulently copied the buyer's authorised signature.'

For his part, Trevor Edwards's first response to Barry's claim is 'What? You must be joking! I had an informal relationship with Barry Tannenbaum, at the very best. He used to live in the Oyster Schelles complex in Umhlanga, and I was the chairman of the board of trustees. So, literally, I only bumped into Barry when he was walking around the complex.'[8]

Never one to miss an opportunity, Barry must have realised his dumb luck at having the CEO of a bona fide pharmaceutical company living in the same block of apartments, so he struck up a conversation about how he was also working in the pharmaceuticals business.

Says Edwards: 'It turned out that he did actually supply some chemicals to

Enaleni, but he never dealt with me, only ever one of my buyers. And if we spent R5 000 a month buying chemicals from him, it was a lot.'

Eventually, Tannenbaum pitched the idea of investing in Frankel, his exclusive scheme that he appeared to be hawking around town, to Edwards. 'I told him, in no uncertain terms, what to do with that offer. I questioned the sustainability of his business, and the fact it sounded too good to be true. And then I also told him that I, as the CEO, can't be in business with any of our suppliers, in any event.'

Undaunted, Tannenbaum approached Edwards again some months later, but got the same brush-off. To underscore his credibility to Edwards, Barry would also reiterate his close relationship with Stephen Saad and Jonathan Louw. 'I said to him, "Fine, you do whatever you want with them, but you're not going to do it with me".'

The last time Edwards saw Tannenbaum was when Barry was packing up his Umhlanga apartment, which he sold before moving to Australia. At the time, he was telling people about the 'horrendous crime' his family had experienced in Joburg. It was an easy story to believe. There are some who doubt this happened, but stories of such searing violence in Joburg are reported every day so it's impossible to say unequivocally that it isn't true.

But those who knew Barry say the actual event was far more prosaic – robbers broke into his house and took his wife's jewellery. The Tannenbaums apparently weren't home. It's the sort of petty burglary that happens all the time, everywhere, even in Australia.

Arriving back in South Africa after a trip to Europe in 2009, Edwards picked up a copy of the *Sunday Times*, and there was Barry on the front page, his Ponzi scheme exposed. 'Thank goodness. It was one of my better judgement calls,' he says.

If any of the pharmaceutical CEOs could be excused for having some kind of relationship with Barry Tannenbaum, it would be Jonathan Louw, head of Adcock Ingram – the company founded by Barry's grandfather. But Louw says that although he met Barry a few times, they didn't have what you would even remotely term a close relationship.[9]

'It depends what you define as a "close relationship",' he says. 'In my mind, that would be when you have had dinner with someone, maybe met their spouse, and socialised together. Now, I've never had dinner with him, met his spouse, or socialised with him.'

Louw did bump into Tannenbaum at one of the Commonwealth Pharmacists Association events, held in Europe, in the years leading up to 2009. 'There were about 20 000 to 30 000 people there, and Barry Tannenbaum was representing one of the companies, so he met our procurement guys there.'

When Tannenbaum did meet Louw, he was careful not to overtly play up his family's role in the genesis of the company. 'Perhaps he didn't have to,' says Louw. 'The original family were among the founders of Adcock Ingram, and are well steeped in our history, so we knew very well what the Tannenbaums meant.'

Louw says that Barry Tannenbaum 'meant nothing to me, or even our older staff because, I mean, they sold out of the company a long time ago, nearly forty years ago'.

Four decades may have separated Barry's family from Adcock Ingram, but the connection was still close enough for Barry to use it as a marketing gimmick.

* * *

The email to Chris became the template for the later brochures that Barry would hand out to investors at lavish breakfasts and champagne-fuelled lunches.

Only, as you might expect, the tales became grander with each year that passed. Three years later, in 2009, Barry's brochure boasted how Frankel, 'through the reputation and history of the Tannenbaum name, grew within the industry and began to acquire new and more valuable agencies across the globe'.

'More recently, we have experienced growth of up to 60% per annum where Frankel Chemicals have been awarded the contracts to procure the antiretroviral (ARV) ingredients for Aspen Pharmaceuticals Ltd in South Africa to combat the spread of HIV/Aids. This business was awarded based on the good relations Frankel has with this customer.'

Prospective investors were given, besides that sanitised profile of Frankel, news clippings about the soaring need for ARV drugs. For example, an Aspen press release from 2008, titled 'Aspen invests R2.7 billion in expanding global business', was included, along with a news report from the *Star* newspaper in 2008, headed 'South Africa awarded B-symbol for its Aids efforts', which informed readers that the country had spent $621 million on dealing with HIV/AIDS. An analyst report from J.P. Morgan, titled 'Aspen wins big from ARV tender', revealed how the company would score R224 million a year thanks to the government tender it had won to supply ARVs.

The message was hammered home: Aspen would make a killing from HIV/AIDS drugs, and its main supplier, Frankel, would obviously be swooped along for the ride.

Nobody knew then, of course, that Frankel didn't actually supply any materials for ARVs. It was an epic lie, cynically exploiting the most tragic virus to hit South Africa in decades, an affliction turned into a plague by the bumbling government of President Thabo Mbeki, which fatally delayed rolling out ARVs.

Estelle Wittenberg hadn't known about the forged invoices, the lies told to investors, the overblown claims that Frankel was a pumping multinational with a finger in every pot and an agent in every port. That is, until she was subpoenaed to testify to an inquiry investigating Tannenbaum's estate in 2010 about what she knew. It was there that she was first shown the fake Aspen invoices that detailed orders for ARV drugs. The lawyers produced evidence of something she had refused to believe had taken place – a clear, outright forgery: a massive order for AIDS drugs on Frankel letterhead.

Estelle was aghast, especially because, she says, 'every single order to Frankel came onto my desk. They showed me an order, and it wasn't an official document. Barry would never have asked [me] to do that for him because he knew I would have refused. I didn't know anything about this.'

* * *

Estelle Wittenberg's history of Frankel Chemicals is a chasm apart from the sexed-up profile of the company passed off to investors. Rather like the yellowed textbooks that the South African apartheid government routinely served on schoolkids before 1994 to sell their story of the white master race, it was a glossy revisionist history that combined half-truths with outright whoppers.

When Barry was seducing a potential investor who was proving reluctant to commit or who wanted extra assurance, he produced an 'investor pack'. This was engorged with just the sort of letters, certificates and official-looking documents detailing Frankel Chemicals' work that you'd want to see if you were ploughing in a few million.

If it's a scam, you'd think it's a damn *elaborate* scam. Then you'd transfer your cash to Barry's account, thinking that, really, the odds on it actually being a scam must be pretty low.

The literature claimed that Frankel Chemicals employed forty-eight people – thirty-one staff in South Africa, including nineteen sales representatives, two in Australia, seven in 'Frankel International', six in Brazil and two in India.

'It was more like half that,' said one former employee, who asked to remain anonymous, dismissing the official documents with a grunt of derision. 'There were probably about five people in South Africa.'

Estelle Wittenberg also scoffs at that figure: 'No. It was myself, a receptionist and a girl that was a secretary to Barry. Then there was a shipping clerk.' Walk around Frankel's anorexic office in Bedfordview, and the first question that comes to mind is, which cupboard would these thirty-one people have to squeeze into? There just isn't the space. Nonetheless, the staff list in those brochures was impressive, trumpeting the blue-chip credentials of Frankel's men and women. Take, for example, Tandy Houseman, the marketing director, who was purported to have held 'senior management positions in a number of multinational pharmaceutical companies, including Boots Pharmaceuticals, Roche Products and Solvay Pharma'.

Robyn Daniel was billed as Frankel's 'responsible pharmacist', a 'well-respected member of the SAPI (South African Pharmacists in Industry)' who 'has strong relationships with the representatives in the Medicines Control Council of SA, which plays a role in insuring [*sic*] the necessary documentation is in place for the APIs'.

Impressive, but false.

'I was never involved in Frankel,' says Robyn, who until recently was chair of the Johannesburg-based SAPI. 'That was one of Barry's bogus documents. I'm not sure if he thought my name lent his company greater legitimacy, but it wasn't true. I even took legal advice on what to do about it.'[10]

Again, it seems that Tannenbaum grabbed at a half-truth and twisted it until it broke. What is true is that Robyn Daniel and Tandy Houseman, both well-respected pharmacists, wanted to set up an API business, so they approached Frankel, which had a relatively solid reputation. Even if you didn't know the Tannenbaums, Kevin Kramer was well known and well liked. It seemed a good match.

'I met them fortuitously and decided to approach them about starting [a pharmacy business],' says Robyn. 'Frankel had been in business a long time, and did actually have a real business going for years.'

So Daniel, Houseman, Kramer and Tannenbaum set up a pharmacy business called Asterix Pharmaceuticals to make drugs. 'Barry was one of the directors … and we were all equal shareholders,' she says.

But Asterix was a completely separate entity from Frankel: as an API trader, Frankel didn't manufacture any pharmaceuticals.

Daniel and Houseman devoted themselves to it. And it worked – at least until Barry emigrated to Australia, and Houseman and a number of other Frankel employees all moved to Australia too.

Unlike Frankel, Asterix did actually produce products, but it was still a fledgling company. (For example, it made an 'energy lozenge' called Wake-Up, which, the flyers said, came in 'four fantastic flavours created especially for your tastes: Berry Blast, Orange Overload, Lime Lazer, and Grape Grenade' and produced 'faster and clearer flow of thought', and 'better general body co-ordination'. It may have *sounded* as hocus-pocus as the API business, but at least there was a physical product in this case. At least it was something.)

At the end of 2008, Daniel had had enough. 'They were all going to Australia. I had a feeling that the agenda had shifted. So I didn't want to be sitting here alone while they sent orders from Australia,' she says. She walked away from the business entirely, getting nothing for her shares in Asterix – a decision that she still describes as 'very hard'.

'The company folded. Asterix was our baby, which we nursed through, and it ended up frozen,' she says. Thanks to Barry.

A few months after she left, the news hit the headlines that Frankel was simply a massive pyramid scheme. It came as a great shock to her that her business partner – a man she described as 'exceptionally caring, and very, very friendly' – was apparently the scheming mastermind of South Africa's largest Ponzi scheme.

'I'd always thought it was a legitimate business. I couldn't believe it. I would never think he'd be capable of doing that,' she says.

Like many who knew Barry, Robyn left the business with nothing. She now works at SAPI, still grateful that she got out before the wheels came off.

Tandy Houseman is still scarred by the experience, and sounds rattled when Barry's name is mentioned. 'I went through an extremely traumatic experience, and I'm pleased to see the back of it,' she says.[11]

The talk is that once in Australia, Tandy figured out the disconnection between Barry's promises and the company's bank account. She confronted Barry about it. The issue remained unresolved and she walked out of the company. She bounced back, though, and was hired by Spirit Pharmaceuticals in Australia in April 2010. She says she doesn't speak to Barry at all.

* * *

Another anomaly is that Frankel did not need Daniel's clout to win support from the Medicines Control Council, the body mandated to ensure all medicine produced in the country is of a proper standard.

Daniel explains: 'Frankel was essentially a broker and they didn't need approval. APIs don't need to be registered in South Africa. They simply sourced APIs and supplied them to the manufacturers. The finished product is controlled, so the manufacturer of the finished product needs approval, not the broker.'[12]

This legal lacuna, the fact that any trader of APIs could essentially fly under the radar, was heavily exploited by Tannenbaum. Yet, if you examine the investor pack, you'll see a letter, written on official Department of Health letterhead, purportedly from the Medicines Control Council. Addressing the 'Managing Director of L. Frankel Chemical Corporation', the registrar of medicines writes:

> This letter serves to inform you that the last inspection report of your company, L Frankel Chemical Corporation, Bedfordview, and your subsequent response to the inspection report were tabled at the meeting of the Medicines Control Council.
>
> Please note that the Council resolved that: The committee is SATISFIED that the APPLICANT is in control to ensure that the medicines are manufactured in compliance with Good Manufacturing Practice, and DOES recommend registration of medicines in respect of quality.

If that weren't enough, there is also a certificate from the South African Pharmacy Council certifying that 'Eurochemicals, which trades also under the names L Frankel Chemicals, has been registered in accordance with the provisions of section 22 of the Pharmacy Act, 1974'. It is signed by the 'registrar' on 18 January 2009 in Pretoria. If you had any further doubt, there is a circular red seal on the bottom right corner, the sort you see affixed to doctors' qualifications in a physician's room. It radiates 'trust me'.

All unnecessary, it seems. But useful if you're intent on buying credibility.

The brochure given to investors says: 'The generic drug market is a key market in which Frankel Chemicals are exclusive agents for the distribution of API materials for many overseas, multinational prime pharmaceutical manufacturers. The primary focus is on Africa, Brazil, UK, South America, Switzerland, France, Russia, Belgium, Spain and India.'

Now, it *is* true that Frankel was an exclusive agent for some companies. In March 2008, Mallinckrodt Chemicals CEO Richard Sherwin provided a letter saying that his company had 'an exclusive arrangement with Frankel Chemicals to market, sell and distribute our products within the Southern Africa region'. Sherwin added that his company had 'been associated with Frankel Chemicals for over 25 years, and [had] been working very closely with Mr Barry Tannenbaum for over 14 years'.

Pfizer provided a similar letter in March 2008, signed by regional vice president Bindert Vriesema, declaring that Frankel 'are our sole distributors for our active pharmaceutical ingredients in South Africa, and this since March 1994'. Vriesema added that 'our main contact with Frankel Chemicals is Mr Barry Tannenbaum'. There are similar letters from the chemical division of Israel's TEVA Group, and from Spanish pharmaceutical company Uquifa.

But although Frankel might have done business with these companies, it's the scale of the business that was grotesquely distorted to suck money from investors. And the grandiose claims of Frankel's global trade are also heavily exaggerated: Frankel really only supplied APIs to South African companies.

Again, it is true that in late 2005 Tannenbaum opened an international office in Hamburg, Germany. That business, called Frankel International GmbH, would be run by a certain Volker Schultz, whom Tannenbaum had met there. But Estelle Wittenberg says the Hamburg office was basically a small operation, opened to solve a problem in sourcing APIs from China. 'Volker had a guy in his office, a Chinese guy, who did all the buying from China through that office. But the Hamburg office was just buying [ingredients] for South Africa,' she says.

And as for the Indian business? Well, Wittenberg says there never was an Indian business.

* * *

The biggest fib in Barry's investor brochure, the moment that the tale of Frankel Chemicals stepped into the territory of a proper scam, was the profits it claimed it made.

In Barry's 'family history', which he emailed to Chris in 2006, he said Frankel's turnover was in excess of $50 million (R450 million). Later, perhaps under pressure to illustrate the immense growth he was bragging about, Barry injected some Viagra into even those sexed-up numbers. A later Frankel brochure, largely based on that initial email, says: 'Group turnover 2008 [was] approximately $450 million and expect [sic] for 2009 in excess of $600 million.'

This is nothing less than an epic fabrication. 'Frankel was small,' says Wittenberg. 'Turnover was between R10 million and R15 million.' Not 400 times that, then.

Barry's brochure says, rather sanctimoniously, that Frankel Chemicals 'does not speculate, and business is carried out on confirmed orders only from blue-chip pharmaceutical companies for API and other associated chemicals'.

Interestingly, the API business was actually relatively strong in the 1990s and early 2000s, but then began to take some strain, according to Adcock Ingram's former financial director, Daryl Kronson. 'That business shrank dramatically over the last ten years,' he says. 'Pharmaceutical companies began to realise, why should they buy the raw materials through an agent, when they could send one of their employees to countries like India and negotiate for it directly?'[13]

So, as a small business chugging along with a few select clients, Frankel could make a steady living. As a multinational conglomerate doubling and tripling business every year, well, that was a story ten years too late.

Yet, investors wanted some evidence of Frankel's fantastic growth. Remarkably, Barry was able to provide them a set of 'audited financials' that attested to the fairy tale.

Those financials are for the 'year ending February 28 2007', and are supposedly signed by an auditing firm called IAPA Chartered Accountants on 8 May 2008.

IAPA said: 'In our opinion, the annual financial statements present fairly, in all material respects, the financial position of the company as of February 29 2008.' It said that it obtained 'sufficient and appropriate' evidence to make its evaluation.

Yet, its 'income statement' said the company had recorded revenue of a staggering R432.8 million for the year ending February 2007. Supposedly, its operating profit amounted to R96.7 million, and there was a bottom-line profit of R6.1 million.

These figures were many multiples greater than what anyone close to the company, like Estelle, say had actually been recorded by Frankel.

The figures had even been cleverly doctored to corroborate the fantasy tale that Frankel was growing by more than 60 per cent, supposedly because of the HIV/AIDS drugs. The revenue of R432.8 million was itself an 87 per cent jump from the R231 million turnover of the 2006 year. Solid evidence of the Frankel success story and signed by auditors, no less. (Needless to say, as fantastically unrealistic as even this was, it was still some distance off the $450 million Barry had claimed. That means there were three sets of figures: the crazy promises doing the rounds in dollars, the elaborately forged figures in the local accounts, and the real figure, which was a fraction of both.)

Frankel's balance sheet – a document that presents a picture of a company's assets and liabilities at a given point, a snapshot of its overall financial health – was an equally audacious work of fabrication. It put Frankel's assets at R1.15 billion, a figure that supposedly included R434 million in cash and R566 million that it was owed by companies it did business with.

But any financial geek would have noticed immediately one glaring problem with Frankel's accounts, fancifully edited though they were. While any accountant knows you can pad 'profits' in many ways – accounting being more art than science at times – the one thing you can't fiddle is a company's cash-flow state-ment. This shows the actual money flowing in and out of a company. Rather like a bank statement, it tends to show the unfortunate reality, rather than the money you wish you had.

However, Frankel's cash-flow statement said it generated only R66.4 million in 'cash from operations' – itself a highly unlikely figure anyway, but far less than the R432.8 million supposedly ringing through the company's tills. Then there is an eye-popping R283 million, which supposedly came into Frankel as a 'repay-ment of shareholder's loan'. This means that Barry Tannenbaum, who was the only shareholder at that time, repaid a staggering R283 million to Frankel. It is this supposed 'repayment' that drove up the company's revenue, and profit.

How was a man who just a few years before had declared that he was earning only R35 500 a month now apparently borrowing and repaying such a staggering amount of money from the company? Even for fictional accounts, this was some-thing of an anomaly. Even for a fantasy novel, this would appear to be a bridge too far.

In 2010, when Estelle gave evidence before the Tannenbaum trustees, she was shown these fanciful numbers. Her response: it's a joke.

So how is it that the auditors, IAPA, signed off on these bogus accounts?

Well, it turns out they didn't. An IAPA director said 'those financials have been altered, falsified and are incomplete'.[14] The company reported this to the Public Accountant and Auditors Board (now called the Independent Regulatory Board for Auditors [IRBA]), the institution meant to ensure the auditing profession remains above board, as a 'reportable irregularity'.

Fantastically, almost like a clichéd gangster movie, it seems Barry kept two sets of books – one he showed to investors as evidence of his fairy tale, and the other, the real figures, were actually the ones signed off by IAPA.

Barry had, through a cunning use of copying, pasting and selective edits of the auditors' report, created an entirely fictional set of books. And the true numbers, as you'd imagine, were far grimmer.

Frankel's true set of accounts for 2007 show it *actually* made revenue of R11.8 million (not R432.8 million as the fake financials said), an operating profit of just R445 576 (not R96.7 million) and a bottom-line loss of R361 702 (not a profit of R6.1 million).

Frankel's true assets amounted to R6 million (not R1.15 billion) and its cash in the bank was only R323 250 (not R434 million).

The company's real accounts show it for what it was: a small enterprise battling to survive with anorexic margins. The truth was that the year before, in 2006, it had actually done better than 2007, clocking up revenue of R12.5 million and turning a profit of R671 392. In 2005, it had clocked up R9.6 million in revenue, recording a profit of R359 786.

Frankel was such a Mickey Mouse enterprise at the time that its 'expenses' for 2005 contain such mundane costs as the R460 spent on 'gifts' that year, R3 704 spent on 'postage', R4 135 spent on 'software expenses' and R21 807 on 'advertising'.

David Grawitzky, the managing partner of IAPA, must have felt his blood run cold when he saw the forged financials with his signature at the bottom, supposedly attesting to the fact that Frankel was an industrial behemoth.

Grawitzky says he doesn't know whether the auditors board followed up the report his auditing firm lodged with the regulator. 'Once I'd done my job [of reporting this], I don't know what they did with it,' he says.[15]

The point is, the public relies on auditors to alert them to problems. They are meant to act as the gatekeepers, the quality assurers who tell if things aren't as they should be. But when they do find something wrong and report it, as in the Frankel case, surely the regulators should do something – even if it is just to alert the public?

The IRBA for years has been criticised as a toothless watchdog, more intent on appeasing the auditing firms – and mostly the big four: KPMG, Ernst & Young, Deloitte and PricewaterhouseCoopers – than taking care of the people who rely on their work. The Tannenbaum case didn't do anything to disprove this claim.

* * *

In 2011 the South African Specialised Commercial Crimes Unit prepared a document they intended to send to the Swiss and Australian authorities, known as a request for 'legal assistance'. This document, though never sent to Austria or Switzerland, spelt out exactly how Frankel, set up decades before, had morphed into the substrate for a massive multinational Ponzi scheme.[16]

'Since approximately 2003, Tannenbaum solicited loans from various investors. The solicitation increased dramatically during 2006,' it stated. At some point, the criminal investigators claim, Tannenbaum 'stole the business identity' of Frankel.

'Although [he] used the Frankel name and business concept, the investigators found no evidence that the loans so obtained ever formed part of Frankel's legitimate business, or were ever reflected in the audited financial statements of Frankel,' the document said.

Instead, 'by using the legitimate business concept of Frankel, Tannenbaum started to act as the head of a consortium that included Leigh and Rees, and that took in investors to fund non-existing transactions'.

Frankel might have been a real company at one stage, they said, but its persona had been criminally manipulated to swindle cash from people. 'In order to use Frankel as the enterprise to obtain loans from investors, Frankel maintained a relatively small legitimate business in importing raw materials for pharmaceutical companies.'

The authorities say Frankel's legitimate business 'recorded yearly turnovers of between R5 million and, in its most profitable year, approximately R12 million'.

The figures Barry gave to investors were exaggerated more than thirty-six-fold. The company was a fraction of the size he claimed it was.

Ask Estelle Wittenberg who she thinks forged those purchase orders and lied about Frankel's mega-profits, and she won't say. Partly, this is because she is still devoutly loyal to the Tannenbaums and maternally protective towards the family she worked with for twenty-three years. She formed something of a familial bond with Harold, whom she describes as 'a gentleman, who treated me like part of his family when I joined'. And she clearly feels the same about Barry. 'It's a sore point, because I gave my life to that business,' she says. 'There are a lot of little things that still hurt, but I'll always love Barry, I'll always love the Tannenbaums. They were a very respectful and loyal family.'[17]

'Little things', like, for example, being diddled out of a pension by Barry. It turns out that despite her twenty-three-year service for Frankel, Tannenbaum never set aside a pension for Estelle. So when SARS closed down Frankel's business, she was left out in the cold. As jilted as any of the investors, but over a much longer period of time.

'Barry said to me, "Estelle, you don't have to worry about money. I'll always look after you",' she says.

But Barry didn't look after her. Or any of the other staff, for that matter. Nor, in fact, did he look after a number of other companies that did business with Frankel and were owed money: when Frankel's doors closed, it owed R1.2 million to several companies, which were most likely forced to write off these debts.

Late one Friday in June 2009, days after the first headlines of 'South Africa's Madoff' had surfaced, a number of agents from SARS arrived at 1 Eastgate Lane. Estelle, who was running the office at that stage, had left for the day, trekking the 107 kilometres back down the N1 to her house in Deneysville, across the Vaal River. There was only a security guard at the office.

Panicked, the security guard called the owner of the property. SARS wasn't taking the locked door as a sign to leave: they threatened to break the door down if they weren't let in. So the tax officials got in and stayed there for hours, dredging through every slip, every file, every record they could find. For good measure, they then packed up everything they could, and disappeared into the night. Effectively, SARS had shut down Frankel Chemicals, a forty-year-old business.

Incredibly, Estelle still blames SARS for what happened to Frankel, rather than Barry. 'They sat there all night, going through all the files. It was totally illegal, they should have had a warrant,' she says. 'It was so scaly.'

Most remarkable is that despite what Barry Tannenbaum did to Estelle Wittenberg – fleeing to Australia and leaving her holding the keys to Frankel, and breaking his promise to provide her with some sort of pension after twenty-three years of service – she still speaks to him on Skype from time to time.

No hard feelings. If anything, she has sympathy for how he had been set up by *someone*, still unnamed.

Barry did buy her a car, though, supposedly to compensate her for her 'loyal service'. But later, struggling for cash, she sold it for R185 000 to cover her 'living expenses', or so she told the trustees.

After Frankel's doors were bolted shut, Estelle tried various ways of making some cash. First, she started her own business trading APIs from home, using the knowledge and contacts she'd got from Frankel. 'That didn't go well because the suppliers associated me with Frankel, so the trust wasn't there,' she says.

Then someone she'd met in the business gave her a job for a few years. In 2011 she retired for good, her last few years soured by the SARS night raid on the office and the lingering sense that her years of sacrifice had been in vain.

Still, she defends Barry: 'I could never say anything bad about Barry. He was, as you would say, a *mensch*. A fantastic guy.'

Like many of those who knew Barry, she finds the idea of him operating a massive fraud highly improbable. Too kind, too respectful of others. In fact, many of those people then reply: but what about Dean Rees?

Not just the rich:
The story of Sherry

The myth is that Barry Tannenbaum only pillaged from the rich, giving to himself, Dean Rees, Darryl Leigh and maybe a few other rich guys, who stashed the cash quickly and efficiently overseas. But the truth is there were almost as many butchers and bakers as there were spoilt trust-fund kids and entitled executives.

Take the case of Sherry – not her real name because she insisted on a pseudonym, as she still hasn't had the heart to confess to her own family how she blew their life savings on a scam.

'If I could just get my hands on that Tannenbaum guy for one minute,' says Sherry today, before adding, somewhat optimistically, 'but I do believe he'll get his comeuppance one day, be it from his marriage or whatever. I just don't know how these people sleep at night. I know I couldn't do what they did.'

Her story is that in 2007 she was retrenched from her job at Ratanga Junction, a creaking amusement park on the outskirts of Cape Town. For months, she battled to find another job, so she ended up scratching into the woeful pension given her by her employer.

'I was basically on the unemployment line,' she says. 'We were renting a place with my two children and my husband, and none of us could find work. The only thing I could do was go work in the UK as a carer for old people, leaving my family behind. I was planning that, when I spoke to an old school friend who told me she'd invested with Tannenbaum, and it had worked for her.'

Sherry only had R30 000 left of her pension, and the family needed it to survive. But on the other hand, if, as the sums showed, she could double that cash in a year, it might just be worth it.

'It was desperation stakes, really, and I agonised over the decision. I discussed it with [a friend] and I said to her, "Look, it sounds too good to be true, but maybe this is our lucky break, maybe this is the one that will get us out the ditch".'

So Sherry, fingers crossed and eyes shut, gave her entire pension of R30 000 to her friend to invest in early 2008. Now that the money they were living on was 'invested', she went to work in London to get cash to send home. From the reports she got from home, it seemed like she'd hit the jackpot. Her friend told her the R30 000 had tripled to more than R90 000.

'It was unbelievable. I immediately said to her, "Let's pull the money out, then we can invest in something more sustainable".'

This was December 2008, five months before it crashed.

Sherry's instincts about the scheme being on shaky ground and unsustainable were bang on. But, fatefully, she delayed drawing her cash. 'Then, one morning my friend called me, and told me the whole thing had gone pear-shaped. She was gutted. I was too, mind, but I didn't blame her for what happened, I went in with my eyes open, I just thought maybe this was our time.'

At this stage, Sherry was desperate to come home. She'd been away from her husband and children for two years. But with her entire cushion swallowed by some magnate in Australia, she had no option: she stayed in the UK for longer, saving as much as she could.

'Tannenbaum really hit me in the stomach,' she says. 'For two and a half years, I was away from home and I had to do it: it was the loneliest existence, but it was the only option I had. So Tannenbaum took far more from me than money. He made me stay over there for longer, he tore into my family.'

Overwrought at being away from her family, Sherry came home and took whatever job she could find. This included a grind as a receptionist at one of Cape Town's seedy strip clubs, full of washed-up Ukrainians and meth-addicted street kids working their way up. 'That was eye-opening. I used to see some of the clients in the streets the next day, and they'd look at me like they knew me from somewhere, but didn't want to say,' she says.

Times have improved for her since 2009. Sherry now has a job as a fundraiser for a research institute. But she's still renting, still supporting her family and still the only one in her household with work.

'What really burns me is that some people are saying, "Oh, this Tannenbaum thing, it was just about the rich getting richer." But it wasn't. There were a lot of us in shit street. There are many more like me out there.'[1]

7

Welcome, Dean Rees

'I've done some research on you. I see you defended that Miracle 2000 guy, and you got him off the hook. Is that how you found out how to get away with running a Ponzi scheme?'   – **Keith van der Spuy, investor, to Dean Rees**

When asked whodunnit, Derek Ziman, the Sydney-based lawyer representing Tannenbaum, replied, 'I think Barry's the victim. He's been an unwitting party to it.'[1]

You might say Ziman, a South African lawyer who specialised in auctions until 1995, when he moved to Australia to start a building business, is doing what lawyers do: defending his client despite overwhelming evidence to the contrary, seizing any smidgeon of doubt and inflating it thirtyfold.

'The spotlight should be on Rees, who we understand has a fleet of Ferraris, a house in Switzerland … and a house in Monaco,' he told the Jewish Telegraphic Agency.[2]

Ziman added that Dean Rees and Darryl Leigh had 'benefited, apparently immensely, from this at a time when Barry has not'.

The thing is, Ziman has a point.

Of all the characters in the drama, of all the potential offenders, no one would have bet on Barry concocting such a sophisticated scam. Barry was the empathetic philanthropist, the jolly, harmless bloke at the party whose name you wish you remembered. The guy you could leave your kids with if you had a family emergency.

As a member of Barry's own family puts it: 'Forget how unlikely it is that the kid I knew would have done this; he really isn't smart enough to have done this.'[3]

No, the smart money would always have been on Rees or Leigh, both schooled in law, both far more versed in how to skirt the fringes of legitimacy. Neither Rees nor Leigh was particularly amiable, or as instantly likeable as Barry. And, crucially, they were not averse to flashing some *serious* moola.

If anyone were to put together an intricate and sophisticated con to make an extra buck – or an extra R100 million or so – it's far more likely to have been Rees or Leigh than Barry Tannenbaum.

* * *

What first strikes you about Dean Rees is his eyes. Set deep beneath rosy cheeks and a receding hairline, his intense but skittish gaze doesn't exactly argue against the stereotype of the fast-talking litigator, sizing up the room for a new angle.

Rees has the rubicund appearance of many South African lads: you have a sense that he'd far rather be outside under the sun fishing, and telling his mates over a beer afterwards the odd tall tale about his day's catch.

Rees isn't even South African by birth. Dean Gillian Rees was born in Porthcawl, Wales, a grimy, if cheerful, seaside town with a population of less than 20 000, overlooking the Bristol Channel and about thirty kilometres from Swansea. The most famous thing about Porthcawl is its seafront, home to one of the UK's oldest amusement parks, called Coney Island, after the New York island, because its first roller coaster was brought to Wales by the Americans in 1918 to entertain their troops during World War I.

Porthcawl was once a major industrial port. But its reputation and cash flow were sucked away in the early 1900s by the nearby town of Barry. Many decades later, as luck would have it, the curse for Porthcawl's sons still seems to be Barry – at least in Dean Rees's case.

'Seems like I should just avoid the Barrys of this world,' Rees now jokes.

Dean's family moved to South Africa when he was ten, so you won't spot a trace of the lilting Welsh accent. Years of schooling – first at St David's Marist College, then a BA degree at Wits University in 1991 and finally a BProc law degree in 1994 at the University of South Africa (UNISA) – tutored Dean Rees in the local vernacular.

What is remarkable is how quickly he made his fortune. He only began practising law in April 1997, but by December that year, he had already been made partner at Goldman Judin and Werner. Little more than a year later, in 1999, Rees started his own practice.

'I was pretty much penniless at the time,' he says. 'I took the clients from the firm, was threatened with litigation and then ran a hugely successful practice. I was twenty-eight so it was a huge risk at my young age.'

By 2009, Dean Rees had become a megamillionaire, was effectively exiled to Switzerland and had a name that anyone who knew anyone tittered about at dinner parties as the real brains behind Tannenbaum. (Or, at least, they were *pretty damn sure* he was, because they knew someone who'd lost big and he'd told them it was all Dean – and anyway, have you seen what Dean *drives* now?)

At that stage, Rees had become a fugitive in his adopted country and a pariah in South Africa's notoriously overstarched legal brotherhood.

This is how it happened. In late 2006, Rees got a phone call from Darryl Leigh, whom he knew well because his law firm was doing work for the Development Bank of Southern Africa, where Leigh was a legal advisor. There is this short-term investment opportunity, explained Leigh. It's sourced through my neighbour Barry Tannenbaum, and you can make a killing on it, he said.

Rees was tempted, but uncertain. After all, he was no stranger to dodgy investment opportunities or even, as it turns out, Ponzi schemes.

Rees says about the incident: 'I was initially dubious about the nature of the transaction and I did not know very much detail, but I had known Leigh for some time.'

No problem, said Leigh, I'll underwrite your investment if this will give you a little more peace of mind. There's no way you can lose.

Rees still wasn't entirely convinced, so he spoke to Tasha Rossen, Darryl Leigh's girlfriend, whom he had represented in a maintenance battle with her ex-husband. 'He asked me what I thought, whether it was legitimate,' says Rossen. 'I told him, Dean, all I can say is that it has worked for me – I've invested and been paid out every time.'[4]

So Rees took a leap of faith, one that would determine his future.

He first stepped onto the treadmill on 8 September 2006, when he deposited R205 000 into Barry Tannenbaum's Rand Merchant Bank account at a branch in Benmore, Sandton. His business partners also invested their money under the company Marble Gold 345.

As Darryl promised, about nine or ten weeks later, Rees was repaid with plenty of interest.

A few weeks later, Rees and a business partner, Ben Jowitt, attended one of Tannenbaum's lunchtime presentations, organised by Leigh. Rees sat next to Tannenbaum and they hit it off. 'We were both so-called technology freaks and enjoy mobile phones, computers and the like,' said Rees. 'I remember giving Tannenbaum my telephone number.'[5]

Within a few months, Barry Tannenbaum called Rees directly to say that there was a shortfall of R600 000 on one trade and could he help. Rees agreed. Again, it all went according to plan. The money rolled in, just as it would if it was a legitimate scheme.

Rees's relationship with Leigh wasn't quite as smooth. After numerous clashes between the two lawyers, Rees had had enough.

Rossen recalls how Dean called her in early 2007 and told her he was going to pull his investment. 'He said he was sick and tired of dealing with Darryl, that Darryl was just constantly rude and aggressive,' she says.

This is borne out by Rees's own court papers. In one affidavit, he says he 'did not believe it was worth the aggravation, given the miscommunication'.[6]

But Tannenbaum had seen something he wanted in Rees. Early in 2007, he called Rees saying he knew he had many connections and asking if he wanted to do a private deal. When Rees asked what had happened to Darryl Leigh, Barry told him not to worry about Darryl. Darryl was 'doing his own thing', he said.

So Dean Rees, Ben Jowitt, Ed Jowitt and Chris Harris had another dip, and again it worked out.

But Rees had an eye for the margin. He realised that Leigh had made a killing from being an agent and punting the scheme to others. Why should Leigh be the only guy to do this, especially when Rees had a bulging wallet of business cards he could leverage into the scheme? So he made some calls to a few of his clients and mentioned the immense returns he had made.

'One transaction led to the next, the investment base grew, the returns flowed, the transactions became bigger in nature and a number of investors were attracted by word of mouth from existing investors,' Rees later said.

Soon, there was a constant flow of money between Rees and Tannenbaum.

Police investigator Piet Senekal says that three years later, by the time the scheme had gone belly up, Rees had 'dedicated most, if not all, his effort into managing 347 investors that he induced to participate in the Frankel scheme'. Essentially, Rees had introduced a new investor every three days.[7]

This illustrates the extent to which Rees jumped in head first – Tannenbaum, the founder who'd been running the scheme far longer, only had about 182 investors reporting directly to him. Leigh – abrasive, truculent and difficult to deal with – had 229.

There are many reasons why Rees was so much more successful than Leigh.

Firstly, Dean is a natural showman, a salesman with an angle on a deal. Secondly, it's because Leigh was such a disagreeable guy that people who invested through Darryl swapped to Dean. And thirdly, Rees 'professionalised' the scheme, providing spreadsheets and fancy-looking documents on letterheads. After all, if it looks like a Ponzi scheme, and pays returns like a Ponzi scheme, at least it's providing investment statements like a real company.

Says Tasha Rossen, Leigh's former girlfriend: 'Darryl bullied his investors and was rude. Whereas I heard from someone who had left Darryl's consortium that Dean was much more professional.'

Dean had every incentive to professionalise the scheme: it made him a fortune.

It meant he would no longer have to do the legal equivalent of turning tricks to make a buck. The lawyer admitted publicly to benefiting from Tannenbaum's scheme by more than R70 million. According to others, he got more than R500 million. Certainly, a lot of cash washed through his accounts – the only question is, how much of it did he get to keep?

Senekal says: 'Amounts in excess of R1.9 billion were deposited in, and transacted through, the personal bank accounts of Rees, either directly through his trust account or through his designated legal vehicle created for operating the Frankel scheme, Suscito Investments.'[8]

Whichever way you look at it, Barry Tannenbaum was Dean Rees's ticket to the big time.

* * *

Rees's office, at 5 Wessel Road, Rivonia, seemed more cocktail lounge than law chamber. Back in 2009, there were the mandatory legal textbooks, but they seemed almost an afterthought.

(Four years later, that office, in which hundreds of investors did their business with Dean, is empty. The furniture is gone; chains prevent anyone stepping inside.)

Within the legal fraternity, Dean's name had never been stamped up in lights. He was still young, a bit-player, someone with an eye on how he could be cut into the next big deal, rather than the person tasked with drawing up the contracts to govern that next big deal.

Speak to those who knew him in his early years as a lawyer, and they'll say that even before he made it big, he lived like he'd won the lottery.

Before Tannenbaum, Rees drove a Porsche, then he swapped it for a Mercedes-Benz and later a BMW. After Tannenbaum, he upgraded to a Ferrari – sunburn red, *Magnum P.I.*-style.

The properties he bought were lavish too. A house he owned in Bryanston (an elite neighbourhood north of Johannesburg renowned for its especially rambling properties) consisted of four bedrooms, three bathrooms, a tennis court, a swimming pool, staff accommodation and a separate bedroom suite.

One person, who knew Rees years before he met Barry, says he was never quite sure if Rees was making a killing on some hidden investment or if he was simply living beyond his means, spending money faster than it came in.

Rees, he says, 'was involved in a lot of property deals before the Tannenbaum thing came up … he seemed clever, but lazy. He had an astute business mind, and seemed exceptionally good at cutting corners.'

Dean Rees's legal practice, Rees & Associates, morphed into Rees Tshabalala Adams Inc. when he partnered with two young attorneys, Reginald Tshabalala and Alastair Adams, and later another young attorney, Steven Merchak. Together they moved into the offices at 5 Wessel Road.

From the start, Rees didn't spend much time in the office. One of his former employees says, 'Dean very rarely passed through that practice. I really don't know what he did with his days.'

Rees says that if people didn't understand what he was doing with his time, it was their mistake. 'I was up to my ears in work, all day, every day,' he says. 'I was running one of the biggest litigation basis in Joburg at the time. I had big clients like Sweets from Heaven, so I was working twenty-one-hour days.'

The clients he did have, such as Investec and the Development Bank of Southern Africa, provided him with a steady trickle of work.

Eventually, Tshabalala, Merchak and Adams offered to buy him out of the practice. The legal firm was on Investec's legal panel, so its value lay in the fact that it would get regular work from one of the country's biggest investment banks.

But Dean asked for more than R4 million for his shares – an amount that no bank was prepared to finance – and he wasn't prepared to settle for less.

This led to an odd incident in 2008, when Rees's wife Dominique stormed into the office, her husband trailing sheepishly behind, and called for a partners meeting. (Quite how she had the authority to do this, the partners weren't quite sure.)

Dominique proceeded to berate the three young lawyers for having not concluded a proper offer, for not raising the funds and for allowing the issue to stagnate. Finger wagging, Dominique lectured them about their craven ungratefulness to Dean and for assuming that just because he was wealthy he would happily sell the practice for little or no value.

Then she stormed out. Dean snuck back five minutes later and apologised for his wife, putting it down to stress caused by their imminent move to Switzerland and her desire to tie up all loose ends.

In retrospect, Tshabalala, Merchak and Adams had dodged a torpedo. Had they bought Rees Tshabalala Adams, the association with Rees wouldn't have won them any gold stars in the legal fraternity.

At the end of 2008, Tshabalala, Merchak and Adams left the practice to go out on their own. This led to another bizarre incident. Dean, who was now living in Switzerland, then sued Alastair Adams for decimating his practice.

Says Alastair today: 'Dean believed he was entitled to be remunerated by me for having allegedly snatched his client base, but in truth, I had been servicing those very same clients for the past four years and they were free to send the work where they wanted to.'

He says that after the three young lawyers left, Rees continued to trade with the law firm anyway. Rees then withdrew the claim, which is just as well, because Alastair wasn't about to be intimidated.

'I welcomed the lawsuit because firstly the claim was ridiculous and secondly, for Rees to have had any chance of succeeding against me, he would have had to come back and testify. And I won't be the only one taking an interest when he eventually does come back.'

* * *

If you're going to construct an elaborate Ponzi scheme, Dean Rees is exactly the man you want as your front-runner. Rees's spending habits – garish and conspicuously flashy – made him an ideal target to absorb the heat when it all came crashing down. Had Barry planned it this way, it could hardly have worked better.

Wayne Gaddin, an investor who said that he and Barry were 'best friends, like brothers, for more than twenty years', described Rees as the 'antithesis' of Tannenbaum. He said: '[Barry] lives in a modest home, not the ones plastered over Facebook [of Rees's luxury home] … There was a change in this when Dean arrived. Then you started hearing how the business was growing.'

Of course, Gaddin refused to believe that his great friend was capable of any wrongdoing.

This isn't to say Barry led an entirely spartan life. By 2007, he had a number of cars: a silver BMW 325i, which he drove; a silver Mercedes-Benz 200k, which Debbie drove; a BMW X5 (this time in black); and a blue Chrysler Grand Cherokee. It's just that, compared with Rees and all his Ferraris, Barry seemed more understated. This made Rees an easy target.

If Barry had duped them, why was it Dean who appeared to be living large on the proceeds? Why didn't Barry have the Ferraris, the multiple houses, the yachts, the million-rand watches, the designer clothes?

These are good questions and the answers are tethered to the motive of the primary architect of the scheme.

* * *

One of the things that makes Rees the perfect patsy is that he is the only protagonist with a clear link to one of South Africa's most successful pyramid schemes.

He was the lawyer for Sibusiso 'Master' Radebe, the mastermind who cooked up the Miracle 2000 scam, which swindled millions from poor black investors (as discussed in Chapter 4).

Like Tannenbaum, Radebe had appointed agents who would get a commission for bringing in new investors. While in the Radebe case, Rees was the lawyer; in the Tannenbaum case, he was one of those agents.

After the magistrate ruled that Sibusiso Radebe need not serve a day in jail, Rees was quoted as saying: 'We believe [the sentence] was fair. Mr Radebe thought he was busy working to the advantage of the community. It was unlike other pyramid schemes where the agents end up stealing all the monies.'[9]

So Rees knew a thing or two about the justice system and its frailties. Sure, Radebe's light sentence was eventually appealed and the Johannesburg High Court sent him to jail for two years. But the point is, the Radebe case represented a university education for Rees in the mechanics of Ponzi schemes. This is partly why many of the investors just don't buy Dean's explanation that he didn't see through the Tannenbaum scheme until it was too late.

Not only did the Miracle 2000 scheme tutor Dean in the ways of a pyramid scheme, it also provided another lawyer, who was also involved in the Tannenbaum case, with some intimate knowledge of how such schemes worked. That lawyer was André Bezuidenhout, an advocate of the High Court, whom Dean hired to argue Radebe's case in court.

Bezuidenhout, representing Radebe on Rees's instruction, faced off against

Gerrie Nel, the legendary state prosecutor responsible for putting corrupt police boss Jackie Selebi behind bars in 2010.

Years later, at the time of the Tannenbaum case, Bezuidenhout popped up on the other side of the aisle as the legal expert hired by the South African Reserve Bank to find out who had used Barry's scheme to siphon money offshore.

Tannenbaum's investors weren't ignorant, however. Unlike the poor Afrikaners who had invested in Krion, or the destitute black people of Spruitview who had poured every cent into Miracle 2000, Tannenbaum's funders had means. They did their homework. Which means that Rees's involvement in Miracle 2000 was known to those of them who'd bothered to perform even a rudimentary Google search before signing over their savings. Months before the scheme folded, Keith van der Spuy, Darryl Leigh's former colleague at Nedbank, met Rees at the News Café restaurant in Sandton – a glittered-up venue where waitresses perch precariously on seven-inch heels and serve cocktails with predictably risqué names, such as the Seductive Strawberry and the Naked Waiter.

He recalls: 'I told Rees, "I've done some research on you. I see you defended that Miracle 2000 guy and you got him off the hook. Is that how you found out how to get away with running a Ponzi scheme?"'[10]

Rees apparently laughed at the suggestion. 'No,' he said, 'this business has been going on for several years; Barry just brought me in to turbocharge it.'

Van der Spuy, who was inadvertently sucked into the scheme when his wife invested R2 million that they'd set aside for their son, ended up losing more than R30 million.

In soliciting investors, Rees stuck to the hymn sheet he'd first heard from Tannenbaum. Obviously, it is impossible for an outsider to say for certain whether Rees had his own private concerns over Tannenbaum's scheme, which he may have shelved for fear of dislodging the bricks on his yellow-brick road.

There is another possibility: some investors believe that Rees might have believed it to be legit initially, but then figured out along the way that it was a laughably implausible scheme – yet decided to ride it for all it was worth until it went pop.

Chris Harris was one of Rees's long-standing business partners who lost a fortune in the end, thanks to Tannenbaum. Harris had been running a property business with Rees since the early 1990s. Rees had been Harris's attorney since 1997 and his property partner since 2004. 'I was his terrier to sort things out,' says Rees. Dean suggested Harris invest, and while Harris was interested, he wanted to know why Tannenbaum couldn't simply approach a bank – the same question every investor asked at some stage.

Rees dished out the stock answer: using a bank would mean a nightmare of bureaucratic delays – which a fast-moving drug business couldn't afford.

Harris took the bait and ploughed R80 million into the Tannenbaum scheme.

At least he had the good sense to withdraw some of it, but still ended up R8 million in the red. To recover this, he dragged Rees to court.

Ultimately, Judge John Horn agreed that Rees had deceived Harris and others, saying that he'd 'spun a web of intrigue' to get people to invest and had kept details of the investments 'under a veil of secrecy'.[11]

Rees, perhaps predictably, disagreed with that assessment. All along he has maintained that he was as much a victim as anyone, that he had been swindled and was now being painted unfairly as a conspirator.

'Why would I be the mastermind of this Barry Tannenbaum nonsense when I was sitting on a screaming fortune in equity in these properties that I could easily leverage,' he says today.

The only thing is, unlike many investors, Rees benefited enormously along the way. It made him rich in a way that MBA students can only fantasise about: champagne-soaked dinners, lightning-fast sports cars and chartered jets became standard.

Indeed, Rees's lifestyle, with its conspicuous absence of restraint, was a tool that Tannenbaum wielded to sway investors. Darryl Leigh may have been crass in the way he spent cash, but Rees, the peacock, was far more willing to boast about it.

This was the way with many who made their riches through Tannenbaum. Like a hedge-fund manager who builds a super-size mansion right next door to his colleague in the countryside to 'escape it all', it was just as important to *show* that you were super-wealthy as it was to *be* super-wealthy.

* * *

If you're looking for one story that tells you everything you need to know about Dean Rees's flashiness, there is no more succinct a tale than that of his trip to Saint-Tropez in the south of France in September 2008.

That trip – ostensibly to dazzle prospective British investors for Tannenbaum's scheme – was so gauche, so fantastically over the top, that you would be hard-pressed to believe it actually took place.

But one of the people who attended the trip, jeweller Mark Gorrie, attested to a twenty-two-page affidavit detailing the events in Saint-Tropez – a document later used by the National Prosecuting Authority's Asset Forfeiture Unit to seize Rees's assets.

Gorrie, in his early forties at the time of writing, started Mark Gold Jewels in Durban and has since become South Africa's version of a celebrity jeweller (if there is such a thing). His clients have included R&B singer Usher, Canadian crooner Celine Dion and British racing driver Jenson Button. His shops were given the right to distribute well-established brands such as Franck Muller, U-Boat and Graham of London. He even has a resort shop at the Fancourt golf course on South Africa's Garden Route and a top-end store in Melrose Arch – a stretch of offices and shops in Johannesburg that shamelessly seek to recreate a high-end London neighbourhood, with all the appropriate snobbery you'd expect.

Gorrie's nightmare began sometime in 2006 when he was working in the store in Melrose Arch. Barry Tannenbaum sauntered through the door and introduced himself and his wife, Deborah. Barry glanced around and seemed impressed. He wouldn't buy from Mark Gold that day, but he told Gorrie that he reserved the right to 'spoil his wife' in future by buying her some jewellery from him.[12]

Yet, remarkably, during that very first meeting, Barry hit on Gorrie to invest in his pharmaceutical scheme. Barry said he was involved in the drug import business and that Gorrie could earn 'lucrative profits' by financing the pharmaceutical deals – in the region of 15 to 25 per cent over a period of less than eight weeks.

Gorrie says, 'I was, at the time, obviously more interested in selling product to him and not open to investing in somebody else's business.'

Equally remarkable is that Barry openly gave the sales pitch to the jeweller in front of Deborah. 'She did not appear surprised at all,' says Gorrie. 'It appeared to me that she was, as Tannenbaum's spouse, obviously aware as to his business dealings.'

Although Gorrie didn't immediately invest, he was intrigued. So he asked his business partner to find out about Tannenbaum. 'He reported back to me that Tannenbaum had a good reputation, and that he came from a family who had made a substantial return from the pharmaceutical industry.'

So, in November 2006, Gorrie made his first investment. It was, as you'd expect, a slippery slope of greed. Soon he was digging into his home loan for more cash to invest and introducing his mother-in-law, his brother and his friends. Altogether, Gorrie ploughed in R6 million.

Gorrie's introduction to Tannenbaum's scheme provides a universe of insight into how the scheme actually worked. For a so-called 'exclusive investment' open only to the 'inner circle' to be so blatantly hawked to someone whom Barry had met just moments before in a jewellery shop says as much as you'll ever need to know about the Frankel scheme and its claims of legitimacy.

Within months, in mid-2007, Dean Rees also began visiting Gorrie's jewellery story with his wife. 'Rees had an insatiable appetite for expensive jewellery and watches. He demonstrated extreme wealth and [was] the typical high-net-worth individual for which my business would cater,' says Gorrie.

Rees became Gorrie's priority client and spent more than R4 million in his store – despite Gorrie's reservations about his integrity. Gorrie says:

He was clearly what I would call a fast talker, very good in selling ideas and clearly someone who was flashy in his lifestyle. I would even describe it as excessive. He was wearing designer clothes, purchasing fine jewellery and driving only the best luxury motor vehicles.

No kidding.

Rees tried to get Gorrie to invest in the Frankel scheme through him, but Gorrie politely turned him down because he was, after all, already heavily invested directly through Barry.

The jeweller was clearly hot property, as he was also approached by Darryl Leigh during a breakfast run of luxury motor cars – a shared passion of Leigh's and Gorrie's. Leigh punted the scheme heavily, pointing out how his Frankel investment had paid for his two Lamborghinis. Gorrie kept quiet.

But it was Rees's magpie-like attraction to jewellery that resulted in him spending many hours with Mark Gorrie – wining, dining and partying.

Rees usually footed the extravagant bills. Once, for example, Dean, Dominique, Mark and his wife, Christy Denn, dined at the Auberge Michel in Sandton, a silver-star boutique restaurant favoured by flashy politicians such as Paul Mashatile. The bill for the four of them that night? A cool R10 000.

The turning point came in September 2008. Rees was planning a trip to Saint-Tropez where he would give Dominique a five-carat diamond ring, worth a not-inconsequential R1.7 million.

On the day of their departure, Dean and Dominique went to Gorrie's shop to try on the ring. But to Dean's dismay, the ring was too small. Gorrie said, 'No problem, we'll resize it.' Dean agreed and promptly invited Gorrie and his wife to deliver the ring to them in France, and join them on a yacht in Saint-Tropez.

But this wasn't just any yacht. The super-yacht that Dean Rees hired for a week, at a cost of R3.5 million, was called *Tommy* – a spectacular Italian-designed vessel fifty-two metres long, able to host twelve guests, and boasting a Jacuzzi, satellite communications and Wi-Fi access. It goes for a minimum of €147 000 a night and even has its own website.[13]

When Gorrie and his wife arrived at Nice Airport (their flights paid for by Rees), they promptly stepped into a helicopter, which Dean had chartered to whisk his guests directly to *Tommy*. (The yacht, as you'd expect, came fitted with a helipad.)

'The sheer size and luxury of the yacht proverbially overwhelmed me,' says Gorrie. 'Whilst I am generally used to high-net-worth individuals spending large amounts of money on luxury items, I was simply overwhelmed by [Rees's] level of spending.'

As soon as they stepped onto the boat, each of Rees's guests were handed a bottle of Château Margaux (costing north of R5 000 per bottle). And limousine rides were standard whenever they hit land.

It seemed that the purpose of the trip was twofold: it was an extravagant birthday party for Dominique; and it was also an act of showmanship for potential investors. Prospective investors who spent a few days on *Tommy* included three British businessmen: Sir Philip Green, and Richard Kirk and his son, Andy. As Gorrie describes it:

> The spending spree was breathtaking. They [Dean and Dominique] ended up at a table in a restaurant which was attended by visitors to a yacht which was moored next to the *Tommy* yacht. During supper the two tables started spraying each other with expensive French champagne. Rees footed the bill for the champagne, [costing] approximately R300 000.

When *Tommy* moored at Saint-Tropez, the Rees party went shopping. Mark's wife wanted to buy a dress for a cocktail party, but the cheapest one she could find in a local store cost R30 000. No problem, said Dominique, I'll buy it for you. Christy politely declined.

Gorrie, already awed by Rees's indulgence, was flabbergasted when the lawyer simply strolled into a Saint-Tropez jewellery store and splashed out on a R250 000 B.R.M. watch. 'Dominique was not to be outdone by this and, in turn, purchased seven pairs of designer sunglasses for herself,' Gorrie says.

The rush to spend money had become a competition in itself. And it appeared to Gorrie to be spontaneous material indulgence of the most sordid kind. But it seemed a contrived spontaneity aimed at achieving a very specific purpose. Rees later confided to Gorrie that these 'entertainment expenses' had been well worth it, given the fact that Richard Kirk invested R105 million after the trip.

The man who introduced the Kirks to the Frankel scheme was a certain James Patterson – a key figure in the scheme. Patterson was Rees's *consigliere*, the man who got stuff done in Europe. It was Patterson who lured the European investors – for which Rees gave him a black Ferrari F430.

Patterson would ultimately earn more than R17 million in commission for greasing the wheels – cash that he used to buy an apartment in Monaco.

Patterson proved to be useful, given his links to overseas investors, but he wasn't exactly popular. In one instance in February 2009, Rees wrote to his Hong Kong connection, Moni Chin, who was helping him and Barry set up companies there: 'Between you and I, does James harass you a lot? He always seems to be sending orders etc., asking questions etc. Sometimes I feel uncomfortable with what he asks.'[14]

Rees said that, in future, he and Moni Chin should 'confer as to what the answers are to [Patterson's] questions. I think it's for the best. He may be involved in the funding, but the private information I would like to keep to between us. He seems to want to know what is going on financially the whole time.'

Moni Chin replied: 'I'm glad that you feel the same way about James. But I think he just wants to be in control, as he is responsible to his investors.'

Though the purpose of Gorrie's trip was to courier the resized ring to Dominique, he also delivered a diamond ring to Patterson and his wife, Deanne.

After the trip, Patterson wrote an email to Gorrie thanking him, and included Rees in the correspondence: 'Thank you so much for making me such an amazing ring, even if it is meant for women. I love it. Deanne is really happy with her flower ring as well.'

Rees replied: 'What do you mean for women! I think diamonds are cool on guys ...'

* * *

It might have cost a pretty penny, but the Saint-Tropez trip had been a fist-pumping, back-slapping victory for Rees and Patterson.

Perhaps wowed by Rees's extravagance, perhaps too starry-eyed to ask more questions, Richard Kirk and his son pumped £17 million into Tannenbaum's scheme – money they never saw again.

This was a significant scoop. Richard Kirk was then CEO of Peacocks, a Welsh clothing firm that later collapsed with £750 million of debt. Kirk was then appointed CEO of budget retailer Poundstretcher.

Richard Kirk apparently acted as the conduit for the Frankel scam to expand into UK boardrooms. In 2012 Richard's wife, Barbara, lodged a claim against her ex-husband in the High Court in London for over £3 million, which she says she lost after his 'persistent advice' led her to invest with Tannenbaum.[15]

Barbara claimed that Richard, who was offered returns of up to 260 per cent a year, acted as a de facto agent for Tannenbaum in Europe's financial centre.

She also said, according to court papers: 'During 2008 and 2009, he was in fact engaged – seemingly as a remunerative sideline from his day-to-day employment with Peacock Group – in systematically soliciting private individuals to invest in the Frankel scheme.'[16]

It is not quite clear whether he did earn commission this way, as she suggests. But what is clear is that a number of other top-drawer UK chiefs ploughed their cash into Tannenbaum's scheme. They included Richard Long, CEO of TUI Travel plc, a travel company worth £3.8 billion and listed on the London Stock Exchange.[17]

After the news broke of the deception, Richard Kirk issued a statement distancing himself from the entire sordid mess – if not convincingly. 'I have a wide range of personal investments and did make a small one in this entity, although this ceased some time ago,' he said.[18]

Patterson, described as a Monaco-based investment advisor 'of growing renown', was fingered by the *Telegraph* in the UK as the man who brokered the

Kirks' meeting with Rees. The newspaper had a photograph of Kirk and Patterson sharing 'sun-kissed smiles and fine wines' together at the Monaco Grand Prix in May 2009, clearly with no idea of the fallout that would take place just two months later.[19]

* * *

After the French trip, Rees went back to South Africa via London, where he stopped off at the Dorchester Hotel on another charm offensive to woo more British investors. As the money flowed in, it was an easy sell.

Back in Joburg, Rees's foot hit the accelerator. He spent more than R5 million on jewellery for himself and Dominique, including, as is now legendary, a R1 million Blue Phantom watch.

Gorrie was struggling to reconcile the nauseating display he saw on *Tommy* with the delays in being repaid his own investments with Tannenbaum. After all, Dean had told him that his own wealth stemmed directly from his involvement with Tannenbaum, so there shouldn't have been such a disconnect.

Gorrie says: 'I explained to [a colleague, Michael Levy] the extreme wealth which Rees was reflecting, and questioned him as to why Tannenbaum, from time to time, needed extensions for repayment on my investments.'[20]

Levy asked Tannenbaum, who replied that he had never received all the cash that Dean had raised.

In December 2008, as fault lines were beginning to show in Tannenbaum's scheme, Gorrie and his wife went to dinner with Dean and Dominique, where Dean opened up about his plans to emigrate to Switzerland.

Dean said he'd just bought a luxury villa in Lausanne for R65 million. He planned to relocate there for a year while he built his dream home on Australia's Gold Coast, where he'd bought land. (Tannenbaum had also put down a deposit on land at the Gold Coast, on Rees's advice – only Barry would later lose that deposit.)

In court papers, Gorrie claims that during dinner one night, Dean had asked for his help to get his watch collection – at that stage, more than fifty luxury watches – and his diamond jewellery out of South Africa and into Switzerland.

As this would have been clearly illegal, Gorrie said no, he couldn't help. He wouldn't even know how, he said. 'At a later point in time, he informed me that he [had] hired a private jet to fly his family to Switzerland with the jewellery and watches on the plane … he informed me that the chartered plane alone cost him more than a million rand.'

Rees continued to drop hundreds of thousands of rands at a time on Gorrie's jewellery. Unwisely, Gorrie had begun to extend Rees credit at the jewellery store and that debt had already rocketed to R1.9 million. Soon after the dinner during which Rees had shared the plans of his Swiss escape, Gorrie demanded that he pay up. Rees offered his Ferrari 599 GTB as security, according to Gorrie.

Five months later, Dean still hadn't paid up. So Gorrie called a luxury-car trader and flogged the Ferrari for R2.8 million. Within months, the Ferrari had been on-sold to Zunaid Moti, a young foul-mouthed businessman often accused of acting more like a gangster than an executive. According to Rees, this just wasn't true, as he sold the Ferrari to Gorrie. In one email between the two in January 2009, Gorrie offers to remake some jewellery for Rees that had been lost, adding that 'we can offset the car, as discussed'.

In that email, Gorrie says 'we have a brand-new style of diamond flower ring which I would love to make for Dom with a matching flower neckpiece, which we can deliver in Monaco, if we [are] still on'. This suggests that in 2009 the relationship was still strong.

Why Rees chose Switzerland, rather than Australia, is unclear. One of the documents from the criminal investigators states that Rees 'applied for Australian residency in the period 2006 to 2008, but his application was declined'.

Rees claims that the decision to move to Switzerland was a natural one:

> My wife had previously lived in Lausanne, Switzerland, in 2000 and 2001, and I had visited her there many times during 2001, prior to us getting married in 2002. I had loved the lifestyle and the country but at that stage it was evident to me that I had no means available to work there or indeed live there.[21]

There is one final vignette that neatly encapsulates the character of Dean Rees. An array of pictures on his Facebook page show him and Dominique enjoying the proceeds that emanated from Tannenbaum's investors.

A few of the pictures show them in a private jet, presumably the one that flew them to Switzerland, revelling in the luxury like children in newly driven snow. In one, Rees studies a newspaper, while Dominique lies on a bed in the bedroom. In another, they are drinking wine and reclining in plush leather seats after a sushi dinner.

There are numerous other pictures of Dean driving his red Ferrari, and some of him in the snow at his villa, 14 Chemin des Graminées in Pully, near Lausanne.

This seems to illustrate a few things. First, that Rees, although he tried to appear the sophisticated legal expert, was really just like a baby in a bath, splashing as loudly and as unselfconsciously as possible in a gigantic tub of money. The fact that he posed for pictures and then posted them on a social-media website to illustrate the extent of his new wealth illustrates his childlike glee at his new fortune.

Second, it seems unlikely that Rees was in the initial stages of patching together an elaborate swindle. If he had been, you'd imagine he would have shown far more discretion. If he had, surely he would have foreseen that these pictures would end up being plastered, embarrassingly, across the centre spreads of magazines as part of an exposé of South Africa's largest fraud?

* * *

Later, in June 2009, after the bubble had burst and the scheme was unmasked as a con, Dean Rees surprised many investors by sticking around in South Africa for a few days. 'The chutzpah!' one investor said. 'He seems to think he'll get away with it.'

After the Routledge Modise meeting, in which he'd broken the news that Frankel was one immense con, Rees held meetings with journalists and forensic expert Steve Harcourt-Cooke.

Despite displaying a perpetual jitteriness, Rees didn't have the air of someone who feared he would soon be staring out from behind bars. He seemed to genuinely believe he'd done nothing wrong. If he had been framed, he didn't realise it.

Nonetheless, at an interview with the *Financial Mail*, he came across as a bundle of nerves: intermittently hostile then charming, taking you into his confidence one minute, then railing against the injustice done to him by the media the next.

Rees is no fool, though. He built a compelling argument for how he couldn't have been the architect of such a scheme, how he couldn't have been the person who spent hours copying and pasting fraudulent words on company letterheads. And he provided witnesses to attest to his story, and said that it was Barry whodunnit.

But then, one morning, he abruptly left.

Whether Rees genuinely believed he'd done nothing wrong or was just playing the game at that point is unclear. But then, with a R1 million watch on your arm, you'd probably feel as if you had some insurance against impoverishment.

In Switzerland, where Rees has stayed, he remains out of reach of the National Prosecuting Authority.

Gorrie says that after the scheme had been unmasked, Rees contacted him a few times. 'He informed me that he was getting involved in the import/export business and in mining. He showed absolutely no remorse for the fact that numerous people had lost large sums of money.'[22]

Jilted investors still tell stories of how Rees has been spotted in Lausanne, enjoying the high life in one of the most expensive countries in the world. He still flaunts his wealth, driving around in a McLaren Mercedes sports car (worth an estimated R18 million).

It's almost like Rees isn't even on the run. Life rolls on as if he were a retired internet billionaire, whiling away his days under the Swiss sun. Dominique still goes to book club.

Many people might see Dominique as a victim in this, but she is no demure shrinking violet, according to documents filed before various courts. Christy Denn, Mark Gorrie's wife, provided an affidavit for one, in which she recounted how she became quite friendly with Dominique over time:

> Dominique is an extrovert, who always made a point of telling me how successful and wealthy [Dean] was and that he was involved in more than fifty businesses. She explained to me that she was his bookkeeper, and that she worked long hours for him. The wealth which Rees and Dominique displayed was staggering.

At one point, Dominique boasted to Christy Denn how she had bought an evening dress for R100 000. How involved Dominique was in the Tannenbaum scheme is a point of debate. She had business cards with the name of Dean's company, which were used to attract investment. And she quite literally wore the proceeds of the scheme in the form of glimmering watches, shimmering dresses and diamond rings.

* * *

To many, Rees seems the most obvious candidate for mastermind of the con. And given his flash and glitz, and the extent to which he tried to take control of Frankel in its final days, it's an alluring argument.

The problem is, Rees got into the game late. He only became involved in the Frankel scheme long after the brochures, hot to the touch with a thick brew of lies, were already circulating among investors. Long after the ludicrously inflated profits were being peddled to wide-eyed patsies as if they were fact.

Rees may have been responsible for turbocharging the scheme, but his first encounter with it was only in late 2006. By that stage, Barry had floated, then shelved, the furniture investment idea. By that stage, the lie was already percolating.

Yet, in another way, Rees was crucial to the scheme's success. Tannenbaum, despite what some people say, wasn't entirely without cunning. He clearly saw that Rees was a man who he could work with. Here was a man perfectly tailored to be the public face of the scheme and, if necessary, to take the fall for it too.

8

'Agents' of destruction

'Mervyn said to me, "Invest in this, and it will change your life." Well, it certainly did that all right.' — **Art dealer Clive Sergay**

Dean Rees and Darryl Leigh may have been Barry's main veins into the public's pocket, but quite soon Tannenbaum had assembled a band of agents who became an equally critical artery carrying oxygen to his scheme.

The criminal investigators say that, altogether, Tannenbaum had eight agents, forming a spider's web feeding cash into the centre.

Besides Rees's 347 investors and Leigh's 229, Ben Jowitt had forty-two investors under him, Craig Delport and his associates had thirty-seven, and about thirteen investors put their cash into the scheme through Mark Gorrie.

Police also claimed the agents included Cobalt Capital – an investment company owned by John Storey (an uncharacteristically self-assured accountant who headed investment company m Cubed until it closed its doors after a nasty tiff with the South African Reserve Bank) and his business partner, Bruce Dunnington.

'We were never agents,' says Storey today. 'To our chagrin, the only thing we did was to introduce some friends to Dean.'

Perhaps the most dramatic tale of any of these agents, the most poignant example of someone whom Darryl Leigh managed to convince to plunge naively and unguardedly into Barry Tannenbaum's sea of sharks, is that of Mervyn Serebro, the former CEO of one of South Africa's most iconic supermarket chains, OK Bazaars.

In the beginning, Barry simply had Leigh as his agent, and the lawyer was a useful functionary. And Rees, like Leigh, was also a means to an end. But Serebro gave Tannenbaum something different. He was a 'name', a man who'd been on the front pages of the business newspapers that Harold had brought home when Barry was growing up in Krugersdorp. Serebro was also a big fish in the Jewish community, a proper *mensch*.

Serebro satisfied Barry's primal need for belonging and acceptance among a certain monied class, which he may have imagined his grandfather had had. So, of all the people dubbed agents, Barry grew closest to Serebro.

Serebro – roughly five foot eight, rotund and bustling with a grandfatherly demeanour – is a cuddly teddy bear of a man. He is also self-made, with the sort of dustbins-to-cufflinks story that was particularly unusual in the class-strait-jacketed South Africa of the 1960s.

Mervyn grew up in Germiston, a low-income industrial town south-east of Johannesburg. His father was an invalid and his mother worked at clothing store Edgars. Their toilet was outside their tumbling-down house, the sort of inconvenience that only black people routinely had to deal with at the time.[1]

When Mervyn finished school in 1963, he was a raw seventeen-year-old with no cash for university and no one else to support his parents. He managed to score a job at what was then Africa's only supermarket conglomerate, the OK Bazaars, working at one of its inner-city Johannesburg branches.

'It was the most gruelling year of my life,' he says. 'We were a group of interns, and they only retained ten of us at the end. I was the only one recruited at the end into the supermarket division.'

That was only the start of the grind. In order to get to work, to earn his R75 monthly salary, Mervyn would wake at 4.30 a.m., take the South African Railways train to Johannesburg, about twenty-five kilometres from Germiston, then climb aboard a bus. When the sun went down, he would do the reverse journey.

Over thirty-two years, Mervyn incrementally climbed the OK Bazaars ladder, in an era where such loyalty wasn't seen as a weakness, or an indicator of feeble ambition. First, he was appointed store manager. Then, after many years, he became managing director of the entire chain.

OK Bazaars had been one of the grandest businesses in the country. But by the time Mervyn took the reins, it was in such poor shape that his most memorable role was to administer its death rites – flogging the entire debt-crippled chain to Christo Wiese's Shoprite for all of R1.[2]

Serebro became a divisional director at Shoprite from 1997 to 2001, before quietly leaving the retail sector. But one of the things he'd done at OK Bazaars was manage one of the country's most accomplished architectural teams, which built Hypermarkets and shopping centres, such as the Menlyn Park and Fourways centres.

This meant Mervyn knew a thing or two about property, so he soon became the CEO of Vusani Property Investments and chairman of South Point Properties.

'I've been a salaried employee all my life. That's all I knew,' says Serebro, adding, 'All I have, really, is my reputation.'

Although Mervyn had hauled himself out of Germiston and had become something of a minor corporate celebrity, his life had not been a breeze. He lost two children, including his son, Darren, to leukaemia – an event that precipitated Serebro's role in creating the South African Bone Marrow Registry.

Fêted as a philanthropist, he still chairs the Reach for a Dream Foundation, an organisation that tries to realise the dreams of children facing life-threatening diseases. Ironically, he was lured into Tannenbaum's own version of a dream-fulfilment enterprise.

But it was Mervyn's efforts to help his friends and family achieve their monetary dreams that led to his reputation being savaged. People like his cousin, David Serebro.

'Mervyn and I were closer than brothers. He was my mentor my entire life,' says David Serebro, who runs a small computer-maintenance business. 'He got me trained up and employed at OK Bazaars. He was instrumental in my entire life: social, career, or just brotherly advice. He was everything to me.'[3]

But this concrete relationship was severed when Mervyn introduced David to Barry Tannenbaum, an introduction that ultimately cost David R500 000. Perhaps not much to someone like Sean Summers – but to David Serebro, it was a considerable chunk of change.

David was one of fourteen people whom Mervyn introduced to Tannenbaum's scheme – a process that led police investigators to characterise Serebro as an agent, alongside Rees and Leigh.

According to Serebro, his intention was simply to spread the good fortune. 'Good things were happening to me because of this,' he says, 'and I wanted to help others close to me. That was all it ever was.' It was a decision that he now says is 'the worst thing to happen to me, ever, in my professional life'.[4]

Mervyn Serebro was seduced into Tannenbaum's scheme back in 2005. He and South Point management chief executive Rob Lowdon had gone to the Development Bank of Southern Africa to ask for funding for an inner-city rejuvenation project. There he met Darryl Leigh, then a consultant to the bank. 'Leigh was very charming at that stage,' he says. 'We met him often, and it was only after about six months that he even mentioned that he had this neighbour, and this neighbour had some amazing investment scheme.'

South Point got the loan – R55 million – from the Development Bank. Serebro, Rob Lowdon and most of South Point's management team got something else entirely: a front-row pass to South Africa's biggest swindle. Mervyn says Leigh kept 'badgering' him for months to invest. A few months after that first meeting, Serebro went to one of Barry's investor breakfasts, which Darryl Leigh had arranged at the Wedge Shopping Centre in Morningside. At the breakfast, Barry was the epitome of the charming confidence trickster. He came up behind Mervyn and put his arm over his shoulder. 'I know all about you and what you've done,' he said, 'and I'm so grateful that you've chosen to invest with me.'

A short while later, Barry called Mervyn directly. 'You're obviously an experienced businessman,' he said, 'so if you have some time, I'd really value your assistance with a small retail pharmaceutical business I have.'

Wowed by Barry's apparent nous, Mervyn readily agreed. He visited Frankel's offices in Bedfordview, where Barry introduced him to Tandy Houseman and showed him the Wake-Up product that Asterix was making.

'They were basically lozenges,' he says, 'and I ate two packets during that meeting and I couldn't sleep that night. Barry had talked to me about helping him market that product in pharmacies, but it never happened.'

Nonetheless, in 2005, Mervyn began investing through Darryl Leigh. His house was paid off, so he registered a mortgage on it and took out R3 million as a home loan – cash he invested with Tannenbaum.

(Shortly before the scheme collapsed, and at the behest of his wife Sue, Mervyn had the extraordinary foresight to pay off that mortgage. In all, Serebro invested R12.2 million with Barry and was repaid R16 million – a profit of R3.8 million. But he then had to pay R2.5 million to the taxman and trustees. 'There are also plenty of legal fees, so in the end, Mervyn will end up a loser,' says his lawyer, Gerald Nochumsohn.)[5]

One day, after Darryl Leigh had been objectionably rude to his wife Sue, Mervyn phoned Tannenbaum. I've had it with Darryl, he said, I'd rather invest directly through you. Soon enough, Barry and Mervyn became firm friends. Their families spent time together in Singapore on holiday, and Barry and Mervyn even started a property business in Australia together.

Clearly, Barry had seen a useful pawn in Mervyn, who was about twenty years older than him and had known of his parents. And – unlike Rees or Leigh – he actually had a reputation of some substance. He could be both Barry's veneer of respectability and a golden thread into boardrooms across the country. Someone to keep the scheme afloat.

Now Serebro beats himself up over his inability to see behind Barry's mask. 'I'm a pretty good judge of character, I think. But obviously I got this one wrong,' he says. 'Tannenbaum wheedled his way into my headspace.'

If trusting Barry was Mervyn's first mistake, his second was to introduce fourteen of his friends and family to the scheme.

Besides David Serebro, these people included Bradley Drue, Clive Sergay, Rodney Horwitz, Stephen Horwitz, Neal Jankelowitz, Neil Novick, Rowan Swartz, Arnold Sharp, Mel Stamelman, Trish Stone, Martin Sweet, Brian Weinberg and Harold Crown.

It turns out, of course, that Mervyn had been blinded by Barry's razzle-dazzle.

'Mervyn said to me, "Invest in this, and it will change your life,"' says art dealer Clive Sergay. He adds, bitterly, 'Well, it certainly did that all right.'[6]

David Serebro says that his cousin Mervyn told him that by investing with Tannenbaum he'd make his family a nice pension. 'Look at the cash I've made, look at what my friends have made,' he supposedly told him.

After fourteen months of what David refers to as 'persuasion ... and convincing me that I wanted to be one of the big boys', he bit.[7]

Mervyn had told him that the minimum investment was R1 million, but David says he could only scrape together R500 000. In November 2007, he transferred the money from his Standard Bank account into Barry's Investec account.

Around March 2008, Barry visited South Africa. One of his stops was Mervyn Serebro's Glenhazel house, where he met David Serebro. Says David: 'Mervyn made me feel in awe of Barry. He told me to treat him with the utmost discretion and humbleness. I was told to treat Barry like a god, and thank him profusely for allowing me to only put in R500 000, rather than the R1 million I was told was a minimum.'

Unlike many others, David wasn't immediately won over by Barry's charm. He says, 'If I met this guy out of those circumstances, I would have thought he was a thug. He comes across smoothly, but you can see he's a street fighter.'

David got his first interest payment, and was then convinced to roll it into the next investment. Bizarrely, it seems that Tannenbaum even urged David to withdraw some of the cash and sent an email to Mervyn in November 2008 to the effect that perhaps it was time for his cousin to cash in some of his takings. But Mervyn told him, 'Leave it, it's growing.'

Was this the first glimmer of a conscience in Tannenbaum? Was the reality sinking in that even people with relatively modest bank balances would end up losing their entire life savings? It's hard to say. Certainly, at that stage, he wasn't advising anyone else to withdraw their cash.

It was about then – late 2008 – that Mervyn Serebro started to get a sense that something was wrong. He was owed R2.1 million at that stage and had asked to be paid. Tannenbaum didn't pay him out. 'At that stage, six months before it folded, Mervyn told me he knew that was going to happen,' says David.

Serebro points out, convincingly, that if he'd had any inkling that the scheme was going to fold, he'd have warned his wife and children to get out. 'I had no clue,' he says. 'Why would I have let my own daughter invest in this if I thought that?'

There were other signs that things weren't as they seemed.

David says: 'When I invested, I was told there were only eight people involved, only eight investors in Barry's whole scheme. Then by chance, I found out that my optometrist, Raymond Schoeman, had been in it for years, through Dean Rees. I was shocked.'

By the time David decided to withdraw his R500 000, it was too late. He and his wife, Colleen, became increasingly desperate, casting around for help from any of the legion of vulture lawyers and investigators who smelt the carrion.

David and Colleen had only recently paid off the mortgage on their house in Victory Park, but thanks to Barry, David took out a new bond on the house.

'I only put in R500 000,' he says, 'but for me, that was a lot of money. My life continued. I was a mushroom, kept in the dark and fed shit.'

Although he believes his cousin should have been more open about what was happening, David Serebro doesn't blame him. He says, 'I don't think he can take responsibility, because I don't think he knew there'd be a real problem. He's not a dishonest guy.'

But they don't speak any more. The fraternal bond that the two shared was shattered by the Tannenbaum affair, and mutual suspicion. Somewhere, Mervyn heard that David had spoken to the authorities about his leg of the scheme, and so Mervyn decided to ice him out completely. Ironic, considering that Mervyn is the reason that David believes his family lost their money.

'He doesn't speak to me,' he says. 'He wants nothing to do with me. I'm sad about it, but what can you do? You have to live with it.'

* * *

Clive Sergay is less willing to forgive Mervyn Serebro. That is, at least until Mervyn bothers to apologise to him for what happened.

'For me,' says Sergay, 'this is not about Barry – he's an out-and-out thief. I got involved because of Mervyn, I blame Mervyn. To those he was close to, Mervyn had a reputation.'

Sergay was so furious about what had happened that he even dragged the former OK Bazaars boss to court, provoking a fire-breathing response from Mervyn and his lawyer, Nochumsohn, for daring to do so.

'Sergay's lawsuit is misdirected, evil and basically bad in law,' says Nochumsohn. 'And the thing is, he knows it.'

You could argue that Sergay's ire was misdirected, that he was trying to punish Serebro by proxy, simply because he couldn't get his hands on Barry. But this wouldn't be entirely accurate. Of course Sergay was angry that he'd been swindled, as were all the investors. But what really fired Sergay, what sparked the blaze in his temple, was what he saw as Serebro's lack of contrition.

Sergay says: 'After this happened, Mervyn was still going on holiday to Mauritius, still driving his big fancy Mercedes, living like nothing had happened. Not once did he call to say, "Clive, how are you doing? Do you have money to buy groceries?" Not once.'

Mervyn says this is nonsense. 'It's not that I didn't care, but the fact is my own daughter lost everything. It was traumatic for everyone.' (He points out too that his car is leased, replaced every five years.)

Clive first met Mervyn Serebro at a wedding in 1992, when Colleen Sergay's brother, Harold Crown, got married. (Crown was also sucked into the scheme, putting in R200 000.)

'Those days, he was a big shot at OK Bazaars,' says Clive. 'He was a big, cuddly person, very affectionate and kind. Him and Colleen became very close, almost a father substitute for her over the years.'

Mervyn and the Sergays began to spend more time together – the odd Friday night dinner, extensive discussions about koi fish ...

Clive claims: 'Then one Sunday night in 2006, out of the blue, Mervyn said, "You know, I love you guys so much. You've seen my lifestyle ... so I want to give you an opportunity to invest with the person I invest with."'

The Sergays were obviously tempted, but displayed the sort of caution that many others with far more investment experience simply didn't. 'Set up a meeting with this Tannenbaum guy,' Clive replied. 'We wouldn't just hand over our life savings to people we don't know.'

Serebro arranged the meeting. Like so many other intimate meetings Barry held in hotel lobbies and Michelin-rated restaurants in 2007 and 2008, this one took place in a suite at the Michelangelo Hotel, an ostentatious establishment in the engorged heart of Sandton's overly bejewelled business district. Suites at the Michelangelo go for around R6 000 a night (around $750) – irrespective of whether you use it for an hour to dazzle investors or stay the night.

Before they walked through the door, Clive said to Colleen that it was her job to assess Tannenbaum's character, that her judgement would determine whether they went ahead or not.

Tannenbaum arrived to meet the Sergays – the shining knight with a spectacular idea and pots of cash he was just gagging to hand out.

'Barry painted a great picture for us,' Clive says. 'He explained how it was for AIDS drugs, and they had these huge orders from Aspen coming in, and how they needed finance for it.'

Then came the crucial question, which Tannenbaum must have faced so many times. 'Why give me the opportunity to invest in this, if it's such a great opportunity?' Clive asked. 'Why not borrow from the banks, then you can make the profit?'

Sergay recalls: 'Barry said to me, "You know how it goes with the banks, so many problems. And the business is so profitable, that I can afford to give away a few percentage points to people I trust, and want to help. I like to help members of the Jewish community."'

Where Barry was particularly astute – and what distinguishes the more accomplished con man from the common pickpocket – was how he summed up his mark. If somebody appeared conservative, he'd offer them a relatively low amount of interest, say 15 per cent over a few weeks. If he thought somebody was a cowboy, he'd radically hike up the returns they were likely to get to around 30 per cent for that period.

The Sergays, who appeared to be cut from a more conservative cloth than some others, were offered 15 per cent. Still, 15 per cent over two months works out to 90 per cent a year, which is fair enough. But it's not the 200 per cent offered to some.

Impressed, but still sitting on the fence, the Sergays left the meeting. As they were leaving, Sergay recalls that Mervyn said, 'Look, you see what a great chance this is, you should take more money on your bond and put it into this, and you should take any offshore money you have and do the same, because Barry is doing a similar thing overseas.'

Ten days later, Clive Sergay handed over R1 million, the cash sucked out of his and Colleen's savings and stocks they'd bought for a rainy day. Unfortunately for them, in their efforts to shield themselves from the storm, they'd run slap bang into the hurricane rolling in from the other side.

Serebro was adamant that the couple shouldn't breathe a word to anyone about the investment. He said that there was a 'very select consortium' of only five or six people invested, so it was imperative that word didn't leak out. This tickled Sergay's antenna, but the excuse was semi-plausible at least. Sergay ignored his suspicions.

Mervyn and the Sergays then became closer, spending the odd lunch or dinner together, discussing how their fortunes were being made while they slept. Sergay pumped in another R2.25 million, and his returns, on paper at least, began to swell. Mervyn told them that he was so convinced of the merits of the scheme that he'd personally borrowed an extra R3 million against his house to invest.

Clive says: 'In 2008 he told me he was personally worth R18 million. I said to him, "Mervyn, why do you have a bond on your house? You should repay it."'

Serebro did pay off his house. He also took his family on fancy holidays and cruises; he refurbished his kitchen; he continued to lease flashy cars. Assuming he was now worth a pretty penny, Mervyn also donated R1 million to a number of charities.

Sergay and Barry began speaking often by email. At one stage, Barry even suggested he was keen to buy a painting from the art dealer. 'I will be back in South Africa towards the end of May and will certainly make the time to come and see you,' he wrote in an email in March 2009. 'I am still very keen on a Chagall. I am not sure if you are still in the industry?' Considering Marc Chagall originals can go for north of $4 million, this was some carrot for Clive to stay invested.

The first time Sergay sensed a disturbance in the irrepressible force was in late 2008. When he got the email laying out his investment return, he noticed that Tannenbaum had 'miscalculated' the return that Clive was meant to get on one particular investment. 'Oh, he's just made a mistake,' thought Clive, especially as Serebro had told him that 'Barry's accounting was atrocious'. So Clive emailed

Barry. Then he emailed again. But the seemingly inconsequential error wasn't remedied. Clive says:

> I was becoming uneasy. So in December 2008, I said to Mervyn that I wanted to draw R1 million. He told me, 'Clive, don't draw it out now, everyone is looking to withdraw some cash for the holidays and festive season, and it's putting Barry under pressure.' He told me that he'd even tried to draw some, and Barry joked that he should go to the back of the queue. Well, it turns out that he'd been taking out money since October 2008.

Sergay took Serebro's advice and waited. But Barry's cash flow only became tighter. There was talk of a restructuring of the investments, and Serebro's investors became nervous. Days before the scheme upended, Mervyn stepped off a two-hour flight from Johannesburg to Cape Town and found that he had fifty missed calls from panicked people querying what had happened to their Tannenbaum money.

It got worse: all the investors got a letter informing them that Dean Rees would be taking charge, and that they should attend a meeting at Routledge Modise. The rest is history. Serebro stood up and told the meeting that he couldn't believe it, that members of his family had pumped everything they had into the scheme.

Mervyn told the Sergays he'd been as unwitting an investor as anyone, that he'd lost everything too.

Clive says: 'He portrayed himself as a huge victim, and a champion of the investors. But I became suspicious when I asked him if he'd lodged a claim [with the trustees of Tannenbaum's estate for what he'd lost], and he said no. If you'd lost out, that's the first thing you do.'

Then Mervyn sent an SMS to people who kept contacting him, telling them to leave him alone. Mervyn's SMS said simply that he was going through an emotional hell and needed space for him and his family to deal with their own devastation.

Clive wrote to Barry Tannenbaum, asking him if he had in fact lost all his cash. On 31 May 2009, Barry wrote to Clive: 'All is fine, and the money is not lost at all. This is only a temporary setback [while] a new structure is being set up.'

Of course, it proved to be more than a temporary setback. A few weeks later, Barry wrote back to Clive: 'Hi Clive, I have been set up terribly here. All I can say is that I will see us all through this.'

He didn't, of course.

In all, Sergay pumped R3.25 million into Tannenbaum's scheme – money he never saw again. He was morose but philosophical about this – after all, it hadn't crippled them, unlike others who'd invested.

But Clive's wife, Colleen, was livid. She was furious at Mervyn and how his handling of the fallout seemed like a betrayal of their friendship.

In 2011, a year and a half after Tannenbaum's scheme was exposed as a fraud, Colleen Sergay died. While Clive doesn't attribute this entirely to the Tannenbaum investment, he doesn't rule it out entirely either. 'I'm over the money,' he says, 'I don't care about the money. The whole thing aggravated my wife, and nothing will bring her back. But show a little empathy. Stop pretending that nothing happened, that you did nothing.'

The episode had irreparably poisoned his and Mervyn's friendship.

* * *

One of the central disputes between Mervyn and his investors is the claim that Mervyn was one of Tannenbaum's 'paid agents', who scored a commission for each new investor he introduced.

Sergay says: 'What I didn't know when I invested, what Mervyn never told me, was that he was being paid commission for every investment I made. That he was getting commission for every investor he introduced.'

However, Serebro furiously denies that he was ever an agent and is unequivocal that he never received a cent in commission. 'I can tell you that just isn't true,' he says today.

While he admits introducing Sergay, Sharp and others, Serebro argues that he did it to share the dosh – not for any grubby reward. 'Never!' says Mervyn, his forehead pulsating with indignation. 'Earning money off my family, my friends? Never. I'd never do that.'

Yet Sergay can hardly be blamed for thinking otherwise. A document titled 'Mervyn Serebro: Schedule of investments 2007–2009', allegedly produced by Tannenbaum, sets out exactly what Mervyn was paid. This schedule records that by July 2009, Mervyn Serebro was owed R33.8 million by Tannenbaum – including, crucially, R3.2 million in 'comm' (commission).[8]

For example, on 8 August 2007 Clive Sergay transfers R2 million to Tannenbaum. That same day, Barry records a R628 000 payment to Mervyn, which is labelled 'comm S&J'. This document is open to interpretation, but you could easily read this as 'commission' for introducing 'S' – say, Sergay – and 'J', which could refer to one of the other investors that Mervyn brought in.

So how does Serebro explain this document then?

'It's a fabrication. It's Barry's document, and it's fraudulent,' he says.[9]

Mervyn points to the fact that his own daughter had invested in the scheme as evidence that he didn't know Barry was running a con, and that he wasn't introducing investors to earn a fee.

'My daughter and my son-in-law sold their house to invest,' he says. 'They lost it all, and it'll take them years to recover. Now, you know family means absolutely everything to me. This has hurt me deeply.'

In yet another twist in the invisible helix that bound Tannenbaum's investors together, Mervyn's daughter was married to Brad Drue, the brother of lawyer Warren Drue from Routledge Modise. As the bubble popped in 2009, Warren's sister-in-law was giving birth to Mervyn's grandchild.

'It's absurd to think that I'd make any money off my own daughter,' says Serebro now. He says that both SARS and the trustees of Tannenbaum's estate now accept that he wasn't an agent, as he didn't collect a cent in commission.

Nevertheless, it isn't just Sergay who believes that Serebro was an agent. In his affidavit, Hawks investigator Colonel Piet Senekal lists Serebro as one of eight people who 'acted as an agent for the Frankel scheme'.[10]

The trustees of Tannnebaum's estate came gunning for Serebro after the scheme popped, demanding he repay the R3.8 million profit he had made over the course of the scheme. In the end, they reached a settlement, which saw Serebro pay about two-thirds of that – R2.5 million – 'in full and final settlement'.

Not all the investors would be so lucky as to negotiate a cut-price settlement offer.

* * *

The anger directed at Serebro is understandable. Many of the investors turned on the people who had introduced them, even if those people had been just as easily duped.

Cobalt Capital, which was co-owned by John Storey and Bruce Dunnington, was also dragged to court by people swindled by Tannenbaum. Storey and Dunnington were late to the game. They'd only found out about the Tannenbaum option in November 2008 through one of Rees's friends, Chris Harris.

Storey, former CEO of the JSE-listed m Cubed, did some limited due diligence, looking at Frankel's financials and deciding it was okay. They then introduced others, with Rees promising to pay them between 2 and 3 per cent of the investment return for each new investor they found.

'We got into it through our mates, who were all saying it was a great investment. So we advanced Barry the money, then almost immediately regretted it. It wasn't anything specific, just a feeling you have in your gut,' he says. Though Storey says it's nasty to have been sucked into a scam, 'you touch a dog, you get fleas'.

Storey introduced his friends Brett Landman and George Yannakopoulos. Dunnington introduced his brothers-in-law Rory Mitchell and Paulo Pinheiro. 'None of these investors lost any capital,' says Storey. 'Bruce and I gave them their capital back and took the losses ourselves.'

Dunnington also introduced his neighbour, Hector Paredes-Taragon, at a party at the latter's house in November 2008. During the evening, Dunnington, whom Paredes-Taragon had known for two decades, sidled up to him and, according to Paredes-Taragon, told him of a 'rock solid' and 'lucrative' investment scheme that was 'open by invitation only to Cobalt's select clients and friends'.[11] (It's a version of events hotly disputed by Storey and Dunnington: 'Bruce never told anyone it was rock solid; all he did was mention that we were investing. Paredes said he had been doing something similar, and asked to be introduced to Rees,' says Storey.)

Whichever version you believe, the bottom line is that Paredes-Taragon was intrigued and decided to dip into the R2.2 million access bond over his house. Two weeks before Christmas, he deposited R1 million into Rees's account. Like magic, a few weeks later on 15 January 2009, he was paid back the R1 million, plus another R110 000 'investment return' – 11 per cent in just a few weeks.

A few weeks later, Paredes-Taragon was offered a deal to invest R1 million for one month, paying 9 per cent. Annually, that would have been a 108 per cent return. So he ploughed in another R1 million – which he never saw again.

Paredes-Taragon went to court to hold Cobalt responsible. He failed, partly because he'd contracted with and paid all his money to Dean Rees, as the agent.

When called to the stand to testify, Dunnington said he'd told Paredes-Taragon that 'there is no sure thing in life, there are no sure investments'. He said: 'If I had known [in] hindsight all the stories that [would] come out, I would have not [advised anyone to get involved] but we were not aware of anything going on, and 2008 was the first that we really got involved in it. We probably caught it at the end of the cycle unfortunately.'

High Court judge Fayeeza Kathree-Setiloane had little sympathy for Paredes-Taragon either. She ruled: '[Paredes-Taragon] became involved in an investment that yielded up to 150 per cent interest per year. Such an investment is patently too good to be true. By the same token, such an investment could not simultaneously be risk-free and yield such an extraordinarily high return if it was above board.'[12]

Storey says Paredes-Taragon was just looking for a soft target from which he could recoup his losses. He and Dunnington might have dodged liability, but they still personally lost out on R2.7 million of their own cash – including the money they spent on refunding their friends – when the scheme eventually ground to a halt.

The thing is, it could have been so much worse for them. In court papers, Dean Rees claims that, at one stage, they made a play to become the 'managers' of the South African business, alongside Rees's own business partner, Chris Harris. This would have made them the hated public face of the con.

'[They] wished to set up a management company to administer the South African investments,' says Rees. Storey and Harris even flew to meet Rees in Switzerland to discuss how to do it. However, in the end, it didn't happen.

Rees says: 'Storey wanted to raise money and bring in investors, but Tannenbaum didn't want him to do this, given the anticipated expansion of the international business and his strategy to whittle down the investor base in South Africa.'

That plan would never have got off the ground. Talking about it today, Storey says the plan was to formalise the scheme, but if they'd put in place even the basic controls that Storey and Dunnington wanted, it would have exposed the deceit.

'At the time, we thought it was legit, so we figured that if you want funding, it's easy to do correctly: you formalise this thing, put in place the right structures and controls, it's something we've got lots of experience doing – bringing in professionals, controlling the assets, getting a top auditor, et cetera. But in retrospect, that was never going to work because the controls required would immediately have exposed the fraud.'[13]

Lucky for them, it didn't work out.

It was the straw that would have broken the camel's back – and not the one to clutch at.

* * *

Friends and relatives were being conned all over the place, and close relationships would splinter when the true nature of the scam emerged.

What galled Sergay in particular was that Serebro was being paid extra-juicy interest rates from Barry for what he invested, while those who invested through Serebro were being offered half that. So, while the Sergays were offered 15 per cent interest by Tannenbaum, Serebro was being paid up to 31 per cent .

For example, in May 2007, Mervyn Serebro ploughed R1.48 million into Barry's scheme, and was offered a 28 per cent return on that investment.

'I don't feel like he was open and honest with me,' says Sergay. 'I later found out that even when Mervyn told me not to withdraw cash from Barry, that it would stress Barry to have these greater demands over the festive season, Mervyn had been withdrawing all the time: while he left as much of his cash invested as he could, Serebro also took out R1 million in August 2008, October 2008 and then December.'

Of course, the truth about Barry's scheme was that the interest rates offered fluctuated dramatically for all investors, depending on the day and the 'deal'. The truth, perhaps, was that Barry changed the rate depending on what he needed on the day.

Today, Mervyn says the first time he drew any cash out of the scheme was 2008. 'It was only because my wife insisted we pay off the mortgage that I drew anything,' he says. 'And everyone knew I was doing that.'

Although Mervyn wasn't aware that it was a scam, his harshest critics say he hadn't told them the whole truth. And that is why he is being castigated now.

The Sergays and the Serebros soon descended from dinner-time companions to participants in an increasingly frosty cold war. In October 2009, Sergay's lawyer sent Serebro a letter, demanding he repay the R3.2 million he'd lost 'as a consequence of your fraudulent misrepresentation, and/or failure to place all the true facts before our client'.

The letter stated:

> Had you been honest with [Sergay] and advised him that you were acting as an agent for Tannenbaum, and that you were receiving substantial benefits as a consequence of such agency, and furthermore had you advised our client that he was not part of an 'elite group of investors', [Sergay] would not have invested any monies with Tannenbaum.

Mervyn's lawyer, Gerald Nochumsohn, responded in a letter on 26 October 2009. Appalled at the insinuations, at the mere suggestion that Serebro had erred, he wrote:

> [Serebro] was unaware of the facts that the scheme was a Ponzi scheme … it is disingenuous and defamatory for you to allege that [Serebro] was less than honest … [Serebro] certainly did introduce [Sergay] to the scheme for philanthropic reasons and not for personal gain.

Serebro's admission, just after that, is fascinating:

> All or any commissions received were unsolicited and were not quantified and related or married back to any specific instructions, rollovers or otherwise. In addition, it should be noted that such commissions were nothing more than a paper entry on [Serebro's] records which were handed to him by Tannenbaum. [Serebro] did not receive the financial benefits or rewards in respect thereof. Neither did [he] expect to receive same.

At best, the lawyers argued, Mervyn introduced 'no more than eight to nine investors' (the truth is, fourteen people invested through him).[14] And even then, they said, 'introduction is far too strong a word', and this had certainly not been done with the intention of getting a commission.

Serebro refused to pay Sergay a cent, and refused to apologise for what had happened. So the stand-off proceeded to the 'lawyering' stage – the stage at which the lawyers loosen their belts and everyone else tightens theirs.

The story goes that at one meeting, Nochumsohn revealed that Mervyn had borrowed R1 million to tide him over this difficult period. Sergay's lawyer said that Mervyn should give it to Sergay, who'd lost everything. Serebro refused.

'Okay,' Sergay said, 'make it R250 000, or even R125 000.' Finally, Sergay said, 'Look, donate R20 000 to a charity of my choice and I'll walk away.' Serebro refused, saying, 'No, I'll donate it to a charity of my choice.'

Sergay, having conceded so much, in his mind, said, 'No, it'll be a charity of *my* choosing.' Now, Sergay says, 'I should have trusted my initial instinct that Mervyn was all flash and no cash.'

Today, Mervyn says this isn't what happened. 'If Sergay had said to me, "Let's each donate R20 000 to charity," I would have jumped at it. Even though I wasn't responsible for Clive's decision to invest in the scheme, I would have jumped at it.'

The truth is, Mervyn Serebro was just never keen to admit that he was responsible for Sergay's predicament.

Nochumsohn says: 'All along, I was aware that we could probably have settled with Clive Sergay for perhaps R5 000 and some half-baked apology, but we weren't going to do that. It's about the principle.'[15]

The principle being, according to Serebro, that he hadn't known Barry was running a con. The principle being that he had done nothing wrong, that he was simply trying to help out his friends and family by introducing them to Barry.

It seems ludicrous that in the context of a R3.7 billion swindle, a miserly R5 000 and plain old ego could prove to be too great a gulf between two people whose families had been close. It's even more ludicrous when you consider that the real reason for both of their misfortune was one man, holed up thousands of kilometres away.

But disagreements are founded on such feeble technicalities. Eventually, towards the middle of 2013, Serebro and Sergay reached a settlement that at one stage looked unlikely. It seemed, for a while, as if they were trapped on a roller-coaster that was inching skyward, with reverse mechanically impossible.

Sergay says now: 'I just really wanted this to be behind me. I don't know why it is that Mervyn just simply couldn't just say from the start, "Sorry, I didn't mean this to happen to you". That's all I ever needed, but he was too stubborn. Whether it's his ego, or his reputation that he was trying to protect, I couldn't say. I just really wanted to put this away in a box.'

Legally, he should be able to do that now. From an emotional perspective, though, he's not likely to be settling down with Serebro over a bottle of wine any time soon.

How the smart were swindled:
The case of Sean Summers

With Dean Rees in the saddle, signing up investors in almost every boardroom in the country and preparing to take the scheme into the big league, the closed circle of initial investors bloated. Tongues loosened, and soon people were talking in shuls, coffee shops and boardrooms about this amazing investment scheme run by this Adcock Ingram guy, Tannenbaum.

As soon as a 'name' signed on, that was a double bonus. Not only did Barry get their cash, but he also got to drop their name into any discussion with other prospective investors. Casually dropping it in, he would use it as a confidence trick: 'Do you think someone like that would invest in something shady?' he'd ask rhetorically.

Mervyn Serebro had been a catch and he was certainly useful. But Barry really lucked out with Sean Summers.

Summers was one of the names that Barry and Dean displayed like an antique collector would a Samurai sword, placing it discreetly on the wall (but never too inconspicuously) to impress would-be investors, and only pulling it off its mantle to flash around when the need arose.

Summers was some catch, not only because of the instant crackle of recognition in someone's eyes when you dropped his name, but also because he had a furnace-forged reputation as a crackerjack executive.

Summers was one of the few businessmen to have quit as CEO of a major company with his reputation enhanced. He joined South Africa's second-largest supermarket chain, Pick n Pay, in 1974, when he was only twenty, as a trainee manager. In 1996 he was made joint MD with Gareth Ackerman – the son of the company's totemic founder, Raymond Ackerman. But, famously, in 1999 Raymond picked Summers, rather than his own son, to replace him as CEO.[1]

Summer's extraordinary anointment jump-started the myth about him. The investment community soon warmed to his sharp eye for the margin, and then began fuelling the myth. When Summers took over, Pick n Pay was stuttering, struggling for new ideas and losing customers to the new upstart Shoprite. Its share price was R4.80. A decade later, when Summers resigned in August 2006, Pick n Pay's share price had catapulted sevenfold to around R32.

This performance outstripped Shoprite, Pick n Pay's biggest rival, whose share price rose from around R4.70 to R25 during those years. (Since Summers left, Pick n Pay has fallen far behind its rivals, its share price dribbling to R47, while Shoprite's stock price has grown more than sixfold to R167. This dire performance reflects the fact that Ackerman's company is yards behind when it comes to investing in new stores.)

Summers wrestled respect from competitors. Shoprite CEO Whitey Basson described him as 'probably one of the greatest retailers in the last twenty years ... Sean was the man who pulled [Pick n Pay] straight'.[2]

Summers even wooed the notoriously dogmatic trade unions, which tend to communicate in hacked-out socialist-era slogans focused on the evils of the capitalist class, rather than soberly assessing the labour deficiencies of a retail industry steeped in exploitation of low-paid black tellers. According to a *Sunday Times* profile, Khulekani Ngubane, former coordinator for the South African Commercial, Catering and Allied Workers Union, said about Summers: 'What you see is what you get. He was honest and hard to bargain with, but he never screwed the workers.'[3]

But where Summers particularly scored points in the public eye, where his name was plastered in banner headlines across newspapers every day, was his handling of the first-ever bioterrorism attack on a South African company. The attempt in 2003 to extort cash out of Pick n Pay still remains one of the most bizarre – not to mention amateurish – bids to swindle money out of a major company in South Africa's history.

It happened like this. On 13 May 2003, the extortionist sent a parcel via registered post to Pick n Pay, containing three items: a 120-gram can of Portuguese sardines, a bottle of garlic flakes and a 155-gram can of pilchards in chilli sauce. A letter in the parcel said that all those items had been poisoned and although customers wouldn't be hurt, similar items would be placed in Pick n Pay's stores unless certain instructions were followed.

Four weeks later, the extortionist called the head office and told Pick n Pay that he had poisoned a can of sardines and placed it in the Boksburg store. The can was found, with a sign that read 'poisoned, do not consume, contact Pick n Pay'. Another letter followed with similar threats.

Summers was still hoping to contain the fallout. But on Friday 27 June 2003, a woman called, saying she'd bought a can of sardines from one of Pick n Pay's stores near Johannesburg and the contents had a 'strange taste'.

Then Pick n Pay went public. It put out an advertising blitz, buying up expensive double-page spreads in Sunday newspapers, to inform customers and ask them to return any of the three items for a 'full credit'. Summers appeared on radio shows, giving out his cell number to any journalist who asked.

'While what has happened is clearly beyond our control, we are absolutely committed to complete transparency with all involved,' he said.[4]

Luckily for Pick n Pay, none of the cans were found to be poisoned. The police's forensic science expert, Dr Murray Coombs, found that 'the hole drilled in the [sardine] tin by the extortionist [had] led to food decomposition, which caused her to feel ill'. The extortionist faded away and was never arrested.[5]

But, rather like Bill Clinton's 'Lewinsky effect', this nasty episode – which should have driven people out of Pick n Pay stores, clutching at their throats with fear – actually helped the company.

John Arnesen, the general manager of the Marketing Federation of Southern Africa, said at the time that he applauded 'the fact that Pick n Pay has chosen to place consumer safety above anticipated revenue losses, and other damaging cost implications'.[6]

This rather gushing response was characteristic of the general reaction, despite the fact that seven weeks had passed between the first attempted poisoning and the firm's PR offensive. Still, there were many other CEOs whose first response would have been to sweep everything under the carpet – the see-no-evil, speak-no-evil brand of leadership.

It enhanced Summers's reputation, though, and fired in him an appreciation of the best way to respond in situations demanding crisis communication. This skill was evident in his first response after the Tannenbaum story emerged and he was outed as an investor.

To his credit, and in contrast to Dimension Data's chairman, Jeremy Ord, Summers immediately admitted his role, savvily referencing his deft handling of the poisoning case. 'Yes, I was a participant, but unlike in the matter of the food extortion issue, we appear to know who the perpetrators are,' he said.[7]

Summers had known Barry's father, Harold Tannenbaum, when he was MD of Adcock Ingram. 'He was a successful member of South Africa's commercial [class],' he said. 'He had a good reputation, and we did a lot of business with Adcock Ingram when I was there, especially early on.'[8]

He hadn't known Barry, though, or Dean Rees. But, having recently left Pick n Pay, and looking for a new adventure, Summers was speaking to a lot of people. And a lot of those people had let slip word of a great new investment.

'It's simple,' says Summers three years later. 'I invested based on the track record of people I knew who were also there. I've made many investments in my life, and this was one of the less prudent investments I made.'[9]

After the scheme went belly up, Summers remained philosophical about the investment, preferring to move on rather than dwell on what had happened.

One of South Africa's top industrialists, a close friend of his, had told him to keep it in perspective. He'd told Summers that anyone who hasn't made a bad decision has not made any meaningful decisions.

There was a lot of corridor chat about what Summers made and lost through Tannenbaum. The bottom line is, he made a net loss of R19.2 million.

Summers invested through two channels: personally, and then through his family trust. Although he invested R42 million personally, and ended up with R94 million, that profit was more than erased by the loss incurred by the family trust.

'There was no difference between the two sources: they were the same money,' says Summers. 'Does one want to lose R19.2 million? No one does. But it's in the past. I made a decision. It just happened to be the wrong one. I'm over it.'

Summers went so far as to say that if any of his R19.2 million was ever recovered, he'd 'donate it all to charity'.

Now Summers works for Steinhoff, a JSE-listed company run by Bruno Steinhoff, with furniture operations in Europe and South Africa. But he keeps a much lower profile in London, where he now lives.

9

Going international

'It is abundantly clear that the [Frankel] operation, which has been functioning for many years, is … one that has functioned properly and within the law.'
– **UK legal opinion on Tannenbaum's scheme obtained for the Concordia fund**

Though late to the game, Dean Rees soon became the Lancelot to Barry's King Arthur, the Tonto to his Lone Ranger.

Emails flowed between Dean and Barry that were toe-curlingly intimate. In November 2008, Barry wrote:

> I trust you equally with my life and am very comfortable with how our relationship has progressed over the last two years. I wake thinking of you and go to bed thinking of you. Don't worry – not in a sexual manner!!![1]

Barry wasn't shy to lapse into greeting-card sentimentality, as if he were penning a Valentine's card:

> There will be times when elements unbeknown to both of us will try and come between us and try and create a tension between us. This has happened in the past and will continue to happen in the future. But we will be strong enough to fight off the demons and continue our good, but very gruelling work. We are building up one very large enterprise, and there will be jealousy, even when we least expect it. I am [an] open book to you – know and fear not as our bond together will conquer anything.

(Anything, except perhaps the unmasking of the scheme as an immense con, and mutual finger pointing as to who was really to blame.)

On another occasion, shortly after Rees had visited Australia, Barry gushed: 'Nice to have had you here – although we didn't see each other, it was comforting to know you are nearby. I look forward to having you here on a more permanent basis.'[2]

Back in 2008 before all the nastiness, the feeling was mutual. In October that year, Dean gushed to Barry: 'On an emotional note, it's amazing how in tune we are and how we both know cash flows so well. We are a very special team. I hope that does not sound arrogant, but I am so proud of what all of us have achieved and what we strive to achieve is very special.' He signs off 'your bestest, the DR'.[3]

Later, in another email, Dean wrote: 'Not many people understand the bond we have,' and added, 'with you through thick and thin, whether you want me or not.'[4]

Even if Barry hadn't wanted him at that stage, he had little choice but to embrace the lawyer. From about the middle of 2008, Barry Tannenbaum began to see only an increasingly ravenous monster in front of him, which kept demanding more and more.

Dean Rees, however, saw only opportunity as new investors signed up daily.

Initially, it had been a scheme contained within a tight circle, but there were so many people joining up that it was in real danger of spilling over the sides. In his frenzied bid to drum up more money, Barry ended up playing Dean off against Darryl Leigh to maximise the amount of investors he could sign up.

Inevitably, his efforts to keep each lawyer from hearing about the other's antics didn't always work. One afternoon, Darryl Leigh was at the Kyalami racing circuit, where amateur racing drivers often had the run of the former Grand Prix track. There he saw Sean Summers.

Darryl stormed over and said to Sean: 'My name is Darryl Leigh, I hear you're invested with Barry Tannenbaum – are you investing through Dean Rees?'

Sean told him to push off. 'It's got nothing to do with you,' he said. Leigh raged that he had exclusivity with Barry, so Summers should be investing through him.

Sean replied: 'I am invested, but through who and how has nothing to do with you. I don't know you.' It was an encounter that neither probably remembers with much fondness, but for Darryl, it was a smack in the face.

As far as Leigh was concerned, there had been only a small group of investors, and he was their conduit to Barry. Now it had spun out of control. Specifically, out of *his* control.

To find out that Rees was running the largest consortium of investors, which included one of South Africa's top businessmen, was something of an unwelcome paradigm shift for the lawyer. He called Rossen, asking what the hell was going on, furious about what Barry was doing to him.

On the other side, Rees too began hearing stories about Darryl's investors, at a time when Barry was trying to make him believe that he, Rees, was his exclusive agent.

In November 2008, Dean got a call from a friend who said he had been approached for a three-week pharmaceutical deal for R15 million at a 15 per cent return. He wanted to know if it was on the up-and-up.

Dean was livid, because he had been led to believe that Darryl was being cashed out – not signing up new investors. He wrote to Barry: 'Either Darryl is diluting out of his ARV deal – which is the last one, please confirm – or this is a new deal ... please can you let me know what's going on here ... I hate hearing s**t like this.'[5]

Barry replied: 'Tell your mate not to touch [it] at all, and to rather work with us directly. Darryl is on the way out and he is clutching at a piece of string to try hang on. He even suggested a dinner for me next week in my honour! I mean, the guy thinks I am so gullible!'[6] (There was some truth in this, it seems. By that stage, Darryl was hardly signing up any new investors – in contrast to Dean and Barry himself.)

Then, insidiously, Barry turned the knife on Darryl, his erstwhile partner, saying to Dean: '[Darryl] is in the process of moving a lot of [his] assets into trusts etc. – something I do not want to get involved with ... he is also wanting to take quite a big chunk of change out the country and [I] think he is using this [to] do so. I am not sure, and do not want to ask or know.'

Jumpy though he was, Dean was placated by Barry's assurances. So he set about implementing his big plan to 'internationalise' the scheme. It was an obvious move: considering the sorts of returns it offered, why not expand the scheme outside the country? Few Americans, Europeans and other first-world investors could dream of ever getting these sorts of double-digit, let alone triple-digit, returns. They'd chew off an arm to be part of this, he reasoned.

Rees hired a number of people to help him implement Frankel 2.0, including James Patterson and Gareth MacIntosh. The plan paid immediate dividends. In June 2008 two overseas investors – Andrew Jennings and Nick Hall – who'd heard about Tannenbaum's scheme came to South Africa to look at it. Deeply impressed, they worked with Rees to set up a global API fund, known as Concordia. The fund would be registered in the Cayman Islands, a place with well-established tax benefits. It started small – $1 million to $2 million – but the plan was to make this a far larger part of Frankel's business.[7]

The glossy Concordia prospectus was impressively professional.[8]

The prospectus set out the size of the API market (expected to grow to €135 billion by 2013, apparently) and the way it would work. It stated that Concordia supposedly had 'an agreement with the Frankel Group to supply up to 50% of all their finance for the API contracts they negotiate'.

Nonetheless, it was the same old scheme, as is clear from the wording: 'Transactions typically take eight/nine weeks at the completion of which, the investment plus profit is either rolled into a new investment or repaid to the fund.'

And, investors would be pleased to learn, it was essentially risk-free. 'Importantly for the fund, there is no speculative purchasing of products as all transactions are secured against legally binding contracts between the pharmaceutical companies,' the prospectus said. No, in fact, it was far beyond mere speculation.

Frankel, the prospectus assured investors, 'have never had an abortive transaction due to the high standards required of suppliers and consumers'.

The prospectus listed some real corporate heavyweights as supporting Concordia. Merrill Lynch in Monaco (where Patterson lived) would supposedly be the banker, PricewaterhouseCoopers would be the auditor, while the fund manager would be Continuity Multi-Fund Management in the British Virgin Isles.

Concordia's prospectus claimed the fund was started in October 2008 and that 'the first dividend was announced in January 2009, paying investors 9.84%'.

Patterson was key to the handling of the Concordia trades. In January 2009, Barry wrote to Patterson with details of the orders placed using 'the trade finance made available from Concordia second week of December 2008'. The trades were apparently for $1.3 million worth of drugs from a veterinary laboratory in Bogotá, Colombia – sourced through Frankel's German office in Hamburg.

That German business, called Frankel International GmbH (as if it were a real company), was 74 per cent owned by Tannenbaum, and 26 per cent owned by someone called Volker Schultz, a German businessman, who popped up mysteriously and has since wisely faded into obscurity, probably keen to put as many miles between himself and Frankel as possible.

In 2009 a liquidator was appointed to wind up Frankel International GmbH, which was dissolved in February 2010. It seemed the company did do some business – it had €155 356 worth of stock on hand and €7 666 in the bank when it was liquidated.[9]

But back then it was unclear to what extent the Concordia trades were legitimate. (For all the assurances of how 'risk-free' Concordia was and how there could 'never' be an abortive transaction, the fund ended up deeply in the red when the scheme went bust. A letter sent by Concordia to Barry on 24 July 2009 told him that 'to date, the losses incurred by Concordia under the supply contracts and/or funding agreements amount to $7.78 million plus legal fees'. Concordia demanded payment by the end of the month which, no surprise, it never got.[10])

Either way, now that the scheme was international, the investors weren't the sort of people who sit around a table at the Mugg & Bean and decide to scrape together R1 million between them to invest. Now you were talking amounts running into hundreds of millions of rands. And these were the kind of people who insist on things like due diligence.

At this stage, Barry lost control of what was going on.

For him, 'internationalisation' would only have been a headache. In the dark corners of his mind, as he hunkered over his computer at 3 a.m. mulling over his options, Barry can only have seen that what was once a self-contained potential disaster was now spiralling out of his control.

But what could he do? He could hardly stop them *now*, because he'd have to explain why. No, Barry's pathology throughout it all was to cause a disturbance, then ride it out to see how it unfolded and deal with what was left standing.

In particular, there were two huge international funds that were considering investing in Frankel Chemicals: an American hedge fund known as Och-Ziff Capital Management, and Barwa, a sovereign fund effectively owned by the Qatari government, which has its shares listed on the Doha Securities Market.

These were both huge coups for Tannenbaum. Och-Ziff is an immense firm of some repute, managing investors' funds worth $36.7 billion – making it one of the largest alternative asset managers in the world.[11]

Och-Ziff, which is listed on the New York Stock Exchange, was started in 1994 by hedge-fund billionaire Daniel Och. According to Forbes, Och is the 163rd richest man in the United States, with a personal wealth of $2.9 billion.[12]

Tall, with a mop of red curls, Och was tutored at the hardest school there is for a trader – Goldman Sachs – where he rose to become head of proprietary trading. He was then recruited by the Ziff family (Robert, Dirk and Daniel), who gave him $100 million of their cash to manage. And Och-Ziff was born.

'We're constantly thinking about where we can expand into new opportunities,' Och told *Pensions & Investments* magazine in 2009.[13]

Indeed.

Och lives as befits the cliché of a hedge-fund billionaire, in a $38-million apartment at 15 Central Park West, the same apartment block that (according to Bloomberg) is home to Sting and Goldman Sachs's CEO, Lloyd Blankfein.[14]

Discussions between Och's company and Tannenbaum started in July 2008, and initially it looked like Tannenbaum would get Och's money.

Barry's brother Michael contacted him in September 2008, saying: 'Small world! I have just come out of a meeting with Anthony Fobel of Och-Ziff – says he met you recently and very impressed with you and your business model and reckons they want to get involved with you – well done, Pooch, nice feedback.'[15]

In January 2009, Rees's assistant, Gareth MacIntosh, emailed Rees, Tannenbaum and Patterson detailing documents they needed to provide to make the Och-Ziff deal happen, including audited financials for Frankel and Frankel GmbH.

'The aim is to finalise this ASAP as Och-Ziff indicated on … Friday that they are prepared to look at some customer purchase orders by the end of next week, as long as all the above [is] finalised and documentation is being drawn up,' wrote MacIntosh.[16]

Och-Ziff's lawyers, Linklaters, sent Tannenbaum extensive contracts and it looked like a 'go'. Tannenbaum, who was struggling for cash at this stage, must have had his fingers crossed. But then it all fell apart. A few months before, in October 2008, Lehman Brothers had collapsed, and while initially it looked like the fallout would be contained, soon the damage had rippled through the entire financial market.

Deals buckled all over the world as financial boffins who would have bet against the sun rising the next day radically cut back on the amount of risk they were willing to take. As a result, as Rees puts it, 'Och-Ziff withdrew from their undertaking to fund the business in approximately … February 2009'.[17]

In an email in March 2009, Tannenbaum bemoaned Och-Ziff's withdrawal: 'We did take the business to higher turnovers compared to previous years in anticipation of the Och-Ziff deal being concluded by end October last year.' He wrote:

> If you recall early July when we met with Och-Ziff, we all decided it was a *fait au complete* [*sic*], and that we must start getting the orders and entering new markets in anticipation of Och-Ziff. This obviously was not concluded on the expectant date and, as a result, we committed to and confirmed many such orders that would have fallen under the Och-Ziff funding structure.

Tannenbaum added: 'Possibly, we were all too eager and excited.'

Had Och-Ziff gone ahead, it would have been hugely embarrassing for everyone, particularly as US government officials would then have lost money to Tannenbaum. Och-Ziff, you see, invests about $500 million that belongs to CalPERS, the California Public Employees' Retirement System.

And if the American government had lost cash to Tannenbaum, you can bet he wouldn't have been allowed to sit tight in Australia for years before any extradition attempt was launched.

The Qatari-government-owned fund Barwa, however, wasn't as lucky as Och-Ziff. Barwa is 45 per cent owned by the Qatar Investment Authority – essentially, a government entity – while public shareholders own the rest. 'Building Qatar's Future' is its slogan.

Barwa got involved thanks to Barry's grapevine. Rees's right-hand man, James Patterson, knew two overseas investors in Barry's fund, who were friends with Barwa's head of corporate finance, Adam Wilson. In late 2008, those investors told Wilson they had invested in this great pharmaceutical business and had done rather well, so he should think about doing the same.

Wilson met Patterson in London, and liked what he heard. Over three days in January 2009, Tannenbaum and Patterson flew to Hong Kong to speak to Barwa's top brass, including Adam Wilson and head of mergers Gordian Gaeta.

They hit it off and Barwa signed an agreement in February 2009 to provide a $40-million 'revolving facility' to be used for the drugs. Tannenbaum must have been giddy with joy.

Initially, the plan was simple. Barwa would finance one initial deal, to test the waters, and Barwa would be repaid within a few weeks with the sort of hefty interest that Barry had promised them. And, if it all worked out well, there would be a lot more to come.

That deal would see Barwa pay $30.2 million for drugs that were supposed to be bought from a Chinese supplier, and then sold to Aspen and another large South African pharmaceutical company called Pharma-Q.

The reality would obviously be very different. In Dean Rees's mind, Barry would use cash borrowed by his Australian company (Bartan Investments) from ANZ Bank to finance the shipments. Barwa's cash would then immediately go to repay other frustrated investors and the Qatari group would then be repaid a few weeks later once the customer had paid Frankel.

In theory, all would be well. And in theory, it was all going according to plan.

On 13 March 2009, Barry sent Dean an email, telling him the first shipment was on track:

Hi, Dean, thanks for this information. I have paid out for the goods today ex-Bartan. The goods are en route to the harbour and will be there tomorrow, Friday. They have been confirmed to sail only end of next week. We will be able to provide proof from our shippers and send photographs if need be that the goods are in the warehouse waiting to board the vessel next week.[18]

The next day, Barry sent another email to Rees and Patterson:

Gents, attached please see the relevant documents for the Pharma-Q order as well as proof of payment ex-Bartan Group. The goods are only arriving at the port on Monday and we will receive the confirmation of arrival of goods and photographs same day. Certificate of analysis and insurance document to follow as well. I will send these documents as soon as I receive the same.[19]

On 17 March, Tannenbaum wrote to Rees:

Please forward this attachment to James [Patterson] this being the first order from Pharma-Q for delivery 4th April 2009. The order has been changed to address FEL [Frankel Enterprises]. The second order from Pharma-Q for delivery 20 April 2009 to follow – that being 350 kg. Customer has agreed we can now ship both orders together under the same bill of lading. Many thanks, best regards, Barry.[20]

Purchase orders from Aspen and Pharma-Q were duly provided.

Only thing was, those purchase orders were forged. No products were being shipped anywhere. No drugs had even been *put* on a ship.

Barwa, of course, was oblivious to this. So the Qatari fund made its first payment of $19 million. The money was then duly disbursed: of Barwa's cash, $5.8 million went to Rees's company, Abated Investment; $2.6 million went to a New York account of Nick Pagden, an investor and executive at Citigroup in South Africa; and another $6.16 million went into Rees's trust account in South Africa.

Barwa would later make much of the fact that this money trail in itself was clear evidence of fraud and that Rees was responsible. And that, to some extent, money provided by Barwa should have been used to pay for the specific transaction.

But, in practice, there were so many investors crying to be repaid, that any cash coming in was swiftly diverted to silence those who cried the loudest. Of course, this doesn't prove that Rees knew the drug deals were all cons – he may have believed that all these drugs were being duly placed on ships destined for Port Elizabeth and Durban, but that it was his job to juggle the cash that was coming in to repay earlier investors.

Later, in court, Barwa's lawyers would argue this point strenuously:

Even if we knew who the investors were, Barwa did not intend to have their money sent off to other people, and the suggestion that it is somehow commercially of no consequence – that if the whole thing had gone through, it did not matter where the money had been in the interim, seems the nicest way that one could put it – is a nonsense.[21]

Instead, Barwa wanted the money used as Barry had initially sold it to them:

It is perfectly clear that Barwa had set up a structure whereby their money was ring-fenced precisely so that it was not a simple matter of handing over $30 million and hoping at some stage that that money would come back with a profit.

Barwa had very evidently been trapped in a textbook Ponzi scheme, Peter's money being used to repay Paul.

* * *

An especial irony, one that delights the financially unsavvy in particular, is how sophisticated investors who peddle money for a living were conned. Had any of these collared professionals bought a business, say, they would first have spent many hours performing due diligence. Ravenous lawyers would have been released from their leashes to sniff out holes in any story and slash any purchase price accordingly.

Yet here, where was the due diligence? Where was the detailed cost-benefit analysis? The Tannenbaum scheme punctured the myth of the omniscient CEO with mystical risk-management skills. For the average Joe, who sees his CEO get paid many multiples what he does, it would have been disillusioning to open the newspaper and read how his boss had just been so easily swindled.

The reality, though, is slightly more complicated than that. Decades ago, all deals were done on a handshake, simply because you trusted your counterpart. A Nedbank director, who had worked his way up the chain from inside a branch, once said: 'When I started at the bank years ago, I was told to look at a man's shoes. If they were scuffed, and if he wasn't wearing a belt, I wouldn't lend to him.'

Nowadays, there's an exhaustive list of legal checks, regulatory filings, due diligence and other hoops that must be jumped through. In part, this checklist is there to protect the executives from fist-waving shareholders if it all goes wrong. But in the Frankel case, the CEOs and millionaires were investing their own cash. They liked to feel they could size someone up, especially someone as seemingly guileless as Barry Tannenbaum.

So, in a sense, there had been some due diligence, even if it was of the primitive belt-and-shoes kind. Many investors had known Barry's family, or they knew others who had invested and been repaid, or they simply trusted someone in the chain. Others, like Cobalt Capital's John Storey, had done a bit of stress testing of Frankel's accounts and found nothing obviously askance.

A few, but not many, prospective investors wanted more assurance. So they hired the best global agencies to dig into Frankel and Tannenbaum to find out how legitimate the scheme really was.

But they too were seemingly duped, almost as easily as any housewife. None of the experts were able to unmask Barry's scheme as a fraud – although they immediately argued how it 'wasn't their brief' in the first place.

These companies were the New York Stock Exchange–listed intelligence company Kroll and multinational auditing firm PricewaterhouseCoopers (PwC).

For Kroll, the largest risk consultancy in the world, this was particularly embarrassing. Based in New York, Kroll is brimming with spooks, former CIA, MI5 and Mossad agents, and boasts of its expertise in exposing cross-border financial crime. A *New Yorker* profile says: 'With its international intelligence networks and their sometimes unnerving abilities, Kroll began to be described as a private CIA.'[22]

Yet, in 2007, Kroll was asked to profile Tannenbaum and Rees for a 'New York-based asset management firm that was considering investing'.

According to the UK's *Guardian* newspaper, 'the due diligence investigation found nothing untoward with either Tannenbaum or Rees, and is said to have shown both men in a positive light'.[23]

The *Guardian* adds that 'the revelation is a blow for Kroll as the American firm is still reeling from the discovery that one of its top investigators gave a similar endorsement to Sir Allen Standford, the Texas billionaire accused of orchestrating a $7 billion Ponzi scheme'.

When asked about it for this book, Kroll spokesman Ray Howell was tight-lipped, playing down his company's role in the scheme. Howell says Kroll 'conducted nothing more than credit checks' on Rees and Tannenbaum. 'Accordingly, it would be inaccurate to characterise such work as an "investigation" or "background screening"', says Howell.[24]

Really? Well, what investor would hire Kroll, whose services probably don't come cheap, to do something they could probably do themselves? Surely they wanted to find out more than whether Barry had paid his bills at American Swiss last month?

Either way, Kroll's findings worked out well for Tannenbaum. Their report was then circulated among investors as evidence that all was above board.

In the glossy prospectus for Concordia, the international fund that Rees planned to launch, there is a section marked 'due diligence'. The prospectus records: 'Full due diligence was undertaken by PricewaterhouseCoopers in 2008. In addition, UK legal council [*sic*] has also been obtained, a copy of which is available to potential investors.'

It is true that PwC did better than Kroll – but the auditing firm also fell short of branding it a con. In September 2008, nine months before it all fell apart, PwC's director, Anton Esterhuizen, produced a report on 'the agreed-upon procedures in respect of the proposed funding arrangement with Euro Chemicals'.[25]

PwC was asked to check three main things: first, that raw-material purchases were taking place, as Barry promised, and were above board; second, that cash was being properly moved between Dean Rees's trust account and his company, Abated Investments. Third, it was asked to 'perform personal and probity checks' on Tannenbaum, Rees, Eurochemicals (which was Frankel) and Abated Investments.

PwC analysed twelve pharmaceutical deals, but didn't check whether Frankel was actually paid by the pharmaceutical companies 'as a result of the structure of transactions being different to the structure originally anticipated'. That was already a red flag. But there was an even bigger red flag.

PwC analysed the flow of cash between Rees's and Tannenbaum's Investec Private Bank accounts between July 2007 and September 2008. It warned that the R200 million that flowed between those accounts was 'substantially less than the indicated transaction values' of the raw-material purchases.

When PwC asked why this was so, it was told that only investment returns were repaid, while the capital remained invested.

'We do not express any assurance on the business of Eurochemicals, Abated Investments, Barry Tannenbaum, Dean Rees or any associated entities,' PwC said.

The separate legal opinion was provided by Lawrence Jones, a UK barrister with more than a quarter of a century's experience. Jones used the PwC report as a basis for his favourable finding, claiming it was 'clear and reassuring'.[26]

So, while PwC raised red flags, Jones's interpretation was that 'it is abundantly clear that the operation, which has been functioning for many years, is a commercial one and one that has functioned properly and within the law'.

In the end, Jones said that he saw 'all documentation one would normally expect to exist' and that all the arrangements 'are effective and are enforceable', while the procedures 'comply with the law'.

Of course, if you look in the fine print, you'll see that Jones's legal opinion is couched by a thousand disclaimers: 'This opinion is not to be relied upon by any third party, including eligible investors ... in any way whatsoever, and should not be construed as giving advice in respect of the suitability or effectiveness of the investment possibilities that may be associated with the business.'

This is the way it works in business. This is my professional opinion, but if I'm wrong, don't blame me.

Although PwC hadn't exposed the scheme as a fraud, there were enough warnings for an investor to want to look deeper, at the very least. Instead, investors assumed that if people whose job it is to find holes in a company's accounts couldn't do so, it must be safe.

They fatefully used this limited assurance as reassurance, continuing to plough cash at an ever-increasing rate into Rees and Tannenbaum's accounts.

10

Fault lines

'The purchase orders are forgeries. Aspen does not order any of the chemicals as described.'
  – Aspen's head of legal affairs, Pieter van der Sandt, writing to law firm
          Werksmans, after one investor queried a R160 million order

The stakes were now the highest they had ever been. Barwa had signed on, and expected to be repaid. As much as Barry may have been reluctant to take Barwa's cash, and 'internationalise', he'd had little choice.

Months earlier, back in 2008, Barry began missing payments to investors as the flood of new cash into his scheme had reduced to a trickle. It hadn't helped that many of the existing investors were no longer happy to keep rolling their investments and demanded to be repaid.

In September 2008, Sean Summers came close to losing it with Rees after there were 'glitches' with repayments. Summers wrote to Rees demanding to be repaid immediately. 'I have told Barry once again in no uncertain terms that he has basically stolen another 3 weeks of credit, notwithstanding his and your commitments. No more bland meaningless emails required. Show us the money. I await your urgent [response],' his email said.[1]

Rees replied, saying the cash wasn't reflecting in his account yet – presumably from Barry: 'I am sure Barry stated that to you too. As soon as cash hits my account, it will be sent to you. I understand your frustration but the end is now imminent. I am doing all I can.'[2]

To some extent, this was just Barry's bad luck. The implosion of Lehman Brothers in New York precipitated a throttling of the financial markets. Banks stopped lending and liquidity all but dried up. And the people who had millions – Barry's target market – started worrying that their wealth was about to evaporate, so they began cashing in investments.

As any banker will tell you, nothing sparks a run on a bank faster than the panic that a bank won't be able to give you back your cash. So when Barry began skipping payments, this rattled his investor base. Until then, many had managed to bury their doubts under the mountain of cash they were getting, or were meant to be getting, on paper at least.

But Tannenbaum was clearly panicking too. In 2008 he had already suggested to Rees that they look at getting cash from Investec. Considering the whole *raison d'être* of the scheme was precisely because it wanted to avoid the banks, this was some rich irony. 'We are still short to settle new orders. I thought of approaching Investec here [in Australia] – they have been trying to get hold of me. What do you think,' he asked.[3]

Investec didn't lend to Barry. Which didn't help his cash squeeze.

Cobalt Capital's John Storey says that when Rees began skipping payments, he got that sinking feeling deep in his stomach.[4]

'There are a lot of crooks out there. I've lost money on deals before, but those are school fees – I don't particularly regret that. But when you get people you know, like Rees, who are outright thieves, who are lying to you, cold-blooded in your face, then it's different.'

After yet another excuse, Storey confronted Rees at the restaurant downstairs from the fancy Michelangelo suites in Sandton.

'I accused him of running a Ponzi scheme. He wasn't giving my money back, but I'd figured out what was happening, and I'm sure he must have worked it out too: he's no idiot. But he swore up and down that he'd been taken too, and swore he'd get our money back.'

Mark Gorrie, the jeweller who had witnessed the distasteful splurging of cash on yacht *Tommy* in Saint-Tropez, wrote to Tannenbaum on 20 February, imploring him to pay up:

Hi Barry, hope you are well. I'm not sure if you got my message yesterday. I require an urgent payment and confirmation which was due over 60 days ago. I have an irate investor who is not being particularly civilised regarding this matter.[5]

Barry wrote back, trotting out the usual excuses:

Hi Mark, thanks for your email and indeed keeping well, considering all the stress. I fully appreciate your situation and doing my best to assist. We are having a very difficult time with our customers taking the liberty of extended payment terms. Their excuses are late deliveries due to port [backlogs] and government not settling them on time for tenders. Unfortunately, this does create the [knock-on] effect.[6]

But delays were becoming the norm. Investors were constantly on the phone to Rees's office or emailing Barry.

Reconstructing events in the final few weeks before the bubble popped reveals that Rees's team was beginning to have acute doubts about Barry's perpetual delays. For Patterson and Rees, who had made a fortune on the back of the scheme, it would have been deeply troubling.

On 2 March 2009, Tannenbaum had a discussion over the phone with them. Patterson wasn't happy and asked Barry to put it all down in an email, which he did next day. Barry wrote:

> I can assure you that collection of monies in South Africa as well as South America is getting under control, and going forward, will prove to be a smoother operation. I have placed a very good chartered accountant now in SA to administer and look after all the debtors on a very regular basis.

It's uncertain exactly who he was referring to, but it seems likely that this person is Arlene Tannenbaum – though her relationship to Barry remains unclear.

Barry continued: 'Aspen holds the largest value in my book, and that is based purely on the ARVs and other such tender items that they rely on funding from WHO and government departments. This is also being sorted out, and as a result, expect large payments for and during March.' Barry added that, with the Och-Ziff money not coming through, 'we have all learnt some valuable lessons here and I suppose nothing comes easy'.

'It is time now to have the fun,' he said.

* * *

By this stage, investors certainly weren't the ones having any fun, as the excuses piled up when anyone asked to be repaid even part of their 'winnings'.

David Croxon, a Nelspruit businessman who had poured as much as he could – more than R1 million – into the fund, had been steadily rolling over his investment. Then, in February, he asked to withdraw what he thought was a relatively minor amount – R10 000. At the same time, his son, Nigel Croxon, a Nelspruit-based Mercedes-Benz dealer, asked for a R660 000 withdrawal.

They had both invested through Darryl Leigh, and began pestering him for repayment. 'We were informed that [Tannenbaum] had accidentally taken the cheque relating to our payments to Belgium but would immediately courier [it] to us,' said David Croxon.[7]

They are still waiting.

Nick Pagden, an executive at the South African operations of America's third-biggest bank, Citigroup, was equally furious. Pagden berated Rees and his assistant, Patrick Ferreira: 'We have been in discussions for ages regarding an interim payout of R1 million – out of the nearly R10 million owed to me – by the week's end. Don't you think I'm owed the courtesy of a response on this?'[8]

Dean did his best to assure Pagden that the cash was on its way, but the Citigroup executive was unsettled. 'I will be a lot happier when this white-knuckle ride is over,' he wrote.[9]

As the grumbling continued, investors who had been sworn to secrecy began finding out about others who had also given their cash to Tannenbaum and who also hadn't been repaid. The myth of the elite inner circle was being punctured.

Richard Goudvis, the lawyer who represented a number of Cape Town investors, wrote to Rees on 29 March 2009:

> Dean, I know you might feel uncomfortable with the number of investors now speaking to each other, but as one said to me today, we never would have found each other had payment commitments been met ... This weekend seems to just be going on and on and it [is] becoming terribly apparent that all investors, yours and ours, are very nervous about being paid out and all that I have spoken to are saying that Barry needs to give us management accounts, debtors and creditors and cash flow with an intended payout programme to investors.[10]

Goudvis said that even though Rees had made certain promises, 'so many of these to your own investors have been breached', so he wanted proof that the business wasn't insolvent. 'For Barry to say this takes time just does not wash,' he said.

Goudvis then demanded that Tannenbaum give permission for people to go to the Frankel office in Bedfordview to verify each payment owing. He said: 'I did hear from one investor there is no business there anymore, a shelf, and no monies either???'

Rees forwarded that email to Barry, trying to alert him to the desperation building up in South Africa. As had become common in his responses, Barry hardly raised an emotional flicker.

But privately, if Tannenbaum didn't know it before, he must have begun to realise how close his scheme was to cracking. And without the Och-Ziff cash, the situation was becoming increasingly desperate.

From Switzerland, but with assistance from Patterson, Rees was scrambling to 'restructure' the scheme (or at least the international leg of it) by 'corporatising' it. But it was proving to be a headache to get his head around Barry's amateurish way of organising the scheme.

On 30 March, Rees sent Barry an email asking for all the lists of investors, which he wanted to consolidate. 'The aim is to make it easier to forecast investor payouts, and relieve the cashflow constraints on Frankel,' he said.[11]

Dean asked Barry for details of Darryl Leigh's investors, the Cape Town investors, the other South Africans, Barwa and the international investors. He wrote:

As a matter of urgency, we need from you the following internal Frankel information – an extensive list including a list of all debtors, a list of all the orders, details of Frankel-specific financing, and management accounts. We also want to set up a clearly-defined communication structure, and I believe that if we have this reporting structure in place and it is kept to – i.e. every Friday morning it is sent out, say by midday – much of the 'stressed phone calls' will be alleviated.

It was the job of Rees's assistant Gareth MacIntosh to gather the sprawl of information and make some sense of it, then draw up cash-flow forecasts.

MacIntosh's forecasts were sent to Barry at the end of March. It must have spooked him, but he covered it well. In an email to MacIntosh on 30 March 2009, Barry wrote: 'Thanks Gareth – a most comprehensive list, I must say. Well done! I will review it carefully, and start responding accordingly as well as adding extra info that I feel is required.'

But simply organising the scheme didn't translate into cash in the bank for investors, who were becoming increasingly frantic and pestering Dean and Barry on a daily basis. Barry, in turn, was desperately waiting for Barwa's cash to clear. His strategy was to promise and delay, then blame the bureaucrats in the banks, the inefficient transmission mechanism, the postal service, and the government.

It was round about this time that the forged emails and fabricated bank letters really began to circulate.

* * *

On 26 March, Barry wrote to Rees: 'Spoke to Deon [Ackerman, a foreign-exchange director at Merchant West]. They have located the one wire and now they are waiting for Reserve Bank to clear and should be available in my account Monday. They are searching for the other two. So we are getting there … Let me know if you hear and get anything from Barwa.'

Rees replied: 'Any way we could move it to today? Monday is a problem.'

Tannenbaum wrote back: 'I'll see what I can do. Will let you know.'

Rees then asked if the cash in the First National Bank (FNB) account could be released to him, so he could start paying investors. He wrote: 'If the cash is there, let's do a letter to FNB to release to me. I will draft it. That way, if you are travelling, it can stream anyway.'

Tannenbaum resisted: 'Not sure if we can, as Reserve Bank have to credit the account it has been destined for. Value is also only Monday. Let me see what I can do. Any news from Barwa?'

Rees replied that Barwa had paid. Barry must have breathed a huge sigh of relief.

To placate investors, Barry then forwarded Rees an email supposedly from Aspen's purchasing manager, Rushda Williams.

'Hi Barry, as per our various discussions, I am pleased to confirm that it is the intention of Aspen Pharmacare to settle your invoice no 7000336 to Frankel Enterprises Limited in Hong Kong the amount of $32 350 000 in full by no later than 8 May 2009,' it read.

Rushda Williams's email was a forgery. Nonetheless, Rees, presumably none the wiser, forwarded Tannenbaum's 'Aspen email' to a few investors. On 27 March, he sent it to Sean Summers, saying:

Hi Sean, here is a confirmation for you. It is obviously confidential, but as you know, the profit on this one alone sorts you out … I control the accounts going forward, which will change things. This confirmation below is proof of what I can do. I need you to back me going forward as I know it will succeed based on the model I have implemented. If we own the business, we can run the cheque book properly.[12]

Rees's email illustrates a number of things. First, it shows the pressure closing in on him from investors. Second, it suggests that Rees believed he could still make a play of the scheme: all it needed, he seemed to believe, was proper management. Well, yes – proper management and a real underlying business.

Dean sent a similar email to another investor, Duncan Simpson-Craib, who had become particularly antsy and was now threatening to go to court to get his money back. Reed tried to calm him: 'All of Barry's funding going forward goes through me. I have worldwide exclusivity. The past is what I am dealing with. It is not the time to push buttons as I am clearing it up as best I can.'[13]

Aspen's (forged) assurance that they would pay by May might have been Barry's way of buying time, but it was still more than a month away. Investors were calling by the dozens, every day. MacIntosh and Patterson, who fielded many of these calls, knew they couldn't hold everyone off for the whole of April.

Patterson saw Barry's email, and wrote back to Dean: 'That will no doubt leave [us] up shit street with additional payments as we have another six weeks without cash …'

'Yep,' Rees replied. Then he added, 'Well, what would you like me to do? …'

But Barry also had little choice. Without the Barwa cash to transmit back to Rees so investors could be repaid, there was nothing he could do. His only option was to string everyone along until Barwa paid.

Again, to make it appear as if it was the bungling bankers holding things up, he forwarded emails to Rees from the banks and gatekeepers who had supposedly trapped his much-needed cash.

Merchant West, a South African forex dealer, was one such company. Tannen-baum forwarded an email dated 31 March from Merchant West's Deon Ackerman saying: 'Forex have resolved the issues apparently and are releasing. I am not sure what the query was, as they will not release the information … Good news is that the $2 million has arrived and that should be available tomorrow for reflection in your account Thursday. We are still waiting on news for the other $4 million.'

But the money didn't arrive.

Three days later, on 3 April, Barry forwarded another email to Rees as an 'FYI' – again supposedly from Ackerman.

It read: 'Hi Barry, the $2 million hasn't cleared through yet – possibly tomor-row. It is a shame as the rand is very strong at the moment and appears to be strengthening against the weaker US currency.'

On 6 April, Merchant West supposedly wrote another email saying: 'The $2 million has not cleared yet. Sure it will be this afternoon.'

It was always the same story – some unfathomable delay, as Barry sorted out new investors to repay the old.

A month later, on 4 May, Barry forwarded an email to Dean, this time supposedly from FNB relationship manager Fred du Plessis. It read:

Hi Mr Tannenbaum, please be aware that we are in the process of converting the funds for you as instructed by Merchant West. The said funds are being queued and the necessary approval has been approved, however we have been requested to review accordingly and hence the delay. This should be sorted within the next 24 hours.

Barry said to Dean that he was 'dealing with the situation and [this] should be resolved imminently. I have experienced this before, and it should not be a biggie. Chat later, best regards, Barry.'

Of course, it later turned out that all the Merchant West emails were forgeries. It was a clever hodgepodge of lies, mixed in with half-truths. While it was true that Barry had actually hired Merchant West, the only service it had provided to him had been to confirm the exchange rates that FNB and Investec had quoted. Merchant West had played no role in transferring funds or getting South African Reserve Bank approval.

Braam Viljoen, MD of Merchant West, says: 'The email correspondence bear-ing Merchant West's company details … has been falsified and did not emanate from our offices … Merchant West has no other dealings with Tannenbaum/ Frankel Chemicals, and we certainly were not involved in any cash flows, transfers or applications to the SA Reserve Bank.'[14]

Viljoen says that when the scale of Tannenbaum's fraud emerged, 'we were as surprised and unaware as everybody else, and immediately contacted the SA Reserve Bank ... and volunteered our limited information and correspondence'.

He needn't have worried – this sort of patchwork forgery was a standard method.

It was the same story with Australian bank ANZ, which had supposedly granted Barry's Australian company, Bartan, a $10.9-million loan.

An email from ANZ Private Bank's director, Kellie Robertson, to Tannenbaum on 9 April said: 'Bartan Group has duly received the amount [but the bank] will only be able to release these funds for onward payment no sooner than Wednesday April 15th.'

Barry was supposedly going to transfer a large chunk of this to Rees's Abated Investments to repay investors, so he forwarded this email as evidence that the cash was coming. Again, the money somehow got stuck. Again, Barry came up with an excuse.

'They wrote the incorrect date!!!!' he wrote to Rees on 30 April, adding that 'it was meant to be 5 May 2009! I am on it ... never seems to end!!!!'

As evidence for this, he attached an email, supposedly from ANZ's Robertson, in which she said that Aspen Pharmacare 'indicate settling you ZAR150 million only on 5th of June 2009. In your application, you stated that these funds would be deposited latest first week May. Please confirm otherwise and request the correct date.'

Rees wrote to MacIntosh, appending Barry's latest excuse: 'I give up.'

Of course, Aspen was never going to pay R150 million to Frankel. This was a fabrication. At this stage, the number of forged emails doing the rounds must have almost been too large for Barry to keep track of, let alone time-consuming to write.

This dragged on for weeks. When the letters from the banks weren't convincing enough, when the excuses just seemed too implausible, Barry upped the ante on the documentation he produced.

As evidence for the fact that the government-owned South African Reserve Bank was the hold-up, he sent Rees a letter allegedly from the central bank to FNB. The letter, supposedly signed by the head of exchange controls, Alick Bruce-Brand, on 15 May 2009, said that the request to release the cash was 'being fast-tracked, and should be released within the next four working days'.

But that letter was also a forgery. South African Reserve Bank's former spokeswoman, Samantha Henkeman, was shocked when shown the letter. 'It is our letterhead and it is the signature of Alick Bruce-Brand,' she said, 'but this was cut and pasted from another document: the reference numbers aren't ours and we don't deal with individual bank branches.'[15]

Not that many people would have known (Rees certainly didn't), but Bruce-Brand had retired at the end of the previous October. This was one of the subtle early clues that the letters were forged, but it was one that few would have picked up on.

While Barry was composing a labyrinth of smoke and mirrors to confuse his agents, not many investors suspected that the entire scheme was without foundation. The cornerstone of their faith was Aspen: a thriving Durban-based multinational company, listed on the JSE, which had soared past Adcock Ingram to become the largest drug company in the country.

Their faith in Tannenbaum may have wavered at times, but they had seen the invoices from Frankel to Aspen, running into hundreds of millions of rands, which they believed underwrote their investments. Newspapers like *Business Day* and the *Star* ran extensive articles about how Aspen had scored immense antiretroviral-drug tenders from government. Surely it couldn't all be fake?

At the height of the cash squeeze, Barry had even produced a letter from Aspen Pharmacare, signed by Bert Marais from the company's finance department on 6 May 2009, underscoring the windfall that investors could expect, thanks to the AIDS drugs. It read: 'Dear Barry. This letter serves to confirm that the amount of R140 058 169.26 will be paid to the nominated account, ANZ Bank Australia on approximately 18th May 2009.'[16]

Some investors, furious at the delays in being repaid, wanted to know why Aspen was stringing Frankel along, and not paying what it clearly owed. Richard Goudvis, the lawyer and property developer who billed himself as 'hands-on, casting slabs, project managing complete jobs and generally learning his trade on-site', was one of them.

Goudvis and his business partner, Craig Delport, represented a number of Cape Town investors. 'We first got involved through Darryl Leigh,' Goudvis says, 'but it was only in November 2008, a few months before it popped, that we told others about it. And it was strictly our family and a few business associates.'

But in May 2009, these investors were asking where their money was. So Goudvis forwarded Marais's letter back to Aspen asking why the company hadn't paid up. This was the first domino that would ultimately tip over Tannenbaum's Frankel scheme.

* * *

When Aspen got the letter, the pharma giant was understandably shocked. Aspen's head of legal affairs, Pieter van der Sandt, immediately booked a flight down to Cape Town to meet Goudvis and Delport at DGS Attorneys' offices.

They met on 14 May, with Goudvis kicking off by saying he was investigating why his clients hadn't been paid. It must have sent a cold shiver down his and Delport's spines when Van der Sandt responded: The reason is that those purchase orders aren't ours. Aspen actually owes Frankel nothing.

Bert Marais also sent Goudvis's firm a written response, a few days later.

'The signature on the letter is false, together with the company letterhead,' he wrote.[17]

Marais pointed out numerous errors in the forged document. For example, his title was wrong (he is senior executive for finance in South Africa), the company name was bungled at least three times and, as he pointed out, 'I do not have authority to sign any documents on behalf of Aspen Pharmacare South Africa'.

But it was the last line of Marais's response that resonated most: 'As of the date of this letter, there are no monies due and payable to Frankel Chemicals by Pharmacare, trading as Aspen Pharmacare.'

Other investors were making their own belated inquiries about the Aspen orders. Law firm Werksmans also investigated, and got the same alarming response from the pharmaceutical company:

> The purchase orders are forgeries. Aspen does not order any of the chemicals as described … from Frankel. Only one of the 'purchase orders' has been purportedly signed by 'S Dana', who does not have the authority to sign purchase orders on behalf of Aspen. In addition, there are subtle differences in the styling of the forged documents and an authentic Aspen purchase order.[18]

In the forged purchase order, Tannenbaum claimed that Frankel traded drugs like niverapine HCL, efavirenz, tamsulosin, zidovudine and lamivudine. The truth was, Frankel sold none of these products to Aspen. Van der Sandt explained: 'Aspen currently purchases coal tar prepared, cellulose acetate petal and betamethasone sodium phosphate directly from Frankel.'

The rest, it seemed, were simply just made up.

That Aspen invoice was entirely bogus – from the letterhead crudely pasted on the top, to the fictional order for antiretrovirals lower down, to the humongous sum involved: R162 million.

Tannenbaum hadn't just stopped at forging purchase orders. To make it convincing, he had concocted a string of fabricated correspondence around the Aspen orders, which he could flash to anyone who asked.

For example, he produced an email supposedly sent from Aspen's Charlene Newton to him on 11 May explaining the delay in the drug company's payment to Frankel. The sheer elaborateness of the explanation should have rung alarm bells. Newton's email read:

> The payment of the invoice is being processed, and due to the fact that Reserve Bank in South Africa approve all foreign transactions of this kind, it does take an extra day or so. The funds then flow through our corresponding bank in New York. Once we have had the approval from Reserve Bank, which should still be today hopefully, we will be able to confirm exact details of the transfer.[19]

There were similar purchase orders floating around from Novartis and Adcock Ingram, the company founded by his own family. They, too, were forgeries.

Sandoz's procurement manager, Shakun Naidoo, confirmed that three Frankel invoices, apparently obliging Sandoz to buy two drugs from Frankel (erythro-mycin phthalate and metformin), were forged. 'You can see that these are faked orders, where the text has been superimposed on a real purchase order,' she said. 'When it comes to erythromycin phthalate, that's not even an approved product that we buy.'[20]

At this point, Tannenbaum must have been so busy forging documents that it's a wonder he had time to sleep. Besides the fake Reserve Bank letter, the Merchant West and FNB letters, and the forged invoices from the drug companies, he even went so far as to forge an airline bill from Etihad Airways confirming the delivery of the AIDS drugs to Aspen Pharmacare Port Elizabeth.

When Adcock's CEO, Dr Jonathan Louw, was shown the invoices indicating that his company had supposedly done mega deals with Frankel, he did a double-take. 'I was quite shocked,' he says. 'The first I'd heard about [this incident] were those invoices, and it was a complete shock.'[21]

To be sucked into the slipstream of the scandal was, Louw says now with characteristic understatement, 'very disappointing'.

He adds: 'It was the biggest fraud in South African corporate history, so we soldiered through it. For the average staff member, I don't think it had too much effect, other than reading some negative news stories that involved the company.'[22]

At the time, few among Adcock Ingram's 2 400 rank-and-file staff members were aware of the irony – that a multibillion-rand scam, which used their com-pany name in an audacious fraud, was being perpetrated by the grandson of the man who had built their company from scratch.

* * *

While the eye-popping truth was beginning to dawn on investors like Goudvis, most still had no clue that it was a scam. They waited patiently, checked their accounts every few hours, emailed Rees incessantly and bit their nails.

By the end of April, Rees had had enough. He decided to take charge. At that stage, Barry was probably more than keen for him to do so, with the walls closing in on him in his study in St Ives in Sydney. So Barry sent an email to investors:

> Due to the large number of investors, Dean and Gareth are being overwhelmed with calls and please excuse them for not getting back to you promptly. It would be a great idea if you could email them and copy me, giving details such as your bank account and contact details and email addresses, and either Dean or Gareth would get back to you within the next few days.[23]

On 27 April, Rees sent a letter to some investors on the letterhead of Suscito Investments, his company, confirming the new arrangement. He wrote: 'As has been communicated directly to you by Barry Tannenbaum over the past week, the investment consortium is going through a time of a positive and a necessary change.'[24]

Rees blustered, in the way that only a skilled lawyer can:

We have reached the situation where our customers view the business as a multinational corporate with virtually unlimited credit resources at its disposal. This, combined with the global economic turndown [sic], makes it inevitable that the payment terms being made to the business will vary.

Rees argued that previously the customers who had bought the pharmaceutical raw materials had paid on a sixty-day basis, but they were now paying after between ninety and 120 days.

'This is largely the reason why we have experienced some late payments over the last few months.' But, to stop people panicking, he wrote: 'We have examined the debtors book and are satisfied with the quality of the debtors ... the business is of good financial standing.'

Rees then talked about the 'restructuring' of the business, saying the 'rapid growth' had caused delays. He said: 'We are currently in the process of setting up a regulated fund with a more structured business model, keeping both the business and the investor's best interest in mind.'

While Rees talked bravely behind closed doors, he was struggling to get anything but the vaguest of promises out of Tannenbaum. As each day went past, the excuses for the delays in payment became more elaborate and increasingly fanciful. The relationship between the two men, almost familial and intimate at one stage, frosted up.

On 17 May, Dean wrote to Barry, clearly angered at the phone calls he'd been getting and what he described as having to 'tidy up the mess'. He stated:

It is not fair that you do not disclose the investors to me outside of the new, consolidated base that I represent, including Gareth, Darryl and International, which James has given himself to. Guys have invested internationally and locally, which was never disclosed your end ... you have been caught out at this. WHY??? ... It is severely embarrassing and ultimately only embarrasses you. If you do not disclose the rest of the [investor] base overnight, I can only assume you have no intent of doing so and then, you are on your own. I am tired of looking like an idiot and getting partial truths from your end.

Rees threatened that he would go to Frankel's Bedfordview offices the following day. He demanded, by the next day, a letter appointing him CEO and details of all Barry's bank accounts, including personal accounts. On this point, he threatened: 'Make sure it is extensive and truthful. I know more than you think.'

He also wanted confirmation of the cash being paid into his account, as well as a date when they could fly to meet Aspen together.

'If I do not get a mail, I will exercise what I need to.'

It provides telling insight into Tannenbaum's character that when confronted with such a hostile email, effectively treating him as one would a delinquent teenager prone to fibbing to get his way, he ignored the insinuation. Instead, Tannenbaum continued as before, sending emails with vague promises.

Four days later, he emailed Rees with a list of the South African debtors (a forged list), which showed that Frankel was owed R1.76 billion by the drug companies. But an edgy Tannenbaum warned in bold type: 'Please keep close on hand and do not send copies out to everyone or give copies to anyone. Even showing them at this stage can be dangerous to us …'

The three-page debtor list, extensively detailed on Excel spreadsheets in numerous columns, must have taken forever to fabricate. The list records that by 21 May, Adcock Ingram owed R71.3 million – R31.9 million of which had been owing for more than ninety days (hence the delay, you see). Merck Generics owed R48.6 million (R21.9 million of which was ninety days late). Pfizer owed $49.8 million, Cipla owed R44 million, Revlon owed R44.6 million, Italy's Uquifa owed €38.6 million, Sandoz owed R32.5 million, and several other Chinese, European and American companies supposedly owed millions.

But the biggest debtor was Aspen's Pharmacare company, which, altogether, was on the hook for R818 million. Supposedly, a whopping R522 million of this had been owing to Frankel for more than three months.

If it were true, that would have been some pretty poor cash management. If it were true, it would be good enough reason for any company to go bust, with debtors just not paying such huge amounts until the absolute last minute.

Yet, in the letter accompanying the debtor list, Tannenbaum pledged: 'I am handling the calls very well to the debtors and feel confident I have a good control in 10 days. Some flows expected next week already, to which I will send you a breakdown tomorrow.'

But the trust had been shattered. Rees clearly didn't believe him. So the next day, 22 May, Rees sent an email to all the investors on his database.

It started: 'Dear Participant. By now, I am sure you are growing tired of the ongoing situation. Please be assured that I and the team, on your behalf, are working hard at resolving the delays in the shortest possible timeframe.'[25]

He rattled off Barry's excuse about cash getting held up in New York, but said cash 'should be available for distribution next week'. Rees also said that to ensure proper 'corporate governance', he had been appointed interim chief operating officer of the scheme. He wrote:

> The first steps I intend to take are to instruct a well-known independent audit firm, who will assess and verify the debtors book, and hence give us an overall picture of the group ... on the face of it, the local debtors book shows an extremely healthy state of affairs, albeit a case where a more active collection strategy is required.

* * *

His scheme was beginning to unravel, but on the other side of the world, Tannenbaum's deception continued.

On Monday 25 May – days after Aspen had revealed to Werksmans and Goudvis that it was all one big scam – Tannenbaum wrote to Rees, claiming that he had 'spoken to my contact at Aspen a few minutes ago, and was advised that the final instruction had been given to the bank to make payment today'. If nothing came through, Tannenbaum said, he'd call Aspen 'first thing Monday morning 8 a.m. to chase for confirmations'.[26]

He promised that a raft of other customers were apparently also going to pay 'imminently'. This included R10 million from Sandoz, R15 million from Merck Generics, R7 million from Le Sel, and R1.5 million from Pharma-Q. That day, Tannenbaum forwarded emails from FNB directly to Patterson, which apparently claimed that 'the transfer was destined to go out on Friday' from Hong Kong.

But word was beginning to leak out that all was not what it seemed with the Aspen purchase orders. Calls flooded into Aspen's Durban headquarters, inquiring why it was late in paying Frankel chemicals. Darryl Leigh, in his customary style, called Aspen and demanded a meeting with CEO Stephen Saad and the chief financial officer. Aspen refused Leigh's request.

That Monday, 25 May, a series of emails flew between the main players – Tannenbaum, Rees, Gareth MacIntosh and James Patterson – illustrating the extent to which Barry was desperately fighting to prevent the situation from spiralling out of control.[27]

When Rees volunteered to call Aspen to get proof of their payment, Barry wrote to the group: 'Trying to get hold of them ... just concerned for Dean to start calling, then they may think I have broken the confidentiality and hence the rumour? Let's see how it goes.'

Rees replied: 'Still can't see what harm me calling does.'

MacIntosh reminded the group that one of the investors, Ian Irvine-Fortescue, was coming for a meeting at 11.30 a.m. Tannenbaum recommended they 'postpone Fortescue for a few days', as he may have been one of the investors who had called Aspen. Rees wrote back: 'Can't avoid him. He is a trigger.' Barry wrote back, a few hours later:

I know. On the phone now to someone close to the ground in Aspen, and we cannot use the Aspen name or Stephen Saad's name anymore. In your meeting, you must not give wind of the debtor's book or how it is made. Stephen [Saad] is apparently furious and looking at legal steps against me as everyone is calling Aspen asking for their money! He apparently said that he will not have this and will not continue business with me should it continue. They are telling very little to investors as a result, but he says I am trashing their reputation and my commitment to them ... we need to be very careful here, and not use their names anymore and say it is a general debtors list. What do you guys think?

Patterson, who appeared to be losing his patience, wrote back:

The only way people will stop phoning Aspen is for the forensic audit to be done to [bring] confidence back into the investor base and the outstanding payments to us to be made, so in turn, we can pay outstandings to investors. Aspen are late with their commitments to Frankel, which is the reason we are in this mess in the first place. On this basis, I have no sympathy on the subject.

Rees concurred: 'The cavalier way in which they choose to pay will result in them having egg on their face if this blows up.'

Barry then again appealed for calm, saying:

They will start paying but we cannot show arrogance ... it will be to our detriment. Darryl [Leigh] apparently also called, screaming and shouting at all of them and leaving very rude messages on Saad's phone! You can imagine their reaction!

Only a few hours later would Patterson find out exactly why they were 'in this mess' – and it wasn't because of Aspen.

The Barwa money had already come and gone, with Rees paying some of the loudest and more litigious investors. But without repaying Barwa, there would be no more where that came from, there would be no white knight riding in with bags of cash.

Tannenbaum, under pressure, had already given Rees the log-in details for his bank accounts, and the contents alarmed the lawyer. 'There seemed to be precious little funding in the accounts,' said Rees.

On Wednesday 27 May, Rees, Patterson and MacIntosh had a conference call with Tannenbaum. Rees described it as a 'heated' exchange, especially after he told Barry that he wanted Deloitte to begin an audit the following Monday. Barry said, 'Let me sleep on it, I'll let you know tomorrow.'

That night, Tannenbaum stayed up until all hours, mulling over what to do about Rees's promised audit and how to break the news to him, how to explain why the Aspen funds hadn't come through – cash desperately needed to pay investors, who were now briefing their lawyers to take this to court.

But in the placid middle-class suburb of St Ives in northern Sydney, the noose was tightening around Barry's neck – and the executioners were the two Cape Town lawyers, Richard Goudvis and Craig Delport. 'We busted him,' says Goudvis today. 'After we had the meeting with Aspen's Van der Sandt, we went to Australia and confronted him.'

As they got off the plane in Sydney, the official email landed from Aspen confirming that its order was forged. Goudvis and Delport met Barry at a coffee shop next to his offices in St Ives. 'Barry, this is a fraud. This is what Aspen says,' said Goudvis, handing him Aspen's letter.

What happened next was illuminating: Barry cried.

I'm so sorry, Barry told the two lawyers as he wept. The doctored invoice was a once-off thing, he said. Cash flow was tight, it was a stupid mistake, he said.

Goudvis and Delport told him he had to come clean: he had to tell Rees and the investors what was going on. Barry agreed, but first he made them promise that when they went upstairs to his office to type the email, neither of them would 'make a scene'. They agreed, and Barry began to write his confession, with Goudvis and Delport standing over his shoulder.

Says Goudvis: 'At that stage, we didn't know the entire thing was a Ponzi scheme. We thought it was just that one invoice from Aspen. We didn't realise how big it really was.'

Barry had no option. Rees's promised audit would soon expose him in any event and the Aspen funds he kept promising were never going to come through.

The excuses had finally run out.

11

Snap!

'In two or three days' time, there'll be a big article in the newspaper, but don't let it worry you too much.'
— Barry Tannenbaum to Estelle Wittenberg

Thursday 28 May

Before dawn on Thursday, Barry sent an email to Dean Rees headed 'Private and personal'. In it, Barry claimed he'd been up all night writing the email, struggling to find the words to say what he needed to.[1]

For anyone who may have been hanging on by their fingernails to the notion that the scheme was somehow still legitimate, it would have been a frightening email. Even for Rees, it must have been chilling. Barry wrote:

Dear Dean, I can no longer put off bringing you into the loop in regard to the South African book debt. Dean, the reality is that the book debt of Frankel Chemicals cannot survive scrutiny on the basis of what has been represented. I have for some time been building up the offshore business, as you know, and the investor funds have flowed to building up Frankel International GmbH. It is for this reason that you cannot allow an audit into Frankel SA's books, that is not where the solution or payment for investors sits.

Tannenbaum explained that the South African investors would be paid from the overseas profits. But he also said: 'The added complication is that if we don't get the offshore funding, the entire business, both in SA and Germany, could come crashing down, and that is in no one's interest, specifically James, you and me.'

He suggested that an independent attorney be appointed to represent him. He then proposed: 'An audit process takes place of all amounts paid to me to fund the various businesses and then we need to negotiate the final figures with each party based on the premise that they sign a settlement agreement and confidentiality for the first payment they receive.'

Tannenbaum clearly had no regard for the trouble he was in. He wrote that he was 'absolutely certain' that the investors would be happy to sign a settlement agreement, giving them a fixed, negotiated sum. For a man who conducted business with so many lawyers, this was remarkably naive.

For the first time, he spoke of the pressure he was feeling to keep the money rolling: 'I cannot carry on like this, and need the certainty of knowing that all investors are tied up ... none of us can afford this to escalate any further.'

Tannenbaum said: 'This is something I have tried to protect you from all this time. But as you said, I must stop protecting you and shielding you from not knowing everything, so now is as good a time as any.'

He wrote: 'I am sure you will be angry with me. I need your help now more than ever, specifically securing the new funds ... and it is probably a good time to come clean and move forward together without any hidden agendas and secrets.'

Rees was shocked by the email. He immediately forwarded it to MacIntosh and Patterson, assigning it high-priority status.

Later that day, Rees, Patterson and MacIntosh held an urgent conference call with Tannenbaum. Rees says that during this call, Barry admitted forging the Aspen invoice.[2]

Patterson has confirmed this version of events: 'We had a conference call with Barry, and he admitted that the invoices were forgeries.'[3]

MacIntosh has backed this up too, saying that, in addition to the forged Aspen invoice, Barry also admitted during the call that 'the debtors book wasn't what he showed us'.[4]

The reality of what was about to happen, the immensity of the problem they faced, had begun to sink in.

Friday 29 May

The next day, Rees sent an email to all the investors he had on his database. He billed it simply as 'The latest update', not revealing much of what he had just learnt from Tannenbaum.[5]

Rees wrote: 'We will be auditing the local company and the international entity to reconcile debtors books and assets, based on irregularities that came to light with the debtors book furnished locally. To this end, we have today appointed Deloitte & Touche to attend. This process begins Monday.'

What he didn't say was that the irregularities weren't just a few typos on the invoice numbers, or that they could very well mean the entire investment scheme was bogus, that everyone had lost everything.

Rees concluded the email by saying: 'We have been informed that there will be some debtor payments over the month-end. This, likewise, will be verified by Deloitte & Touche.'

But behind the scenes, Rees was clearly beginning to realise the enormity of Barry's 'confession'. So he wrote an email to Barry and Volker Schultz:

Hi Barry and Volker, it has come to all our attention that there were, at the least, irregularities on certain deals with Frankel Enterprises. James [Patterson] and I were not parties in that regard, were unaware and same came to our attention and was reported to the financiers today. We are reconciling same via an independent audit firm … we are very concerned.

Dean then asked for all the details of those deals by that Sunday, 31 May:

Based upon both of your representations, as admitted by Barry telephonically, in our investigations there are transactions that you have performed which these funds have been used for independently of the funder's intent. These transactions, I believe, have not been disclosed.

Volker Schultz forwarded Rees's email to Barry, saying 'FYI – what to do?'.

One could argue that Dean's email was just a belated attempt to cover himself, that he was grabbing at the first opportunity to place his denial on the record. But the tone of his email betrays his panic. It turned out that those who'd been telling him for months that it was a scam were right all along.

Sunday 31 May

Rees didn't get the details he had asked from Tannenbaum, so he tried to log into Tannenbaum's bank accounts with passwords Barry had given him. One account had been entirely blocked. The passwords of all the others had been changed. It was a clear omen that Barry wasn't going to roll over that easily.[6]

Monday 1 June

Rees arrived at Frankel's pokey Bedfordview office to begin the long-promised audit, but he was met at the door by a lawyer supposedly representing Tannenbaum, Charles Valkin from Bowman Gilfillan. 'There will be no audit,' said Valkin. 'Your power of attorney has been revoked. Please leave.'[7]

On his way out, Rees bumped into the accountant, Arlene Tannenbaum. She said that they had had great fortune bringing down the debtors book and chasing up clients. 'It's now down to R2.5 million,' she said. Needless to say, there's a fair degree of light between R2.5 million and R1.76 billion.[8]

At the same time, James Patterson – perhaps still hoping something could be salvaged, perhaps just wanting to get it on the record – contacted Aspen's Rushda Williams, who supposedly authorised the payments.

Patterson emailed her and asked: 'Hi Rushda, please confirm whether this invoice … and payment of $32,350,000 to Frankel Enterprises in Hong Kong is due? Please revert ASAP.'

Williams replied a bit later, apologising for missing his call. She said: 'Pieter van der Sandt will revert with further matters regarding the Frankel account.'

Van der Sandt emailed Patterson the next day pointing out that the invoice was 'in all probability a forgery'.[9]

Tuesday 2 June

Rees sent another letter to investors calling for an urgent meeting at Routledge Modise in two days' time, 4 June. He gave scant details, but enough for investors to know there was something seriously wrong. His letter began ominously:

> The writer's status as chief operating officer and general power of attorney were revoked yesterday. The commencement of the audit yesterday by Deloitte & Touche was not allowed ... We had a brief meeting with Arlene Tannenbaum, who is the accountant in the Frankel Bedfordview office. The writer presented her with a book debt analysis furnished on 21 May 2009. She claimed to have never seen same, and further reported that the total book debt outstanding locally was R2 million.[10]

It got worse. Rees reported that the copy of Frankel's accounts in his possession had been sent to the auditors, IAPA, and they had responded that the numbers were 'overstated, but they were not the author of those figures'.

The purchase orders placed with Frankel were forgeries, Dean told the investors, and the debtors did 'not owe the amounts claimed'.

Julius Preddy was an investor and worked as an orthopaedic surgeon at the Life Hospital in Johannesburg's kitsch new-money district, north of Fourways. He described Rees's letter as 'largely unintelligible', although it was clear that the scheme was 'in a state of collapse'.[11]

Thursday 4 June

After the fateful meeting at Routledge Modise on Thursday morning, there was an unseemly scramble from lawyers, liquidators and investigators to sign up desperate and confused clients. Having just found out they had invested in an illegal Ponzi scheme, investors were justifiably wary of Rees's plan to form an investors' committee to probe their options.

As a journalist for the *Financial Mail*, I contacted Tannenbaum on his cellphone in Australia and told him about the meeting at Routledge Modise. He appeared nonchalant about being branded the mastermind of the country's biggest con and was seemingly unaware of the storm that was brewing. He made polite small talk, as if I was an air hostess asking him if he preferred chicken or beef.[12]

He seemed surprised to learn that Rees himself was at the meeting and he remarked offhandedly, 'If I go down, [Rees] is going with me.'

When pressed, Tannenbaum admitted that 'the debtors book was overstated', before adding, 'but I have never said the Aspen invoices are frauds'.

When asked how that overstatement happened, Tannenbaum asked me to put the questions in an email to which he would reply.

After I'd sent him written questions, he replied without showing any urgency: 'I will work on it over the weekend. Have a good day. Kind regards, Barry.'[13]

For the next few days, he continued to dodge my calls and emails – defer, defer, defer. 'Been very busy this side,' he wrote at one stage in the early hours of the morning in Australia. 'Been in meetings all day with very important guys. Will try you later. Looks like I am winning the race!' he said another time.

Shortly before the magazine went to print, he claimed he was 'in meetings', so he emailed a comment that, in legalese, is dubbed a 'bare denial': 'All I can say is that I deny the truth of the aspersions that have been levelled against me, and the fanciful allegations that are being made.'[14]

He added: 'I am not sure who the responsible parties are, but intend finding out.' He said he was gathering information to 'support my evidence', and would be in touch shortly. Laying his hands on this evidence must have been tricky indeed, because, nearly four years later, Barry has yet to provide any of it.

Investors who contacted him that week were equally baffled by his apparently calm demeanour.

About the only signs that he was stressed by his imminent unmasking were the times of his emails: 2 a.m., 3 a.m. in Australia. What could Tannenbaum have been doing on his computer while everyone else slept? What could his wife, Deborah (presumably fast asleep next door), have thought?

It was almost as if Tannenbaum wasn't quite aware how serious his exposure would be, how utterly his life would change. However, it is possible that he was faking this stoicism with the same panache he had shown when fabricating invoices.

One of the few outward indicators that he acknowledged the scale of the looming fallout was that he called Estelle Wittenberg, the woman who had worked for Frankel for twenty-three years, and warned her about the impending media storm.

Says Estelle: 'He phoned me and said, "Estelle, in two or three days' time, there'll be a big article in the newspaper, but don't let it worry you too much." That was the first time I knew something was happening.'[15]

It clearly wasn't worrying him too much. Not nearly as much as it should have been.

Friday 5 June

Sports-car enthusiast Chris Leppan wasted no time in rushing to petition the Johannesburg High Court (now known as the South Gauteng High Court) for Tannenbaum's sequestration. Leppan said that when he arrived at the Routledge Modise meeting the previous day, he had been amazed: 'So many people were present … I had, at all times, believed that the number of investors was limited to a maximum of 100.'[16]

Leppan also didn't buy Rees's plan to form a committee (headed by him, naturally) to probe what investors should do.

'I am suspicious of his motives,' Leppan said in an affidavit. 'I believe that the committee suggested by Rees and accepted by the other investors is merely a ploy to enable [Tannenbaum] to obtain sufficient time to remove whatever assets he has in this country to Australia.'[17]

Judge Thami Makhanya agreed with him and granted the order. Makhanya could not have known that this would open the door to years of squabbling among lawyers, trustees and liquidators for control of what little cash Tannenbaum had left in South Africa.

But the vultures knew. Because of the quirky design of South Africa's liquidation laws, the first person to rush to court will steal poll position. This means they can nominate their chosen liquidator who should, in theory at least, be an independent trustee to look after all creditors.

In practice, however, this liquidator is all too amenable to the first creditor's propositions above everyone else's – having been nominated by him or her. The early bird pretty much steals the liquidation.

In retrospect, the only surprise was that there wasn't a queue of Barry's investors outside Judge Makhanya's chambers that Friday morning. A queue that would have stretched down the grimy court staircases, through the gloomy passages and out into the chill winter sunshine bathing the vendors hawking socks, potatoes and shiny cellphone covers on central Johannesburg's Market Street.

Wednesday 10 June

At midday, news broke of a massive Ponzi scheme that had suckered South Africa's wealthiest and most successful. The *Financial Mail* hit the shelves with a hazy picture of Tannenbaum on the front cover, with the headline posing the question: 'South Africa's Madoff?'[18]

The next day, Johannesburg's biggest newspaper, the *Star*, ran with the Tannenbaum story as its lead. Journalist and veteran investment writer Bruce Cameron called it straight, immediately dubbing it a Ponzi scheme.[19]

Investors (now seeing their exclusive investment scheme splashed all over the front pages and dubbed a scam) flooded Tannenbaum with emails, begging him to answer them, to deny what the media was reporting.

Nigel Croxon, a Nelspruit Mercedes-Benz dealer, for example, sent him an email two days after the story broke:

Hi Barry. I don't know where to start. Can you at least answer your phone, return an email, or just tell us you fucked up so we can carry on with our lives. I have to explain to my father that he will never see any of his hard-earned money, 65 years of it. What really amazes me is when you accidentally deposited R2 million into his account, he called you and notified you of the mistake. Please just drop me an email to let me know what you intend doing. Kind regards.[20]

Although Tannenbaum had strung me along for days without responding to my questions, he now leapt into action and effectively branded the entire mess a monstrous mistake orchestrated by unnamed enemies.

He replied to Croxon's email the next day: 'Hi Nigel, thanks for your email. I am working fast with a large team to bring down the person responsible for this fiasco. This will of course prove my innocence and eventually get us back on track. I will not let anyone down. That is for sure. I will keep you updated. Thanks and regards, Barry.'[21]

Investors rushed to the banks with the cheques they had been given by Barry. But the banks simply returned them, stamped 'account closed'.

The consternation among the investors was almost tangible. People were forced to confront their greed; they mentally beat themselves up for not having withdrawn their cash earlier; and they desperately cast around for any vulture lawyer who promised to recover everything.

Friday 12 June

Assailed by journalists, Barry put out a press release – anorexic in its detail, but bristling with self-righteous platitudes:

As has happened with other companies that have from time to time found themselves in a financial predicament, particularly in the present climate, I have found myself in such a situation … However, I have read with amaze-ment that I have been guilty of a multibillion-rand scam, and that I am compared to Bernie Madoff in the USA. I am not prepared to embark upon an exercise of attempting to refute allegations in respect of which I have been provided with no substantiation whatsoever.[22]

Tannenbaum described the claims against him as 'conjecture' and 'speculation', saying that when the hype died down, 'the extent of the exaggeration [would] become apparent'. He said: 'Time will demonstrate that I have defrauded no one.'

Unfortunately for Barry, time hasn't been that generous to him. If anything, it has only calcified the public's view of him, which was still malleable in June 2009, as a con man – a pre-eminent scamster whose name is now etched into South Africa's corporate folklore.

As Tannenbaum's statement hit the news wires, an unprecedented meeting was taking place in Pretoria, a few hundred metres from the office of the newly inaugurated president, Jacob Zuma.

Barry Tannenbaum, although clearly unintentionally, had managed to do what a thousand political pledges couldn't: provide the gel for five crime-fighting agencies to work together. South Africa's crime-fighting efforts have been traditionally haphazard: disparate agencies clumsily stomping on one another's toes; one arm of the law doing secret plea-bargain deals with crooks to put other crooks in jail, unbeknown to the other arm of the law, which was doing its utmost to put the first set of crooks behind bars.

(Exhibit 1: A few months before, the crack crime-fighting unit, the Scorpions, had struck a plea bargain with the renowned drug dealer Glenn Agliotti, and three thugs who had gunned down Brett Kebble. The deal had been made in order to nail the police commissioner, Jackie Selebi, who had been taking bribes from Kebble. Sure, Selebi was a scoundrel – he had even asked Agliotti for cash to host his election as the head of Interpol. But was this the only way to put away the police boss? To grant a blanket amnesty to some of South Africa's most notorious criminals?)[23]

At that Pretoria meeting of the justice department's top brass, a decision was taken to form a special task team made up of the police's Serious Economic Offences Unit, the South African Revenue Service, the South African Reserve Bank, the National Prosecuting Authority and the Financial Intelligence Centre.

The task team, government said, would conduct a 'high-level investigation into serious allegations, including possible fraud, money laundering, tax evasion and foreign-exchange violations against Barry Tannenbaum and associated entities'. Initially, the task team would 'assess' the claims 'as reported during the week'.[24]

Then, the Reserve Bank hired auditing firm KPMG to assess whether Tannenbaum had carried out 'the business of a bank' – which would have been illegal because only banks registered with the central bank can do this.

Government's regulators had abjectly failed to detect Tannenbaum's scheme at its height, despite billions flowing through the country's bank accounts. They weren't so keen to be embarrassed again.

Saturday 13 June

The news of Barry Tannenbaum's scam had finally made it across the Indian Ocean, traversing the 10 000 kilometres between South Africa and Australia.

Australians woke up to the front-page headline in the *Sydney Morning Herald*: 'Exposed: The Sydney man accused of $1.5 billion scam', along with a picture of Tannenbaum, taken the previous day at his Sydney office. That Friday, Tannenbaum had invited the newspaper into his office and, when asked if he had run a multinational Ponzi scheme, he declared, 'Absolutely not.'[25]

The newspaper, however, also displayed pictures of his St Ives mansion on its front page and reported how his former business partner, Kevin Kramer, remembered him as 'sometimes ostentatious with money'.

Bloomberg's Renee Bonorchis was also by then running a series of stories for a fascinated American audience, who couldn't believe how eerily the case echoed that of Bernie Madoff.

Hendrik du Toit, the CEO of Investec Asset Management, told Bloomberg that both the Madoff and Tannenbaum cases illustrated how investors completely forgot the relationship between risk and return. Du Toit said that the cases showed the 'naivety of investors who were prepared to back, with vast amounts of their savings, an almost entirely unknown entity, in an investment offering ludicrously high returns, without any comprehension of how those returns were to be justified and without any form of operational due diligence'.[26]

Tannenbaum, initially so reluctant to answer questions from journalists, was now putting out statements on a daily basis. This seemed entirely in character: manage the disaster rather than prevent it.

On Saturday, responding to the growing pile of media articles, Barry said: 'Having been publicly vilified, tried and pilloried, there seems to be little reason for me to offer comment because clearly the adage "Do not let the truth get in the way of a good story" applies here.'[27]

Sure, except for the fact that when asked to answer questions, he avoided answering anything specific. And, except for the fact that he'd had plenty of chances to correct the story, but chose not to.

Tannenbaum said the claim that he had spirited away his assets was an 'outrageous and unsubstantiated piece of drivel'. He added: 'I have no intention of leaving Australia, I have no intention of disposing of whatever assets I possess and I, in fact, assure whoever requires such assurance that I will not do so.'

But then, his tactic became clearer. 'Why all the focus on me, and me alone?' he asked. 'In fact, I state categorically that I am not sitting with millions. I have not amassed some fortune that I have spirited away, and in due course, an audit will bear out this statement.'

Barry then referred to the article in the *Sydney Morning Herald*, which, thank goodness, he said, 'published one piece of information that must raise a question mark over the suggestion that I, singlehandedly, if at all, spearheaded a massive scam'.

The passage he was referring to stated: 'Two Johannesburg lawyers, Dean Rees and Darryl Leigh, are said to have made millions of rands by signing up investors.' Said Tannenbaum: 'Maybe some attention will then be given to others who might have made millions.'

Rees fired back with a predictable, if convincing, response: 'If I'd had any hand in orchestrating this, why would I have taken the actions I did, like coming back to South Africa to speak to investors or pursuing further investigations into his criminal activities? Why would I have asked for a forensic audit by Deloitte?'[28]

Leigh hunkered down, refusing to speak to anyone.

But while Tannenbaum was furiously and publicly protesting his innocence, there was a sideshow taking place behind closed doors that immediately exposed him as a liar.

The depressing case of Professor Peter Beale

Paediatric surgeon Professor Peter Beale is an unfêted legend of the highly regarded South African medical profession, which has trumpeted itself to the world on the coat-tails of Dr Christiaan Barnard, who performed the world's first heart transplant in 1967.

Unlike many surgeons, who become tired of the constant brutality, anaemic resources and constipated salary cheques of state medicine, Beale has done public service for the better part of three decades. He is head of paediatric surgery at Johannesburg's main public hospital, Charlotte Maxeke, and has done extensive stints at the country's busiest state hospital, Chris Hani Baragwanath. He is a former chairman of South Africa's Association of Paediatric Surgeons.

In 2007 the Health Professions Council of South Africa awarded him an 'excellence in healthcare award', describing Beale as someone who has 'made a profound impact on the health and well-being of children', someone regarded as 'possibly the world's most experienced paediatric surgeon' in the wider field.[1]

Dr Simon Huddart of Cardiff University's Hospital of Wales describes Beale as 'one of the most gifted technical paediatric surgeons'.[2]

Beale, some would say, has an almost overdeveloped sense of responsibility towards the country he lives in. He, alongside a determined social worker, helped establish a rape crisis unit at the police station in Alexandra, a poor township area squatting next to Sandton. He also started a fund called Surgikids to raise cash to buy surgical equipment to treat disadvantaged children. As a result, the Baragwanath paediatric theatres now have surgical instruments that should help narrow the time taken to operate on babies born with birth defects.

Forget fast-talking finance traders scraping to flog warrants to one another for a small margin to make a buck for themselves to buy a bigger SUV: their contribution to society is less than nothing. Instead, it is people like Peter Beale who actually make a difference to South Africa. He is the sort of man about whom movies should be made and books written.

As part of his service to medicine, Beale has seen eye-watering brutality that would cow lesser souls. When he operated on the horrifying injuries sustained by six-year-old rape survivor Lerato in 2002, Beale challenged the *Star* to print pictures of the injuries to shock the country into finally doing something about child rape. Needless to say, the *Star* declined. The maxim for a newspaper to decide on its top story is that if it bleeds, it leads. Unless it bleeds a little too much, and for a little too long – then readers start spitting out their cornflakes.[3] Instead, the *Star* printed a white box on its front page, signifying where the picture would have been placed, were it not too gruesome.

In a clear indication of the poverty of police leadership at the time, police commissioner Jackie Selebi threatened that Beale's possession of the photographs amounted to 'distributing child pornography', brushing off the rape as the sort of case that police see 'every day'.

It didn't surprise many when it later turned out that Selebi had the sort of malleable moral fibre that would make a Colombian drug lord blush. The police chief was sentenced to fifteen years in jail for corruption in 2010, but he only ended up serving seven months before being paroled because of 'kidney failure'.

(On a side note, Lerato's attacker, Reuben Modiba, was sentenced to life imprisonment in 2004. Prosecutors said they would have asked for the death sentence had it been in force. The thug, Modiba, claimed to have had 'amnesia' and couldn't remember it. Welcome though his life sentence was in a country where someone is raped every twenty-three seconds, it represented just a drop of rain in a desert.[4])

Beale's bad luck was that he had known Darryl Leigh for more than two decades. Every Sunday morning, Beale and a group of friends would gather at a nearby tennis club. Darryl played tennis too.

Eventually, Darryl drifted away from the tennis club, preferring to spend his Sunday mornings driving fast Ducati motorbikes. Says Beale: 'Darryl wasn't likeable, and he was a loudmouth. But even after he left the tennis club, every now and again, I'd get a call from him wanting a prescription for something or other. At the same time, I kept hearing these stories about how he'd become very successful, and was making all this money in some business or other.'[5]

Then, in 2008, Beale addressed a *Top Gear* festival event in Durban, where Jeremy Clarkson, the presenter of the BBC motoring programme, was the star attraction. Beale's charity Surgikids was a beneficiary of a gala dinner held at the festival, and the surgeon told the crowd a compelling story. Somewhere in the middle of the audience, Darryl Leigh stood up, his head swathed in a red bandana – reminiscent of *Easy Rider*, perhaps. 'I've known Peter Beale for many years,' said Darryl, 'and he's a crap tennis player but an amazing surgeon. If there's any charity we should be supporting, it's Surgikids,' he said. Leigh made the first donation, and others followed, stirred into action by his words.

That day at the *Top Gear* festival, Surgikids raised more than R300 000 – the single biggest injection it had ever received from an event. 'I was thrilled, and felt I had to thank him, so me and my wife invited him to dinner,' says Beale.

Leigh, as you'd expect, pitched up in his Lamborghini, dropping insinuations of his wealth like a clumsy thief leaving fingerprints all over a house he was robbing.

'Leigh told us we shouldn't be working ourselves to death,' Beale recalls. 'He said he can show us how to make some real money. He told us how he'd establish a charitable foundation for us and everything. He was persuasive, he sucked us in.' Leigh told them there was room for only 100 investors in the scheme. 'He told us we were lucky; we'd just got spot number 98,' says Beale.

Beale went to that breakfast meeting at the Pigalle restaurant at Morningside's Wedge shopping centre, where Darryl paraded Barry to the prospective investors.

'It was a meeting to tell everyone how safe their money was. But right from the beginning, I felt uncomfortable, like something wasn't right. In retrospect, it was so obvious what they were doing, pretending we were all part of a small group and telling us we shouldn't speak to anyone else.'

Barry was convincing. 'He reeled us in. You look at it now and you think, how was I fooled by this? It was an absolute Bernie Madoff move, Madoff-style modus operandi. But you just don't see it at the time.'

When Beale asked for his money back, nothing happened. Leigh ignored all the calls; Barry ignored emails. Then the bubble popped.

'After that, I became seriously depressed about the whole thing,' says Beale. 'I started sending Darryl Leigh numerous SMSes, which got him severely rattled. So he called me, and suggested a meeting with his lawyer so they could put the screws on me.'

The meeting began badly, and quickly escalated. Darryl tried to placate Beale, saying they had a friendship that went back decades, which shouldn't be thrown away. 'I'm no friend of yours. You have no friends,' Beale snapped back.

It ended, as you'd expect, badly.

Leigh was probably feeling a scalding degree of heat at the time. Some of the SMSes that Beale sent to his phone were dark, red-hot with the anger of betrayal. 'You're going to look very good in orange pyjamas,' said one. Another read: 'I'm just confirming your booking for Sun City. Unfortunately, it's a room without a view.'

It's a threat of some menace. Sun City is the local euphemism for Johannesburg's most notorious prison, near Soweto – so-called as much for the fact that it's a million miles from the luxury holiday resort of the same name, as for the constant glare of the prison floodlights.

Beale then gave statements to the National Prosecuting Authority, expecting them to act. They dithered. Now, he's trying to move on with his life, but has no time for Leigh or Tannenbaum.

'I learnt a lot from this episode. Someone who knew Darryl Leigh said, "He's a stranger to the truth" – and that's probably right. Me, I'm just continuing with my life. But I want to see them held responsible.'

Back at work, Professor Peter Beale remains nothing less than an entire pillar of South Africa's public healthcare system. Despite Barry Tannenbaum's attempt to bring the temple down around him.

12

Admissions

'A number of documents including invoices, bills of lading
and emails were altered or fabricated by me.'
– Barry Tannenbaum's statutory declaration

While Barry Tannenbaum was outwardly pledging to investors that he would
'make this right' and find 'those responsible', he had been secretly spilling the
beans to a gaggle of lawyers acting for Barwa in Perth.

Barwa, hot with embarrassment and humiliation, hadn't wasted any time.
The Qatari fund had immediately hired hotshot lawyers and packed them on a
flight to Australia. Their task: to wring a confession and repayment plan out of
Tannenbaum before it all blew wide open.

Tannenbaum's naivety was at times mind-boggling. Confronted by Barwa's
lawyers, he had signed a statutory declaration in which he gave the game away,
admitting all sorts of illicit behaviour. Any lawyer worth his salt, had he been
asked, would surely have told Barry it would be suicide to sign the document.

Reading the content of the declaration, you would struggle to believe this was
the same person who was simultaneously putting out such withering, offensive
press statements, and metaphorically shaking his head at the temerity of those
who dared accuse him of forging anything or deceiving anyone. Yet his signed
statement, which was leaked to the *Financial Mail*, began:

> I, Barry Tannenbaum, admit responsibility and promise to make full resti-
> tution to Barwa Real Estate ... Frankel, Frankel Enterprises Limited and I
> ran into financial problems because of overtrading over a long period. These
> difficulties continue. I accept and acknowledge that with my knowledge and
> consent and participation and that of Frankel, a number of documents includ-
> ing invoices, bills of lading and emails were altered or fabricated by me and
> Frankel (and other connected companies) with the intention of diverting
> or retaining funds owed to Barwa. These actions were taken with the active
> encouragement and full knowledge of Dean Rees, who acted on behalf of
> Frankel and connected companies. Funds received from or owed to Barwa
> were transferred to accounts controlled by Mr Rees or entities under his
> control, including Abated Investments and Bartan.[1]

Tannenbaum then agreed that he would repay Barwa $1 million on 11 June and $2 million on 17 June. The rest, presumably, would follow.

It is a statement that Tannenbaum must surely regret having made. Any number of times over the next few years, he must have wished he had held his tongue. But there was no way he could wriggle out of it: it was also signed by lawyer Larissa Strk-Lingard from law firm Mallesons and attested to by a commissioner of oaths, Philip O'Hanlon-Creed.

To make matters worse for Tannenbaum, he had also signed an acknowledgement of debt to Barwa on 10 June, setting out all his assets for the first time.

Barry Tannenbaum, a man said to have made billions in an HIV/AIDS drug Ponzi scheme, stated that his total assets were worth only A$37.4 million.[2]

This included $8.8 million in property; about $7 million for the value of his Australian company Bartan (would you trust Barry's valuation at this stage?); $2 million in property belonging to Sertan Investments (the joint venture with Mervyn Serebro); and assorted cash in various bank accounts.

Sure, that is a lot of money – but where was the rest? If billions had flowed into the scheme, as appeared to be the case, where was this cash? Had Barry splurged it, and, if so, on what? Was it stashed somewhere? Or did someone else have the loot?

Pointedly, Tannenbaum admitted in this document: 'I estimate that Euro-chemicals has a current annual turnover of $12 million to $15 million, trading at a margin of approximately 15 to 22 per cent.'

So, not $600 million then – as the Frankel brochures peddled to investors had brashly claimed.

* * *

Barwa's lawyers couldn't believe their luck. They immediately set about squeezing a more comprehensive statement out of Tannenbaum. Based on what he told them, the lawyers drafted a twenty-two-page document.

However, by that stage, Tannenbaum had managed to speak to his South African lawyer, the streetwise Darryl Ackerman.

Ackerman, tall with silvery hair and an inherently combative air, came across like a retired air-force major with a voice that barked efficiency and procedure.

Although he ran his law firm from a first-floor office in Johannesburg's rarefied suburb of Illovo – one of the wealthiest square kilometres in Africa, where law firms are wedged up against private-equity companies and boutique chocolatiers – Ackerman knew a thing or two about what went on in the murky substrata of corporate South Africa.

He had, after all, worked for Warren Goldblatt's corporate investigations company, SSG, a few years before. Under its previous guise as Associated Intelligence

Networks, SSG had been accused of all sorts of things – ranging from illegal phone tapping to unlawfully bribing clerks to draw people's bank records.

Since forming his own firm, Ackerman had had his fair share of celebrity clients – Nelson Mandela's grandson Mandla Mandela for one. But Tannenbaum would be his most high-profile and challenging case.

One thing Ackerman did know was that there was absolutely no profit in making admissions early on – especially the forehead-smacking concessions that his new client had just made. So he smartly put a stop to it.

He couldn't do much about the first statutory declaration, but that second twenty-two-page affidavit – well, that would remain unsigned and unsworn.

Which is a pity. The second declaration is a sensational, extensive affidavit, nothing less than a 'how-to' manual for international corporate forgery. Notably, it sought to shift the blame entirely to Rees and Patterson. Barry, as this version of events tells it, was simply a puppet on a string, twisting and dancing to Rees's every instruction.

In the document, Tannenbaum sets out the origin of the scheme, beginning in 2005 when he 'initially obtained trade financing privately through Darryl Leigh'.[3]

He stated: 'Then approximately two years ago, I met Dean Rees through Leigh. Rees … expressed an interest in funding my business much the way Leigh had done.'

Barry said: 'Rees was generally reluctant to discuss or to reveal to me the sources of some of the funds he provided me. But I knew from discussions with him that he had many investors.'

Tannenbaum said that in December 2008, he had received a phone call from Rees, who informed him that Patterson had met the Qatar-based Barwa in London and they were keen to invest.

'In the end,' he said, 'Barwa was defrauded into making payments for fake transactions on the basis of falsified documents provided to Barwa by Rees, Patterson and me.'

This second affidavit goes much, much further than the first, sketching out a scenario in which Rees becomes the mastermind of the con, pulling the strings behind the scenes to produce enough fake drug invoices to fill a warehouse.

* * *

So, here's what it looks like inside the boiler room of an immense global con. This is how to dupe a large international firm, according to the pages and pages of documents and emails that soon tumbled out of the cupboard.

In February 2009, Dean Rees wrote to his Hong Kong connection, a woman known as Moni Chin, who was on the payroll of his company Abated. Dean told her to set up some Hong Kong companies, presumably for the Barwa order. Rees wrote: 'Can we open a second company called Lin Ping import export too. I need no trace to Barry and I though, and no-one knows about their existence save for you, Barry, Volker Schultz and I. It needs to stay that way.'[4]

Moni Chin replied: 'What you are saying is that you don't want me to prepare any paperwork to show the beneficial ownership of the shares ... will it be problematic though if I sign for these two companies' bank accounts, as some people know that I work for you? Shall I use a completely different signature?'[5]

The suggestion was very clear: Rees, apparently with the knowledge of Tannenbaum, was setting up sham Hong Kong companies to make it look like they were independent suppliers of pharmaceuticals sold by Frankel. The implication was that investors like Barwa would be shown 'invoices' from these Hong Kong companies as 'proof' of drug deals.

So Moni Chin created two companies called Xing Wild and Lin Ping – and both immediately started invoicing Frankel for pharmaceutical deals. The invoices, it seems, were all cooked up by Volker Schultz, in Frankel International GmbH's Hamburg office.

On 20 February 2009, Schultz sent an email to Barry, subject matter: 'Invoices and Proformas'. Schultz said: 'Hi mate, as discussed. Let me know if everything is ok. Cheers, Volker.'[6]

Attached to the email were a number of invoices, including one from Lin Ping dated 20 February and titled 'Commercial Invoice'. Ostensibly, this invoice was charging Frankel International $2 050 000 for 20 000 units of lincomycine HLC, an ingredient used in antibiotics.

It is unclear who signed Lin Ping's invoice, but Lin Ping says Frankel should 'pay us per the following instruction' to an account at HSBC in Hong Kong, a bank account set up by Moni Chin.

However, attached to Schultz's email is another invoice, in which Frankel International billed the Brazilian pharmaceutical company Farmabase Saude Animal $2 590 000 for that same order of lincomycine.

The upshot is that it looks like Lin Ping is selling pharmaceuticals to Frankel, which is then on-selling them at a big profit to Farmabase. Only this was not the case.

It's even more blatant in another invoice attached from the other sham company, Xing Wild Pharmaceutical Company. Xing Wild sent a 'pro forma' invoice to Frankel International GmbH for 4 525 kilograms of diphenhydramine, an antihistamine. Xing Wild's total invoice is $510 193 – about R5.18 million at the time.

What appears to be incontrovertibly damning is that Schultz's email also contained a complementary 'purchase order' from Aspen Pharmacare in South

Africa to the supplier, Frankel Chemicals. This purchase order asked for that exact amount – 4525 kilograms of diphenhydramine – at a cost of R8.5 million. (There are similar matching Aspen and Xing Wild orders for other drugs too.)

That Aspen order was fake. Presumably, the Brazilian order was too. This seems to be clear evidence of exactly how invoices were forged, paired to an 'order' from a sham overseas exporter, and then passed on to investors to corroborate the investment story.

In his unsigned but comprehensive statutory declaration, Barry explained how this happened: 'In February 2009, Rees discussed with me an idea that he had of creating some Hong Kong-based companies with names that sounded like API suppliers so that those companies could issue fake invoices for APIs, which could then be used to fraudulently obtain trade finance, including from Barwa.'[7]

Barry said he then gave instructions to Volker Schultz to 'prepare a purchase order and related invoice which met Rees's specifications'. Said Tannenbaum:

> Schultz sent me two emails and a number of attachments comprising invoices from companies known as Shudu, Lin Ping and Xing Wild, and Aspen Pharmacare … The Xin Wild and Lin Ping invoices were fake in the sense that those entities had never received, and would never fill, any orders for the APIs identified in the invoices. The Aspen orders attached to the emails, which appear to record that Aspen has ordered APIs to be supplied by Xin Wild and Lin Ping were also false.

Shudu was a real company that did buy drugs from Frankel – just not the quantity Tannenbaum said. 'The weight on the packing list, and bill of lading had been altered by Schultz on my instructions in order to increase the value of the shipment,' said Barry.

Equally, Schultz apparently forged a certificate of marine insurance to the tune of $21.3 million, as well as a host of other documents.

'Rees was aware that the Barwa money was not going to be used to pay Shudu … as Barwa had understood,' according to Barry's unsigned affidavit.

Barry said Volker Schultz forged the Aspen and Shudu invoices, which were then shown to Barwa, to justify its $30 million investment.

So how does Rees respond to this? The evidence appears compelling that, at the very least, he was involved in creating sham Hong Kong companies specifically to deceive investors. Rees's answer, in his affidavits, is that Tannenbaum told him to set up the companies 'for invoicing purposes only, to keep apart the Israeli suppliers such as TEVA, or so I was told, from the Arabic financiers, such as Barwa. If the one knew of the existence of the other, this would have created trading difficulties for Frankel International.'[8]

He added: 'I was not included or copied-in on any of the emails regarding the creation of fictitious invoices. This was something that occurred solely between Tannenbaum and Schultz.'

Rees argues that if he was part of the forgeries, surely Barry would have copied him in on the emails to Schultz. 'If [the invoices] had been created on my instruction, one would have thought that Tannenbaum, being the dutiful servant he holds himself out to be, would have copied in the master who he alleges furnished the instruction.'[9]

* * *

Even if Rees argues that he had no idea the invoices were not backed up by physical orders of drugs, Barwa soon produced a number of other emails that looked pretty bad for the South African lawyer.

In another string of emails, Dean wrote to Barry on 31 March 2009 saying: 'Hi mate, hope all ok. I need an order and invoice on a 60-day payment basis for $3.1 million. Can you send to me today? Just doing admin ... D.'[10]

Tannenbaum, in his unsigned declaration, said he understood this to mean that Rees 'expected me to provide falsified invoices of the kind described'.

Rees denied this. 'What I was asking for from Tannenbaum was an order that would match such an investment – it did not matter where the order emanated from, but what was important was to obtain an order that matched the investment criteria. The request was certainly not a request to Tannenbaum to create a fictitious order.'[11]

In another case, Rees apparently called Barry and said: 'Barwa won't accept multiple orders – we need a single order. If you can get me one, then leave it to me. Do up an order in a big amount, just under $20 million.'

So Barry called Schultz, apparently, and told him to create an invoice that met these specifications. Schultz duly rustled up the fake invoice.

A few days later, Rees called Barry, apparently, and said that Barwa wouldn't pay because there was no proof that the drug company Shudu had bought the APIs. Barry replied: 'We can just tell them we've paid.'

'They'll want documentation,' answered Rees. 'Just get something going.'

So Tannenbaum then instructed Volker Schultz to create yet another fake transfer receipt for $19.4 million.

Tannenbaum's statement says that, in numerous other cases, Rees told him what to do – usually peddling fake invoices to fool investors.

On 17 March, for example, Barry had sent an email to Rees attaching an order from Pharma-Q for $8.2 million -- the value of which was 'significantly more than the underlying value of that transaction, and that order was altered by Schultz at [Barry's] instruction' to get extra cash from Barwa.

The Reserve Bank letter, said Barry, was also forged: 'Rees told me he needed to provide [an] explanation for the delay in payment and instructed me to falsify that [document].'

Tannenbaum's unsigned affidavit provides a seductive and neat version of events. And yet there are some rather obvious contradictions.

For one thing, why would Tannenbaum email Rees on 13 March to tell him that the drugs were 'en route to the harbour' and 'confirmed to sail only end of next week', if Rees was supposedly in on the scam?

Rees argued furiously in the court case against Barwa that Barry's second statement was simply the 'hearsay evidence of an admitted fraudster and forger', saying that Barwa's reliance on the unsigned statement was 'reprehensible'.[12]

The lawyer pointed out that in the first document, Tannenbaum had admitted forging the Reserve Bank letter, but in the second he claimed Rees had told him to do it.

'I had no role or liaison with suppliers,' Rees said. 'Not a single email or other document has been produced to show that I had any awareness of the forgeries ... until well after the event.'

Rees argued that his own behaviour was 'inconsistent' with the notion that he was an accomplice. Why, for example, would Tannenbaum have emailed him that 'Private and Personal' confession at the end of May, in which he implored Rees not to start an audit because 'the book debt of Frankel Chemicals cannot survive scrutiny', if Rees had known what was going on all along?

Rees's arguments are compelling, especially as there was no obvious smoking gun linking him to the forgeries, whereas Tannenbaum had already admitted the fraud in a signed statement.

Nevertheless, not everyone was convinced of Rees's innocence – and the lawyer's own ego was partly responsible for that. In addition to the flashy spending, the Ferraris and the villa in Switzerland, he had also claimed repeatedly that he had taken charge of the scheme.

This was a similar bluster to the player who claims after the match that, but for his deft skill on the wing, the game would have been lost. But the hero of the win is far more likely to be blamed as the villain of the next loss.

After Barwa had made its second payment of $10.9 million, Rees sent the confirmation of payment to his partner, Chris Harris, boasting: 'My next deal ... Just done this one Harry.'[13]

However, Rees's bigger problem was that Barwa provided money for a specific deal, which he then used to repay other investors, like Nick Pagden.

In his court papers, Rees said he saw nothing wrong with that: 'At the time, I believed I was entitled to pay out such funds by virtue of not only the transfer of ownership of the funds in question from Frankel Enterprises to Bartan, but also by virtue of the representations made to me by Tannenbaum in relation to the existence of an ANZ banking [facility].'[14]

He also argued that Barwa knew the deals would not happen 'strictly in accordance with the provisions of the facility agreement'. And he said that if Aspen and Pharma-Q had actually paid up, Barwa 'would have commercially been none the wiser'. The only reason it didn't work out was because Barry had forged the purchase orders.

In truth, it seems the arrangement had been fast and loose between Barry and Dean for some time. Explaining how it worked in his court papers, Rees said: 'Things went so well that on a number of occasions I had received, or had available, investors' money without Tannenbaum having arranged a specific trade. In those circumstances, I would have asked him to undertake a particular trade to meet the investors' investment criteria.'

With such a fluid arrangement and with Dean willing to take credit for virtually every deal done, it was little wonder that Barwa had him pinned as the bad guy.

* * *

Some investors, at this stage, still had their fingers crossed that they would soon get some of their money back, that perhaps their cash was simply trapped in a snarl-up at a pharmaceutical warehouse in Durban thanks to a management tiff between Rees and Tannenbaum. But a few weeks after its unmasking, it was pretty clear where the chips had fallen.

In October 2009, finance minister Pravin Gordhan stood up in Parliament to deliver his mid-year budget speech. Gordhan confirmed that the task-team investigation had found that it was just one immense Ponzi scheme, and he revealed that arrest warrants had been issued for both Tannenbaum and Rees. 'It now appears that the scheme involved R12.5 billion in financial transactions,' he said. 'We know that one individual received more than R800 million returns and, in all likelihood, is not paying tax on those returns.'[15]

Gordhan cited the sum of R12.5 billion – more than five times the original estimate and multiples more than the losses incurred in other scandals, like Fidentia and Leisurenet.

So where was this money?

Rees was peddling hard to sell the story that he was an innocent patsy, duped by Tannenbaum, but his arrest warrant was clearly a setback.

In an affidavit submitted to court to defend himself against Barwa, Rees attacked Gordhan's arrest warrant, saying it was 'unlawful and issued in question-able circumstances, which warrants further investigation by the head of the National Prosecuting Authority'.[16]

Rees's argument was that the arrest warrant had been issued as a result of the complaint from Chris Leppan – but Leppan had lodged the complaint against Darryl Leigh, not Dean Rees.

Secondly, Rees said he had then tapped some friends at the South African Police Service 'whose identity I am not at liberty to disclose', and that their crime administration system did 'not reflect the issue of any arrest warrant for my arrest'. Rees even obtained a police clearance certificate, ostensibly confirming that he wasn't even being investigated.

But all this merely served to illustrate the yawning disconnect between South Africa's law-enforcement authorities: the police, the prosecutors and the politicians. (And this wouldn't be the last time the cops would be embarrassed in this case.)

The thing is, there *was* an arrest warrant for Rees, just as there was one for Tannenbaum. The warrants had been requested by Advocate Glynnis Breytenbach, head of the Specialised Commercial Crimes Unit, and approved by the deputy director of public prosecutions on 27 October 2009.

Glynnis Breytenbach isn't tall or physically intimidating, but when angered by a recalcitrant witness or suspect, she has a penetrating scowl that could cause paint to surrender its hold on nearby walls. 'You don't want to bullshit me,' she would say menacingly after asking a question – and you believed her. You could easily picture Glynnis Breytenbach as the uncompromising cop in a 1970s TV crime show, the person for whom there are never grey areas when it comes to justice. There are good guys and bad guys, and the latter sure don't want to hear from her.

As the lead prosecutor in the case, the fiery Breytenbach would be the public face of the state's fight against Tannenbaum. Her later misfortune – as a casualty of the political forces shaping the top echelons of South Africa's prosecutions service, which will be examined later in this book – spelt grim news for the country's efforts to extradite Tannenbaum.

But before that, in October 2009, it was Breytenbach's name dotted over the paperwork on the arrest warrants for Dean Gillian Rees and Barry Deon Tannenbaum on suspicion of 'fraud, theft, forgery uttery'. ('Uttery', an anachronism still used as a legal term, conjures up images of a lunatic shouting incomprehensible insults on a street corner. But in the legal sphere it means to publish something that is false, like a forged invoice.)

When Breytenbach found out that Rees was disputing the fact that he was a 'fugitive', she fired off an email to his lawyer, Bryan Biebuyck, the tone of which was consistent with her tough, unbending character. She said it was her 'public duty as the lead prosecutor in the investigation' to inform Rees that 'several criminal complaints [had] been filed' against Tannenbaum, Rees and Leigh.

Breytenbach's message was clearly threatening: 'The [police] clearance certificate indicates that [Rees] does not have previous convictions. This certificate was obtained in circumstances unknown to me. I point out that in view of [Rees's] knowledge that a warrant of arrest has been issued against him, he can no longer rely on the clearance certificate to support his claim that he is not a fugitive of justice.'[17]

* * *

With all the frantic finger pointing, it is surprising that Dean Rees and Barry Tannenbaum both still had full vision. Barry was spinning as best he could to pin the blame on Rees, while the lawyer, now in Switzerland, was doing the same thing to Barry.

Furious millionaires needed someone to blame. And Barry's laughable contention to Bloomberg in the weeks after the scandal broke publicly – that he was living from day to day, with only the 'support of friends and family' to pull him through – had served its purpose. The guy to pursue, the only person living large on what was presumably investors' cash, was Dean Rees.[18]

Barwa, now with Tannenbaum's statutory declaration in hand, hit the Royal Courts of Justice in the UK, specifically the Queen's Bench Division of the British High Court, days after the news emerged, in pursuit of Rees.

'Barwa's money has been lost. It has been taken,' Barwa's lawyers argued to Justice David Steele, reinforcing the point repeatedly, just in case Steele was hard of hearing or happened to think that 'stolen' had a particularly South African meaning, other than the universal one. 'We have not had it back. And in the respect of the involvement of Rees, of Tannenbaum, of Patterson and everybody else, the simple fact of the matter is that we are out of pocket.'[19]

Steele was suitably moved and promptly froze all Rees's assets worldwide.

In South Africa, Barwa tried to sequestrate Rees, arguing that he set up 'sham corporate entities' designed to 'spirit away his ill-gotten gains'.

Rees fought as hard as he could, but judges aren't inclined to side with people involved in a scam, even if their argument is that they had no idea it was happening. A few weeks later, however, Justice Steele was forced to recant his ruling – but only because Rees had too few assets in the UK to justify hearing the case in that country.

In August 2009, Steele ruled: 'With some regret, I have come to the conclusion that it is not appropriate to continue this worldwide freezing order.'[20]

That seemed favourable for Rees – but it only appeared that way. Far more crucially, Steele had clearly placed Rees in the centre of the fraud.

'The more the entirety of this material is considered, the more I am satisfied that there is a good arguable case that Rees was a party, and a successful party, to the conspiracy to defraud Barwa,' Steele said.

His logic, reasonably enough, was that Barwa's cash went through Rees's accounts and Rees ended up using that cash.

It couldn't have worked out better, even if Tannenbaum had planned it. While Barry largely morphed into the background, Rees became the target.

So why hadn't Barwa targeted Tannenbaum?

Well, firstly, Tannenbaum had stepped up to help them, giving them the affidavit they were now using to pursue Rees. Secondly, Tannenbaum simply didn't seem to have much money on him. 'You should see how he's living,' said one person close to Tannenbaum at the time. 'Unless he's hidden it all very well, you just can't see how he made millions.' Barry had also, under the acknowledgement of debt he signed in June, ceded everything he had to Barwa anyway.

But there was a crucial third reason – and it infuriated Rees. Astoundingly, Barwa had actually gone into business with Tannenbaum, an admitted fraudster, in order to trade its way towards recovering the rest of its cash. Barwa had essentially taken over the running of Frankel International GmbH in Hamburg as part of the acknowledgement of debt.

Tannenbaum's Australian lawyer, Derek Ziman, wrote a lawyer's letter in September saying: 'Barwa have in fact received some re-imbursement. They continue to receive funds from the company operating in Germany and have also taken charge over the assets of various Australian companies.'[21]

On 15 November, Barwa CEO Ghanim Bin Saad Al Saad, held a press conference in Doha saying he expected to recover between '70 per cent and 75 per cent of the money invested with Barry Tannenbaum' – partly because Barwa was now running the German business.[22]

Emails between Barwa's corporate finance boss, Adam Wilson, and Tannenbaum in August 2009 (two months after the scheme was exposed as a fraud) show that swindler and victim appeared to have grown rather close.

Wilson emailed Barry saying he would be in Hamburg for a meeting (presumably of Frankel International) on 24 August, landing at 10 a.m.: 'I have yet to book a hotel room, Barry where did we stay last time???'[23] Barry replied, as if this were the most fundamental problem he faced:

I always stay at the Four Seasons Hotel, also known as the Fairmont Hotel Vier Jahreszeiten. You may want to discuss with Volker as there is a country estate hotel, where we had the conference room last time we were in Hamburg together, nearby the office. It is called the Steigenberger Hotel. I prefer to stay in the city, so the Vier Jahreszeiten is ideal. Let me know if you need help with accommodation.

Wilson wrote back, asking Barry to please book him a room at the Four Seasons, pointing out that he was also 'flying to Cape Town today, nothing to do with Frankel, I assure you', and signed off, 'Kind regards'.

Barry wrote back: 'Travel well, and my best to Cape Town. I do miss it there!'

As part of the same exchange, Barry emailed Barwa's Gordian Gaeta and asked him if he wanted help booking accommodation.

Rees was incensed. His lawyers wrote to Barwa accusing it of duplicity in its dealings with Tannenbaum, saying the Qatari company was pursuing Rees despite the fact that they were already being repaid by Barry.

Of course, there is nothing more deliciously passive aggressive than a handbag-slinging contest between two well-educated lawyers. Barwa's lawyer, Mohamed Randera, sniffily replied: 'It does not behove your client to complain of duplicity given his admission that he misappropriated at least $12 million from our client.'[24]

At that point, Rees spoke repeatedly of the injustice of the situation. Tannenbaum had branded him the mastermind of the scam but had provided no evidence of this – other than the undeniable fact that the money went through his trust account.

Yet the courts had bought the argument. On 28 October, the Johannesburg High Court placed Rees under provisional sequestration, at Barwa's request.

In a later case, when Rees was sued by his former business partner Chris Harris, Judge J.P. Horn of the Johannesburg High Court was scathing about Rees, saying there was little chance he hadn't known what was going on:

[Rees's] allegation that he knew nothing about the fraudulent nature of Tannenbaum's scheme does not sit easily. [He] was intimately involved with each and every investment. He had intimate knowledge of Tannenbaum's business. He approached the investors and prompted them to invest in the scheme. He dealt with investors personally. He vetted each and every investment. All payments were made directly to [him] and he treated all investments as his responsibility and dealt with them through his trust account.[25]

Judge Horn said the inference was 'irresistible' that Rees had been a 'willing participant in a grand scheme to defraud investors'. He added:

An innocent man in the circumstances of [Rees] would not have abandoned the investors. He would have stayed in the country, if only to assist with investigations and to clear his name ... leaving the investors in the lurch as he did made a mockery of his claim that he always had the interests of investors at heart.[26]

Rees's estate was sequestrated, his bank accounts frozen, and his property seized and auctioned. Later, in 2011, the Johannesburg High Court struck him off the roll of attorneys allowed to practise law. This completed his slide into pariah status.[27]

Rees was given the order: 'Immediately surrender and deliver to the registrar of this honourable court [your] certificate of enrolment as an attorney.'

Darryl Leigh also had his life upended. The government's Asset Forfeiture Unit, the purpose of which is to seize the proceeds of crime to give to the victims, had gone to court and frozen R44 million of Leigh's cash.

Yet, all this time, Tannenbaum was living in Australia, virtually untouched. Sure, investors like Chris Leppan had rushed to court to sequestrate Barry's estate in South Africa, but there was precious little they could immediately liquidate. Instead, the trustees appointed by the court to wind up Barry's estate would have a long, slow grind to trace all his assets. Anyway, Barwa had essentially been given the rights to virtually anything Barry owned.

Barry, who had owned up to orchestrating a massive con worth many billions of rands, may have been preparing to go on the run, but it wasn't because his door was being beaten down by jilted investors.

* * *

While pledging to recover what he could for investors, Barry was going out of his way to recover what he could for himself.

Frankel Chemicals, by this stage, had its doors bolted shut. But Barry appeared to be concocting yet another dubious scheme to keep it going, *in absentia.*

On 13 July 2009, about six weeks after the scheme had been exposed, Barry sent an email to Estelle Wittenberg with the subject heading 'Names of Companies':

> Hi Estelle, hope you well and had a good weekend. I have been thinking of names for the new company. I have thought of names similar to this:
> - South Seas
> - Ocean Air Group
> - Southern Star
> - Pine Forest Investments
> - South Sun
>
> I will try think of some more. I will also let you know about the agency letters and the diversion of commissions letter. Have a good morning. Best regards, Barry.[28]

That same day, Estelle replied: 'I don't like your names, will register Core Procurement Solutions as discussed. Speak to you later.'[29]

The next day, Barry replied: 'Morning Estelle, Please see attached draft for letter to suppliers. Let me know what you think. Any luck in forming the company?' The draft letter read:

Dear Supplier, you are no doubt aware of the circumstance in which I find myself, which has had the unenviable consequence of Frankel Chemicals effectively having to cease business.

I am not sure what the future holds for the company and, at this stage, continued operation of the company would seem to be unlikely, even though the company has not been placed under liquidation and could have continued as normal, that is if the department of customs and excise had not interfered – in my view, in an unwarranted and unnecessary fashion.

I commend to you Estelle Wittenberg, who was part of Frankel Chemicals for many years and who has indicated a wish and intention to commence in a similar business for her own account. I have no doubt that Estelle, with all of her years of experience, will acquit her task more than adequately and will be able to service all of your business as I and my company did in year's past. She is well known to most, if not all of you, and there is no reason why she should not be in a position to continue rendering you a proper service.

Estelle will be advising you on her new details, including email addresses, physical and postal addresses as well as her bank account details for her new company. Please feel free to contact me at anytime should you wish to discuss this matter. I wish Estelle all the success in her new venture and I will be in touch with her very often to assist where I can.

Regards, Barry Tannenbaum

Estelle sent two emails to Barry, saying 'the letter looks good' and then suggesting he 'maybe back date the letter to 1 July 2009'. She also suggested to Barry that they delete the bit in the last paragraph where he said he'd remain in touch with her. 'Please don't feel offended by me asking you to delete [the] wording in the last paragraph. We must show them that I am totally independent, as we discussed on yesterday [sic].'[30]

Barry made the changes, and sent out the new letter on a Frankel letterhead, dutifully backdated to 1 July.[31]

* * *

'[Tannenbaum] has suffered severe mental anguish as a result of what has happened. It is obvious that he has been tried and convicted in the press,' said his Australian lawyer, Derek Ziman.

Ziman was responding to Mervyn Serebro, who, ill-advisedly, had gone into business with Barry in Australia. Barry and Mervyn had started Sertan Investments together in October 2007 to invest in property in Australia, each supposedly investing A$800 000 in Sertan Unit Trusts.

Sertan bought two properties – a plush modern-looking apartment in Rose

Bay, on the eastern side of Sydney, for A\$1.1 million in 2007, and an equally fancy apartment at Newhaven Place, around the corner from Barry's house in St Ives, for A\$870 000 in 2008.

Though the plan was for Sertan to be a property business, it turned out that Barry's uncle, Norman Miller, ended up living in one of the apartments, with Bartan apparently paying A\$2 383 every month in rent to Sertan. This 'formed part of Norman's salary package', said Barry.

Sertan's financials for 2009 showed that it was making a loss – clocking up A\$76 134 in expenses that year while only bringing in A\$64 383. The ledger shows just how porous the accounts were – cash flowed in and out of Sertan's accounts like alcoholics moving through a soup kitchen.[32]

Serebro, who had introduced a number of his own friends and family into the scheme, was now being pilloried back home in South Africa. So, in September 2009, Serebro's lawyers wrote to Ziman, effectively accusing Barry's company Bartan of stealing about A\$106 000 of the cash in the Sertan Unit Trust.[33] 'The purported lending of money to Bartan is of special concern to our clients. That company has allegedly been used by Mr Tannenbaum in connection with a notorious fraud, which is presently the subject of investigation by both South African and Australian regulators.'

Serebro then demanded that Barry quit the Sertan Unit Trust and hand over its shares, or he would act against him for breach of trust.

With remarkable chutzpah, Ziman fired back: 'Mr Tannenbaum is extremely disappointed in the actions and behaviour of your client. [He] is of the view that [Serebro] has no capacity to sit in judgement of him, and ought to be aware of the immense strain that he and his family have endured. Given their close prior relationship, Tannenbaum was expecting far more from [Serebro].'

Ziman then referred to Barry as 'mentally drained', which probably wasn't a lie, and said he had suffered 'the brunt of bad publicity', which was also true.

He said that Barry's offer to pay A\$800 000 to Serebro was 'hereby withdrawn'. Instead, he said there was roughly A\$2 million worth of property, with mortgages of A\$1 million. Barry offered to pay the debt and walk their separate ways with A\$500 000.

Then came a threat to unmask investors who had broken the rules themselves. Ziman wrote:

Many investors who invested funds with Rees and Leigh ... have in fact made handsome profits from their investments.

Whether or not these investors disclosed to the authorities the nature and extent of their investments, and the fact that certain of these investments were offshore, is a matter which has obviously concerned them.

Like he'd earlier threatened Rees: if he was going down, he was going to take others down with him. Barry's response to Serebro shows two things: firstly, that Barry knew right from the beginning how some people wanted to use his scheme to break the rules and, secondly, his eagerness to shift blame away from himself and paint himself as the victim.

Serebro's lawyers eventually went to court to force Barry to quit as a director, and they ended up taking control of the Sertan Trust.[34]

Barry had begun June by admitting his role in the scam to Barwa in his statutory declaration. But, in keeping with character, he soon tried to wriggle out of that. The fact that he had signed it clearly meant nothing. Perhaps that's no great surprise – he had, after all, signed hundreds of documents he would later claim not to remember.

In court in 2012, Barry said of the Barwa 'declaration': 'This statutory declaration was signed in Perth, and under duress and … I did not have any legal representation at the time, and I was prepared to really sign anything on that day just to assist Barwa, for Barwa to assist me.'[35]

That's vintage Barry – say anything, do anything, to get what you want – no matter how illegitimate it may be.

13

Hiding in plain sight

'This incident has completely destroyed him.'
– Mannie Witz, lawyer for Meir Levin, who now
lives in New York, and invested millions

One thing that tycoons don't like is details of their flashy spending splashed on the front pages of newspapers. But what they *really* don't like is being made to look like fools on the front pages of newspapers, and being depicted as greedy, credulous and desperate.

So when asked whether they had gone for the Tannenbaum investment option, many of them simply lied. Others headed for the bunkers, avoiding calls and emails, eyes squeezed shut and fingers crossed that their involvement would never come out.

Few had the fibre of Sean Summers, who owned up to what had happened. Jeremy Ord, the executive chairman and founder of Africa's largest IT services company, Dimension Data (Didata), was one who furiously denied any involvement. When first contacted in June 2009, Ord said: 'I'm not an investor [but] I know some people [who invested].' He even said he felt sorry for those who had lost money. Yet Ord's name kept cropping up in emails, invoices and documents. When asked again, Ord said that claims he had invested with Tannenbaum and made money were 'totally untrue'.[1]

This wasn't the whole truth, however. One email, sent from Ord's Didata email account to Dean Rees in March 2008, read: 'I haven't heard anything from you with regard to my latest investment … I understood payment was due last week, and that we would be receiving 2% extra interest per week. What is the status, when are we going to get paid?'[2]

Then, in August, Ord got an email from one of Tannenbaum's agents confirming that for one deal he had put in R10 million in capital and had been repaid R7.5 million. Ord replied, again from his Didata email address: 'Does this mean the 6 [R6 million] outstanding will be repaid by tomorrow? Regards Jeremy.'[3]

Ord, a laddish cycling fanatic, is a much-fêted entrepreneur with the sort of success story that would launch a thousand books. Ord started Didata with two mates from Roosevelt High School, in western Johannesburg, in 1983 with a loan from FirstRand Bank. Didata grew to the extent that it now has operations on every continent and is one of only six global partners for Cisco Systems.[4] It survived the dot-com crash of 2000, which shredded the ambitions of many bigger tech firms.[5]

Ord's fortune grew along with his company. It's no surprise that he now lives the life of a tycoon. He bought a jet and built the Waterford Estate in Stellenbosch in 1997, which sells about 40 000 cases of top-notch wine every year. 'We do our own distribution [of the wine], with very much a personal touch,' Ord told IT website TechCentral in September 2009, three months after the Tannenbaum balloon had burst.[6]

Perhaps Ord really believed his investment would stay quiet. But then, he did have a lot to lose. At the time of Ord's denials, Didata was still listed on the JSE and the London Stock Exchange. In 2010, a year after the Tannenbaum affair became public, Didata was bought for R24.4 billion (all cash) by Japan's Nippon Telegraph & Telephone Co. in one of the largest buyouts of a listed company in South Africa. Ord himself made $21 million from the sale, given his large share-holding in Didata.[7]

His exposure was inevitable. On 26 May 2010, Ord was subpoenaed to testify to Tannenbaum's trustees. There he confirmed to the inquiry that he had paid Rees, but 'was investing with Barry Tannenbaum'.[8]

In all, Ord said, he had invested R20 million in two equal tranches. He was repaid R25.3 million – a handy return for a few weeks' 'work'. But quite whether the trustees believed him is unclear – in the minutes of the inquiry, they said: 'We must take a careful look at these profits.'

Perhaps it's something in the water coolers at Didata's headquarters, a picturesque arrangement of offices surrounding a cricket oval in the wealthy Joburg suburb of Bryanston.

Bruce Watson, a Didata executive who is in charge of the global Cisco relationship, also dabbled for a short time in Tannenbaum's scheme. 'I've been told I shouldn't chat to anyone about it,' says Watson. 'But the truth is, I was in and out of there about five years before, so it was all above board.' Watson had heard about it from friends – 'and we trust our friends,' he says.[9]

But Ord wasn't the biggest winner in the scheme – not by a long margin. The person whom Pravin Gordhan had spoken about in his budget speech, the man reputed to have made over R700 million in profit, was a reclusive IT entrepreneur called Arnold Sharp.

KPMG's analysis says that Sharp's companies invested R88.2 million and ended up with nearly ten times that – R823.2 million. This was through First Technology, which supposedly invested R76.8 million and was repaid R273 million, and Berniebee Investments, which invested R11.4 million and was repaid R550.2 million.[10]

But Sharp, a chartered accountant, vehemently denies this, claiming initially that those figures were 'completely wrong'. He refused to say how much he made from the scheme, denying he had invested at all, in fact.

In 2013, he told *Moneyweb*: 'It is now an established fact that neither I personally nor First Technology were ever investors with Barry Tannenbaum.'[11]

Clearly, Sharp's idea of an 'established fact' differs from many other people's. After all, Sharp had arrived at the Tannenbaum inquiry in October 2010, and the record of the inquiry reads: 'He confirmed the Berniebee Investments and First Technology ins and outs.'

Sharp apparently said that Berniebee made a profit of R4.9 million, while First Technology made a R22.5 million loss. The inquiry minutes say:

> Sharp stated that although many payments were made and received through the First Technology account, in excess of R300 million, those payments all related to Berniebee. It is difficult to accept such an explanation as during the period January 2008 to October 2008, Berniebee and First Technology were making payments to, and receiving payments from, Tannenbaum.[12]

Clearly, SARS did not buy that explanation, recording in Tannenbaum's tax assessment that Sharp received more than R800 million from the scheme. The true facts around Sharp's investment have yet to be determined. Though KPMG tried its best to nail down the exact amounts people were paid, it was a tricky job, and not all the numbers were spot on.

But perhaps the biggest undisputed winner from Tannenbaum's scheme was a company called Jawmend Rossi – formed by the troika of businessmen, Jonathan Jawno, Michael Mendelowitz and Rob Rossi.

For many people wondering where Barry's money went, the answer is partly to Jawmend Rossi. This company invested R601.4 million with Tannenbaum and was repaid R740.4 million – a spectacular profit of R139 million.

Jawmend Rossi's story is unique among investors, partly because it predates almost all the others. Mendelowitz was called to the inquiry and arrived with his lawyers, Sharon Wapnick and Arnold Subel. He didn't give much away, but what he did was intriguing: '[Jawmend Rossi] became involved with Tannenbaum as from 2004. The investments made with Tannenbaum were short-term special opportunity investments at high returns.' This according to the transcripts of the inquiry.[13]

Now, this is long before most other investors got involved. Jawno, Rossi and Mendelowitz were with Barry from virtually the beginning. If anyone knows how it worked, how Barry duped all the other investors, and can provide insight into his motivation for doing so, it is them.

But if the trustees were hoping to wrestle an easy settlement from Jawmend Rossi, they would be bitterly disappointed. A terse note by the trustees after Mendelowitz's testimony said: 'We can accept that they will not pay ... and we are preparing the necessary summons.'

Jawmend Rossi's argument is that they simply provided 'trade finance' to Tannenbaum – and that he repaid what was owed. But if the trustees expected to be repaid the R139 million profit, they might as well whistle for it.

At the inquiry, Mendelowitz described Jawmend Rossi's business as that of 'investing in special opportunities'. They don't come more 'special' than an AIDS-drug Ponzi scheme offering returns that many seasoned investor should know were ridiculous.[14]

The clash between Jawmend Rossi and Tannenbaum's trustees would become one of the epic encounters that would define the mopping-up operation of the scheme. But more on this later.

* * *

Perhaps the most fascinating 'large' investor is Meir Levin.

Levin remains indecipherable, doggedly avoiding the media as if it were leprosy. The soft-spoken lawyer was born in what was then Rhodesia. He attended Milton High School before moving to Johannesburg, where he studied law at the University of the Witwatersrand.

In what would later become something of an irony, Levin studied alongside crusty state prosecutor Glynnis Breytenbach, the woman leading the Tannenbaum probe. After passing the South African bar exam, Levin moved to the US, and in 1989 was admitted to the New York State Bar. He now lives on Staten Island, the time-warped forgotten borough of New York. A short ferry ride takes you across New York Bay from Manhattan, past the Statue of Liberty to Staten Island, a middle-class throwback to the 1950s, where kids bounce balls in the streets and stay-at-home mothers swap cake recipes. A tacky version of *The Stepford Wives*, perhaps. He still retains his southern African accent.

Although he lives in the US, he keeps in contact with South Africa. His relative, Dr Shlomo Levin, still practises as a general practitioner in Johannesburg's eastern suburbs. And Meir remains well connected, especially among Joburg's Jewish community.

Levin works mainly from his surprisingly austere office at the top of an intimidating high rise at 521 Fifth Avenue, New York. 'He's hardly ever in the office,' explains the secretary, 'but leave a message and he'll get back to you.'[15]

But Levin, spooked into a state of metaphorical paralysis by the Tannenbaum fallout, never calls back if he thinks it has anything to do with the Ponzi. Messages to his house also fall on deaf ears.

Levin made headlines when he, sensationally, claimed that he was owed $825 million by Tannenbaum – an immense figure, amounting to more than R8 billion. This seemed implausible, even in the early days after the scheme was unmasked, when just about every wild claim at least seemed possible.

Someone who knew Levin says, 'Meir had actually met [Tannenbaum] before ... It's a small community and everyone knows everyone. So, a friend comes to you and says he's got a good opportunity to invest, you don't think he's conning you.'

Levin's story begins in March 2004, when a friend of his, dentist Greg Spark, said he'd been providing loan finance to Barry so he could import pharmaceutical components – the earliest known investor in Barry's scheme.

According to court papers that Levin filed in a British court in 2013, he said Spark told him that 'the returns were very good and typically yielded 10% to 20% interest over a four-month period'.

'The deals had grown to the point where [Spark] could no longer provide sufficient finance by himself and was looking for others to assist in providing the necessary money,' said Levin in his particulars of claim.

So, on 22 March 2004, Levin lent $90 000 to Barry. The loan was repaid on 6 June that year, along with interest of $10 980 – a healthy return of about 13 per cent over three months.

Wowed by the fact that it had actually worked, Levin lent another $80 000 to Barry on 4 August 2004, underwritten by an 'acknowledgement of debt'.

He'd taken the bait and, from then on, Levin and Barry grew closer, spending hours on the phone discussing Frankel's drug business. Barry told him that Frankel was a 'large pharmaceuticals importer and manufacturer' that needed large chunks of cash.

The lies got grander too: at one stage, Barry said Frankel had an exclusive deal to provide 60 per cent of all the raw materials needed by Stephen Saad's Aspen to make antiretroviral drugs.

In one email to Levin, Barry wrote: 'We are in a very profitable situation, but cash flow is tight. That is due to the fact we purchase material from China and India and sea freight the goods in.'

But, Levin asked, how do I know you are not simply repaying me with 'new money' you're getting from each deal? It was a good question. If there was any time, early on, for Barry to come clean, it was then.

He didn't though, obviously. Instead, Barry answered: '[The] answer [to] your [question] is simply trust. All I can respond to you on this one is by saying that it is not my intention to fool you or anyone else, including my brother, by using new money to pay for previous deals.'

That's pretty unequivocal. Untrue, sure, but definitive.

Levin said in his court papers: '[I] asked why Frankel could not simply borrow money from established lending institutions [and] Barry explained that the banks did not understand the business, [they] offered rates of interest that were unattractive and were too slow.'

Then in mid-August 2004, Barry asked Levin for a much bigger loan – $475 000 for a 'once in a million' risk-free deal.

This made the lawyer jittery, but Barry was quick to placate him, offering up his brother as a human sacrifice for his Ponzi scheme.

The way Barry sold it to Meir Levin was that Michael Tannenbaum, the financial director of Westcity plc in London, was 'still involved in Frankel', was 'a man of means', and continued to 'back Barry in the business'.

In an email to Levin on 14 November 2004, Barry said Michael 'is still being looked after financially' for his help with certain deals.

Fine, said Levin: if Michael Tannenbaum can guarantee this investment in Frankel, then perhaps we can do a deal. Barry replied that Michael was 'willing and ready'.

Had that deal been legit, it would have been a windfall for Levin: he would provide $475 000 and be repaid by 10 December, along with $87 875 in interest.

Speaking today, Levin's lawyer Mannie Witz says Meir only lent the money based on Michael's involvement: 'Meir reckoned that Michael had lots of money and was the director of a fancy property company, Westcity, so he figured that if he got guarantees from Michael, his money would be safe.'[16]

Barry asked an old family friend, Cecil Wulfsohn, a bespectacled lawyer from Joburg law firm Edward Nathan Sonnenbergs, to draw up the guarantees obliging Michael to make good for any cash that Meir provided to Barry.

In all, Meir Levin got fifty-two 'guarantees and indemnities' from Michael Tannenbaum. Comforted and apparently protected from any fallout, Meir started lending increasingly large sums to Barry, supposedly for pharmaceutical deals. He would transfer the cash from his American bank to Barry's account. Usually, Meir chose not to be repaid in full, instead 'rolling over' the capital into the next deal. In all, Meir entered sixty-nine separate 'loan' deals with Barry.

By May 2008, Meir Levin had, on paper at least, a mammoth investment in Frankel Enterprises and Barry Tannenbaum. At that stage, Barry signed a letter confirming that Meir had provided a loan 'facility' of $400 million – roughly R4 billion at today's exchange rate. It was an immense sum, dwarfing the annual revenue of most companies in South Africa.

By the time the scheme went bust, Meir's own court papers record that he was owed a giddy $728 million – more than R7 billion.

But then, as it inevitably did with every investor, the relationship began to sour. At Meir's request, Wulfsohn began asking Barry to repay some of the loans. In February 2009, Barry said he would repay $4 million from Commerzbank and another $13.7 million, which he said would be paid from 'a recent facility of US$40 million' – presumably the money coming in from Barwa.

The money, of course, never materialised.

So, on 12 May 2009, Levin started asking Michael Tannenbaum to stand good for the loans based on his guarantees. He sent a lawyer's letter, demanding $47.4 million from Michael.

When Michael got the first lawyer's letter, he was astounded, not to mention nauseous at the numbers involved. He called Barry and asked what the hell this was all about, but Barry said it was all 'a big mistake', that Levin was bullying him and that he should 'leave it' with him.

'I genuinely thought that Barry was sorting things out,' Michael says.

Michael called Wulfsohn, who had delivered the guarantees. 'I remember asking him what on earth was happening here,' he says, 'why I have never been contacted during all the years since the alleged guarantees ... were executed, and why I had not been copied into any emails or letters. Crucially, why had no one asked for a statement of assets and liabilities, given how ridiculously large the sums involved were.'

Wulfsohn couldn't answer, saying he thought that Barry was keeping him informed. He appeared to be just as shocked as Michael.

There are some fascinating elements to the Meir Levin sideshow that have greater resonance for Barry's scheme.

First, it is clear that Levin began investing in early 2004 – even before Barry began touting the furniture investments – and the bait even then was an investment in pharmaceutical products. This is before Darryl Leigh, Tasha Rossen or any of the ostensible 'early investors'.

Secondly, it would appear that Michael Tannenbaum was part of Barry's scheme. But the thing is, it just looks that way. With Barry, nothing is ever what it seems.

When first confronted about this, Michael Tannenbaum explained to the *Sunday Times* that Barry had asked him 'to give one, perhaps a couple, of modest personal guarantees in respect of Levin's loans, as part of the company's expansion. I did this in good faith, and was told at the time that the loans were repaid and the guarantees fell away.'[17]

But strangely, a rash of new guarantees then appeared using Michael's name. These included guarantees for five investments made by Levin, worth R47 million, in 2006. These were blatant forgeries.

Says Michael Tannenbaum: 'It is obvious that the signatures on these documents are not mine, and bear no relation to my signature.'

When asked who did this, he said he had 'no idea'. He probably did know. But Barry was in so much trouble as it was.

What this shows is that Barry was clearly forging documents right from the start, long before the Aspen purchase orders. What it also shows is that Barry clearly had no qualms using his own brother's position to flog his Ponzi scheme.

The 2004 furniture investments had been another instance of Barry peddling forged documents implicating his brother directly in a cash-for-furniture business in the UK. But the 2006 faked guarantees show it was no accident.

Michael Tannenbaum says he only became aware of the furniture scam in 2010, after fabricated emails supposedly from him surfaced.

'I do not know who faked these documents,' he says. 'I suspect it was Barry, but I certainly did not know anything about them. I called him, that [was] the last time we spoke, and I went crazy ... I told him he was ill.'

So what did Levin do? What could he do? The first thing he did was go to a London court to sue Michael Tannenbaum, based on the guarantees. But that wasn't exactly a roaring success, given the murk around which documents were forged and which weren't. At the time of going to print, the case remained mired in court.

What is interesting about Levin is that for a man supposedly owed so much money, he has been notably shy about pressing his case. Though he initially contacted a number of 'investigators' in South Africa asking for their help to get back his cash, he dodged calls and emails from the media as if they were hand grenades.

'That guy is the most secretive guy you'll meet,' says one of his friends. 'It's not because he's done anything wrong, he's just like that. He's an attorney, he's different. He knows all about my life, but I know nothing about his.'

Although Levin avoided the media, he still wanted his cash back. So he hired Mannie Witz, a round-faced, bubbling, fast-talking lawyer with a celebrity client list that included some of the country's most colourful characters, and not just a few public villains.

Strip-club king Lolly Jackson, who was gunned down in 2010, was one. A tacky, low-rent brute, Lolly, who was born Emmanuel Zachary, looked like every inch the cliché of debt-collector thug: permanently sweating, puffed out, hair greased back – as if by the river of slime he swam in.[18]

Lolly liked to bully others by throwing down briefcases of cash just to illustrate his influence. But he died respected by nobody except the sycophants who worked for him. Certainly not by the eastern European strippers he exported from places like Bulgaria to work at his Teasers clubs, women who then effectively became slaves while he kept their passports and demanded huge amounts from them every week in 'rent' and other concocted fees. It's so they 'don't run away with a rich farmer', he argued.[19]

Jackson, the son of Greek refugees from Mobutu's Congo, ran Honest Lolly's Motors before he hit on the idea of a strip-club franchise. It was anything but honest. He is said to have removed the rear-view mirrors from the beaten-up wrecks he flogged so that customers taking cars on test drives couldn't see the smoke choking out of the exhaust when they started up.[20]

Witz doesn't have a kind word to say about him now. Though it's hard to feel much sympathy for Lolly Jackson. When the public first heard how Lolly had been taken out in a hit, people kind of nodded. It made sense.

Witz's other clients included South Africa's former national soccer team captain Steven Pienaar, who was accused of assaulting someone in a nightclub. Although he often works for villains – men like Ping Sung Hsieh, a former business partner of Grace Mugabe, the wife of the Zimbabwean president – Witz says there's a line he won't cross. 'I'll never lie for a client,' he says today. 'If someone is guilty, then he must plead guilty. He must go to jail.' Which isn't exactly what you'd expect to hear from a gun-for-hire.[21]

In Joburg's old-school-tie legal community, everyone knows Mannie Witz, a legal eagle, the type you'd picture sipping a whisky on the balcony of a Cape Town mansion, debating why South Africa's Springboks are too over-reliant on kicking the ball, rather than running with it.

Though he isn't tall, Witz used to be a semi-professional soccer player, and still loves the sport. He is not shy about taking a flutter on the horses, and even used to own racehorses until he called it quits a few years back.

Given his profile, it's hardly surprising that a number of investors hired Mannie to fight in their corner – including Meir Levin.

That $825 million figure that Meir was 'owed', says Witz, isn't what he invested, but includes all the interest he says he was meant to be paid by Barry. 'He initially invested far less,' says Witz. 'The $825 million includes all the interest payments he was owed, so the amount he actually lost was far smaller.'[22]

Rather than cashing out everything he was 'owed', Levin apparently kept rolling this cash into new investments. The figure involved might not add up to R8 billion, but it is still immense. KPMG's audit says that, in South Africa alone, Levin 'invested' R368 million, and was only repaid R77.5 million.[23]

But the problem is that he was also paid money from Australia. Balance sheets from Barry's Bartan Group show that Meir and Jennifer Levin were owed A$38.8 million. Witz puts Meir Levin's real loss at 'somewhere between $5 million and $7 million'.

When it all went belly up, Levin was distraught. Unsure who to contact, he got in touch with a number of private eyes. None could help him. 'This incident has completely destroyed him,' says Mannie Witz now. 'It's a huge amount of cash, and he was really torn up about it.'[24]

* * *

There is a fascinating private email exchange between Barry and Michael Tannenbaum in August and September 2009 – months after the scheme had been exposed – that provides rare insight into Meir's case. Not only does it expose Barry's machinations to protect himself from investors' claims, but it also raises some awkward questions about Michael Tannenbaum's explanation that he was only tangentially involved.

On 12 August, Barry writes to Mike about Levin's efforts to claim back the cash: 'Signatures don't worry me, as if they pursue what is the jurisdiction and also they have already gone civil and cannot change to criminal. We are updating the figures and Meir has been paid back quite a chunk.'[25]

(Though Barry's email is garbled, it seems to suggest that Levin's lawyers raised the issue of the forged signatures, which constituted a criminal offence. But Barry says that Levin has already chosen the civil route, so is unlikely to press criminal charges of fraud.)

Mike responds, but the text is hidden. Barry then replies that he has heard nothing: 'Let's hope it stays that way. I don't think they have anything to go on. What do you think?'[26]

Mike replies, saying: 'Probably right – the signatures worry me and there could be a case there – but if most has been repaid, who knows … they did have a helluva go at me – at least 7 heavy letters and serious allegations over a 2-month period but my lawyers were very sharp.'[27]

Then, a month later, on 9 September, Barry emails Mike to wish his daughter a happy birthday. Mike then says that Levin 'hit me [with] a huge witness statement and a full file, they want my bank statements, correspondence between you and me regarding him – they can't work out what guarantees are still outstanding'.

Mike adds that 'they are making all allegations about conspiracy, fraud, etc – getting so sick of it!'

To which Barry responds: 'I know the feeling. At least we know nothing through accounts, and we had no correspondence on it between us.' He also apologises, saying, 'Sorry it has come to this. Never in my wildest dreams would I have thought as much. Let me know your thoughts.'

Mike replies: 'Okay – must be careful on emails.'

Barry responds that in future 'we messenger', presumably referring to a hard-to-track internet messenger service.[28]

These emails are awkward for Michael to explain, even if they stop short of being outright damning. Barry's statement 'at least we know nothing through accounts' suggests money might have changed hands covertly. Mike's statement that Meir's lawyers 'can't work out' the guarantees doesn't look good for him either.

In his court case, Levin argued that those emails are evidence of the fact that Michael 'was in regular contact with Barry', that they were 'doing business together', and that he was 'involved in and benefitted from transactions of the type for which funding was ostensibly obtained'.

When asked about this correspondence by the *Sunday Times* in 2010, Michael Tannenbaum admitted that these emails, unlike the furniture ones, 'are genuine'. But he doesn't see them as incriminating at all: 'The emails reflect my frustration that I have personally become embroiled in this fraud investigation when I have done nothing wrong.'[29]

Again, he reiterates that the later guarantees were fake, and that 'these further signatures will be shown to be fake along with those of the alleged witnesses'.

Michael says the email discussion had started because Barry was saying Levin had tried to 'stitch him up', and that the reference to 'nothing through accounts' was simply referring to the fact that Michael had not received any money from his brother.

On 14 June 2013, Michael filed court papers in London defending himself against Meir Levin's $47.4 million claim. 'I was absolutely horrified to receive this claim, without warning, in March 2013,' he said. 'I have not heard from [Levin] since late in 2009. I assumed that [he] had finally realised that I had nothing to do with the guarantees and fax correspondence that were forged with my name.'

This claim, he said, would devastate him. 'I am by no means in a position, financially, to guarantee the sums mentioned in this case, even the smaller ones. If [Levin] had bothered to do any due diligence on me, he would have found out that I am far from a man of substantial means,' he said.

In his court papers, Michael said that even if he sold everything he had, including a £3 million home (with a mortgage of £1.4 million still on it), he wouldn't even be able to pay the smallest loan he supposedly guaranteed for $425 000.

Michael says that while he used to get on well with Barry until he got married (Debbie apparently didn't get on with the rest of the Tannenbaums, so things became 'strained'), they don't see each other any more.

'I have seen very little of Barry over the past eight years,' he says. 'We had a family falling out at the end of 2007 over his and his wife's mistreatment of my son who went to stay with them on his gap year for a few weeks. Since [then] I have hardly spoken to or communicated with Barry and his family.'

Even though Barry used to visit London often – eight times in 2008 – he only contacted Michael twice during those trips.

'When I asked my parents about this, he told them that he avoided me as I was too inquisitive and would always lecture him on conservative business practice,' says Michael. 'I now realise exactly why he avoided me whilst using my name and reputation on all the forged guarantees.'

'At the end of the day, Barry was my brother and I trusted him – even if I now realise that this was misplaced.'

* * *

But there is far more to the Meir Levin story, revelations that might explain the lawyer's reluctance to press too hard for repayment – even though the fact he hired Witz meant he wasn't going to roll over completely.

Investigators say that some of Barry's 'repayments' to Levin were made in Israel, out of the prying eyes of tax officials in both South Africa and the US. Barry cunningly asks his brother in one of the emails to let slip to someone, presumably one of the lawyers, that Levin was repaid in Israel. 'You need to somehow intimate that I have mentioned to you that I did settle large sums to him in Israel,' he writes. 'I am sure the IRS [the US Internal Revenue Service] would like to get wind of that.'[30]

Sly, Barry.

Mannie Witz admits that some of the payments to Levin were made in Israel, but seems to think this is an irrelevant detail: 'These were only very small amounts paid in Israel. And why would it matter anyway? You can transfer money from the US to Israel, and from South Africa to Israel. That's not a problem, so I don't see how that was relevant.'[31]

Documents show that Barry actually applied for exchange-control approval from the South African Reserve Bank for loans made to him by Meir Levin. One document, for a $5 million loan from Levin, states it was for eighteen months, and the terms were that Barry would repay Meir the prime rate plus 0.25 per cent – around 15 per cent at the time.

The bigger problem for Meir Levin might not even be the IRS. It is that he appears to have invested on behalf of a larger group. Says one person close to Levin: 'It's difficult to say for sure, but it seems he wasn't just investing for himself. It looks like it was an investment group of religious folks he knew. How's he ever going to get their money back?'

Ultra-orthodox New York lawyers are not, you would imagine, the kind of audience who would take lightly to someone they trusted losing all their cash in a Ponzi scheme.

* * *

A key element of a multinational scheme like Barry's is that it allows someone to invest in one country and then be repaid in another. This is clearly what Tannenbaum is referring to when he talks about Levin being repaid in Israel.

And this is what got the South African Reserve Bank interested. If people are externalising cash, especially in a state that still has an archaic regime of exchange controls to limit how much cash people can take out of the country, then such a scheme will attract plenty of interest from the country's central bank.

Many investors were summoned to the Reserve Bank and told to come clean or face some very nasty legal action. Some investors described this as harrowing, saying they were told by the Reserve Bank's lawyers that they were the real crooks seeking to smuggle cash out of the country.

Of course, the investors you really want to interrogate are all sitting overseas already, like Meir Levin. And Avin Lieberman.

Lieberman is a South African property wunderkind, a quantity surveyor with an honours degree in finance who made his first real-estate fortune in his early twenties.

Lieberman founded a company called Zenprop in 1998 (when he was twenty-seven), alongside property fundis Jonathan Beare and Rodney Weinstein.

A *Financial Mail* profile in 2008 said that Lieberman and Weinstein had 'built a portfolio of top-quality offices, warehouses and retail properties worth somewhere between R5 billion and R8 billion'.[32]

Then, in 2008, Lieberman abruptly left for Australia, where he ran an environmental-services company called CTG Holdings.

Lieberman also scored an absolute fortune from Tannenbaum's scheme. KPMG's figures show that he invested R186.1 million with Tannenbaum, and that he was repaid R222.9 million.[33]

In 2007 Lieberman spoke at a fund-raising event organised by charity Helping Hands. He talked about how Zenprop's founders were 'paranoid' about doing bad business, so had forgone questionable deals, rather than put themselves at risk.[34]

Building a business, Lieberman told the *South African Jewish Report*, is a 'physical and emotional roller coaster'. This was about two years before Tannenbaum's scheme was exposed. If simply doing business was a roller coaster, you can just imagine how Lieberman would have described *that*. So much for forgoing questionable deals.

* * *

Investors' responses to the collapse of the scheme provided rare insight into the characters involved. A number of CEOs, for example, weren't even willing to admit they had invested in the scam – despite their names appearing on the initial spreadsheets.

This may be, it seems, because some of them lent money to Suscito Investments – Dean Rees's company – rather than to Tannenbaum directly.

This appears to have been the case with Brett Landman, the CEO of Satrix, the company that provides all South Africa's exchange-traded funds for investors on the JSE. Landman is pretty clued up when it comes to investment. Satrix is 100 per cent owned by South Africa's life-insurance giant Sanlam, and small investors wary of buying a particular share can instead choose to pump their cash into the Satrix-branded low-cost exchange-traded funds, which have been described as 'pre-packaged investing for the lazy'. Lazy it may be, but it's working. At last count, investors had put more than R12 billion into Satrix's exchange-traded funds.[35]

Gareth Tindall, the chief executive of recruitment company Kelly Group, also appears on KPMG's spreadsheets, which say he made an investment of R1 million.

Tindall used to be a sales director at Jeremy Ord's Dimension Data before he joined Kelly. Considering that a number of Dimension Data hotshots, including Ord himself, invested in the scheme, it's no great leap to see how Tindall ended up investing – even if it was through Rees.

Then there are a number of other corporate hotshots who, understandably, are not keen to discuss their investments at all, but refer to it as a painful experience that they would rather put behind them.

Take the case of Litsa Roussos, another recruitment doyenne and former Businesswoman of the Year finalist, who invested R10.2 million and was paid out R17 million. Though in her sixties, Roussos could pass for someone twenty years younger. You could imagine her power walking earnestly every morning along the beach in Camps Bay, one eye on her pulse rate. She is granite hard, and that seems to be how she wrestled her way to the summit of the notoriously cut-throat recruitment industry.

Roussos's studded thirty-seven-year career saw her build a company called Emmanuels Personnel, which she sold to Adcorp, a rival to Gareth Tindall's Kelly, in 1997. She became a director of Adcorp for a few years before quitting to start a recruitment training company. Some people just don't fancy reporting to a boss.[36]

When asked about the Ponzi scheme, Roussos was furious. 'I don't want to have anything to do with Barry Tannenbaum in any shape, size or form. Don't call me again,' she said, slamming down the phone.[37]

Perhaps she's still scalding over having invested in a Ponzi scheme. Yet, six months after Barry was exposed, she was willing to share her investment wisdom on Twitter, saying 'invest in the right people, not just the business'.[38]

Other investors were equally keen to bury the past without fanfare. There's the case of Farida Parsad, who ran the Institute of Training Excellence. The institute provided a number of training courses for companies and individuals, covering call-centre skills, sales and marketing, real estate and general business.

Bizarrely, Parsad appears to have invested the institute's own funds with

Tannenbaum – cash she then lost. When contacted, Parsad said they'd had an awful time. 'Unfortunately, it's been such a traumatic experience for us, with the whole investment and everything. We're just getting over the hurdle of it, dealing with SARS and everything, so we don't want to talk about it,' she said.[39]

Ironically, the words that Parsad used when she refused to discuss her experience were: 'I don't want to participate, thank you.'

A bit late to learn those words, you would think. A more judicious time to decline participation would have been a few years back, when Darryl Leigh had first proposed the investment.

But Parsad's case illustrates the phenomenon that it wasn't just individuals who invested: companies also ploughed cash into Tannenbaum's scheme.

Ed Jowitt, the brother of Dean Rees's good friend, Ben Jowitt, is the marketing director for a company called the Sysman Group. Sysman invested R32.9 million with Tannenbaum and was paid out just north of R17.9 million.[40]

Then there was direct-marketing company Glomail. Like its American peers, Glomail is famous for its implausible television adverts showing people suddenly unable to do a simple task without falling victim to some spectacularly gory injury. It's for this reason that you need Glomail's products, like the EZCracker, a plastic contraption that 'instantly releases the egg from its shell with one simple motion'. A steal at R9.95.[41]

If that's too elaborate, for R399.90 you can get the Celltone with snail gel extract, which was 'discovered by farmworkers who, when harvesting snails, noticed the healing effects on their hands', or Bobble Off, a 'hand-held lint remover that makes your clothes look like new', for just R99.[42]

Glomail's former CEO Alan Ber invested with Tannenbaum. Yet the liquidator's documents said Glomail itself invested. Ber referred all queries to his lawyer from Werksmans, Bernard Hotz. But Hotz said that Glomail itself didn't invest – it's just that Ber used a loan account with the company to put some of his money into the scheme.

Not such a wise investment, it turns out. The numbers show that Ber invested R11.5 million and was repaid only R4.2 million.[43]

* * *

In the days after the scheme's collapse, as every news outlet scrambled to report on the Barry Tannenbaum Ponzi, every news item led with the same names. It was a variation of this: 'A scheme in which Sean Summers, Tom Lawless and Howard Lowenthal invested …'

Of course, Summers, Lowenthal and Lawless were the names that had been recycled since that first-ever Routledge Modise meeting. The thing is, though, there were far wealthier and more influential company bosses whose names had remained hidden for many months.

For example, there was Duncan Simpson-Craib, a former employee of British Petroleum and head of strategy at black empowerment company Safika, founded by former ANC national executive member Saki Macozoma. Simpson-Craib was one of the largest single investors. According to an affidavit he signed, Simpson-Craib invested R113.8 million and was repaid R127.4 million. He testified before the liquidator's inquiry, and the minutes say 'he understood that at all times, he was transacting with Tannenbaum'.[44]

What this means is that Simpson-Craib was a net winner to the tune of R13.6 million. Now, that's a large chunk of cash. When people ask who got the Ponzi cash, you'd do worse than to look to people like Duncan Simpson-Craib.

Lawless now shrugs off the fact he was held up as the emblem of the corporate top brass duped by Barry. 'I suppose if I hadn't put my name down at that meeting, it might never have got out,' he says.[45]

Chances are, it would have emerged anyway. A greying, but fiercely articulate accountant, Lawless had appeared stunned during those first few days in June 2009 when he learnt it had all been a scam. He says he felt foolish – no different from hundreds of others.

Lawless was the man responsible for steering one of the country's most important investment institutions, the Bond Exchange of South Africa, which, by 2009, was registering a truly mammoth turnover of R19 trillion. This made it one of the largest emerging-market debt exchanges in the world. If government wanted to raise cash by issuing a bond, or a large company wanted to list a corporate bond, they would stop at Lawless's office. It was a position of some responsibility, so you would expect the man in charge of it to know a thing or two about investing.[46]

What you wouldn't expect was for that man to be putting money into an investment promising to pay more than 100 per cent a year. In the end, Lawless ended up losing with Tannenbaum. He invested R900 000 and was repaid R410 000.

* * *

It turns out there was a healthy cross section of professions represented among Barry's investors. For example, it will please some to learn that lawyers and estate agents were a key target market for Tannenbaum.

Take Warren Drue, a lawyer with Routledge Modise. The site of that first investors' meeting, Routledge Modise, wasn't an arbitrary choice of venue. Drue, who stood up and defended Dean Rees at the meeting that cold June morning, also got swindled.

Records show that Drue ploughed R610 368 into Tannenbaum's scheme in 2008, and got out R589 750.

Drue had known Tannenbaum since their university days and their two families went on holiday together to Singapore, the lawyer told the *Jewish Chronicle*.[47]

'I had Barry at my offices in October,' Drue said, 'and he basically told me that I'm missing out on the best opportunity of my life – how can I not be putting money behind him, don't I have faith? I discussed it with my wife, and we decided we'd put a little bit of money behind him. We thought perhaps it was the right thing to do for a friend and I thought I was hopefully making a wise investment.'[48]

Drue then described Tannenbaum as 'the most charming, wonderful person you've ever met', kind and a really good father. 'It just saddens me that he got himself caught in this mess,' he said. 'I don't think it started out intentionally as such. It's very very upsetting.'

There were many other lawyers too – Richard Goudvis and Craig Delport, Rees and Leigh, and former Bowman Gilfillan partner Eric Truebody.

Representing the estate agents, you have Leigh's girlfriend, Tasha Rossen, and Sarah West and others.

The country's diamond dealers were represented by Trevor Temkin (a director of the Diamond Dealers' Club of South Africa and himself a dealer for more than three decades), who invested R250 000.

The booze industry had Charles Kramer, brother of Solly Kramer, who started the liquor chain of the same name, before selling it. Charles and Solly then started Norman Goodfellows, the sort of top-end store where, on a Friday afternoon, you'd find Ferraris and Porsches parked outside, as their millionaire owners rifled through the shelves of single malt for the weekend's poker parties.

Like many, Charles Kramer doesn't want to talk about it: 'It's a chapter of my life that's now closed.'[49]

Leroy Tulip, at the time an advertising planner at the Jupiter Drawing Room, the only advertising agency in Africa to be named as 'one of the world's leading independent agencies', ploughed in only R100 000 – which he lost. (It speaks volumes that when Tulip invested, in February 2009, Barry was willing to take anything – even R100 000, the sort of amount he never would have stooped to accept two years before.)

Tulip explains: 'My car was stolen, so I got some money and I knew some guys who had invested. So they suggested I could do quite well out of this. Now I've basically been robbed twice.'[50]

Tulip, who now runs his own agency called Black Tulip Productions, doesn't expect to see his money again. 'With the liquidators and everyone involved now, I think I've got more chance of landing on Mars,' he says.

Barry Tannenbaum did not discriminate: if you were rich and willing to suspend your cynicism for a few extra rands, he'd take your cash – regardless of whether you were a liquor-chain owner or the CEO of a major corporation.

And although it can't have been Barry's plan, he also inadvertently ended up with some of the poor on his laundry list.

For many people, seeing the rich fleeced thanks to their own poor judgement sparked a comforting dose of *Schadenfreude.* As talk-radio shows like the Johannesburg-based 702 ran long pieces on the Tannenbaum Ponzi scheme, callers dropped in words like 'greedy', 'ironic' and 'justice'. (Justice, of course, wasn't how you could describe any of what happened. Justice wasn't exactly what the investors got the first time, or the second time, when the liquidators came calling.)

But there were other calls to the radio stations too. These were the less privileged victims who had been taken for a ride and were now living without cash. One woman, too ashamed to reveal her identity, broke down on air, describing how she had been forced to move in with her family. They had to choose between buying food for themselves or for their dog. They chose the dog.

Inevitably, it had come at an awful time. A recession was beginning to infect the country, so people were losing their jobs as companies contracted.

'Things have been tough. There just hasn't been as much money around as there used to be,' says Allon Rock, a tennis coach in his early forties. Rock is a veteran, having started coaching in 1991 after a tennis scholarship saw him spend a year at Washington College in Maryland (which, incidentally, was America's first college, inaugurated in 1782).[51]

Rock bumped into Tasha Rossen and her boyfriend Darryl Leigh at the tennis courts. He says that Tasha eventually 'convinced me it's what I should have been doing with my cash'.

Her advice was, go big: this is your one shot at the big time. You don't want to be a tennis coach all your life, she argued. So Rock cashed in an endowment policy he had taken out years earlier and got a second bond on his house. He ploughed it all into Tannenbaum's scheme.

A tennis coach doesn't have the sort of disposable income as the likes of Sean Summers. Nonetheless, Rock was able to invest R350 000 in October 2008 – less than a year before it all went bust. Though Rock did get some money back, it was only R72 000 – part of which the liquidators then took. 'For us, it was a big loss,' he says.

When Rock pitched up at that Routledge Modise meeting and saw his so-called 'small club of investors' packing the auditorium, he had a sinking feeling that he had lost the rest.

With two children heading into teenage years and a daughter who needed pricey orthodontic treatment, the Rocks had to make new plans.

Four years later, Allon is just glad it's in the past: 'It didn't sink us, thankfully. It was money we couldn't afford to lose, and it put us back a few years, but it wasn't the end.'

He continues to give tennis lessons, though. Though he describes Leigh as an 'arrogant narcissist', he says he doesn't blame him for what happened, because it was Barry 'who screwed us royally'.

Besides small investors, there were others who found their names flashing up in reports as having received Ponzi cash.

Sue Fowlds, a teacher who had worked at various special-needs schools around London for five years after 2000, started her own special-needs school in 2007 from her home in Johannesburg's working-class northern suburb of Randburg.

It's expensive to start a school. So a generous lawyer called Dean Rees provided R2 million in initial seed capital, and became the main shareholder of the school property.

The school is now kaleidoscopic. Rainbows hang above the doors; swings and gym equipment are suspended from the ceilings; wooden jungle gyms, orange stools and turquoise trampolines give it the air of a children's refuge.

Only thing is, was Rees being generous with other investors' money?

'Of course there's that question,' says one person with insight into the case. 'Was this done with dirty money, with Ponzi money? But, you know, Dean denies knowing that it was a Ponzi scheme.'

Where it becomes tricky is that the school is flagged in KPMG's list as having received money – at least R270 000. Should liquidators decide to claw back any money that Dean might have paid to the school, that might very well spell bad news for the children.

After lawyers got involved, Rees signed over the property to Fowlds, which at least removed the prospect of the liquidators seizing it as an asset.

In any other scenario, the donation of the money to the school would have reflected well on Dean Rees. Nowadays, however, you don't see Rees's name on the school's sponsor list.

* * *

For Mike and Jeanette van Ginkel, an elderly couple in their seventies, Barry Tannenbaum was a particularly unwelcome intruder in their twilight years. Described as 'colourful and intrepid veteran South African adventurers', the Van Ginkels had been married nearly five decades and neither was averse to taking risks.[52]

Mike, born in the sleepy Eastern Cape at the bottom of South Africa, got his pilot wings in 1955, learning to fly on Tiger Moths. Over the years, he led the sort of 'Out of Africa' existence that young boys plan to live before they're sucked into real life. Besides piloting charter flights across southern Africa, Mike did such exotic things as fly old Dakota planes spraying pesticide to eradicate tsetse fly in Botswana's sprawling Okavango Delta, before starting his own airline, Avex Air. He clocked up more than 29 000 flying hours, finding time to get his national colours in aerobatics in 1968.[53]

Jeanette was Mike's perfect foil. She had met him when still a schoolgirl, referring to him as 'angel baby' her entire life. They married the year he got his pilot's licence. But Jeanette was far from the demure wife who stayed at home baking scones and waiting for her husband to touch down. Initially a ballet teacher, she became South Africa's first licensed hot-air-balloon pilot, representing the country at the World Championships in England in 1976.[54]

Together, they won the President's Air Race in 1969 and 1972, a forty-eight-hour 1 000-mile race, in their Twin Comanche ZS-EVB.

Fifteen months before Tannenbaum's scheme was exposed, the couple took off on a rollicking adventure chronicled in a ten-part television series – *Silver Spirit: The Epic African Adventure*, the sort of undertaking that would have scared off people five decades their junior.

On 30 March 2008, the Van Ginkels hopped into a 1981 Rolls Royce Spirit, with the plan to drive it from Cape Town to Cairo, a 15 000-kilometre trip across some of the world's most forbidding terrain.

It was an epic adventure made possible, ironically, because of Barry's investment scheme. The Van Ginkels financed the drive themselves, something they believed they could do as they were theoretically doing quite well, thanks to Barry.

In Kenya, Jeanette said she dodged 'gullies a metre deep every kilometre'. In Ethiopia, they experienced the terror of an Ethiopian soldier running at them with an AK-47 rifle (though, his purpose, they learnt later, was just to stop them driving over an unsafe bridge that could have collapsed and seen them plunge 100 metres into the Nile). And in Sudan, they had to drive through 'dangerous bandit territory with a real risk of ambush and hijack', according to Mike.[55]

Not the sort of daily diet of knitting and philately you would expect of the average septuagenarian grandparents. Just the sort of taste for risk that would drive people into a Ponzi scheme.

Jeanette told one reporter how the Cape-to-Cairo drive was essentially just something to keep them busy. 'We had to have a dream and something to look forward to. Michael didn't want to be a commercial airline passenger after being a pilot all his life, so we started thinking of a trip to London in our Rolls Royce.'[56]

Another way to find adventure: invest in South Africa's largest scam. Jeanette used to run an interior-decorating business, and her bad luck was to have a lawyer called Darryl Leigh as a client. 'One day, Darryl was driving me to an apartment he wanted me to furnish,' she recalls. 'I mentioned to him that my husband, Mike, had just given me a cheque for R1 million, so Darryl said to me, "I know just what you should do with that".'[57]

(Interestingly, Jeanette is one of the few people who have only kind words to say about Darryl Leigh, describing him as an upstanding individual she would still have over for dinner any time.)

On paper, their investment worked out well. So well, in fact, that they decided to mortgage their house in Parkhurst and invest that money too.

On paper, the Van Ginkels ended up making a small profit of R355 000 – but they soon ended up on the wrong side of the liquidators of Tannenbaum's estate.

Along with numerous other investors, the Van Ginkels were hauled before an inquiry and threatened with having to repay R810 000 – all the money they had received in the last six months before the scheme popped. Never mind the fact that this was far more than they had made from it.

And this wasn't even the worst news for Jeanette. A few weeks before they were subpoenaed to appear in October 2010, Mike van Ginkel died at the age of seventy-nine from kidney failure. It was Sunday 1 August, Jeanette's birthday.

After his death, the tributes for Mike van Ginkel gushed with praise for a rare individual. Noel Otten, a former student at Mike's flying school, described how in August 1965 he took flying lessons from Mike at the Rand Airport, south of Johannesburg: 'You asked me when I wanted to go for my "next" lesson, Saturday or Sunday? I was shocked … people worked on a Sunday? I always believed Sundays were religious days. I will never forget your reply: "Sonny, flying is our religion! Now, do you want to fly on Sunday?"'[58]

The liquidators of Tannenbaum's estate were far less generous. Mike's widow, Jeanette, now alone after fifty-five years of marriage, was forced to appear before their inquiry.

A report from the inquiry, held on 4 October 2010, states icily: 'She was married in community of property to Michael van Ginkel who passed away approximately one month ago … demand was made for payment within 14 days. We are confident that [her lawyer] will approach us with a settlement offer.'[59]

She had been swindled and widowed, and was out of pocket, but the liquidators weren't shy to stick the knife into Jeanette van Ginkel one more time. 'Barry Tannenbaum has completely forced me to change my life,' she says. 'It turns out that when Mike died, he left an insolvent estate and since we took out a bond to invest with the scheme, it looks like we owe more than R4 million.'[60]

At the time of writing, Jeanette van Ginkel's family home was 'under execution', which meant the bank was in the process of selling it to repay her debts.

Barry's impact on people like Jeanette was far more brutal than on the likes of Sean Summers or Mervyn Serebro. 'But for Tannenbaum coming into our lives, it would all have been fine,' she says. 'We would have managed. Now, things are really tough.'

Rags to riches:
The story of Kate Hoggan

The prevailing theory is that Ponzi schemes are pretty bad things.

Take Bernie Madoff: not many people delivered glowing assessments of how the episode had helped them buy that house they had always wanted, that great car they had seen advertised on TV, or a new kitchen.

Kate Hoggan, a friend of Dean Rees's wife, Dominique, went from marginally above the breadline and driving a beaten-up old jalopy to the rank of multi-millionaire in the space of two years. For her, Tannenbaum had been the straw to clutch at.

It didn't turn out that way for her brother, Graham Evans, or her father, Trevor Evans, who both invested in Barry's scheme with less fortunate results. 'It was a complete disaster – easily the biggest mistake of my life,' says Graham today. 'But, you know, it taught me that if something sounds too good to be true, it is.'

Kate's experience was different. She arrived at Dean Rees's law offices relatively green, just having turned thirty. She had drifted from various jobs, having worked at drug firm Pfizer, fertiliser company Omnia and Daewoo Electronics.

At the time, she was living in Johannesburg's western suburb of Weltevreden Park in an apartment bought for R250 000 – an affordable option for the ambitious but cash-strapped up-and-coming professional.

It all changed when she spoke to Dominique Rees. Dean did her a favour and hired her in 2006. A year later – apparently at her insistence, according to someone who knows her well – Dean made her the MD of his company Suscito.

'Kate dealt with the bulk of the investors daily and was the person responsible for all the administration of [their] investments, including accountants, auditors, and she coordinated it all,' says one person who worked at the company.

The talk was that Dean was paying her a massive salary – R150 000 a month. This is many times more than the R11 000 or so paid to personal assistants, the R8 000 paid to office administrators or even the R25 000-odd paid to an operations manager.[1]

She married Kurt Hoggan, whom she apparently hired to work at Suscito. And she began putting her own money into Tannenbaum's scheme. At the last count, the KPMG analysis revealed that she made R9.5 million from an investment of just R295 000. Kurt made R13.5 million, according to the KPMG figures.

Those who knew her say Kate made far more – some estimates suggest she got R43 million in all. This catapulted her into the elite class.

Within a few years, Kate had moved into a house in Johannesburg's posh, round-vowelled suburb of Parktown North that she and her husband bought in December 2007 for R8.2 million. There was no bond, suggesting it was paid for with cash.

The Hoggans also bought two holiday homes in the ultra-luxury resort of Zimbali. Kate had made it to the big time.

'She went from being a nobody to running Suscito for Dean. It was a big transformation,' says someone who knew her well.

Kate Hoggan won't discuss the experience. 'I have no interest now in talking about it,' she says. Which is a pity: it would have been fascinating to hear her tell how a humble office assistant scraping by on a mediocre wage became a mega-millionaire in a flash. It's a twisted Cinderella story, a fantastical fable only made possible through the prism of Barry Tannenbaum's epic swindle.

14

The banks that greased the wheels

'How did such a scam, which seems to have been well exposed to regulated institutions (like the banks), escape the attention of the Financial Services Board and Financial Intelligence Centre for as long as it did?'
— Institute of Security Studies researcher Hopolang Selebalo

Bernie Madoff could have been busted nearly a decade earlier – if the American regulators had cared enough to do their work properly.

Henry Markopolos, a chartered financial analyst, worked as a portfolio manager at Boston's Rampart Investment Management. Described in Jerry Oppenheimer's book *Madoff with the Money* as a 'genuine financial wizard, mild-mannered and studious', Markopolos was asked by his boss to replicate Madoff's returns. At the time, the aim was simple: swoop in and snatch Madoff's upper-crust clients.[1]

The thing was, Markopolos just couldn't seem to reverse-engineer Madoff's model. The numbers, implausibly, increased in an impossibly elegant 45-degree arc, whatever the market did. It was either a fraud or Madoff was fiddling the numbers.

So Markopolos filed a complaint with the Boston office of the American regulator, the Securities and Exchange Commission (SEC), in 2000. He said there were two options – either 'the returns are real, but they are coming from some process other than the one being advertised' or 'the entire fund is nothing more than a Ponzi scheme'. No response. The SEC had no idea how to even start to verify this.[2]

A year later in March 2001, Markopolos filed another complaint with the SEC. This showed that Madoff had only had three months of negative returns, against the twenty-six months in which the US stock market had dropped. The numbers, Markopolos said, 'really are too good to be true'.[3]

Still no one picked up the phone. An enforcement lackey sent an email internally saying simply: 'I don't think we should pursue this matter further.'

In November 2005, Markopolos sent the regulator a twenty-one-page document titled 'The World's Largest Hedge Fund is a Fraud', a comprehensive dismantling of Madoff's business model highlighting thirty red flags and arguing that it was 'highly likely' that Madoff was running a Ponzi scheme. The sharp-eyed regulators nevertheless again turned their blindest eye.[4]

SEC investigators fluffed the probe, partly because Madoff 'did not fit the profile of a Ponzi scheme operator'. They dismissed Markopolos's concerns, saying he 'doesn't have the detailed understanding of Madoff's operations that we do, which refutes most of his allegations'.

In May 2006, Madoff testified to an SEC committee, but the officials were hopelessly green. When they asked Madoff about his strangely consistent returns, he replied: 'Some people feel the market. Some people just understand how to analyze the numbers that they're looking at.' The SEC investigators nodded obediently.[5]

Later, after it was exposed as a Ponzi scheme, the regulator's own report described that incident as a missed opportunity to put Madoff on the spot: 'Because of the enforcement staff's inexperience and lack of understanding of equity and options trading, they did not appreciate that Madoff was unable to provide a logical explanation.'

Still, one simple inquiry, had it been made by the investigators before the scheme was exposed, could have changed it all. Madoff testified to those regulators that all his trades were cleared through his account with the Depository Trust Company – so the SEC investigators asked for that account number. Had those SEC investigators then used that account number and called the DTC to verify the trades, Madoff's lie would have been exposed. But they didn't.

Speaking after he was busted, Madoff said this was the moment he had most feared: 'I thought it was the endgame, over. Monday morning they'll call DTC and this will be over ... and it never happened.' Madoff said he was 'astonished'.[6]

In all, the SEC received no fewer than eight complaints – and not just from Markopolos. In May 2001, a magazine called *MARHedge* raised some pretty tricky questions about just how it was that Madoff's investment returns were so smooth, so predictable. 'Experts ask why no-one has been able to duplicate similar returns using Madoff's strategy,' the journalists wrote. *Barron's* magazine followed with a hard-hitting article titled 'Don't ask, don't tell: Bernie Madoff is so secretive, he even asks investors to keep mum'. Again, nothing happened.[7]

Markopolos kept plugging away, getting more desperate. In June 2007, he warned that 'when Madoff finally does blow up, it's going to be spectacular'. The SEC filed it in the drawer they reserve for tip-offs from lunatics.

After Madoff was uncovered, the regulators came under heavy attack for looking the other way for so long. So the SEC commissioned its own investigation, and fessed up. The final SEC report on the Madoff scheme found that 'credible and specific allegations regarding Madoff's financial wrongdoing were repeatedly brought to the attention of SEC staff, but were never recommended to the Commission for action'.[8]

There were so many conflicts of interest, you could have picked out any of them as a reason for the regulator's failure. For a start, Madoff himself served on the SEC's advisory committee. And there was also the fact that his own niece, Shana Madoff, had married the SEC's assistant director, Eric Swanson.

The failure to verify any of the trades with anyone outside Bernie's office was described as the SEC investigators' 'most egregious failure'.

'If someone has a Ponzi and they're stealing money, they're not going to hesitate to lie or create records,' said one SEC examiner. So the only way to catch them out is to verify their trades.

Had the regulator taken even very basic steps any time from the first complaint in 1992, 'the SEC could have uncovered the Ponzi scheme well before Madoff confessed'.

* * *

In the case of South Africa's biggest scam, the regulators had been blissfully unaware that anything was going on. Investors had, reasonably enough, asked how it was that, in a country with an arsenal of regulatory task forces and oversight bodies, nobody was able to stop this train crash from happening.

Even police colonel Piet Senekal said:

> What is most striking in this investigation is that no notifying suspicion was raised by investors, auditors, financial institutions or other role-players within the six-year period during which the Frankel scheme apparently operated. The police and other government agencies were blissfully unaware as to the existence of the Frankel scheme.[9]

Well, it wasn't our responsibility, said the Financial Services Board, the government agency that is tasked with overseeing all investment schemes in the country. The regulator's spokesman said 'in a case like this, we can't do much other than refer this to the police's commercial crimes unit'. The investors, one board official explained, had simply 'loaned' the money to Barry, who'd then 'invested'.[10]

Perhaps, but then isn't that exactly what a bank does? And banks need to be regulated – a point underscored by the 2008 financial crisis.

Later, in February 2010, auditing firm KPMG reported to the South African Reserve Bank that, yes, Tannenbaum, Rees and Leigh had effectively been running a bank: taking deposits from individuals, and then paying them interest. That in itself is a breach of the Banks Act.

The auditing regulator, the Independent Regulatory Board for Auditors, also did not appear to have done anything about Frankel's faked financials. Glenhazel-based accountants IAPA had, after all, reported the fact that Barry had produced a fake set of financials for Eurochemicals to the auditing regulator as a 'reportable irregularity'.

What a regulator shouldn't do, in those circumstances, is nothing.

Bernard Agulhas, CEO of the Independent Regulatory Board for Auditors, says that by the time he got the report from the auditors, it was late in the game. 'As soon as we got it, we reported that RI [reportable irregularity] to the police. The police then, according to the information we have, interviewed the auditor.'[11]

However, that report from IAPA was only lodged on 8 June 2009 – after the meeting at Routledge Modise, at which Rees had told the investors it was a Ponzi scheme, and after Aspen had confirmed the invoices were forged. In other words, after it was too late to do anything about it.

'Before that, we had no report against [Tannenbaum], and there were certainly no charges against the auditors,' says Agulhas.[12]

Unlike some of his predecessors, Agulhas isn't one for covering up infractions of the country's auditors. So it wasn't as if the auditor's board failed to follow up signals – it's just that the report they got arrived too late.

In most corporate scandals, like Fidentia, Madoff or Enron, the first wail of anguish from investors is: Where were the regulators? How could they let this travesty of economic justice occur?

With Tannenbaum, few investors beat their chests on this point. Which is probably only right: it would have been extreme chutzpah for them to have complained. After all, many of them will surely have been aware of the fact that this sort of scheme was an unregulated, 'off-the-books' investment. If they didn't, they should have: what investment scheme doesn't even give you a contract, but hands over only post-dated cheques from the scheme's CEO? Estate agent Sarah West admits that 'it was a gamble from the start'.

But on another level, you have to ask what sort of regulator doesn't even spot a scheme this massive, with such influential people involved? How could South Africa's largest corporate fraud have taken place right under their noses?

If the Financial Services Board should have been keeping its ears to the ground, it was more likely to have been on the pavement fast asleep.

Perhaps a more appropriate place to look for accountability is to South Africa's banks. After all, more than R3 billion went through Barry Tannenbaum's and Dean Rees's accounts at RMB Private Bank and Investec.

How is it that, despite tough Financial Intelligence Centre Act laws obliging banks to report any suspicious behaviour, none of the compliance boffins at the banks considered the billions flowing through the accounts as odd? The Act says a transaction should be reported to the authorities if it seems likely to be the 'proceeds of unlawful activities' or 'has no business or lawful purpose', among other things.

A KPMG audit confirmed that R6.6 billion flowed into eight of South Africa's banks – nearly $1 billion at the time. Yet, in all that time, only one 'suspicious-transaction report' was ever submitted to the Financial Intelligence Centre, and that was by RMB. A single report. Once.[13]

Every cheque that Barry Tannenbaum sent to an investor was issued under the stamp of RMB Private Bank, which falls under the umbrella of South Africa's FirstRand Group, one of the country's largest banks, worth about R190 billion.

One investigator describes RMB Private Bank's actions in only lodging one report under the money-laundering laws as outrageous. 'Barry Tannenbaum was issued with literally hundreds of RMB chequebooks, yet these cheques never came back. They didn't think that suspicious?' he asks.

FirstRand won't comment on this case at all now. But FirstRand's investor-relations director Sam Moss rejects the view that her bank didn't do what it should have. 'We complied with all our obligations,' she says. 'We have co-operated with the investigating authorities and continue to do so.'

RMB Private Bank might have only lodged one report, but that was back in 2007 – two years before the bubble burst. Yet the Financial Intelligence Centre, which was set up specifically to detect, prevent and deal with money laundering, hadn't done a thing by the time the scheme ground to a halt.

If the aim of the money-laundering law is to stop money laundering, the Tannenbaum case exposed this catch-all net as pockmarked with holes. If a major international con man can easily sidestep this law without even stretching, then what good is it?

As the table below shows, the scale of the cash flow through the banks was immense, and right across the entire system.

Bank	Cash inflow
Investec	R4 065 705 474
RMB	R1 634 220 879
Standard Bank	R491 665 381
Nedbank	R246 560 826
First National Bank	R158 651 749
Bidvest Bank	R14 180 814
Mercantile Bank	R9 400 459
Absa	R2 518 103
TOTAL	R6 622 903 685

Source: KPMG report to South African Reserve Bank

But if RMB Private Bank should have done more than lodge a single report, what about the other banks? Especially because – as is evident from KPMG's figures – one bank was clearly Tannenbaum's preferred financier. One bank alone acted as the conduit for nearly two-thirds of all the Ponzi cash: Investec.

* * *

Not for nothing has Investec, the home-grown investment-banking success story, and sponsor of Test-match cricket and international rugby, developed a reputation as South Africa's Goldman Sachs.

Investec's corporate insignia is a zebra, but if even half of the wild tales of its predatory tactics are true, a far more appropriate option would be a hyena. If there's a quick buck to be made, its critics argue, Investec can be counted on to do the deal, whatever the reputational cost.

Many of those who have done property deals with Investec, for example, have a story about how they were shafted by the bank. In many cases, it's more myth than reality. In some cases, it's just the bitter ranting of people asked to make good on money they borrowed. But the point is, with Investec, people can believe these tales.

It was this way when Investec 'bailed out' con artist Brett Kebble in 2005, lending R460 million to his two companies – JCI and Randgold & Exploration – to allow them to survive. But Investec only did that as a quid pro quo for a deal in which they would get 30 per cent of the upside of every asset sold by JCI and Randgold's new management. Kebble dutifully stepped down, and a month later was assassinated on a highway overpass.[14]

Investec made a mint from the Kebble estate. Unlike the investors in JCI and Randgold, from which Kebble had brazenly pillaged R22 billion worth of assets.

Raised on the taste of fresh blood, Investec seems, at least to its harshest critics, to skirt an uncomfortable ethical line. But in the Tannenbaum case, now that's something different. Here, Investec's officials appear to have done some really questionable things indeed – even though the bank has since tried to spin it as decisions taken by rogue officials of which the bank itself officially had no part.

But the criminal investigators saw it as rather black and white. 'After what they did, we wanted Investec to be named as an accused on the provisional charge sheet,' said one advocate close to the case. (Of course, no such charge sheet exists as yet. And quite whether the authorities will have the appetite for a tussle with Investec when a charge sheet is finally lodged in court remains to be seen.)

The KPMG audit showed that R2.4 billion was deposited into Barry Tannenbaum's personal bank account at Investec. Tannenbaum also had Investec loan accounts and two treasury accounts. This was aside from the R1.9 billion that went into Rees's twelve accounts, including accounts with Investec.

Despite the fact that Tannenbaum had declared his income a few years back at only R400 000, this appeared to raise no alarm bells at Investec. Damningly, Investec filed not a single suspicious-transaction report. 'That, to me, was surprising,' says one Investec staffer. 'With so much money going through those accounts, it must have popped up on someone's radar. Someone must have ignored it.'[15]

It wasn't just Barry either. All Dean Rees's main accounts were at Investec. The lawyer's bank account at Investec had ended up being the conduit for billions flowing between investors and Tannenbaum. Again, no suspicious-transaction report was lodged for Rees's accounts.

RMB Private Bank, which filed exactly one report, might not have appeared as the model of diligence either, but at least it was more awake than Investec.

There is actually one reason, arguably, why Investec never lodged a single money-laundering report about the rivers of cash washing through Barry Tannenbaum's and Dean Rees's accounts. It is an answer that can partly be found amid the velvet-covered cushions of Investec's Private Bank. Specifically, it comes from the mouths of two Investec 'private bankers': Kamini Moodley and Peta-Jane 'P.J.' Muller.

A commerce graduate, Muller slogged away at Investec for sixteen years from October 1994, edging her way up a notoriously dangerous ladder, with each rung patrolled by cut-throat investment bankers and traders, eager not to be supplanted on their own climb to the top.

By the time she left the bank in 2011, Muller had become a senior financial consultant in the private bank, specialising in property finance. It was here that she met Dean Rees.

There weren't many Investec brass above her at this point. She had organised some mega property deals for clients, and was trusted by the bank's credit committee, which included CEO Stephen Koseff. Her word carried plenty of clout at these credit committee meetings.

One of Muller's clients at the private bank happened to be Chris Harris, Dean Rees's partner and good friend. Harris's property deals ran into hundreds of millions of rands – yet because much of this was vacant land being developed, he wasn't yet earning much income on this property.

So, Investec's credit committee wanted to know how Harris was meeting the interest repayments on his loans. Muller asked him. She came back and relayed Harris's explanation to the full credit committee, including directors like Koseff and Ciaran Wheelan: he was paying his bills thanks to a private investment scheme, something to do with a Barry Tannenbaum. It was an explanation she had to give a number of times.

Muller's boss, Mike Leisegang, didn't think this made much sense, but another senior executive said he had heard about the Tannenbaum scheme, and it had been going on for a number of years.

Investec's directors – Koseff, Wheelan and others – couldn't see how the scheme was working for Harris. It just didn't make sense. But hey, while it was working, at least the loans were being serviced.

As a veteran, Muller knew other former Investec boys who had invested and seemed to be doing all right: John Storey and Bruce Dunnington were two of them.

At one stage, Investec even considered financing Tannenbaum's business directly, at Harris and Rees's instigation. An Investec staff member recalls: 'They said to the bank, at the moment we're using individual investors. It doesn't make sense. Investec should be involved in the trade financing of this, and it could make a killing.'

Always open to such an offer, Investec organised a meeting between Rees, Darryl Leigh, Harris and some senior members of the bank staff. Says one Investec insider with knowledge of what happened: 'It was a Friday afternoon, and Darryl Leigh arrived wearing shorts, a vest and gold chain. And then, none of them could answer any of our questions about the actual business. So we said, "No thanks".'

Undeterred, Rees managed to get Tannenbaum an appointment with Investec to ask for more funds. 'Again, they couldn't answer the tough questions, so the bank decided against financing the trades,' says the insider.

Which is more than a touch ironic, considering that one of Barry's self-righteous selling points for the scheme was that he would never approach a bank, given the time lags and bureaucracy involved at these institutions. What he never mentioned, the fact that would have shot his entire bogus story to pieces, was that none of the banks would touch *him*.

Nonetheless, even though Investec demurred, Muller saw the returns that Harris was clocking up. So when she was given a hefty bonus one year, she took R1.5 million and invested it with Rees.

This was notable for the fact that Rees had big property loans with Investec, where Muller was a top executive handling private clients' property deals.

For this reason, criminal investigators flagged Muller's investment immediately: if she was handling Rees's accounts, then by investing in the scheme, surely this was an overt conflict of interest? If you are looking for a reason why Investec didn't lodge a single suspicious-transaction report, could this be it?

Today Muller says she had 'absolutely no insight' into Rees's accounts, as she was in a 'different division completely'.[16]

'His lawyer's trust account [through which Tannenbaum's money flowed] was handled by a different division and [his] accounts handled in property finance were handled by Kamini Moodley,' she says.

Muller says she did not have access to the finance systems, and didn't get involved in any payments unless they specifically related to a property deal.

Muller's authority, she argues, stopped at presenting property deals to the credit committee. 'Plus,' she says, 'I disclosed my investment fully at the time to my boss, Mike Leisegang. He said there was no problem with it.'

In the end, Muller ended up losing R750 000 of her R1.5 million investment – money that, she says, 'as a single mother, [she] couldn't afford to lose'.

About a year and a half later, Muller took a sabbatical from the bank. Then she was effectively forced out – something she attributes to hostility from her bosses. Quite whether this was related to the Tannenbaum affair is hard to say. If so, it wasn't overt.

After leaving Investec in 2011, Muller bounced to various places, including property financier Paragon, before settling down at the High Street Auction Company in late 2012 as a business-development manager.

In her LinkedIn profile, Muller describes herself as a 'deal maker' within property finance, listing her specialities as 'thinking out of the box to enhance returns'. To some extent, investing in Tannenbaum's scheme would fit this description. It was certainly 'thinking out of the box', at any rate.[17]

But Muller wasn't the only Investec banker to plough money into Tannenbaum's scheme. The case of Kamini Moodley was more blatant, according to investigators.

Moodley was one of the bankers responsible for Rees's account at Investec. But seeing as she was also an investor herself, she would hardly have been in a position to keep her professional distance from his investment scheme.

Says one Investec insider: 'What really shocked some of the Investec people was when it emerged that Moodley hadn't just invested: she'd taken a loan from Dean Rees to invest. I thought she'd be fired for that.'

The sums involved might have been nominal – the records show that Moodley invested R52 364 and was paid out R100 000 – but the issue was the conflict of interest. After all, Moodley would hardly have been likely to report the oceans of cash flowing through Rees's account as 'suspicious transactions', would she?

Moodley's name is dotted all over the paperwork. For example, it was Moodley who provided the information to PricewaterhouseCoopers for their limited due diligence on the scheme – an investigation that failed to expose Tannenbaum.

When contacted, Moodley also denied that she had any real authority over Rees's accounts. 'I didn't handle his accounts, no. I just worked with the woman who handled that account, P.J. Muller,' she said.[18]

When contacted again about her own involvement in the scheme and the fact that she allegedly took a loan from Rees to finance her investment, Moodley simply refused to speak: 'I'm not interested in talking about it, no.'

Moodley, like Muller, is no longer with Investec, having also apparently chosen to leave the bank. But how is it that bank officials are allowed to invest in investment schemes run by their clients?

One senior Investec executive says that the bank didn't have any rules specifically precluding its staff members from doing business with people whose accounts they handled. In the Tannenbaum case, Investec claims its risk-management staff did in fact flag these transactions. 'Our compliance guys did look at these transactions,' he says. 'But in the end, they decided nothing was wrong.'

The entire episode didn't work out particularly well for Moodley or Muller. And neither did it work out well for Investec: Rees used the bank to finance most of his property deals. So when he left the country, Investec was owed a bundle of cash.

In June 2012, the bank sued him for R34 million and, being Dean Rees, he decided to fight them in court. Reveal nothing, spare no quarter, battle each claim.[19]

First, Rees said Investec had 'manipulated the [company's] debtors and [Rees and his co-directors] into defaulting in terms of the loan agreements by unlawfully freezing their accounts'.

He then accused Investec of having a 'collusive relationship with [his] former business partner Chris Harris'. Harris, he said, had entered 'negotiations' with Investec to protect himself from defaulting, while throwing Rees to the wolves.

Then, he said, Investec colluded with the liquidators and auctioneers, like Auction Alliance, to sell his properties 'for prices below their true value' – without accounting for it.

In the case of one specific property, Rees still owed R6.9 million to Investec. The liquidator sold the property for R30 million, giving Investec R26.6 million of that, after taking off his fees. But Investec credited Rees's account with only R25 million, from which it then deducted the R6.9 million. So the question is, what happened to the other R1.6 million? Even the judge said this raised a question of 'some substance' over the claim.[20]

It wasn't the first time Investec had been accused of breaking the allegedly sacrosanct bond of trust between a client and a bank to protect itself.

Nonetheless, in March 2013, acting Johannesburg High Court judge Ross Hutton ruled in Investec's favour. Hutton said: 'What is strikingly lacking from Rees's affidavit is any allegation that the principal debtors would, but for Investec's alleged breach of the banker-customer relationship, have been in a position to discharge their indebtedness to Investec.'

Hutton said the way that Rees fought the case 'seems to be the work of a man attempting, as best as possible, to expose himself on as narrow a front as possible'. The judge said that 'sweeping assertions of misconduct are made in Rees's affidavit [against Investec], but are not backed up with anything of substance'.

Which doesn't, of course, mean his claims weren't true. It's just that it becomes so much harder to take the word of a man hiding out overseas with a warrant of arrest hanging over his head.

* * *

When asked about its involvement with Barry Tannenbaum, Investec clams up, refusing to give anything away. 'We are communicating with the regulators and the National Prosecuting Authority. A great deal of information has been, and will continue to be requested from us and Investec remains committed to co-operating fully with the authorities,' according to a statement its PR agency sent in response to fourteen detailed questions.[21]

If that sounds like an answer that has been lawyered out of meaning, well, it is. But it does illustrate that the bank is worried. 'We cannot provide any information outside of that which is already in the public domain,' it says.

When it comes to Muller and Moodley, Investec says they invested 'in their personal capacities and without the knowledge of Investec until well after the fact'.

'From the facts at our disposal, it appears they genuinely believed in the legitimacy of the investment opportunity,' the bank says.[22]

As if that somehow makes it okay. Pointedly, the bank does not say their actions broke any of its rules. What this means is that, according to Investec's rules, any banker would legitimately be allowed to step across the divide to invest in a client's scheme. When asked, Investec did not respond to this implication. Instead, it said: 'Due to our operating model, various consultants would have engaged with Tannenbaum and Rees.'

Investec's head of investor relations, Ursula Nobrega, points out that Investec 'did not profit from the Tannenbaum scandal and did not prevent any reporting on the matter to make any profit'.

That might very well be true, but the issue is why Investec didn't alert anyone sooner to the large amount of cash flowing through Rees's and Tannenbaum's Investec accounts. How is it that the bank didn't think this suspicious?

Says Nobrega: 'The scandal, as you know, duped a large number of high-profile and sophisticated investors [and] no money flowed out of South Africa because of Investec [in this case].'

But for an institution which was remarkably eager to bank a sudden windfall of billions for a crook, you'd have expected better. You'd have expected, at the very least, for its compliance systems to have flashed red.

* * *

The 2009 financial crisis had crudely destroyed the myth of the studious, diligent banker, risk-averse and ethically unshakeable. The Tannenbaum case took it one step further: it shattered the notion that bankers were somehow more sage on investment matters, more knowledgeable than the rest of us.

It wasn't just Investec's staff who invested. A number of top banking executives personally stashed their own cash with Barry. And they carried on as though nothing had happened.

As discussed earlier, the investment made by Nick Pagden, a banking executive at Citigroup's South African office, proved to be one of the pressure points that caused the Ponzi scheme to crack open. Pagden had been putting Rees under intense pressure in mid-2009, so one of the first things the lawyer did when he was paid Barwa's cash was to sluice $2.6 million into Pagden's New York account.

Quite how much Pagden put in and got out is unclear. The analysis of the South African accounts shows he put in R8.25 million in South Africa, and was repaid R7.7 million. But it doesn't reflect the money that went into the US bank accounts.[23]

At the inquiry, Pagden said he made a loss of R460 000 through Tannenbaum – though he also invested in Hong Kong, through Rees's Abated Investments.[24]

Clive Douglas, the former head of Standard Bank's top-end private client business, which looks after the accounts of South Africa's super-elite, was another one who was suckered. Since 2005 he has run his own business, Douglas Investments. Douglas is an easy-going, accessible guy – unlike many of his peers – and recounts his tale with a shrug. 'Barry bluffed a lot of us,' he says today. 'He kept telling us it was an offer he'd made to just a few people, so in the end, we were keeping secrets from each other.'[25]

Douglas says that, in retrospect, this only helped Barry conceal the nature of his scheme for longer. 'When you look at the conditions we were prepared to accept from the guy, like not saying a word to anyone, it's clear we were duped. Intuitively, we trusted him – when that was the last thing we should have been doing.'

The figures show that Douglas made a profit of just under R4 million on the Tannenbaum option – probably a lot better than most Standard Bank clients will have done out of the Adcock Ingram heir. On paper it looks like Douglas invested just over R27 million, but this includes 'rolled-over' investments, so the real figure is probably closer to R10 million.[26]

On 4 May 2010, Douglas was subpoenaed to the inquiry by the trustees of Tannenbaum's estate, who were desperately trying to salvage what they could. A report from that day recorded that Douglas was 'extremely willing to settle the matter, but his problem lies [in that] he has already paid SARS tax on the profit made'.[27]

Speaking today, Douglas says that he was dragged to just about every inquiry there was: SARS, the liquidators – you name it, they wanted him to testify. 'I've been through the ringer on this,' he says.

There were other bankers who invested too – at least one from First National Bank, the turquoise-branded banking group owned by the highly rated First-Rand Group. However, FirstRand also owns RMB Private Bank, whose cheques Barry handed out to all the investors as 'security' for their investment.

You could argue that, like Investec, the fact that FirstRand's own staff invested with Barry meant the lack of any money-laundering reports was understandable – but this would be a stretch.

The truth is probably far more prosaic: RMB Private Bank must have thought they had done their duty by lodging that single report. You could imagine it was not so much a conspiracy as apathy – and a desire not to do anything that might spook a client responsible for bringing billions into the bank.

The Institute for Security Studies, a non-profit research organisation, says the banks have 'heavy compliance and vigilance responsibilities'. Yet none of the financial institutions emerged with any glory from the Tannenbaum saga.

The institute's Hopolang Selebalo says it could have all been very different if, back in 2007 when RMB Private Bank submitted its suspicious-transaction report, something had been done. 'It could have been established that the transactions cited by Tannenbaum as supporting the high returns for his investors did not make economic sense,' she says.[28]

The money-laundering legislation itself is fine – according to the institute it just 'needs to be implemented diligently and with a bit more imagination'.

Ponzi schemes, Selebalo writes, 'thrive in the country on account of sloppy regulators or regulators who collude with them'. It's rare, she says, for a regulator to expose a scheme before people lose money.

The question that has yet to be answered is one she poses in her research: 'How did such a scam, which seems to have been well exposed to regulated institutions [like the banks] escape the attention of the Financial Services Board and Financial Intelligence Centre for as long as it did?'

Just imagine how different it might have been had RMB Private Bank or Investec flagged each suspicious transaction Tannenbaum made, and the authorities had acted on it. Such as the tens of millions transferred to Australian-based property entrepreneur Avin Lieberman or New York lawyer Meir Levin. Had that been the case, the money-laundering authority, the Financial Intelligence Centre, might have launched an investigation. Then the police might have acted. Then Frankel Enterprises might have been stopped before Tannenbaum had run out of money, or before he'd had the time to place his knights and rooks where he wanted them. It's a long shot, but it might have happened that way.

If the banks had done their job.

15

Crime and punishment 1:
Liquidators and tax collectors

'This is them coming to stab the wounded.'
— **Howard Lowenthal, investor in the scheme, discussing how
SARS and the trustees targeted the most vulnerable, while
Tannenbaum, Rees and Leigh continued to live large**

Howard Lowenthal knows a scam when he sees it. The brawny chartered account-ant was virtually brought up on the trading-room floor, as the son of Norman Lowenthal, former chairman of the JSE, Africa's largest stock market.

In the late 1990s, Lowenthal clashed with Jack Milne, a self-promoting, two-bit investment guru, who ran an 'investment school' called the Progressive Systems College (PSC). The tussle got so heated that Lowenthal even dragged Milne to court for defamation, but the case was chucked out. 'I knew Milne wasn't legiti-mate from day one,' says Lowenthal.[1]

As it turned out, Lowenthal's instincts were spot on. In 2000, Milne started his own investment fund called the PSC Guaranteed Growth Fund. It immediately seemed fishy. One red flag, for example, was that Milne wouldn't reveal how his PSC Guaranteed Growth Fund was making apparently supersonic returns for his investors. Milne doggedly refused to say which shares his fund had invested in – information that would have allowed people to stress test his model. When he was asked, Milne replied that it was a competitive secret.

But despite the fact that the PSC fund was as transparent as cement, more than 4 000 investors shunted R250 million into it, blindly trusting Milne. Which proves that long before Barry Tannenbaum was operating, a fool and his money were always itching to part ways.[2]

In the end, it turned out there was a damn good reason why Milne wouldn't reveal how his PSC Guaranteed Growth Fund made cash. The fund, it turned out, contained exactly two shares – Tigon and Shawcell, both companies listed on the JSE by the slippery but charismatic Pietermaritzburg businessman Gary Porritt.

Worse, the PSC fund was the engine room for one of the most epic frauds to smack the South African stock market, all made possible thanks to Milne's complicity.

Milne had lied by claiming in PSC's prospectus that the fund would invest in a 'wide range' of shares, bonds and other investments. Instead, by investing in just two, Tigon and Shawcell, PSC was an elaborate fraud set up to boost the share prices of Porritt's companies.

This is how it worked: Milne, as Porritt's stooge, was simply taking investors' cash and, through a series of front companies owned by Porritt, putting in buy orders for shares in Tigon and Shawcell. When people are pumping so much cash into buying shares, the stock price inevitably climbs – creating the illusion of wealth.

PSC's investors saw great returns for a while, but when there's no more cash coming in to finance new buy orders, the shares stop climbing in value. Then, when people want their money out and the sell orders start piling up, there's a crash. It was as inevitable as morning.

In December 2002, Gary Porritt was arrested and later charged with 3 160 counts of fraud. His lieutenant, Sue Bennett, was arrested a few weeks later. PSC Guaranteed Growth capsized, drowning more than a few of its 4 000 investors.[3]

Milne freaked. He packed a rucksack and fled from his small farm, north of Johannesburg, into hiding. It took journalist Vernon Wessels weeks to track him down to a small cottage a million miles from anywhere. But when he opened the door to Wessels, Milne broke down and confessed to everything.

'The idea to start PSCGG came from Porritt,' Milne said. 'Not all the funds went into Tigon shares, and Porritt, without my knowledge, began moving the funds into the Tigon general account and, I suspect, used the money to finance his acquisition spree ... I began to juggle the market to keep as many sellers happy as possible.'[4]

Under Milne, PSC Guaranteed Growth had become nothing less than a pyramid scheme, secretly supporting one company. So it came as no great surprise, except to his most hardened acolytes, who refused to believe it was possible, when, in February 2004, Milne pleaded guilty to fraud as part of a plea bargain with the prosecutors.

He was sentenced to five years in jail, a sentence he spent in Krugersdorp, the small town west of Joburg where Barry Tannenbaum was born. Barely ten months later, Jack Milne was paroled. He didn't have to spend a single Christmas behind bars. More than a decade later, Gary Porritt has yet to be tried.[5]

Nonetheless, the Tigon and Jack Milne story remains one of South Africa's headline investment frauds. And right from the start, one man who didn't trust a thing Milne said was Lowenthal.

Which makes it ironic that a decade later, Lowenthal was conned into investing in a pyramid scheme himself, reeled in by Darryl Leigh, whom he had known for decades, and Tannenbaum, whom he first met in the early 1980s.

'I've known Darryl for about thirty years,' says Lowenthal. 'We both had boats at the Vaal Dam. We got on well together, we spent a lot of time together.'[6]

Over drinks one day, Darryl mentioned to Lowenthal that he and a few well-chosen friends had this sensational investment opportunity. Magnanimously, Darryl said he would try to get Lowenthal into this inner circle too, if he was keen.

Howard wasn't sure, though. The scheme seemed to be working all right, but there were some pretty pertinent questions that needed answering before he would plug in anything. So Darryl invited him to one of his famous 'investor breakfasts' to meet Barry to discuss the mechanics of the scheme.

'It didn't make sense to me that we'd effectively be lending to Tannenbaum,' Lowenthal says. 'I mean, why wouldn't we just lend directly to Frankel? But Darryl's answer was that Tannenbaum was only a 50 per cent partner in Frankel, and so by lending to him directly, Barry would be getting a greater share of the profit. Which made sense to me.'

So Lowenthal gave Leigh R1 million to invest. 'A few weeks later, like clockwork, I got back R1 050 000. So, I went in again. Soon, I was just rolling the capital, and taking the interest.'

It confounded his expectations, but the scheme was clicking over perfectly, just as it had been sold to him. So Howard introduced his father, Norman, the one-time chairman of the JSE.

Their involvement was a handy trump card for the scheme's promoters. Investors would later describe how Rees and Leigh would boast that Norman Lowenthal was involved. It was a windfall of instant credibility. After all, if your scheme is supported by the man who ran the JSE, the symbol and citadel of South African investments, how could it *not* be safe? Investors reasoned that this Lowenthal guy surely must know more than them, and if he was satisfied, who were they to question it?

This isn't to say that everything Norman Lowenthal touched turned to gold. 'I've got no issues with Norman,' says Sasfin Securities deputy chairman David Shapiro, 'but before the market collapse in 1987, Norman's company put a lot of crap on the market. But all of us listed rubbish back then. None of us were that discerning. It's just how things were.'[7] While some of the companies that the Lowenthal's listed might have folded, others prospered – including Shapiro's employer, Sasfin Bank.

But back in the 1980s, investment was less technical in the wild west mining town that was Joburg at the time. Then, investing was more of a poker game, with insider knowledge being traded over brandy in smoky rooms at the stately Rand Club on the corner of Commissioner and Harrison streets – a 'gentlemen's club' founded by Cecil Rhodes in 1887, which, after much furious debate, reluctantly opened its doors to women in 1989.

The Rand Club is the kind of place that still has large oil paintings of England's monarchs, the place where Rudyard Kipling and Winston Churchill used to retreat after a day in the dust to reconnect with the essence of Mother England. Anachronistically, a portrait of Nelson Mandela hangs uncomfortably opposite that of Queen Elizabeth. A bust of former ANC leader Albert Luthuli is plonked next to one of Paul Kruger, the Boer who caused all the trouble for the British at the turn of the twentieth century. You can imagine neither would have been particularly happy with the arrangement.[8]

Back in the 1980s, it was a different investment world. You couldn't hop onto Google to trace the dividend history of Apple's stock or price-to-earnings ratios. Every month, fly-by-night companies were raising cash by listing shares on the JSE, and then subsequently folding. That's how the game worked.

Aware of what can go wrong in an investment scheme, Norman Lowenthal and his son played it relatively safe with Barry Tannenbaum, at least early on.

Says Howard: 'I was very conservative. I kept taking out the interest and re-investing the capital, so in the end, I only lost about 5 per cent.'

By the time the scheme collapsed, Howard Lowenthal had invested R2 million, as had his father. In all, they had been paid R1.9 million in interest, so even though they hadn't been repaid their capital, they weren't too badly injured.

But the really nasty surprise for Lowenthal, the cobra in the sock drawer, only emerged after the scheme was exposed. The surprise was that while Tannenbaum may have been the first to swindle Lowenthal out of money, the 'authorities' appointed to clean up the wreckage were going to extort even more.

Already brutalised by Barry, the investors were now in for a real thrashing.

* * *

In every corporate calamity there are vultures circling, about to make it a whole lot worse for anyone unlucky enough to be trapped under the carcass.

As soon as the Tannenbaum bubble burst, the sleazy undertakers of corporate South Africa slithered out of their holes.

First to descend were the ambulance-chasing lawyers. Desperate investors who had already lost their money were cold-called by shady attorneys, offering to act on a contingency basis to recover their cash. They would whisper to these investors that if they could get their friends to sign up too, then the odds of getting cash back would be greater.

Right behind the litigators were the liquidators, sensing a pot of gold at the end of a R12.5-billion rainbow. Within days of the news that Tannenbaum's estate was being sequestrated, there was a mad scramble within liquidation circles for the right to act as trustee on his estate – 'trustee' being just a fancy word for liquidator.

Liquidations in South Africa are traditionally a rotten business. Baggage handlers at Joburg's O.R. Tambo International Airport, who run criminal syndicates flogging what they can steal from your luggage, would blush at the tactics of some of South Africa's liquidators. Tattooed tow-truck drivers have to make fewer moral compromises on a daily basis.

It works like this: if you can get enough support from those owed money by an estate – say, investors owed millions by Tannenbaum – then you can ask the master of the High Court to appoint you as a liquidator, or trustee, to that estate. It ends up being an undignified race to chase creditors to give you a signed requisition, supporting your appointment as liquidator.

The good news is, that's the hard work done. Once you are in the door, once you have been appointed as a liquidator to an estate, the cash just starts bucketing in: for every moveable item he sells, like machinery or furniture, the liquidator pockets 10 per cent; for anything immoveable he sells, like a building, for example, he pockets 3 per cent.

In the Tannenbaum case, the trustees appointed to sequestrate his estate would first try to track down as much cash as possible to divide among all those owed money by him. The taxman is always at the front of the queue, but then all those investors owed money would typically get to share the rest.

But with R10 billion at stake with Tannenbaum, the dash to be appointed as trustee of the most high-profile investment disaster in the country was even less dignified than the usual stand-on-your-grandmother tactics used by liquidators.

Enver Motala, a liquidator who had a close relationship with former justice minister Penuel Maduna and scored a bucketload of lucrative liquidation jobs at the time, was quick to poke his snout out.

Days after the scheme was exposed, a group of about 150 investors met at the offices of forensic investigator Steve Harcourt-Cooke, desperate for some coordinated plan to track down their cash. Immediately after that meeting, Motala called Harcourt-Cooke, telling him to hand over the names of the investors.

Motala, mercifully, wasn't appointed to Tannenbaum's estate. Good thing too, considering that two years later, he would be struck off the roll of liquidators when it turned out he had been convicted on one count of theft and ninety-two counts of fraud back in 1978. In fact, it turned out that Motala wasn't even his real name: it was Dawood. He had had his name legally changed in 1981, presumably so the criminal charges wouldn't emerge.

You couldn't make it up: in 2012, Motala then applied for a presidential pardon from President Jacob Zuma, parlaying the sort of outrageous explanation for the fraud charges that his outlandish situation demanded. According to the *Mail & Guardian*, Motala's plea was that he had taken the rap for an activist uncle, Advocate Yusuf Patel, who had used a stolen credit card to get cash so he could escape the apartheid government.[9]

Motala apparently wrote in his petition to Zuma: 'Patel was a practising advocate at the time and intimately involved in the struggle for a free and democratic South Africa – following his arrest and brief detention, he was convicted of defeating the ends of justice and sentenced to undergo four years' imprisonment. He had committed these offences as part of the struggle.'[10]

Motala wasn't the only liquidator chasing the Tannenbaum case. Many sleaze-bags put on their ambulance-chasing boots, aware of how much money was involved.

Eventually, the Tannenbaum trustees were appointed: lawyer Shirish Kalian, KPMG veteran Gavin Gainsford and Vincent Matsepe were mandated as joint liquidators.

They set about tracing the cash, first hiring Harcourt-Cooke. He was the right choice: a smart, streetwise certified fraud examiner, Harcourt-Cooke had designed the only pyramid scheme 'reconciliation' system, which he used to track down every investor and every cent that had changed hands in the Krion scam. It was his evidence that helped convince the judge to sentence Krion mastermind Marietjie Prinsloo to twenty-five years behind bars in 2010.

'In the Krion case, these were all poor whites from the Vaal Triangle region,' Harcourt-Cooke explains. 'In the Tannenbaum case, it was far more complex. There were many rich people, some of who made a lot of money out of it, and with lawyers who were happy to help them hide the cash, it was a lot trickier.'[11]

Thankfully, the cops had at least woken up for this case. The government task team, made up of five law-enforcement groups, was by now trying to put together a workable case they could use to extradite Tannenbaum.

Of course, each agency approached it from a different angle. The Financial Intelligence Centre wanted to know how Tannenbaum had skirted the freshly minted money-laundering laws; the Reserve Bank was keen on finding out how he had dodged exchange controls; the police's serious economic offences unit had to pull together the evidence; the National Prosecuting Authority had to prepare the case; and the revenue service, SARS, well, they just wanted to see what tax they could grab from the rich white folks who seemed to have too much cash and not enough sense.

This task team appealed to investors to come forward with information. It suggested that investors lodge suspicious-transaction reports with the Financial Intelligence Centre. As ever, they were one step behind events, and two steps behind Tannenbaum and Rees.

Four years later, the law-enforcement authorities are still tripping over their own tail, talking tough about extraditing Tannenbaum and Rees, and issuing warrants of arrest that have yet to be served on anyone.

* * *

If it sounds like the net was closing, it was: but only on the investors who had already been fleeced. The big guns had been dusted off and loaded – but their sights were trained on the hedgehogs, because the foxes had long since fled.

To the bleeding investors, it was soon pretty clear that the trustees, the taxman and the police were all just looking for a piece of the smaller investors, looking to take a bite out of the easy meat. Neither the trustees, nor the taxman nor the police, it seemed, had the appetite, or perhaps the ability, to net the real culprits. Perhaps it was just too hard.

The first unsettling indication that the liquidators wouldn't exactly be seeking to track down investors' money from the real culprits emerged almost immediately after Kalian, Gainsford and Matsepe were appointed.

The trustees first turned their eye on charities to which Dean Rees had donated about R2 million before he left for Switzerland. Rees had given R25 000 to the Johannesburg School for the Blind, Low Vision and Multiple Disability Children, and made numerous other donations – including to a centre for abused women and children in Krugersdorp.

Yet, Kalian told *Bloomberg News* that 'if we find, eventually, that whatever monies those charities received were from ill-gotten gains, then investors would require us to go and get the money back – even if it sounds morally repugnant'.[12]

Kalian said that the trustees would be 'shot down by investors' if they didn't try to retrieve this money, though he added that the odds of the trustees seeking to raid the charities were 'remote at this stage'.[13]

Which is an odd justification. Investors would surely begrudge the liquidators far more for holding endless 'inquiries' – paid for out of what is eventually recovered – than they would for losing R25 000 in Ponzi money to a charity for blind children.

The blind school was started in 2003 by the Children of Fire charity, which itself was set up to help children who had been badly burnt. It started thanks to British geologist Bronwen Jones, who met a young girl called Dorah Mokoena, who had been savagely burnt in a squatter-camp fire when only seven months old.[14]

Dorah's story is heartbreaking: three hospitals turned her away, convinced she would die, and partly because of the delay in getting treated, she lost her nose, eyelids, lips and bones in her hands and forehead. After the child was abandoned by her mother, the doctors wanted to remove her eyes in 1997 because they said she was blind, and the dressings used to protect her eyes were too expensive. But a British campaign in *The Times* to raise cash saved her eyes, and this is how Children of Fire began.[15]

Bronwen Jones described Rees's donation as 'really kind of him', saying 'it helped us to continue'. The school and the charity, she said, were 'on the brink' of collapse.[16]

Four years later, the blind school remains open, which is good news for the children who are accepted when, according to the school's website, 'government can't or won't teach' them. It seems to have survived, no thanks to the trustees.[17]

* * *

'Morally repugnant' would be exactly the way to describe the trustees demanding they be repaid this money. 'This is them coming to stab the wounded,' Lowenthal says, from his small broking and trading office in Oxford Road, Rosebank.[18]

Framed on the walls of Lowenthal's office are original share certificates for South Africa's first listed companies, dating back to the early 1900s. Back when times were simpler, and you saw a man's factory before you gave him your cash.

'There are three silos – the liquidators, the tax authorities, and the criminal authorities – and all three of them have just been trying to screw over the investors right from the start,' he says.

When the trustees were first appointed, they spoke bravely of getting the Ponzi money back for the investors. No mention was made at the time that the very people they would be targeting for this cash would be the investors themselves.

The trustees first needed to get a handle on where the money was, and who had got what. So they appointed Alec Brooks, a veteran of companies gone bust, to track the cash.

Brooks had had plenty of experience in this field: he was the lawyer who had tried to track down the R161 million belonging to the 4 000 investors of Jack Milne's PSC Guaranteed Growth Fund on behalf of the liquidators of Milne's fund. Brooks spent many days grilling Tigon's boss, Gary Porritt, about where PSC's cash had gone, but it was fruitless. Porritt ran rings around him and, more than a decade after Milne's fund crashed, investors still haven't seen a cent.

You could argue that PSC was an exceptional case. But the truth is, it wasn't the first time lawyers and liquidators ended up collecting big fees from the estate, while the investors ended up with nothing.

Brooks admits today that no funds were recovered for PSC investors in the two years he worked for the estate. But he points out that he agreed to act on a contingency basis, so he would only have got paid if he'd recovered cash for investors – which he didn't.[19]

'Accordingly, I acted for free for nearly two years, which included 39 trips to Pietermaritzburg [from Johannesburg],' he says. 'The investors only paid for disbursements.'

Brooks argues that the information he got from Porritt in the inquiries did help the investors, but because the PSC liquidators ran out of cash, they couldn't take Porritt to court.

In the Tannenbaum case, the liquidation inquiry ran for months, and some investors whispered conspiratorially that they were sure the lawyers were string-ing it out inordinately long so they could levy big fees on the estate. Of course, it's difficult to say for sure. Neither the trustees nor Brooks would answer any questions about the Tannenbaum liquidation, almost going out of their way to stymie any press inquiries.

But from the outside, it appeared that rather than going for the real culprits, Kalian, Gainsford and Brooks concentrated on the small fry. Investors were sub-poenaed and grilled in front of a commissioner at Alec Brooks's law office in Rosebank. Every tedious detail was examined as the hours ticked past.

Some of the big investors refused to cooperate. If you had made R100 million, you could simply ignore Brooks's subpoena. But if you had made R1 000, you were sure to be hauled to the offices of Brooks & Brand, and grilled for hours.

'I called him a thug to his face, and the guy from KPMG,' says Lowenthal today. 'I told him you're unethical.'

It was a common sentiment. 'I heard at least six investors refer to Brooks as a bully,' says another person who sat through many of the hearings.

And every day that went past, the lawyers clocked up another bill – an account that would be settled from any money recovered supposedly for investors. Screwed over once by Tannenbaum, many felt they had been screwed over again.

Brooks used section 29 of the Insolvency Act, which provides for liquida-tors to demand repayment of any amount paid by the estate in the six months before sequestration. So, if Tannenbaum had paid anything whatsoever to anyone between February and July 2009, Brooks demanded they repay it.

This infuriated some of the investors: already out of pocket as their capital had not been repaid, they were then ordered to repay any smaller 'interest' pay-ments they might have got.

Howard Lowenthal had one bad-tempered meeting with KPMG trustee Gavin Gainsford and Brooks. 'I told them, I'm a creditor to the estate because Tannenbaum owes me R2 million for the capital I put in. The R1.9 million I got back was the interest I was owed. Brooks said to me, "Nonsense, in fact you're a debtor to the estate, you owe us".'[20]

Brooks then demanded R1.3 million from Lowenthal, for what was paid to him in the six months before Tannenbaum's estate was sequestrated. A furious Lowenthal refused.

Some investors owed cash by Tannenbaum – creditors to the estate – were told to pitch up at the 'first meeting of creditors' on 3 February 2010. Only thing is, not all the investors were told about all these meetings – Lowenthal, for one, wasn't – so he didn't arrive to lodge a claim for the R2 million owed him.

It reeked of a determined effort to sideline people who might ask for a share of any loot recovered, he says.

Instead, the Lowenthals were told (by a registered letter sent by KPMG) that a creditors' meeting would take place on 16 March, so that people owed money by Barry could then lodge their claim. Fingers crossed, if any money were recovered, those who had lodged their claims would get a portion of their cash back – even if it was 10 cents for every rand they were owed.

When the Lowenthals pitched up at that March meeting, they were shocked to discover that all claims against the estate had already been voted on at the general meeting that had taken place in February. KPMG's James Galloway apologised for 'any inconvenience that the creditors may suffer as a result'.

Not that it mattered, said Brooks, because the Lowenthals were debtors – they actually owed Tannenbaum money, not the other way round – so their claims could be rejected. The official who headed the inquiry simply took Brooks's word, dutifully snuffing out the Lowenthals' claim without a second glance. Despite the fact that they had made a R100 000 loss.

This seemingly arbitrary decision appears to have closed the door on the Lowenthals getting their cash back. Norman Lowenthal was so incensed by the way in which KPMG acted (the firm that employs Gainsford and Galloway) that he wrote to KPMG's then chairman in New York, Timothy Flynn.

The letter creates the impression that KPMG, Kalian, Matsepe and their lawyer, Brooks, tried to extort whatever cash they could from investors, while going out of their way to stop any claims being lodged against the estate.

Lowenthal says the error about the dates, where he hadn't been told about the first creditors' meeting in February but only the meeting a month later, 'must be a remarkable error for a firm of your standing'.

He writes: 'Your claim that we are debtors is total nonsense ... Our records clearly show that we are creditors, not debtors. We are extremely surprised that you could even contemplate such an assertion, as you are a highly respected and competent accounting organisation.'

KPMG were having none of it, basically ignoring Lowenthal's protestations. Brooks took the Lowenthals to court, demanding repayment of the R1.3 million to the estate. Eventually, they settled with the trustees, paying them less than that. But it still left a bitter taste.[21]

Speaking today, Lowenthal says the most absurd thing about this case is that Tannenbaum himself – the man who cooked up the scheme – could end up making a mint from the investors, thanks to the way the trustees have handled the matter.

'Barry could end up very rich, this time legally,' he says. 'Because the trustees prevented most of the investors who were owed money from registering their "claims" on what is recovered, there's only a small group who will get to divide what is recovered. If there is any extra money, it gets returned to the insolvent – in other words, Barry.'

Perhaps the most telling indicator of the spirit in which Brooks and the trustees ran the inquiry was that of the 200 investors subpoenaed to give evidence, it seems that more than 90 per cent of them apparently initially refused to settle and repay the estate. Even after a further round of what was described as 'out-and-out bullying', there were still indomitable investors holding out against the lawyers' letters and threatening phone calls.

So Kalian, Gainsford and Matsepe took many of them to court, often for tiny sums. Hilton Anthony, a businessman who runs an office-furniture company, was dragged to court to get him to repay R56 500. Just the cost of defending the case would have been much more.

Jody Bloch, a widow living in Johannesburg's Victory Park, was summonsed to the same court for R215 000.[22]

Accountant Leslie Sher, for example, had invested R850 000 with Tannenbaum, and was repaid only R770 000. Nonetheless, the trustees went to the High Court demanding he repay R670 000 of it. Sher mounted an ingenious defence. First, he argued that Tannenbaum had given him a 'gift', and, second, that because the NPA had obtained an order in the High Court against Leigh, the trustees couldn't take any action until the criminal case was finalised.[23]

Other investors hauled to court argued that the court that sequestrated Tannenbaum in the first place, at Chris Leppan's request, didn't have the jurisdiction to do that.

Mark Harris, who invested R3.59 million with Tannenbaum and appears to have been repaid R32.1 million, even cheekily lodged a counterclaim, saying that because he lent money to Tannenbaum, the estate must now repay that 'together with interest of 15.5 per cent'.

You can just imagine that Brooks was not amused.

While giving testimony in court against Dean Rees in October 2013, Brooks detailed how the trustees had actually been very conscious of the costs and had many off-the-record meetings to 'speed up the process'. Brooks said that '90 per cent of the investors were helpful and cooperated with the process'.

It's difficult to say where the truth really lay. Certainly none of the investors would have been charmed at having to hand back any cash they'd got. Their view of Brooks and the trustees would have been tempered by that. But at the same time, some of their complaints about the lack of transparency and legal threats would have riled many people – whether they were investors or not.

In some cases, the trustees' demands even seemed perverse. This is neatly illustrated by the case of Mark Read, the curator and owner of arguably the country's top art gallery, the Everard Read Gallery, in Rosebank, Johannesburg.

'I was flabbergasted by what they can do,' says Read, speaking today. 'Do you know that if a Tannenbaum investor had gone and bought a Mercedes-Benz, for example, that car dealership can be approached and told to give back the money, even though they'd never heard of Barry Tannenbaum?'[24]

What had happened was this: one of Tannenbaum's investors, who had coined it, took a stroll through Read's gallery and decided he wanted to buy a piece of art worth R1 million. But he put it like this: rather than me paying you directly, why don't you invoice this company that owes me money, called Frankel, and they'll pay you?

'It turned out that I was charging a Tannenbaum company,' says Read. 'If someone had asked me what a Ponzi scheme was back then, I would have said I haven't the faintest idea.'

Read was summoned to Brooks's 'inquiry', and told he had to repay the R1 million. Not a chance, swore Read: this can't be legal. Yet it was: even his own lawyer conceded that he would lose the fight. So he reached a settlement with Kalian and Brooks, repaying them R600 000. He remains bitter: 'It was just unbelievable. It means that, if you take it to its most ridiculous conclusion, you could go to the corner cafe, and demand they give you money they were paid because it was stolen Ponzi money.'

Luckily for Read, the investor who had bought his painting had done other business with the gallery. So when he later asked the gallery to wrap one of the other pieces he had already paid for and send it overseas, Read said no way: 'I told him, you've got more chance of being hit by an iceberg than of me exporting this for you. He wasn't a bad guy – he was a repeat customer for us – but he was maybe just a naive person.'

* * *

Brooks and the liquidators, perhaps you can understand. After all, they get paid depending on how much they get back, so there is an incentive for them to gobble the low-hanging fruit. But KPMG is a company that is supposedly a bastion of upright ethics. It's the corporate equivalent of a Catholic nun. It has a 'code of ethics', a charter of 'values' and a mission statement. On its website, KPMG trumpets a corporate ethos straight out of a governance textbook: 'We lead by example at all levels,' it boasts, adding that 'we respect the individual'. KPMG also pledges to 'seek the facts' first and remain 'open and honest in our communication, sharing information, insight and advice frequently and constructively, and managing tough situations with courage'.[25]

'Above all,' it vows, metaphorical hand on its metaphorical heart, 'we act with integrity.'

'Integrity' isn't a word you'll catch many of the investors using when describing their interaction with KPMG, however. You are more likely to hear words like 'ruthless'.

Former SA Bond Exchange CEO Tom Lawless says KPMG should have been acting on behalf of the investors. Instead, they became debt collectors for the lawyers, leaning on the smaller investors for cash, craning their necks around every bend in the search for carrion. 'They've been making plenty of money in fees, but they won't reveal a thing,' he says. 'I've been asking them to communicate, but the last time I heard from them was two and a half years ago.'[26]

So much for 'open and honest' communication. So much for 'sharing information'.

Though it was Gavin Gainsford from KPMG who was appointed by the court as a trustee, somehow another KPMG employee, James Galloway, managed to manoeuvre his way into the Tannenbaum case.

Galloway's derision for any media query is palpable. 'What you media people don't seem to get is that it is the individuals who are appointed to be the trustees, not KPMG,' he says.[27]

Sure – only Galloway wasn't appointed as a trustee, Gainsford was. So why was he the one contacting the investors, attending the inquiry, and even going on overseas fact-finding missions for the Tannenbaum estate? And if Galloway's suggestion is that KPMG isn't involved, well, KPMG hasn't gone out of its way to keep this distinction intact. Galloway bills himself as a 'senior manager at KPMG' on his LinkedIn profile, yet he also says he has 'been in the profession as a liquidator for forty-three years'.

So who gets the fees? Does KPMG not make *any* money from the Tannenbaum liquidation? This rather hazy distinction isn't clear in the public's mind either. In August 2011, *Business Day* said that 'doubt has been expressed as to the role of KPMG Services as represented by Gavin Gainsford or James Galloway'. The newspaper asked whether Gainsford and Galloway were not both acting as trustees, adding, unhelpfully, that Alec Brooks 'says Gainsford acts for KPMG Services, and that Galloway is his assistant'.[28]

Really? So how does Galloway's claim that Gainsford was appointed as an individual to be a trustee tally with Brooks's answer that KPMG was appointed? And how would Gainsford have decided that it was right that the Tannenbaum estate should pay Galloway too, who, after all, is on the same payroll as him? Surely this would be a conflict of interest? How exactly does it work?

No one will say. The trustees are all media shy. When asked for assistance with this book, the trustees said they 'have taken legal advice from senior counsel' that they should not provide any of the documents at the time.

When asked to clarify the relationship, KPMG's head of communications, Carl Ballot, ignored the question. Instead, he said KPMG was 'not going to respond to any of your detailed questions' and threatened that 'all our rights are reserved'.[29]

A day later, however, Ballot did provide some scant elucidation, revealing that Gainsford is a director of KPMG, while Galloway is an employee. But he again refused to say whether KPMG made any money from their role in the Tannenbaum estate.[30]

He said 'our choosing not to engage in certain discussions should not be construed as antagonistic, but rather a decision based on sound professional judgment and what we believe to be the most appropriate response'.

This seems a remarkably weak response – unless KPMG is just not able to defend its position. Ballot's explanation is hardly helpful, saying that 'we typically cannot explain or defend our position fully for reasons of client confidentiality'.

So, not very 'transparent', not exactly 'honest and open in our communication'. Which is probably why many investors believe corporate mission statements aren't worth the paper they're written on.

But then perhaps you can understand their skittishness. Gavin Gainsford has, after all, ended up on the wrong side of some media coverage in the past. Gainsford was axed as a liquidator of a mining company called Pamodzi Gold, along with his co-liquidator, Enver Motala (better known now as Enver Dawood). The Department of Justice fired Gainsford and Motala in May 2011 'to safeguard the integrity of the liquidation process, and the company, workers and creditors' after questions were raised about why they had decided to sell Pamodzi's assets to a politically well-connected company called Aurora.[31]

It doesn't take much to guess the reasons for the sale of Pamodzi's assets. Aurora's top brass were political heavyweights and its directors included Michael Hulley (President Jacob Zuma's lawyer), Khulubuse Zuma (the president's nephew) and Mandla Mandela (grandson of Nelson Mandela).

Aurora didn't have the cash to buy the assets, yet Motala and Gainsford let them take control of Pamodzi's mine without any money because they were 'preferred bidders'.

After they were fired as liquidators, Motala raged that it was 'frightening' how the Department of Justice had removed them, calling it 'completely unconstitutional, completely irregular and totally unlawful'.

But far more frightening was what happened to the Pamodzi mines under Gainsford and Motala. After they handed over control to Aurora, the mines were stripped, employees weren't paid, and one mine worker committed suicide – this while Aurora's owners led flash lives and donated money to the ruling party, the ANC.[32]

When Gainsford was asked about Aurora, he refused to answer, instead directing all inquiries to KPMG's communications czar, Carl Ballot. Which seems a pretty farcical thing to do, considering that KPMG is adamant that trustees like Gainsford are appointed in their personal capacity, and the company isn't involved.[33]

Well, it turns out that KPMG *does* get involved in estates if the heat on their 'independent agents' like Gainsford gets too high. Then they can, it seems, step up.

So Ballot answered for Gainsford: 'The legal dispute concerning the removal of Gainsford as a liquidator was amicably settled … it had become clear that

Gavin's removal had been [the result of] a misunderstanding by him as to the requirement to answer the Master's inquiries, which was then clarified.' The master of the court continues to 'hold Gavin in high regard and in good standing', he said.

Unlike investors in the Tannenbaum estate, who feel rather differently.

Kalian has also faced some heat. In 2013 he was accused of theft and fraud by Anglo Platinum, the world's largest platinum-mining company, for his role in the alleged disappearance of R30.8 million, which was meant to be used to buy property. Rustenburg Platinum Mines, a joint venture between Anglo Platinum and Royal Bafokeng, had placed the cash in the trust account of the practice that Kalian shared with another lawyer. But when Rustenburg Platinum asked for it to be repaid, only R10.8 million was returned.[34]

Though investors angry with the Tannenbaum case frequently point to this incident as evidence that the trustees aren't to be trusted, it's a red herring.

It was Kalian's partner who was the one in charge of Anglo Platinum's money, not him. 'I appeared before the Law Society and was found not guilty, and my name was cleared,' says Kalian. 'The partnership was terminated soon after I became aware of the alleged misappropriation.'[35]

The full story on Aurora is still to be told. Nevertheless, the case underscores the fact that liquidations are a notoriously filthy business, blemished with vested interests and accusations of the worst kind.

The Tannenbaum liquidation was probably no worse than the rest. But it illustrates that investors couldn't exactly be faulted for believing the trustees were only looking after themselves.

* * *

If you survived a skirmish with the trustees and you still had your shirt, there was always the next challenge: the tax authority, SARS.

Tom Lawless might be furious with KPMG, but he's equally scathing about the taxman's role in turning the screws on the smaller investors. 'KPMG have behaved very badly,' he says. 'And SARS, well SARS went beyond being completely unethical and outrageous.'

Perhaps predictably, the taxman has few friends among the top brass of corporate South Africa. But in the Tannenbaum case, SARS moved one notch lower in the estimation of the investors by behaving, as one investor put it, 'in a way that was nothing less than outrageous'.

What didn't help is that SARS apparently changed its mind on how to tax the investors. First, it sent a letter to all investors saying they would only be taxed if they were a 'net winner' – in other words, if they'd made money from Tannenbaum.

The letter came from SARS team leader for investigations, Molibinyane

Makwakwa, who told at least one investor on 9 December 2009 that some people 'made a huge profit from the scheme and others incurred huge losses'.[36]

SARS said that people would only have to pay tax on the capital gains: 'For example, a taxpayer who paid R100 000 into the scheme and received a net amount of R150 000 from the scheme will be assessed on the R50 000.'

SARS added that people who 'received less than the capital amount paid into it, at this point in time ... will not be taxed on any amount received from the scheme'. Essentially, if you lost money on the scheme, you won't have to pay tax.

It might seem weird that tax even comes up in the context of a Ponzi scheme, which is, after all, illegal. But this was the legal position after Krion, where the Supreme Court said that investors still had to pay tax 'notwithstanding that the scheme was illegal'.

Sure, if you had made a profit from the scheme, you might end up in a tricky position: first, the taxman would claim his cut, and then the liquidators would also demand their cash back. But at least SARS wasn't going to hit you for tax if you had lost money overall. Which seemed fair enough.

Then SARS changed its mind.

In December 2012, three years after its first letter to investors, SARS manager Elle-Sarah Rossato sent another letter to some investors: 'SARS considers that the amounts received from the scheme for 2007 to 2010 tax period constitute an income receipt' – but then added that these 'receipts' should not be 'of a capital nature'.[37]

This was far more serious for investors. This meant that even if Tannenbaum didn't repay your initial capital, investors would still be taxed on what they had been paid out – even if they were net losers.

Practically, if you had invested R1 million, and had only been repaid R600 000 in interest, you would still be taxed about 40 per cent of that R600 000 'income' – about R240 000. Never mind that you're R400 000 down. Sure, you could offset your capital losses against your capital gains – but at a much lower tax rate.

Bottom line – you'd still be screwed over.

SARS's decision to treat the Tannenbaum cash as 'income' rather than 'capital' is problematic, not least because, if it was just a scam all along and there was no real business, then how could anyone have made any 'income'? Surely it was just the same money being recycled?

So why did the taxman change tack? Predictably, each investor had a theory, the malevolence of which depended on his or her own animosity towards the tax authorities.

The most prominent theory revolved around the fact that SARS isn't collecting the amount of tax it used to get from the public, as more people are unemployed and the economy has slowed to a tortoise crawl. At the same time, more and more people are being supported by social-welfare grants.

About fifteen million South Africans get some form of grant – because they are old or poor, have lost their jobs or have never had one in the first place. That's nearly one in three South Africans on welfare, and a sixfold increase since 1996, when only 2.4 million people got welfare. And the number of taxpayers isn't growing as fast as the number of people on welfare. The non-profit Institute of Race Relations points out that in 2001, there were on average 3.3 taxpayers for every person on welfare; twelve years later, there are more people getting grants than taxpayers.[38]

How do you finance this deficit? Tax. Companies pay more; individuals pay more; Tannenbaum's rich victims pay more.

SARS manager Elle-Sarah Rossato says the tax authority's processes have never been driven by social or community economic situations. '[The complaints] sound more like disgruntled taxpayers, who invested in an illegal scheme and thought they would not be taxed on the receipts,' she says. 'SARS is purely fulfilling its legislative mandate of collecting taxes. Nothing more nothing less.'

Something had to give. If you listen to Tannenbaum's investors, they will say it was common sense and equity. 'SARS are behaving like any agency that has run short of revenue, taking on all the little guys, rather than the people they should be going after,' says Lawless.

Lawless was forced to sell some of his investments to repay the taxman, even though he disagreed with their assessment. 'They've been pretty close to ruthless,' he says. 'I had to pay them eventually after they threatened me repeatedly. I lodged an objection, but I had to pay them.'

Howard Lowenthal's case eloquently highlights the perverse result. Having invested R2 million each, he and his father Norman each got back R1.9 million. Already R100 000 in the red, Gainsford and the trustees then hit them for another chunk of cash for what they got back in the last six months before the scheme went bust. Then SARS came knocking, and wrestled another payment from each of them for tax on their 'income' of R1.9 million.

Add in the R250 000 they paid to hire lawyers, and Howard and Norman Lowenthal are suddenly more than R1 million down – a loss exceeding R2 million for the family.

It seems iniquitous. But Johann van Loggerenberg, SARS's head of investigations, says the tax authority did not change its mind – nor did SARS decide to arbitrarily nail the rich.

'From word go, we stated that the position of SARS was that the investors were afforded the opportunity upfront to come to us and disclose everything,' he says. 'Their behaviour in doing so would dictate the consequences they face. Anyone who ended up in a fight with us, it's a fair bet they didn't disclose what they should have in the beginning.'[39]

Van Loggerenberg says the principle did not change: 'All we tried to do in the second letter was clarify the position. We did so because it became apparent in our interactions with some of those who came forward that SARS's position was not clearly understood. Different people had different interpretations.'

What complicated things, he says, was people invested over multiple tax years. 'So if you receive a payment in one year, you're taxed on that as gross income,' he says. '[Investors'] obligation is to report their gains or losses per year to SARS.'

Those who now feel aggrieved, he says, were precisely those people who failed to declare the Ponzi-scheme income in the relevant years: 'It only became an issue when SARS came knocking after the scheme collapsed. Had that not happened, they would have happily continued to benefit and not declare the income to SARS.'

Van Loggerenberg is also adamant that SARS's position is the right legal position, as established in the Krion case. None of the investors, he points out, challenged the tax authority in court.

Most of the investors, says Van Loggerenberg, sorted out their tax affairs pretty smartly. 'It was almost the reverse of a Ponzi scheme,' he says. 'As soon as the first guy came forward, and investors saw the consequences weren't too dire, there were queues at our office.'

And it was easy to see exactly who had put what amount into Tannenbaum's scheme. This made it very different from Krion, a scheme where a lot of poor South Africans had given Marietjie Prinsloo and her agents hard cash to invest. With Barry, the sophistication of his investors and the fact that many of them insisted on acknowledgements of debt and post-dated cheques, made it pretty easy for SARS to trace everyone.

But it left a sour taste in the mouth for many investors. Says Howard Lowenthal: 'They must just see a bunch of rich white Jewish guys, and think, well, let's just get whatever we can. What SARS should have done is said, "Look, you guys who made a loss on an illegal scheme, we'll leave you alone. The ones who made a profit, we'll tax those."'

One of the wealthiest people conned by Barry says he told SARS that it had effectively become just an extension of the Ponzi scheme. 'I told them, you guys know now that there was no underlying business making any real money, yet you're taxing this as if we'd made income? You're pretending it was a real business – you're just part of the Ponzi.'

* * *

In 2013 SARS finished its investigation into Tannenbaum's affairs and his 'illegal multiplication investment scheme' for the years 2004 to 2009.

For investors, it wasn't nice – mainly because the taxman is first in line to hoover up whatever is left in an estate. This meant that Brooks, Kalian, Gainsford and Matsepe would have to first pay tax from Barry's estate, then divide up whatever was left for the investors.

'SARS's findings are that [Tannenbaum] grossly underdeclared his taxable income ... during the relevant years,' wrote Pieter Engelbrecht, the coordinator for financial investigations at SARS. (Engelbrecht had also addressed the letter to KPMG's James Galloway. SARS must have also assumed he was appointed as a liquidator.)

Engelbrecht said that Tannenbaum had failed to declare 'taxable income' of a staggering R444.7 million. This was made up of R152.1 million, which was the difference between what investors paid him and what he had paid out, and a R292.6 million increase in his 'net assets'.

SARS has developed a reputation for squeezing people who 'under-declare' their income by even a few thousand rands. So imagine the giddy joy of a tax inspector who discovers that somebody has failed to reveal an extra R444.7 million.

So the taxman said that Barry owed R177.9 million on that amount. Add in penalties of 200 per cent of the sum, interest and some other bits and pieces, and Tannenbaum's total tax bill came to a spine-chilling R747.9 million.

But what was intriguing was SARS's revelation that there was a R152 million difference between the R3 160 million that 'investors' had ploughed into his bank accounts, and the R3 008 million he had paid out to them.

This suggests that the story that poor, impoverished Barry didn't make a cent from the scheme, while Rees and Leigh pillaged investors' funds, is yet another fairy tale. It suggests that Barry either blew an immense amount of cash, or he siphoned that cash into other accounts.

The SARS assessment provides an alluring, if flawed, analysis of how much money flowed in and out of Barry's scheme. Flawed, partly because the tax authorities only analysed what happened in South Africa, which meant that investors like Meir Levin, Avin Lieberman and others, who were paid in other countries, were not included in the calculation.

Flawed also because certain investors have taken serious exception to some of SARS's figures. Arnold Sharp, for one, the director of First Tech, continues to vehemently deny that he was paid out R884 million.

The trustees did score one major coup for investors, however, which should temper the rabid criticism of their antics.

In September 2013, SARS drastically lowered its assessment of what Barry's estate owed, reducing it from R747.9 million to R32 million. 'That was a major settlement for the estate,' says one person who was part of the negotiations with the taxman. 'Some of the SARS estimates were incorrect and there was double counting. In the end though, a settlement of R32 million is far less than SARS initially wanted, and means there's more money in the estate for investors.'

Or for the lawyers. Nonetheless, the fact that SARS eventually agreed to take about one-twentieth of its initial R747.9 million tax bill is some mighty concession.

But it also means that investors will be justifiably fuming if they end up paying more to SARS than Barry's estate had to. Tannenbaum was the guy who, after all, had taken all their cash.

Luckily for the investors, SARS has not hit any of them with criminal charges for either dodging tax or fraud – though Tannenbaum, Rees and Leigh won't escape this fate.

'This was an understanding we had with the investors. And we have stuck to it,' explains Van Loggerenberg.[40]

Nonetheless, Van Loggerenberg has some harsh words for the investors: 'Probably the biggest indictment on most of the investors is the way in which they were so keen to invest to begin with on the basis of a very flimsy prospectus and scant detail of what exactly they were investing in. In interviews with investors afterwards, I asked them this question – why would you invest so much into something that so little is known of or demonstrated to you? None were able to explain it to me. I saw a lot of bowed heads and blushing faces when I asked this.'

Greed, he says, remains the driving force. 'Tannembaum's scheme was not the first such scheme and certainly will not be the last in the world. I hope people take a leaf from this and apply greater care and due diligence in future when they invest their money.'

Not that many of the investors will be thankful for Van Loggerenberg's advice. Many grumble that his institution has simply shafted them. Speak to a few of them and, inevitably, the name Dave King comes up a lot. It would though – there is no more totemic a figure for anti-SARS sentiment than King.

A truculent Scotsman, the son of a former policeman in Glasgow, King came to South Africa in 1976 with only R170 in his pocket. But he made himself a billionaire by listing a company called Specialised Outsourcing on the JSE at 50 cents per share. Then, after the share had rocketed to R70 per share, he aroused the fury of the other investors by secretly selling all his shares in the company.[41]

Unethical, perhaps, but it scored King R1.2 billion. King reckoned that, at the time, this profit was a capital gain, which was essentially tax free. The tax authorities, on the other hand, reckoned it was revenue – taxed at close to 40 per cent.

So King fought. He fought in almost every tribunal in the land, clocking up

322 criminal charges for fraud and tax evasion, and a tax bill (with penalties) of a preposterously immense R2.75 billion. The charge sheet alone ran to thousands of pages – packed into separate boxes, it took up an entire wall in the court.

After eleven years, the NPA still hadn't been able to prove a thing against King, despite having effectively publicly branded him a tax cheat and a crook. So it wasn't surprising that in August 2013, King reached a 'settlement' with the state agencies, agreeing to pay R718 million and plead guilty to forty-one minor tax charges.[42]

After the settlement, King put out a statement saying: 'When this tax dispute arose many years ago, I took a conscious decision not to cooperate with the authorities. That was a mistake. I regret not engaging with the state sooner as I have found them to be extremely firm but fair in their dealings with me.'

No one believed this was really what King thought. Clearly, this 'press statement' had been meant to sugar-coat the authorities' embarrassing retreat. No one bought it.

'Dave King was right,' says one of Tannenbaum's investors, who invested more than R20 million, but didn't want to be named. 'Only the guys with the big bucks can take on SARS. Everyone is living the life of Riley here, except for the smaller investors. Tannenbaum, Rees, even KPMG and Alec Brooks are making money off it. The only ones paying for it all are the investors.'

You have to consider this kind of whinging in its proper context, though. You have to bear in mind that many people who invested with Tannenbaum never planned to pay tax on their investments and were particularly resentful when SARS came knocking at their door. Nobody likes being caught out.

SARS's Van Loggerenberg believes that the wave of anger directed at the tax authority over Tannenbaum is essentially misplaced frustration that the real culprits appear to be getting away with it, and frustration over the fact that the NPA hasn't been seen to be acting against Tannenbaum or Rees, as people would expect.

'From a SARS perspective, no one has got away with anything,' he says. 'It is public record that we have concluded our investigations against Tannenbaum and Rees and assessed them accordingly. We've finished the tax investigation and we know exactly what we're doing – irrespective of what the criminal-justice system is doing.'[43]

He says he understands the investors' frustration. 'Look, it's hard for these guys to see the remainder of their money getting eaten up by Tannenbaum and Rees. What is needed as a matter of urgency is for the criminal-justice leg of the investigation to begin to deliver.'

The first step, he says, would be for the prosecuting authority to file its request for mutual legal assistance in Australia and elsewhere. Secondly, extradition applications must be lodged.

'A big part of the problem is that the prosecutor who was dealing with this case right from the start is no longer there. It's a major problem, because the case files for the criminal case run into the hundreds. SARS spent significant funds on a very capable legal team to not only assist, but to ensure that all evidence collected through the various investigations by the different departments were compiled and ordered in a manner that would assist the NPA.'

Now, Van Loggerenberg says, it would take a new prosecutor quite a while to get up to speed on the case.

'It is not a simple matter. This is international fraud in its purest form spanning jurisdictions such as the USA, United Kingdom, the United Arab Emirates, France, Switzerland, Australia and South Africa. These countries have distinct and different legal systems and each comes with their own challenges.'

Van Loggerenberg is right about that, and the inexplicable filibustering from the NPA is hard to understand. Until, that is, you shine a light into the inner workings of the prosecutions service. Then you will see exactly why it is that the NPA has been effectively paralysed from doing anything to anyone about anything.

The paralysis is all the more damaging, given how crucial the NPA has been to the Tannenbaum case. The prosecutions authority, after all, represented the third gauntlet that investors had to run. If an investor was able to shrug off the heartless liquidators, and keep SARS's wolves from the door, there was still the frightening prospect of the third tier of interrogation: the NPA.

But it was an agency in crisis, and its flailing approach to Tannenbaum eloquently told this story.

Jawmend Rossi
and the R140 million bonus

You wouldn't pick them out in a line-up, but three of South Africa's most inconspicuous power brokers made a killing, thanks to Barry Tannenbaum.

Scan through the list of investors, and you'll spot an obscure company called Jawmend Rossi that made – no kidding – a profit of R139 million from Barry's scheme.

Between 2004 and 2009, Jawmend Rossi ploughed in R601.4 million and got back a monstrous R740.4 million in 124 separate 'loan transactions'.

So who is this Jawmend Rossi and what did they do with the money? It turns out that three friends, who all knew each other from their days at fledgling micro-lender African Bank, formed Jawmend Rossi. The company's name is a conflation of Jonathan Jawno, Michael Mendelowitz and Roberto Rossi.

Jawno, Rossi and Mendelowitz are very well connected. Most of South Africa's business elite have done business with one of them at some stage.

'They're smart businessmen,' says one person who knows them well. 'Would they do something if they thought it was a scam: I don't think so. But I can tell you they wouldn't have done anything unless they were completely covered.'

From different backgrounds, the three met as colleagues at African Bank, which fills a gap by lending cash to people who don't qualify for credit from the major established banks. African Bank did this by extracting an almost unconscionable interest rate, ostensibly to cover risk. The rate has dropped over the years, but in 2002, if you borrowed R1 000, you could be expected to repay R2 350 over the course of a year.

Jawno and Mendelowitz were both accountants – Jawno at Arthur Andersen (the company that imploded after it emerged that it had tried to hide the fraud at Enron) – and Mendelowitz at Deloitte & Touche. In 1995 they started a company called Stratvest, which was eventually bought by African Bank.

Rossi, an engineer and lawyer, had started a company in 1991 called Miners' Credit Guarantee, which was also acquired by African Bank.

As you would expect from people who worked at a bank, Jawno, Rossi and Mendelowitz knew a lot about interest rates and lending terms. You couldn't put them under the banner of gullible investors who didn't know better.

Yet, in October 2004, their company took a gamble on Barry Tannenbaum's scheme. Bank records show that Jawmend Rossi Capital first deposited a cheque of R500 000 into Barry's account in Sandton, followed a few weeks later by another R500 000.

Quite why Rossi, Jawno and Mendelowitz thought it was prudent to give this man with no track record such a large amount of cash has never been explained. People close to the three say it makes perfect sense: 'It was a normal business transaction done in blithe ignorance of the fact that Tannenbaum was the consummate con artist and fraudster,' says one person. Either way, it worked out: a few months later, in January 2005, Barry made the first repayment of R317 500. It was the start of a wonderful relationship.

The deposits grew larger. By January 2006, Jawmend Rossi was slapping down R4 million; by August 2006, it was R14 million (the return: R4.2 million); by August 2008, it was R33.6 million (the return: R8.06 million).[1]

In 2012, when Barry was subpoenaed to testify in a court in Australia, he said: 'I had a relationship with Jawmend Rossi Capital for quite some time. Initially, [the way] it would be done, they would loan me the money and I would set up the guarantee.'

So how would Barry possibly repay Jawmend Rossi – unless it was a Ponzi scheme? 'Well, I would rely on some other funds coming in,' he explained, when asked that exact question in court.

From where? 'Possibly from other lenders,' he said.

So, the lawyers asked, if there were no more deals to be done, Barry would not have been able to repay Jawmend? 'Probably not,' he admitted.

So how is it that the three investors missed this fact? Especially as, being at the sharp end of credit lending, they should have been aware that returns of more than 100 per cent are, to say the least, only given to lenders where the risk is immense.

Again, Jawmend's defenders say they didn't miss a thing – they just did simple, garden-variety trade-finance deals. 'It's ridiculous to annualise returns on short-term, high-risk trade-finance transactions,' they argue.

Perhaps. Or perhaps they reasoned that whatever the merits of the scheme, a watertight 'lending agreement' would cover them anyway. So Jawmend Rossi put in place hundreds of 'acknowledgements of debt' signed by Barry for 'participating in the procurement and sale of various pharmaceutical products and dossiers'.

These contracts encapsulated Barry's (justifiable) paranoia about being found out by stipulating that neither party should 'disclose' any of the details 'to any person, firm or company or to the media'.

Some of the deals looked ridiculously lucrative for Jawmend Rossi. For example, in a transaction on 25 July 2007, Jawmend lent R5.048 million to Barry for the 'procurement and sale of certain dossiers from Adcock Ingram to Aspen Pharmacare Holdings' for thirty-four days. It would be repaid at R7.75 million on 29 August – an interest rate of 53.5 per cent.

Annualise that, and it comes to a spectacular 574 per cent return. You have to ask how it was that the seasoned lenders at Jawmend Rossi believed this to be 'in the normal course of business'. You have to ask where else in South Africa you'd find this rate of return.

When I raised the question, Jawmend Rossi told me that the interest charged 'was appropriate to the quantum, the risk and the repayment period, as is usual in such trade-finance transactions'. Only, you won't find too many trade-finance deals offering those terms anywhere else.

An expert report filed at court stated that Barry used funds from Jawmend Rossi to 'repay earlier investors, gamble, pay his wife's Barclaycard and reduce the scheme's bank overdraft'.

Mendelowitz is a director of Bayport, a company that claims that he has 'developed, over many years, the skill in identifying great owner-managed companies'. Only, he wasn't so shrewd with Tannenbaum.

Surprisingly, when I asked them, Jawmend Rossi claimed it 'did not invest money in, or otherwise participate in the alleged Tannenbaum scheme'. Despite all evidence to the contrary.

'[We] advanced loans to Tannenbaum. Each short-term loan was made in the ordinary course of business and supported by ... supporting documentation,' they argued. To secure this debt, Jawmend Rossi said it had even ceded a policy over Tannenbaum's life.

Jawmend Rossi's biggest success was starting a company called Transaction Capital, which then listed on the JSE. Like African Bank, Transaction Capital included a micro-lender – Bayport – as well as a firm that lent funds to the people who 'run' South Africa's roads: minibus-taxi owners. Like New York's yellow cabs, or Bangkok's tuk-tuks, minibus taxis are a defining feature of South African traffic. Every day, 180 000 of these hurtle down the busiest roads in the country, ferrying twelve million people to work and back.

SA Taxi provides the finance for 18 000 of these, making a handy return – even if it's nothing like the 574 per cent that Barry would have paid Jawmend Rossi.

As was the case with the other investors, Gainsford and the other trustees came knocking, demanding that Jawmend Rossi repay the R139 million to the estate.

So was the Tannenbaum Ponzi cash used to capitalise Transaction Capital? No, say Jawno, Rossi and Mendelowitz: 'This is purely speculative and not true.'

In their summons, the trustees claimed that the agreements were 'sham transactions' that enabled Jawmend Rossi consistently to earn exorbitant annualised returns of between 125 and 1 437 per cent.

They argued that Jawmend Rossi 'knew that Tannenbaum was conducting an illegal Ponzi scheme and that it participated [in the scheme] to continue to earn the abnormal rates of return'.

Tannenbaum 'paid returns to Jawmend Rossi from money paid by subsequent investors in the scheme, rather than from profits earned by legitimate business activities,' the trustees alleged.

Jawno, Mendelowitz and Rossi told them to take a hike. The three entrepreneurs provided a number of arguments. First, they said, if 'Tannenbaum was the author and architect of the illegal scheme', then his estate shouldn't be allowed to recover a cent because of this illegality.[2]

They also argued they had paid the cash to Barry 'in good faith', and he took their cash 'in the ordinary course of business'.

More convincingly, they argued that if Tannenbaum was running a Ponzi scheme, he would have been insolvent from the very first payment. This stands to reason: if you owe people more than you have coming in, you're effectively bankrupt from the start.

Jawmend Rossi even got University of the Witwatersrand professor Harvey Wainer to testify for them, putting forward the argument that the three businessmen couldn't have known it was a scam. 'It would be peculiar and unlikely for a person who was party to a vast-scale fraud to studiously account for the transactions in formal records ... this would be analogous to a thief keeping a full ledger, management accounts and financial statements, and declaring all his thefts for tax purposes,' said Wainer.

It's probably true that Jawmend Rossi didn't know it was a scam. But if their argument is that they are somehow 'different' from the other investors, it's a hard line to swallow.

When asked in court why they lent Barry money, their answer was for a number of reasons, including the 'procurement and export of certain furniture in [a] consortium for a residential property development in London', and to fund 'antiretroviral orders for Aspen Pharmaceuticals'.[3]

But there were other things that Jawmend Rossi funded, including the purchase and sale of 'certain vaccines in a consortium led by Biovac Holdings [and the] on-selling of such vaccines as part of a government tender'.

Basically, exactly the same things the other investors thought they were financing. The only difference is that Jawmend Rossi was a registered credit provider, which the other investors weren't.

But then this would have given them insight that the other investors didn't have. As the trustees argued, 'Jawmend Rossi's directors and managers had particular fields of expertise, knowledge and experience of the lending industry – including the market-related rates of return.'[4]

They pointed out numerous 'abnormal' features of Jawmend Rossi's investment, such as the fact that they earned, on average, more than 300 per cent a year, and that they lent to Barry directly, rather than to Frankel, which needed the cash.

In one of the numerous preliminary court tussles, in February 2013 Judge Mathopo said that 'evidently, this was a classical case of robbing Peter to pay Paul' – which, of course, it was.[6]

But if you were being asked to pony up R140 million, your response might also be 'sue me'.

People who know them say the troika aren't worried about the case. 'Mendelowitz told me he doesn't even know what's happening with the case,' says one businessman who went to school with him. 'His lawyers are handling it all. If I'd made a profit of R140 million, you can be sure I'd be fighting it.'

16

Crime and punishment 2: All the president's men, and the prosecutor who didn't know when to quit

'This reminds me of walking into a bank to deposit R12 million. You put it on the counter, the teller takes it and gives you a receipt. Then a gunman walks in and robs everyone. He takes the money, the R12 million, even the watches on your arm. Then, after the gunman has made his getaway, the police arrive and arrest everyone in the bank. It's exactly like that.'

**– Investor Keith van der Spuy on how the
authorities treated the investors like thieves**

Travel up to the seventh floor of a dilapidated government building at 228 Visagie Street in a creaky elevator, and that's where, a few years back, you would have found the muscle behind the National Prosecuting Authority's Specialised Commercial Crime Unit.

There, some of the country's most knotty, convoluted white-collar crimes were dissected, documented and prepared for court. If you walked into the spacious office of the state prosecutor, Advocate Glynnis Breytenbach, you'd have seen a wall of files, each containing the story behind the headlines of some of South Africa's biggest cons, each building a meticulous, prosecutable case.

There were dozens of files. For example, South Africa's top construction companies were there, accused of doing sordid back-hand deals to divvy up tenders before the 2010 World Cup, which was held in South Africa. The World Cup was an event that cost the country R33 billion, and on which South Africa ended up making a loss – primarily because of the immense cost of building white-elephant soccer stadiums that now largely lie empty, robbed of their *raison d'être* once the tournament had ended.

It turned out that the construction firms that built those stadiums – including household names like Murray & Roberts, WBHO, Stefanutti Stocks and Aveng – had been colluding for decades, submitting dummy tenders and splitting up contracts between them. Projects worth more than R46 billion were involved. In 2013, South Africa's antitrust authority, the Competition Commission, fined them R1.46 billion collectively.[1]

But the biggest set of files in Breytenbach's office was labelled 'Project Frankel'.

These contain the efforts to bring those responsible for the Tannenbaum scam to book. It's a teetering effort on the part of the country's crime fighters, crippled as much by the police's steady erosion of financial expertise as it is by President Jacob Zuma's war against the National Prosecuting Authority in his banana-republic-style bid to sideline those he saw as hostile to him during his criminal prosecution for corruption, and to promote those who were loyal to him during his darkest days.

It may be too much to say, as Zuma's critics do, that a fledgling kleptocracy could yet be his single biggest legacy as president. But what is less contestable is that politically connected stooges and members of the ANC have scored a colossal amount of government business and mining rights awarded by the state. Little wonder that morally corrupt companies have fallen over their own polished shoes to sign up Zuma's inner circle in their 'empowerment deals'. A cynical ploy for a fickle age.

As the most experienced prosecutor, Glynnis Breytenbach was tasked with unravelling just one such case. It was a case that would prove to be her undoing, and a case which would leave her, and the Tannenbaum prosecution, on ice.

The story goes like this: to mine gold, one has to first apply for a mining right, which has to be renewed once it has expired.

Kumba, an iron-ore company that is 65 per cent owned by the world's third-largest mining entity, Anglo American (now worth R310 billion), had applied for the rights to mine the 21.4 per cent of Sishen it didn't already control on 4 May 2009.

Out of nowhere, a shelf company spirited into existence only months before called Imperial Crown Trading 289 popped up, and claimed that it too had lodged an application on 4 May. Under the arcane mining-rights rule, the first to lodge the application gets it, unless they are lodged on the same day, in which case government can decide, taking into account things like black economic empowerment.[2]

Because both applications were (supposedly) lodged on the same day, Imperial Crown got the licence.

Which sounds fine. Except for the fact that Imperial Crown *hadn't* lodged its application by 4 May, which should have disqualified it. It was missing key documents, like a title deed for the Sishen mine, which had to be included in the application. What appears to have happened is that someone in the Department of Minerals and Energy managed to get hold of Kumba's application, took the title deed (which had been stamped by a commissioner of oaths), photocopied it, and stuck it in Imperial Crown's application so that it could lodge the application on the same day.

It was such an amateurish job that to hide the official stamp on the photocopy, which would have identified it as Kumba's copy, someone had simply put a card over the stamp.[3]

It appeared to be blatant fraud, designed to steal a mining right that some said would have been worth R800 billion over the course of Sishen's life – which is why it ended up in Breytenbach's office.

The problem for Breytenbach was that Imperial Crown's politically well-connected shareholders included Gugu Mtshali, the long-term partner of Deputy President Kgalema Motlanthe, as well as Jagdish Parekh, an associate of the powerful Gupta family, who are known to be close to Zuma and who are not shy about bragging about it.

The prosecutor took her career in her hands when she touched that case. First, Zuma's appointee as national director of public prosecutions, Menzi Simelane, tried to suspend Breytenbach for 'inappropriate behaviour' in prosecuting the case. But Breytenbach thwarted Simelane by immediately assigning another prosecutor.

Though Simelane might have tried another route to ice Breytenbach, he was kicked out of his job when the Supreme Court of Appeal ruled that Zuma shouldn't have appointed him, implying that he was not 'fit and proper' – an unfortunate consequence of the fact that Simelane isn't always so scrupulous about telling the truth.[4]

Next, Zuma appointed Advocate Nomgcobo Jiba, who had herself been suspended from the NPA some years back for unprofessional conduct and dishonesty for plotting to thwart a criminal probe into former police commissioner Jackie Selebi. Selebi went to jail, but Jiba was reinstated.[5]

Jiba wasted no time in suspending Breytenbach from duty in April 2012. For more than a year, Breytenbach sat at home on full pay – with the exception of some jaunty interludes on the days when her 'disciplinary trial' was on. Breytenbach's advocate, Wim Trengove, took apart the NPA in that disciplinary hearing. The lacklustre NPA officials appeared as uncomfortable as a butcher given a calligraphy pen. The disciplinary hearing ultimately threw out the fifteen charges against her, ordering that she be reinstated. Jiba appealed this finding to the Labour Court, despite earlier pledging in an affidavit that 'if Breytenbach is found not guilty, it will be the end of the matter'.[6]

Instead Jiba filed three new complaints against her, throwing every hurdle in the way of her returning to work. Predictably, the files that Breytenbach handled – such as the Imperial Crown case and another against former police crime intelligence boss Richard Mdluli – have gone nowhere.

And when it comes to Tannenbaum, it was Breytenbach who was leading Project Frankel. It was Breytenbach who was the guiding hand behind the arrest warrants for Rees and Tannenbaum. With her out of the picture, thanks to some transparently political gamesmanship, the dice had rolled in Tannenbaum's favour.

* * *

As any of the investors who were summonsed to Pretoria to answer questions about Tannenbaum will attest, Breytenbach is a fearsome presence.

Seemingly perpetually trapped between a furrowed scowl and an eye-glinting smile, she can be terrifying if you are on the opposite side of the desk to her – even to her friends. Standing at not much more than five foot five, Breytenbach has a demeanour that shifts from genial air hostess to storm-cloud fury in less time than it takes to crack open a skull with a spanner. And she has black-robe fever: as soon as she pulls the legal gown over her head, she only sees one thing: you are her opponent.

Perhaps it is inevitable that a lifetime as a public prosecutor erodes your patience – a lifetime of unravelling lies strand by strand, painstakingly decoding the facts. Breytenbach's approach is this: tell me what you did, and tell me now, and maybe I'll be nice. Or nicer than I would have been, at any rate.

The formidable Breytenbach has a prosecutor's soul, a strong belief in who are the good guys and who are the bad guys, an unshatterable diligence when it comes to pursuing a case, and an almost unfathomable respect for a judge's decision on cases she handles.

Speak to the Tannenbaum investors, and they all have a story to tell about their interaction with her. Their voices betray equal amounts respect and fear for Breytenbach.

To illustrate her style, after the arrest warrants were issued, Darryl Ackerman, Tannenbaum's lawyer, headed to Breytenbach's office. Whether he planned to float the prospect of a deal or simply test the waters over the consequences of cooperation is unclear. Breytenbach said to him: 'Look, your client can come back now voluntarily, and we'll offer him a nice jail cell. Or he can fight us, and we'll put him in a cell with forty angry Zulus.'

It's an offer she has made to many others. In a country where people trample all over the law, no one tramples over Glynnis Breytenbach. No one gets anything but the barest compromise from her.

A lawyer relates the story of discussions with Breytenbach about Dean Rees, who offered to cooperate with the police but wanted certain assurances before he left Switzerland to return. 'We won't need bail,' said Breytenbach. 'We'll take his child.'

In November 2009, Rees's lawyer wrote to Breytenbach suggesting it would be possible to do some sort of deal, in which he would testify against Tannenbaum – surely the real scoundrel of the piece. Breytenbach replied in a letter dripping with scorn: 'It is the normal attitude of the state not to negotiate with fugitives from justice.' But having said that, the prosecutors would be travelling to Switzerland anyway soon, she said, and 'assuming your client has not yet been arrested/extradited, then it will serve a useful purpose to speak to him'.

To a large extent, Breytenbach *was* the state's case against Tannenbaum. What is clear is that her suspension castrated the NPA, removing perhaps their strongest weapon in the fight against corporate crime, their spear guarding the citadel of honest business.

It would be stretching the point to suggest that with Breytenbach suspended, it's a free-for-all for ingenious corporate crooks – but it's not far off. 'Look at the biggest frauds in the last ten years, and ask how the prosecutions authority has handled it,' says one government employee from another department, who is scathing about the lack of muscle at the NPA. 'In none of those cases has anything ever come of it. Not a single one.'

He's right of course. There's Brett Kebble, the mining boss who systematically robbed the shareholders of his mining firms, JCI and Randgold & Exploration, of more than R2 billion over nearly a decade. Kebble was assassinated before he got to trial, which was lucky for the prosecutions service, as this probably saved it some blushes.

There was Saambou, South Africa's seventh-largest bank, which collapsed in 2002, causing great anxiety for its 520 000 customers (though they later got their cash) and 1 746 employees (who all lost their jobs), and big losses for the hundreds of shareholders, who lost most of their investments.

The bank's CEO, Johan Myburgh, and two other executives accused of sinking it were hit with thirteen criminal charges of fraud, insider trading and theft involving R640 million, and with breaking the Companies Act.[7]

The Saambou prosecutors must now wish they hadn't even tried in the first place. It took so long for the state to stitch together a case that Myburgh had already died of cancer by the time it finally came before Judge Willie van der Merwe's court in Pretoria in 2008. Not that the delay had improved the prosecutors' case: Van der Merwe chucked out the charges entirely once it became clear the prosecutors weren't able to pin anything on Saambou's bosses – the ones who were still alive, at any rate.[8]

Kobus Rossouw, the lawyer who represented one of the Saambou executives, told *Moneyweb* at the time: 'The case was thrown out without any of the accused even having to give evidence. Basically, it's a case that should never have been brought to court.'[9]

Then there's Fidentia, an investment fund that plundered more than R600 million that belonged to 46 000 widows and orphans of mineworkers. The penalty for the mastermind, J. Arthur Brown: a R150 000 fine. In May 2013, the NPA accepted a plea bargain with Brown for two relatively minor fraud charges, ones that the judge described as 'an extremely diluted version' of fraud. It was a far cry from the ninety-odd charges he had initially faced.[10]

Judge Anton Veldhuizen, who heard the Fidentia case, was disgusted. During the hearing to decide on the sentence, he flayed the prosecutions authority for effectively trying to lead new evidence. 'I think the state has mismanaged this,' he said.[11]

Veldhuizen asked why the prosecutors hadn't called Dawood Seedat, an expert witness who worked at the regulator, the Financial Services Board, and who knew all about Brown's machinations with the Fidentia cash. 'If you had done so I might not have accepted this plea,' he said. 'I may well have forced the state to proceed with prosecution. This is wrong. How can I sentence the accused on facts that indicate there has been theft when there has been no conviction for theft?'[12]

It was the right question. But overworked, harassed prosecutors, often with little ability to balance their own bank accounts let alone decipher complicated accounting trickery, are just no match for the silver-tongued litigators that dirty money can buy.

Brown's mild-mannered accountant, Graham Maddock, who had such a minor role in the Fidentia drama that he was all but invisible, had already struck a plea bargain and gone to jail for two years for acting as an accomplice. Yet the man he testified against didn't see a day behind bars. Rather like Tigon – Milne served jail time while the supposed mastermind of the con, Gary Porritt, looks increasingly unlikely to see a single day in a cell.

With Breytenbach at the helm of South Africa's serious-economic-crimes cluster at the NPA, it would still be a tricky job to put the well-heeled crooks behind bars. Without her, it looks impossible.

* * *

Within weeks of Tannenbaum's scheme going bust in June 2009, Breytenbach summoned investors to testify about what happened and began to gather evidence.

Some of the investors were terrified and stumbled through the interviews, unable to recall precisely what had happened. Others were furious about how they had already been rushed-up by the liquidators and SARS. And now the NPA had summoned them and accused them of being complicit in a criminal enterprise.

Howard Lowenthal, the tell-it-like-it-is stockbroker, was one of the latter. When he walked into Breytenbach's office, he was greeted by no fewer than nine officials: Breytenbach, Advocate André Bezuidenhout, officials from SARS and investigators from the Hawks.

Armed guards stood at the exit – perhaps just in case one of the suit-and-collared investors got so intimidated they bolted halfway through.

'Mr Lowenthal,' Breytenbach began, 'are you aware that you're living on the proceeds of crime?'

Howard, sitting on the one side of the desk, facing an army of state resources, all staring at him, replied: 'Firstly, it's Howard: only my children call me Mr Lowenthal. Secondly, that's fantastic news to hear. That means I can come sit on that side of the desk, and go and find out who committed this crime against me.'

They all laughed. But the interrogation continued for three hours. The questions were the same as they had been at every other forum he had been called to, like the liquidators' inquiry: Who got you into the scheme? How much money did you make? Did you know Barry well? Did you take any of the proceeds overseas?

Eventually, Breytenbach said to Lowenthal, 'You know you're going to have to give it all back, everything you got?'

By now, Lowenthal had had enough. From when he was paid his first amount of 'interest' by Barry, he had paid tax on it. Of the first R50 000 in interest he had got on his first investment of R1 million, he had declared it to SARS and paid tax of R20 000 on the income.

In all, Lowenthal 'invested' R2 million with Tannenbaum, and was paid R1.9 million in 'interest' over three years. So, effectively, he was already R100 000 down. His net losses at that stage were R120 000, if you included his first SARS payment.

But to compound his misery, liquidators Shirish Kalian and Alec Brooks then came calling, and tried to sue him to recover every cent he had ever been paid by Barry.

Then SARS came calling again, giving him a new assessment: you owe us R800 000, they said.

So when Breytenbach told him again that he would have to repay the cash, Lowenthal was prepared for another assault. 'You must decide who wants my money – there's only so much to go around,' he said. 'Alec Brooks and his crowd, they wanted it all, then SARS wanted it. Now you [the NPA], you want it all. Not everyone can have it.' He then pointed at the female representative of SARS, 'In fact, you, Mrs SARS, I want my R20 000 back that I paid you.'

That was met with a stony silence.

Lowenthal stood up to leave, demanding that the guards let him out: 'Look, you can stand on your head, the bottom line is I lent my mate some tom, and he didn't give it back to me.' With that, he walked past the guards, into the rickety elevator, and out of the building. No one stopped him.

* * *

'The only thing [Breytenbach] didn't do was shove a torch up my arse to see if I was hiding anything,' says Keith van der Spuy, Darryl Leigh's former colleague at Nedbank, who ended up losing about R30 million in the scheme.[13]

One day, with no warning, eight officials from the police pitched up at Van der Spuy's house. They barged in and swept up everything they could see. Every computer, every electronic device containing movies, virtually anything that could be plugged into a power socket.

'They came back sheepishly six weeks later and handed it all back,' he says. 'They basically turned my life upside down – you try operate without a laptop for six weeks if you're running a business. I could have told them they'd find nothing: a lot of guys had hot money in this, but I didn't.'

Van der Spuy was called to the same inquiry with Breytenbach, facing off against a room full of state law enforcers. 'She basically told me that we were the criminals, that we were the ones who had all the illicit money,' he says. 'Yet, where was Barry Tannenbaum? Where was Dean Rees?'

Van der Spuy, angry about the way it was turning out, told Breytenbach it was a perversion of justice:

> I said to them, you know, this reminds me of walking into a bank to deposit R12 million. You put it on the counter, the teller takes it and gives you a receipt. Then a gunman walks in and robs everyone. He takes the money, the R12 million, even the watches on your arm. Then, after the gunman has made his getaway, the police arrive and arrest everyone in the bank. It's exactly like that. Why have they done nothing to get Tannenbaum, to get Rees?

Cobalt Capital's John Storey says it cost him R500 000 to defend himself against the NPA – all while Tannenbaum and Rees are 'running around Australia and Switzerland as if nothing happened'. He says:

> It's been far more horrific than actually losing the R2.7 million [which he lost in the scheme]. They sat us down, and told us we were terrible people, that we were profiteering from kids dying of AIDS. Yet, we never did anything wrong, we never took any money out the country, we paid our taxes, we never broke any laws, and yet the NPA pursued all the major victims of the fraud.[14]

The NPA's apparent pursuit of the easy targets is all the more galling for the investors who saw Fidentia mastermind walk away with a R150 000 fine. (Brown actually tried to buy one of m Cubed's companies, but was ultimately rebuffed – so Storey knows him well.)

Says Storey: 'Given how they couldn't prosecute Brown, I don't think the

NPA know how to deal with the Tannenbaum case, to be honest. Everyone is after whatever they can rape you for, but what has happened to the main perpetrators? Nothing.'

Like a cumbersome ox-wagon hauling itself up a hill, the special task team set up to unravel Project Frankel in 2009 crawled along after Breytenbach was suspended in April 2012. Six months later, it creaked to a halt.

Squabbles broke out among the three groups – the prosecutors, the taxmen and the Financial Intelligence Centre. 'They just couldn't agree who should be paying for this,' says one insider close to the task team.

In August SARS sent a letter to the other task-team members, telling them their funding had come to an end. The kitty was empty, so the law enforcers were told to go back to their day jobs.

It was an act of numbskullery that could only have been fashioned deep in the bowels of some government office by some calculator-jockey, sacrificing the bigger gain to balance the books of some cost centre. A slap on the back from the bookkeeper was nothing compared to pursuing a probe that could have recovered billions.

Sure, they still had Darryl Leigh's R44 million that the Asset Forfeiture Unit had confiscated. But Willie Hofmeyr, the head of the unit, was buggered if he was going to release that cash to fund the investigation. 'The upshot was that we all went our separate ways, the task team was unbundled,' says that insider.

At the time of going to print, no request to extradite the ringleaders had been lodged, though there were constant threats to do so. Requests for mutual legal assistance, a necessary formal bureaucratic process, were only just creaking into action.

'I hold out no hope,' says one investor. 'Are they going to show any more interest in getting Tannenbaum than they've shown in getting those responsible [for corruption] in the arms deal?'

It's a rhetorical question, obviously.

* * *

Few people know this, but the National Prosecuting Authority did actually prepare papers to kick off the extradition process for both Rees and Tannenbaum.

Draft documents, titled 'Letter of Request for Legal Assistance … Suspects: Barry Deon Tannenbaum, Dean Gillian Rees and Darryl Leigh', were prepared on letterheads of the Specialised Commercial Crime Unit.[15]

Both letters were dated 1 December 2011 and addressed to the authorities in Australia and Switzerland, where Tannenbaum and Rees were living, via the high commissioners of those countries. The Swiss letter runs to twenty-nine pages, the Australian one to thirty-one pages.

But neither of the letters was signed; neither was sent to the authorities in Australia and Switzerland. (The letters were handed over to me by people close to the process who are furious that nothing has happened for years, when all that was apparently needed was a signature.)

There are gaping holes in the letters where some magistrate is meant to sign, as well as Sibongile Mzinyathi, the North Gauteng director of public prosecutions. You couldn't fault the documents for a lack of detail. The letters describe with tedious precision exactly which laws have been broken (the Banks Act, Companies Act, Credit Act, Income Tax Act, Unfair Business Practices Act, Financial Institutions Act, Financial Intelligence Centre Act, and the Financial Advisory and Intermediary Services Act), as well as the legislation in terms of which countries can ask for legal assistance.

Almost absurdly, on the last page, there is a section headed 'urgency', which reads: 'The request is urgent. Both Tannenbaum, his wife, Deborah Tannenbaum, Rees and his wife, Dominique Rees, are currently fugitives from justice, Tannenbaum in Australia and Rees in Switzerland. The information is needed to finalise the investigation prior to extradition applications being finalised.'

By late 2013, more than four years after the scheme was exposed, even the preliminary steps to extradition have not been launched.

The 'request for assistance' is nothing more than a diplomatic hoop that law-enforcement authorities must jump through before they start interfering with someone living in another country. In this case, the NPA wanted to be allowed to 'interview the witnesses', subpoena bank statements in those countries and lay their hands on whatever evidence they could.

It remains unclear why the letters were never signed. Those requests were twice submitted to the former director of public prosecutions, Menzi Simelane, but he refused to sign them, saying they were incomplete. Quite why, Simelane couldn't explain.

Simelane's reluctance was all the more mysterious given that those requests were 'unofficially' given to the Australians and the Swiss authorities, who were apparently quite happy with them. But in the absence of the signed, official requests, the Swiss and the Australians could do nothing. Colonel Piet Senekal, a veteran policeman now with the Hawks priority-crimes unit leading the Tannenbaum case, is a no-nonsense and methodical policeman. Each page of every affidavit is stamped, signed and checked in laborious detail. But even Senekal appears to have been wrong-footed by the drama over Breytenbach's suspension.

When asked about the delays in launching extradition proceedings for Tannenbaum and Rees, the Hawks offered no explanation.

'It is not our policy to report progress on an ongoing investigation such as this one,' said Hawks spokesman Captain Paul Ramaloko. 'We will be able to talk once this investigation is finalised in court.'

Even a particularly injudicious gambler would think twice about betting on that happening anytime soon. Especially as the drama around Breytenbach shows no sign of settling down.

Though Breytenbach was cleared in May 2013 of the fourteen disciplinary charges against her, the acting head of the NPA, Nomgcobo Jiba, 'transferred' her to another office – effectively stripping her of her title as head of the Specialised Commercial Crimes Unit. Again, Breytenbach had to go to court to protest.[16] This has cast a chill over the Tannenbaum criminal case. In the letter, under 'responsible officials', it names Glynnis Breytenbach as the 'lead prosecutor'. But with her out of the picture, the layer of dust gathering on the files marked 'Frankel' is growing thicker by the day.

With the NPA at war with itself, SARS looking to the estate for any back taxes and the trustees furiously pursuing the investors, the main protagonists – Tannenbaum, Rees and Leigh – are quietly going about their business as if nothing has happened.

17

The forgotten men

'He's not very bright.'
– Australian lawyer Derek Ziman, describing his client, Barry Tannenbaum

As KPMG and the liquidators trained their artillery on the low-hanging fruit, Barry Tannenbaum had managed to slip out of the spotlight entirely.

Weeks after the first newspaper headlines, Barry claimed he had received all manner of death threats. And he probably wasn't lying. 'If I'd ripped off this many rich Jews, as a Jewish man myself, I'd be very security-conscious,' says one person who knew him well.

Barry's wife, Debbie, later said the family 'moved out quite quickly because we were being threatened and we had people following us, and walking around our home, and my children and I were really scared'.[1]

So he fled Sydney and his mansion in St Ives, and his 'stuffy little office above a strip of shops around the corner from his ... home', as the *Sydney Morning Herald* put it.[2]

Where did Barry go? Where would anyone go who was seeking to duck furious investors, the law, and court officials with attachment orders?

Runaway Bay, on Australia's Gold Coast. The irony was palpable. It was almost like a dare to the bungling law-enforcement authorities: catch me if you have the stomach – I'll be in Runaway Bay, waiting.

It became almost an in-joke in Australia: 'Take a stroll along the Runaway Bay marina today with its views of the Surfers Paradise Manhattan-esque skyline and bobbing yachts at berth, and you might pass Barry Deon Tannenbaum, now a resident of the palm tree-lined suburb,' wrote former South African Larry Schlesinger on his blog, Freshly Worded.[3]

Look up Runaway Bay on Wikipedia, the online crowd-sourced information network, and you will see that the only 'notable resident' is alleged Ponzi mastermind Barry Tannenbaum.

Hardly surprising. It's a neglected little patch of Australia's Gold Coast, with just about 9 000 residents. It's essentially a gold-plated retirement village: the average age of residents is fifty – compared to an average of thirty-seven for the rest of Australia.[4]

Runaway Bay was once just 180 hectares of wetlands until 1972, when two developers turned it into a residential estate.[5]

Now, it's a luxury resort with its very own fugitive. It was an obvious place to go. The Tannenbaums had earlier put down a deposit of A$335 000 on one of the Soul apartments in Surfer's Paradise, about ten kilometres away. It was Dean Rees who convinced them: his company had also bought two apartments at Soul. (Had the sale gone through, just imagine Rees bumping into Barry in the elevator.)

(As an indication that Barry wasn't as naive as some might think, all the properties he owned were in Debbie's name: the holiday flat in Umhlanga on South Africa's east coast, the St Ives mansion, and the property in Surfer's Paradise.)

'He had lots of property in Australia,' says one person who used to be close to Barry when he was living in Sydney. 'He put down lots of money, including a big deposit to build his dream house on the Gold Coast.'

The Soul apartments market themselves as a 'world of refined opulence', a place 'unmatched anywhere else in the world'. Marketing bumf aside, it does look like the sort of place where an international fugitive would be quite comfortable whiling away his days. Its seventy-seven floors rising 245 metres into the sky, tropical gardens and an indoor and outdoor pool on the third level, as well as a wine-tasting room, create the feel of a luxury hotel.

But apartments at Soul, which was finally completed in 2012 at a cost of $850 million, don't come cheap. Soul holds the record for the most expensive apartment traded in Australia, at $16.75 million – sold in September 2006 to 'an undisclosed south-east Queensland businessman'. All of the apartments have sold for more than A$1 million (around R9 million).[6]

Tannenbaum's lawyer, Darryl Ackerman, says that 'long before any problems arose, it was Debbie's hope to purchase a property on the Gold Coast. The transaction was not then, and has never been finalised.'

It's a dream that appears to have fallen flat. Ackerman also says that 'neither Barry nor Debbie are in any financial position to finance any grandiose idea of a new home'.

Later, in court, Debbie admitted that she and Barry had hoped to buy an apartment on the Gold Coast, but they 'didn't think that everything would go so wrong'.[7]

The reason the deal was never concluded, according to Barry, was that he just ran out of cash. You would think, having masterminded a grand scam, Barry wouldn't exactly have any money issues. You would think he'd be rolling in it. But the fact is, it just didn't appear to be so. All the anecdotes recounted by people who met him during this period suggest that, contrary to all expectations, he didn't seem to have a cent.

For example, after receiving death threats in Sydney, Barry packed up all his documents and placed them in a storage unit in north Sydney. But he ran out of cash and couldn't pay the storage fee, so the company told him they would destroy his files.

Even the two fancy BMW X5s were repossessed after he stopped making the payments. The Tannenbaums then rented a car from Hertz.

They sold their furniture on auction in 2011; some was hawked on eBay, like a leather chair for which he got $150. Barry pawned Debbie's jewellery on Nobby Beach, on Australia's Gold Coast, at a place called Cash in a Flash. He got A$5 000 for Debbie's diamond ring and A$2 000 for her bracelet.

One person who knows him well recounts an intriguing late-night conversation with Barry: 'I said to him, "Barry, it's just you and me here. Tell me where you've stashed the cash, and we'll see if we can find a way to keep most of it." He said, "Look, I really don't have a thing." And I believe him.'

The fact is, no one has been able to uncover the hidden pot of gold that Barry has supposedly ferreted away.

In October 2013, Alec Brooks testified in a Johannesburg court that despite looking under every rock they could find, they hadn't been able to trace any further assets belonging to Tannenbaum. 'Despite all our efforts, we just haven't found any further assets,' he said. 'The forensics have done an analysis of Mr Tannenbaum's bank statements. Had there been any major assets ... that we hadn't known of, we would have traced it.'

Brooks said the investigators were so scrupulous that even if Tannenbaum had bought a 'chair or a couch for R4 000', that would have been highlighted.

Even his brother, Michael, in his own court papers, says he doesn't see how Barry could have made millions, 'especially when I hear from my parents that he is struggling to put food on the table in Australia'.

* * *

Now on the Gold Coast, the Tannenbaums set about reconstructing what they could of their life – ostensibly without much cash and even less of a plan.

Barry opened a bank account using Debbie's maiden name, Blou. Debbie explained in court: 'We didn't really want to use the name Tannenbaum. We had had people threaten us, and when people heard the surname, they recognised the name, and we were trying to make a fresh start and a life for our children away from all of the problems.'[8]

They flitted from house to house, but always stayed within a few kilometres of Runaway Bay. First, they lived in a complex called Allisee on Bayview Street – an upmarket apartment with views over the marina and three swimming pools, a sauna and a spa in the complex. Allisee's drawcard, besides the 180 metres of direct water frontage, is that it is 'two minutes' drive to the local village, Paradise Point/Runaway Bay marina for a variety choice cuisine'.[9] It wasn't cheap, though, going for between A$2 400 and A$5 000 per month.

Then the Tannenbaums moved a few kilometres away to a suburb called Coomera, before moving again to another luxury block called Salacia Waters in Paradise Point. Salacia Waters was just as plush as Allisee. With waterfront views and close to golf courses and the casino, it boasted its own mini theatre, gym and spa. They moved soon enough to an apartment on Main Road in Surfer's Paradise.

Despite Barry's protestations, the money must have been coming from somewhere: those apartments weren't cheap to rent.

Having sold the St Ives house, and still occasionally jetting off to Germany to 'help Barwa run Frankel GmbH', Barry didn't appear to be as impoverished as he made out. And besides the fancy apartments, he also rented an office in Surfer's Paradise.

Even more mysteriously, on 12 October 2009 – four months after Barry's scheme was exposed as a con – Deborah Tannenbaum signed a deal to buy vacant land on Royal Albert Crescent, in Paradise Point. The purchase price on the contract was A$1.1 million, with a deposit of A$55 000 and the rest to be paid within two months. Where did Barry believe this cash would come from?[10]

One theory is that he was using cash that had been paid to him in Australia by investors – both existing South African investors, who transferred money offshore, as well as newer Australian investors in his Bartan Group. (Bartan, in a typical Tannenbaum convention, is a conflation of the names 'Barry' and 'Tannenbaum'.)

Barry moved his family to Sydney in early 2007, and it appears he used $31 million to capitalise Bartan.

Bartan was 100 per cent owned by Bardeb Nominees, controlled by Barry and Debbie Tannenbaum. It was first registered in January 2007, shortly after the Tannenbaums arrived in Australia.

The move to Australia cost them plenty too. The Tannenbaums brought all their furniture, including mahogany lounge suites and cabinets, and a leather desk, worth more than R250 000. They also brought ten pieces of art, which Barry had bought for more than R120 000. (Debbie said they had sold all but two of the artworks by 2010 – and furniture – 'to be able to put food on the table for my children and pay school fees'.[11])

But once that $31 million was in Bartan's account, $14 million of it was spirited away into other accounts controlled by Barry.

There are a lot of murky areas in this story, but what is clear is that money from the Ponzi scheme ended up in Australia. As Australian Federal Court judge

John Logan said in a judgment in August 2012: 'There is no doubt on the evidence that substantial funds sourced from South Africa were transferred to Australian entities controlled by him and his wife.'[12]

The real questions are, what happened to this money? Where did it go? Why did the Australians not follow the money?

* * *

South Africans love to bemoan the disintegration of their criminal-justice system, the dilution of forensic-investigation skills, and the fact that known crooks end up thwarting police and prosecutors and writing books glamorising their lives, like Glenn Agliotti.

They don't tend to think of Australia, the archetypal nanny state, as a jurisdiction that would give crooks an easy ride. Yet, how else would you explain the fact that Barry managed to rip off numerous people in Australia and wasn't arrested or charged? His Bartan Group had a similar investment scheme to the South African one, and its balance sheet showed a long list of investors. So why was it being left to a flailing South African prosecutions service to bring him to justice?

The request for legal assistance prepared by South Africa's National Prosecuting Authority, which, as mentioned, was never signed or delivered to the Australian authorities, stated that 'approximately 25 Australian investors have been identified'.[13]

Was the Australian business, by any chance, legal? Could that be why the Australians never acted? The South African authorities don't think so. The letter of request reads: 'Tannenbaum, upon his arrival in Australia, opened offices in St Ives and registered various entities, employed staff members and opened bank accounts through which he proceeded to conduct and further his illicit business.'

Barry was also a director of nineteen companies linked to Australia, including Bartan and Oxygen Pharmaceuticals, and he had nine bank accounts at ANZ Bank. Bartan's balance sheet listed investors in Australia from whom it took money or paid money to. The largest investors on the Australian list were two South Africans who emigrated – New York–based lawyer Meir Levin, who was owed A$38.8 million (R355 million), and Zenprop founder Avin Lieberman, who was owed A$11.9 million (R110 million).[14]

And there were others. Under the grouping of 'individual investors', for example, there is Alex Glasenberg, the man who appears to be the financial director of large Canadian-owned pharmaceutical company Apotex (owed A$2.3 million, or R21 million).

Then there is Brad Shofer, a Johannesburg-born tech boffin who made a mint in Australia, and subsequently got quite close to Tannenbaum. Shofer made his cash after he started Australian software firm MYOB (Mind Your Own Business) back in 1991. MYOB sold an accounting software package that became one of Australia's best-known brands, and when it was listed on the Australian Securities Exchange in 1999, it raised A$500 million.

Shofer left MYOB in 2003 with a mountain of money and too much time. So he whiled away his days looking for new companies to invest in, such as Ingogo, which made a system to book taxis over your phone, and Dinosaur Deals, an online discount company.

Speaking about his two partners in Dinosaur Deals, Shofer says his role has been to teach 'fiscal responsibility' – not exactly what you would expect from someone who ploughed millions into a Ponzi scheme. 'I just realised straight away they were more willing to take on risk than I had ever been,' he was quoted as saying. 'They stretched me a bit in some areas and I introduced that fiscal responsibility – that you needed to look at every deal. I guess I brought them back a bit and we met at a comfortable middle ground which has worked really well.'[15]

Shofer certainly learnt a bit about risk – thanks to his new friend.

Shofer told *The Australian* newspaper in 2009 that he'd first got to know Barry in 2007 because both of their children went to the Masada College Jewish day school in St Ives, Sydney. But Shofer said he 'no longer had dealings with him'.

'He wanted to start a company and distribute pharmaceuticals and we had plans but we never did anything with them,' he said. 'I'm thrilled it didn't go anywhere.' Shofer ended up with 25 per cent of the Australian arm of Frankel International, but quit in August 2008. That company didn't actually trade while Shofer was there, so he never made any money from it.

'He was a fellow [South African] immigrant and I was trying to help him out and settle in,' Shofer told the newspaper.

So what happened to these investors? Bartan was put into liquidation in March 2010, and a liquidator called Trevor Pogroske, from Grant Thornton, was appointed. But when he asked Barry for specifics about Bartan's assets, liabilities and books in his post-liquidation communication with him, Tannenbaum obfuscated. The written list of debtors was wrong, he said. Barry's explanation is that he did not have 'funds to pay anyone to regularise these records, which are obviously incorrect'.[16] Barry added:

I say that because, under individual debtors for example, SE Abrosie was a South African lender who lent money to a South African company and was repaid by the Australian company. I was given to understand that an adjustment was made in the records of the two companies. SE Abrosie should not appear in the books of Bartan. There are other names which are in the same position. The data has obviously been incorrectly inputted.

That was the essence of Barry: everything was always somebody else's fault, there was always another excuse for why things were not as they seemed.

When Pogroske took over, he estimated that Bartan's total liabilities were A$132 million. It was insolvent.[17]

The odds of Bartan repaying its debts looked slim, as there was pretty much no money anywhere. The books showed that Bartan had only A$150 in its accounts at Liaki Bank. Bartan had no stock, no property and no petty cash. Barry added that Bartan was owed A$21 million by Frankel International, Eurochemicals and Asterix. (He put the value of the investment in Eurochemicals at A$481342.)

Even the BMW that Barry drove hadn't been fully paid for.[18] Barry provided some responses to Pogroske about Bartan's position, and it painted a desperate picture of a company in ruin.

'Desks, chairs and cabinets were given to the landlord in lieu of rent arrears,' said Barry. '[The landlord] credited A$4000 to the rent accounts after locking the company out of the offices at the beginning of December 2009. I had received death threats, and had moved from Sydney at the time.'

Bartan's three Apple laptops were sold, 'one to Bradley Miller in lieu of salary, approximately A$1500 owed to Norman Miller, his father … the other two were sold to JFK Security in lieu of invoices in arrears'.

Barry had by then sold his St Ives house for A$1.765 million, but, as Pogroske's lawyer pointed out, the home was in Debbie's name: 'We doubt, on the sale, there was much, if any, equity after payment of [the mortgage] and the costs on sale.'[19]

But, crucially, when asked why Bartan had failed, Pogroske listed in the official report: 'Fraud, poor financial control including lack of records, poor management of accounts receivable, poor strategic management of business, inadequate cash flow or high cash use.'

So if the liquidator had felt convinced enough to blame its collapse on fraud, you would imagine that would be more than sufficient incentive for the Australians to act against Tannenbaum.

But even if they hadn't acted against him, even if they had scrunched their eyes shut and pretended it was all above board, at the very least, what you *wouldn't* have expected Australia to do, is give citizenship to the man who ran South Africa's largest cross-border scam. Yet, this is exactly what happened.

Three months after the Ponzi scheme was exposed, Barry Tannenbaum sat the citizenship test in Australia. On 14 September 2009, Tannenbaum's Australian lawyer, Derek Ziman, wrote to a law firm that specialises in immigration, explaining that 'the reason [Barry] would like the matter handled by a migration agent who is well versed in these matters is because, as we explained to you, there is some degree of urgency involved in his obtaining Australian citizenship'.[20]

The urgent reason Ziman cited is that Barry travelled to Europe and other countries often, for which he needed visas, and, he said, Barry 'anticipates that there will be serious delays in him obtaining visas from the South African authorities'.

(There are, you would be correct in thinking, a few pertinent details missing from that motivation – like his desperate desire to get citizenship to avoid landing up in a South African jail.)

A letter from Australia's Department of Immigration and Citizenship confirms that Tannenbaum was due to sit the citizenship test on 16 September. The Australian lawyers replied to the effect that while they could help lodge the application, 'there is no certainty' that they would be able to expedite the immigration process.

At about the same time though, Ziman wrote to an Australian barrister, Anthony Bellanto, saying that Tannenbaum wanted to consult with him about 'the possibility of Mr Tannenbaum being arrested and incarcerated, the possibility of him applying for bail, and the possibility of him being extradited to South Africa'.[21]

Said Ziman: 'Once he is an Australian citizen, this will effectively put an end to any efforts to extradite him, but until that happens, it is anticipated that steps might be put into place for his extradition and he might be arrested at any time.'

Tannenbaum, Ziman said, had been living on a permanent-residence visa, but his wife was an Australian citizen, as were his two children. Ziman then told the Australian barrister about how Barry stood accused of running a multinational Ponzi scheme. But Ziman summed up Barry's response, which was to pin the blame on everyone else:

> [Barry] says that he came under the influence of two South African lawyers, Darryl Leigh and Dean Rees, who elected themselves as being responsible for attracting investors into his company. These investors parted with their money based on certain representations made by Leigh and Rees to [them], and our client and his companies were minor beneficiaries.

That is a predictable enough course of action. But to get citizenship in Australia, you need to have a letter from the police proving your 'good standing' – that is, that you're not an international crook, or the sort of guy who would run an international Ponzi scheme. No problem for the South African Police Service, which duly provided the letter.

The story gets even more outlandish: Barry Tannenbaum ended up getting a job in Queensland selling insurance for a company called Qantum Capital. Call the company's toll-free hotline, and the person on the other end of the line, advising you to leave a message, is Barry Tannenbaum himself.

Qantum was only registered in November 2012, but is 100 per cent owned by an Australian, Brian Upton. Barry appears to be Brian's right-hand man – pictures of them both chatting to prospective clients at a Gold Coast business expo in 2013 dot Qantum's Facebook page.

Qantum says it is 'passionate about taking care of you', with advisors who are 'risk management specialists' offering insurance to ensure 'your family's financial well-being and security'.

Not that Barry had been able to ensure much financial well-being or security to those who had previously come into contact with him. (Unfortunately, Barry did not respond to the messages that I left for him at Qantum.)

Of all the jobs that you would imagine an international fraud mastermind should *not* get, selling insurance to the public must be pretty high up on the list. There are clear guidelines that say people who sell insurance should be 'fit and proper'. Barry is quite clearly neither.

* * *

Tannenbaum claims that he moved to Australia after a horrific crime incident at his house in Joburg. Of course, that's not entirely implausible in a country where forty-two people are killed every day – a rate of 30.9 for every 100 000 people, which is around the same level as Colombia.[22]

But a far more likely explanation is that he immigrated to Australia to get out of the sights of the South African police. Judge John Logan, in his Federal Court judgment in Brisbane in August 2012, said as much:

> It may very well be that his decision to quit South Africa was inherently bound up with a desire not in the future to be dealt with under the law of that country in respect of his involvement in the scheme described, and a related desire to enjoy the benefits of proceeds repatriated to Australia.[23]

This isn't the way Tannenbaum's Australian lawyer sees it. In fact, Ziman says that Barry didn't do anything wrong in Australia, so there's absolutely no reason why he should be propping up a jail cell in New South Wales or Queensland. 'I can tell you, proper competent people have looked at Barry's behaviour, and found nothing wrong with it,' he says. 'After Bartan went into liquidation, the liquidators conducted all sorts of investigations and canned the investigation after a while, because they found he hadn't done anything wrong.'[24]

Really? Well then, who possibly could be responsible for this fraud that the liquidator found, one wonders. Not Barry, says Ziman. The lawyer tells a story about the tsunami that ravaged Thailand in December 2006, which, he says, has huge resonance for the Tannenbaum case.

'After the tsunami, there was lots of aid money coming in that needed to be spent. So what happened? A thousand little businesses, homes and people popped up saying, yes, thanks, I'll need some of that. So what's the moral of the story? When there's a big cock-up, everyone gets involved.'

The point is, everyone is now after Barry for cash, even those who have no legitimate claim to it. Everyone is willing to pin everything and anything on Barry to cover themselves, Ziman says.

But with Barry firmly not breaking cover, ducking requests for interviews, there's no other narrative that would provide a better explanation.

* * *

In a Ponzi scheme like this, few people think of the impact on the perpetrator's family. In the Bernie Madoff case, for example, one of his sons hanged himself – a move that was attributed to the 'shame' of being his son.

In the Tannenbaum case, many of his family members have spoken of their shame, of how they have been ostracised. One of them describes walking down the central aisle of a plane, where all the passengers already seated were holding open the *Star* the week the scandal broke publicly, with large pictures of Barry pasted across the front of it. 'It was surreal,' he says, 'it was like I was living in a movie.'

Another family member says this case 'ripped apart our family'. Which is understandable, given how Barry sucked them into the eye of his personal tornado.

In 2010 the police issued an arrest warrant for Barry's older brother, Michael. His younger brother, Hylton, also copped serious flack, from both the advertising profession in which he works and the trustees of Barry's estate. They had traced payments between Hylton and Barry's accounts, so they dragged the advertising executive to court. The court papers say Hylton paid R576 000 to Barry between 2004 and 2009, and he had got R1 702 240 in cash from Barry. But these payments had nothing to do with the Ponzi scheme. For example, Hylton had bought a car from Barry, and Barry had paid his brother for marketing some products he tried to launch.

Hylton says he had also borrowed some cash from Barry, which he planned to pay back: 'I was having a tough time in a competitive industry and needed some support. Over the course of a few years, during lean months, I loaned money from Barry as I believed, like many others, that my brother was excelling in the legitimate business world.'

It was these loans that sparked the trustees' curiosity. Hylton might not have been an investor, but nevertheless it was cash paid from Barry's account – money that Gainsford, Kalian and Matsepe wanted back. So Hylton settled, repaying them what Barry had lent him. 'This was at great personal emotional expense and legal costs,' he says now. 'I haven't spoken to Barry since August 2009.'[25]

* * *

If Tannenbaum had, unaccountably, been allowed to roam free in Australia's Gold Coast and turn a buck hawking insurance, Dean Rees had a far tougher time in Switzerland.

Each time he turned around, the Qatari-based investment fund, Barwa, was lurking with another sequestration order, another liquidation application.

'I've spent the best part of the last few years trying to clear my name,' says Rees today. He has spent hours compiling documents, chronicling his fall from grace and plotting against Tannenbaum. It doesn't take a genius to figure out why Barwa pursued Rees so vigorously in court, rather than Tannenbaum. For one, Barwa's lawyers had already come calling on Barry, and taken everything he had – which turned out to be not much.

To investors, however, Rees was the one who got away with the loot. Along with Darryl Leigh, who got R114 million, and investors like Jawmend Rossi, who profited to the tune of R140 million.

Barwa's view was that Rees was 'the principal architect of the fraud on Barwa' – notwithstanding his 'protestations of innocence'.[26]

But how much cash did Rees actually have? How much had he made from the scheme? It's tricky to say for sure. Rees admitted that he handled Barry's 'acknowledgements of debt' to the tune of R3 billion. And in one court action, Rees admitted that he had personally made more than R70 million in 'commission' from the scheme, but he claimed he'd been 'independently wealthy' before Barry came along.

Totting up his various assets disclosed in the UK courts, puts Rees's net worth at easily north of R70 million, just by his own admission. By June 2009, Rees had about R16.4 million in cash in four accounts at the Hypo Swiss Private Bank in Geneva.[27]

When it came to cars, Rees drove a McLaren sports car (value: R2.4 million), a Mercedes GL420 CDI (value: R1.1 million) and a Mercedes Suzuki Swift (value: R275 000).

But it's in property where he keeps most of his cash. In Switzerland, for example, Rees's villa near Geneva was estimated to be worth R46.7 million in 2009 (about R33 million of which was mortgaged). In Australia, his company Doggered Investments holds property worth R16 million, including land on the Gold Coast and two properties in the ultra-chic Soul development, on which Debbie Tannenbaum had put down a deposit.

In South Africa, Rees also had a number of properties, worth more than R20 million in total. These included his mansion in Wilton Avenue, Bryanston (worth about R6 million, but with a bond of R5.7 million with Investec), the offices at 5 Wessel Road, Rivonia (worth maybe R30 million, but with a bond of R15 million) and Silver Armor properties (in the black to the tune of R2.5 million).

He might have already made a pretty sum, but the arrest warrant and Barwa's freezing order has iced him out of any further business. The freeze on his bank accounts, Rees said, meant that 'my law practice has lost all its staff as I was unable to pay salaries'. The loss from this: an estimated R100 000 per month. And, unable to develop properties he owned, Rees's net worth was rapidly dropping.[28]

By 2013 Rees was still living near Geneva, reportedly discussing setting up new businesses in Europe, and plotting revenge against Barry. 'There isn't much that's going on,' says Rees now. 'I'm still here doing my thing, trying to prove that it wasn't me who put this thing together.'

A court case argued in Johannesburg's South Gauteng High Court in October 2013 provides some insight into the fortune that Rees made from Tannenbaum.

Here, the trustees of Tannenbaum's estate took Rees to court, demanding he repay them R159 million. (Rees, obviously, wasn't going to come back from Switzerland in person, but he hired a crack squad of lawyers to go and fight his corner in that Joburg court.)

The figure of R159 million was based on the trustees' analysis of Barry's bank statements, which showed that Dean had transferred R411 million to Barry, and had been repaid R570 million. (If accurate, this would have put Rees above Jawmend Rossi, who got R139 million, as the biggest beneficiary of the scheme).

Rees, however, says that just because this amount went through his trust account, it would be a glaring error to assume that this is what he 'made' as a profit from the scheme. 'If I took all this profit, how did the investors make money?' he says. 'They weren't doing this for no return. The profit wasn't mine – the investors made profits.' This seems a valid point: Rees would have had to pay out at least some of the investors from his own account from the cash transferred to him by Barry.

Alec Brooks, the lawyer for the trustees, testified in the case, painting an unflattering picture of Rees as an unscrupulous liar who made off with everyone's cash. Brooks testified that before the scheme went belly-up and he began acting for the trustees, he was hired by one of the unlucky investors, Ian Irvine-Fortescue to wring his cash out of Tannenbaum.

On 25 May 2009, Brooks said, he met Rees at a restaurant in Sandton – about a week before the scam was exposed. Even though Brooks says he alerted Rees to the fact that the Aspen orders were forged, Rees still spoke to other investors days later as if he was oblivious to the fact it was all a fraud.

Brooks said: 'I would have expected an honest person to say to Mr X, Mr X here's a big problem. The whole basis of this investment has a big hole in it. There are no debtors.'

Rees hit back at Brooks and the trustees, saying they were simply intent on 'building their own pyramid of inadmissible and illegally obtained evidence'. He said that Tannenbaum's version of assets was 'inherently unreliable' as it was the account of a 'self-confessed liar and fraudster'.

Rees added that Brooks was 'one-sidedly' focused on just getting whatever cash he could for the estate. He recounts in his court papers how Brooks told one investor, 'We are vultures feeding on a carcass' and 'I like to ask for money.'

Brooks probably feels equally enamoured of Rees.

Nevertheless, at least that R159 million provides some quantifiable number of how much money Rees had made from his association with Tannenbaum.

But there was another intriguing element to the trustees' tussle with Rees: bizarrely, Brooks even asked Barry Tannenbaum if he would return to South Africa to testify against Rees – his former partner. Had he done so, it would have been particularly galling: the architect of the scheme becoming a star witness against one of his agents.

But this wasn't to be Brooks revealed in court that Tannenbaum's lawyer Derek Ziman said that 'Mr Tannenbaum would be prepared to come and give evidence if we could guarantee his safe return to Australia,' in other words that there are no warrants for his arrest'.

When Brooks contacted Colonel Piet Senekal, he confirmed that the warrant for Tannenbaum was still out. So Brooks got what he described as 'the obvious answer that he won't come'.

* * *

Of the three central protagonists, however, Darryl Leigh has had by far the roughest time. But that was inevitable, as he was the only one whom the authorities could touch. Although it wasn't exactly a lynching at dawn.

Despite the fact that Leigh was named as one of the prime suspects in the National Prosecuting Authority's draft request for legal assistance, the grumpy lawyer has not yet been charged. Instead, he continues to lead his life as before, living in the same townhouse block, Le Mistral, existing on what is understood to be a 'stipend' given to him by the authorities.

The reason that Leigh is being paid a stipend is that the Asset Forfeiture Unit swooped down in 2009 to seize the R44 million that Leigh had in his Standard Bank account. They then seized three of his properties: the Morningside townhouse, the R8 million Camps Bay property he had bought in 2008, as well as another property there registered in his daughter's name.

That sprawling 1520-square-metre property at 3 Medburn Road, Camps Bay, was bought by Leigh's daughter, Laura Danielle, in November 2007 for R8.8 million from wine producers Hamlin House. There was no bond on the property, suggesting it was bought by Leigh for his daughter using his 'commission'.

Six of Leigh's cars were also seized, the Lamborghini Murciélago Roadster, a Lamborghini Gallardo Spyder, two Mercedes-Benz SLKs, and two BMW X5s.

For good measure, the Asset Forfeiture Unit also seized a Moomba speedboat and two jet-skis. 'Darryl used to boast how [his boat] was the biggest on the Vaal Dam. But it sold on auction for barely R250 000,' says one of his erstwhile friends.

But unlike Tannenbaum or Rees, Darryl Leigh signed a 'settlement agreement' with the trustees led by their lawyer, Alec Brooks, in August 2010. It was a remarkable agreement, partly because the truculent lawyer finally confessed to the amount of cash he had got from the scheme – even if he stopped short of admitting his culpability for what had happened.[29]

Nonetheless, the magnitude of the amount he made over four years made for a staggering confession, immediately undercutting Leigh's contention that he did nothing wrong.

In a signed statement, Leigh admitted that he had made a 'total profit of R114.1 million from the investments in the scheme', cash purloined directly from the investors. The mechanics of this, according to the statement, were that Tannenbaum had paid R145 million into Leigh's bank account, and Leigh had repaid him R30.9 million.

Yet, anomalously, Leigh says in the statement that he 'denies that he, in his dealings with Tannenbaum, in any way acted unlawfully and/or wrongfully, and he disputes that the [trustees] are entitled to the relief claimed'. Quite how Kalian, Gainsford and Matsepe allowed Leigh to sign a statement denying any culpability whatsoever is breathtaking.

Especially since in the agreement that Leigh signed, it says the scheme was 'illegal' and that Tannenbaum had asked for money to use 'for his own benefit and to repay earlier investors their capital and interest'.

This again underlines how the trustees were after the cash, not ascribing responsibility – which was, to be fair, the job of the police and prosecutors. The trustees probably had dollar signs in their eyes when Leigh agreed to sign over everything he had to them, including €380 000 held in a Lloyds Bank account in Switzerland, R1 million in a UK bank account, and the R44 million already seized by government.

It also included that fleet of cars, which would have made a retired Formula One driver envious.

Then there were his properties and other assets, including his 50 per cent share of Tann Leigh Properties (the company he co-owned with Barry), his 50 per cent of his townhouse in Morningside, and his right to reclaim money lent to four friends.

The question is, did Darryl Leigh admit everything he had got from the scheme, openly and honestly declaring all his assets?

Well, it appears that Leigh may have had other assets that no one initially detected. For starters, the Hawks investigator probing this case, Colonel Piet Senekal, says that R326 million flowed through Leigh's six Standard Bank accounts

– R264 million alone through his current account – between January 2003 and June 2009. This is far more than the R145 million highlighted by the trustees.

On 30 June 2008, Leigh transferred R1.96 million from his Standard Bank current account to an international 'endowment' fund run by Momentum, situated in the tax haven of Guernsey. Says Senekal: 'The funds transferred from Leigh's Standard Bank account to ... Guernsey originated from funds which formed part of the illicit Frankel scheme, and are therefore the proceeds of criminal activities.'

One document shows a payment of $370 000 to Leigh's German bank account, while the trustees apparently also traced cash paid to Leigh in Australia.

Luckily for Leigh though, he had already reached a 'full and final settlement agreement' with the trustees of Tannenbaum's estate. Having done a quick and dirty deal with Leigh, it probably won't be easy for them to lay their hands on any cash that surfaces later – money that could have ultimately been split among the rest of the investors.

Leigh could probably never have foreseen this back in 2005, when Barry first spoke about stepping in to provide trade finance, but people close to him had ridden the roller coaster to extreme wealth, and back again.

On paper, Sharon Haarhoff, Darryl's ex-wife, looks like she made a killing. Her story is perhaps the best illustration of how Barry's scheme created immense, life-altering fortunes for some. Not always in a good way.

Sharon, remarried and living in Somerset West in the Cape, invested just R367 350 in the scheme, but over the course of three years, she was paid out nearly R5.7 million – a stratospheric return of 1 455 per cent.[30]

You'd imagine she would be comfortable for life. But Sharon says today: 'It's quite the opposite. I've lost my home because I had to pay everything back to the trustees and to SARS. I had to get rid of everything, and after that, I had no more money to fight it.'[31]

Darryl first suggested she should invest in 2006, so she put in R100 000 in February that year. As the returns clocked up, she invested another five times. She probably couldn't believe her luck with the amount she got back – such as the R3.7 million paid to her in September 2007.

But after the scheme was exposed, SARS were first at Sharon's door, followed quickly by Gainsford and the other trustees, demanding it all back. She resisted, so they dragged her to court. Eventually she gave up.

Now she's retired and lives in the Cape, but says she is lucky to have a husband who is still working. The husband after Darryl, that is. But Haarhoff doesn't blame Darryl so much as other people, like her accountant: 'My accountant told me it was a perfectly legitimate scheme. I wouldn't have got involved otherwise.'

Sharon, unlike many others, doesn't have much bad to say about Darryl: 'Obviously I've been divorced from him for a long time, but from what I know, if Darryl had thought it was a Ponzi, I can tell you there's no way he would have got involved.'

Tell that to the cops.

* * *

Reading through the court papers, the series of hapless missteps and epic faux pas, you're left with only two options: either Barry Tannenbaum is one of the most sophisticated con men ever, or he's very, very stupid.

Derek Ziman calls it straight: 'He's not very bright.'[32] His former lawyer says that in many cases, Barry simply fails to appreciate the gravity of a situation. Take Barry's actions when Dean Rees launched a bid to sequestrate him in Queensland in September 2009. Barry approached Ziman: 'What can I do to stop him?' Barry asked. 'Give me some money, and we'll file a defence,' Ziman responded. Barry disappeared. No defence was filed – so Rees got a default judgment against him.

Again, Barry approached Ziman: 'What can I do now?' he asked. Ziman replied: 'Well, we're already behind the game, so we can apply to set the order aside, but we need to move quickly and I'll need money to do it.'

Barry disappeared again. Rees then went to execute the judgment and got a bankruptcy order against him, which, in Australia, means you have only a few days to pay.

So Barry approached Ziman again asking what to do. Ziman laid down the law and impressed on Barry the gravity of a bankruptcy order, which could then be satisfied internationally. This time, the message seemed to have penetrated.

The thing is, Barry didn't appear to have any cash. In the end, he appeared without legal representation before a judge in Queensland, and got the bankruptcy order reversed.

Barry just didn't seem to get it. He couldn't grasp the consequences of his actions, or, in this case, inaction. But then, this wasn't exactly a new symptom.

Ziman seems to believe that had the Barwa money not disappeared (well, been used to pay other investors, mostly), then everyone would have been paid. It all would have been just swell. This seems a bit naive. After all, the 'purchase orders' from Aspen, Novartis and Adcock, which were backing the 'trade finance' deals were fake – so there never would have been any money coming through.

'It's never been necessary for us to get into that sort of detail about forged orders,' he says. 'The real issue is, who's got the loot?'

But what about the numerous forgeries with Barry's name on them? How can that be explained? Ziman has an answer: 'Dean used to just arrive at Barry's place with documents, and put them under his nose to sign. I mean, reams of documents. He didn't know what he was signing half the time.'

This seems like a very convenient excuse. You won't find many judges who will sympathise with someone who's argument is that he was a patsy, given a pen and told to initial whatever was put in front of him.

However, many investors still agree with Ziman's sentiment – that this was a legitimate scheme somehow laid low by over-zealous police, know-nothing journalists, a grasping tax authority and two shady lawyers guzzling too much cash out of the scheme in 'commissions'.

But by June 2011, forensic investigator Steve Harcourt-Cooke had finally finished his expert report on the wild ride that Barry had taken since 2004. His report showed there was nothing legitimate about it. Harcourt-Cooke's finding was that

> less than 0.05 per cent of the funds invested in the scheme were used for the purchase of pharmaceutical raw materials ... The scheme had no legitimate underlying business, and generated no income except for a small amount of interest earned. The scheme's true business was to obtain new funding from investors to repay earlier investors.[33]

In fact, for every single month between 2004 and 2009, while Barry was charming investors, buying new houses and new BMWs, and flying around the world, he was insolvent.

To reach these findings, Harcourt-Cooke had painfully trawled through every one of Barry's bank accounts, Rees's accounts, Leigh's accounts, documents provided to the auditors, tax submissions, reports from the trustees' inquiry and every other scrap of paper with the word 'Tannenbaum' on it.

In all, investors had paid R3.67 billion into his accounts over those years, part of which he then squandered. But if, as Michael Tannenbaum believes, Barry doesn't have much of this cash, why would he have constructed the scheme?

Crucially, Harcourt-Cooke's findings revealed a missing chain of evidence that would provide keen insight into what had driven Barry Tannenbaum to create such a scam.

Until then, Barry's true motivation for cooking up the con had been indecipherable. But it would soon become blindingly clear. And it would be an astounding revelation that would take everyone by surprise.

Ian Irvine-Fortescue:
Twice bitten, not shy

Ian Irvine-Fortescue has the distinction of owning the most expensive iPhone in South Africa. He moved to South Africa from the UK in the early 1980s, and is something of a serial entrepreneur.

The unwritten rule of entrepreneurship, though, is that for every smoking hot investment, there are three fly traps waiting to suck up all your cash and give you nothing.

As trim and alert as you would expect a black-belt karate enthusiast to be, Fortescue has had more than his share of bad luck. Just before he put money into the Tannenbaum scheme, he got drawn into a nasty little investment in Africa's only ski resort, Tiffindell, perched on a 3 000-metre-high peak south of the mountain kingdom of Lesotho, landlocked in the middle of South Africa. His accountant, Andre le Roux, had just invested in the ski resort, and needed bridging finance. Just for a few weeks, he said. So Fortescue coughed up.

It wasn't a great move. Le Roux ended up in court fighting the former owners, and the African ski business wasn't about to break any revenue records. Tiffindell isn't exactly the Alps, with a spluttering snow-making machine doing most of the work, and only the occasional smattering of natural snow helping cover the 1.5-hectare slope.

'I got most of my promised money back eventually,' says Fortescue, 'but it took a lot longer than anyone expected. So when my friend John Miller told me about the Tannenbaum opportunity, I left the letter in my briefcase for a year.'

Fortescue's reasoning was: sure, there's risk – but this Tannenbaum thing can hardly go any worse than Tiffindell. The sort of words that, five years later, you would want to cut out and frame.

Miller was one of Darryl Leigh's first investors, from the days when Barry was still hawking furniture investments, ostensibly in partnership with his brother Michael. Ian had also known Darryl for many years.

'Initially, I wasn't particularly interested,' he says. 'But I'd got this money from a property sale that I wanted to set aside as my "pension investment", and was looking for a place to put it. The returns sounded great, so I called Leigh.'

Fortescue attended three of Barry's investor breakfasts, but was never really convinced at any stage. 'At one of them, I sat next to the tennis coach [Allon Rock] and he was asking me if I thought it was a legit investment. I said to him, "Look, I have no idea if it is, or it isn't".'

Barry spent some time chatting with Fortescue at that breakfast, and noticed the Brit – now a naturalised South African – was quite taken with his iPhone. 'You like it? Would you like one?' Barry asked.

'Of course I'd love one,' said Fortescue.

That same afternoon, an iPhone was delivered to Fortescue's office. As simple as that. No contracts, no complications – just Barry being Barry, delivering.

Only thing was, Fortescue got an iPhone, but Barry got R8.4 million of his money. In the end, as the KPMG figures show, Fortescue was paid out R1.2 million, but this still left him R7.2 million in the red.

Each time, Leigh would call him with a new offer: 'Barry's got a belter,' he'd say, then rattle off the number of weeks, investment limit and return.

But towards the end of 2008, the excuses became more regular than the payments. By November 2008, Fortescue had figured out it was a con.

'Look,' he says, 'I'd always been cynical, but some of the excuses he gave me were rubbish. But then I became quite obsessed about how to play this so that I'd still get something back. I had to keep up the pretence to get my money.'

This pretence even saw Fortescue ploughing in extra cash into a new deal, even after he thought it was a scam. 'I was trying desperately to out-think him. If I let on that I suspected, it might fall apart. I took the view that I had to put in a little, to get out a lot.'

Reading through the emails between Rees and Tannenbaum, it's clear that Fortescue had piled plenty of pressure on them to repay him. Once, Barry told Ian he'd made a mistake, repaying two lots of capital into his bank account. 'He called me up, and said, "Please won't you transfer half of that back." There was no way I was giving him back a cent though.'

He called Leigh, and asked if he could put some pressure on Barry. Leigh's response: I'm having my own problems getting paid, I can't help you.

By early 2009, Fortescue lost patience. 'I figured there were three options: get some underworld hoods to go to Sydney and beat my money out of Barry, continue applying pressure, or go the legal route. Well, I don't know any hoods, and the pressure had got me nowhere.'

So he hired a lawyer who had a reputation of getting cash out of hard cases, a man named Alec Brooks. Brooks launched a court case against Tannenbaum in late May. Then, Brooks called up Fortescue and said he had to step down as his lawyer because of a 'conflict of interest'.

'I got Brooks involved,' Fortescue says, 'but I think he then realised just how big this was, and how much money he could make on the other side of the fence. So that's why he jumped ship.'

Instead, as mentioned earlier, Brooks was hired by the liquidators of Tannenbaum's estate, where he would stand to make a lot more money by suing the investors to recover cash.

Fortescue, ironically, then got a letter from the trustees demanding that he repay some of what Barry had paid him in the last few months before it popped. At least Brooks had the good grace not to send the demand himself.

Fortescue told them to take a hike. 'Honestly, I'll fight that to the end. All they're doing is milking the small guys while they collect fees. I can bet there'll be nothing left in the estate in the end.'

Luckily for Fortescue, the loss of the money wasn't terminal. His company, Reef Business Systems, a stone's throw from Adcock Ingram's offices in Midrand, is doing well selling office equipment. But he could have retired early on the basis of what Barry had promised him he would earn. Something he can't do now.

'You could look at it, and say, wow, I was rich! But the truth was, it was all virtual money anyway. If you'd added up all the [bounced] post-dated cheques I had, I'd be very wealthy. But it was all a lie.'

He shrugs philosophically: 'If you're looking for sympathy as an entrepreneur, you won't find it – even your mates laugh at you.'

He doesn't use the iPhone that cost him a princely R7.2 million any more. It's no consolation to think that if he had invested that cash in shares of Apple, the iPhone maker, he would have more than R21 million today.

18

Flushed out

LAWYER: Who loaned you the money to gamble?
BARRY TANNENBAUM: Friends.

In mid-2012, Shirish Kalian and the trustees scored a significant goal, and did something that the entire South African government law-enforcement services hadn't been able to do: they got Barry Tannenbaum into a witness box to testify about what had happened.

Tannenbaum was subpoenaed to testify before Katie Lynch, the registrar for Queensland, in the Brisbane Federal Court.

This was Kalian's first trip to Australia, and he says he was struck by how Rolls-Royce the courts seemed – velvet trimmings in the courtrooms, efficient court-case management, online court files. Even a room with a bed for exhausted lawyers to crash.

First, Debbie Tannenbaum was called to the stand. But she couldn't answer anything. Looking tired, and without make-up, Debbie knew nothing. She didn't know how her signature had ended up on documents setting up companies; she didn't know what Barry did with his time; she didn't know why they were even on the run. All she knew was that the wolf in the forest was 'Mr Rees'. She wept repeatedly on the stand.

Look, Barry told the lawyers, she knows nothing. Let me answer your questions. And answer them he did. For three days, Barry poured out his soul to the lawyers, in front of the registrar, nailing home the point that he was simply an unwitting party, manipulated by others.

* * *

The picture that was painted of Barry during the hearing was that of a bumbling, hapless character, as likely to stumble accidentally into the middle of a gang war as he was to launch the biggest Ponzi scheme in South Africa.

When asked for his financial records, Barry said he 'did try' to account for his finances, but he just 'did not have any of those records whatsoever'.[1]

'Are you then able to complete a statement of affairs?' asked the lawyers.

'I don't know,' he replied. 'I can attempt to do that. As I said, I don't have any of the exact records … for some time back, but I can certainly attempt to do so.'

It was difficult to say where Barry's ineptitude stopped and his efforts to dodge the questions began.

But first, his wife testified. It was an excruciating, painful process. Each time the lawyers pulled out some document she had signed – the purchase of a house, for example – she would say she had no idea how it worked, that she had just signed whatever her husband put in front of her because she 'trusted him'. Given that she was the registered owner of all the properties – the Johannesburg town house, the Umhlanga holiday flat, the St Ives mansion – you would think she would at least have a basic understanding of how it all worked. Not so. She said: 'I take no interest in the financial dealings, I really just concentrate on my children. That sounds really pathetic, but I am a mother who is a home mother who looks after the children.'[2]

Nor was Debbie aware of precisely why they had ended up on the run, ostensibly penniless. 'I'm sorry. I am quite an ignorant person because my focus is on my children and I am [a] fashion designer, and I am sorry I don't understand all those terminologies,' she said.

Well, what about the houses? the lawyers asked. You must have signed the papers? 'I must've signed something to enable the sale, or Barry wouldn't have been able to handle the sale,' she replied.

She had no idea where the A$1.6 million had come from to buy the St Ives house in the first place, and said the decision to put the houses in her name was done 'under the instruction of the accountant … That's just what I've grown up knowing. My mum had [the] house in her name and that's all I've ever known as well. I didn't know you weren't meant to do that, it's the way [in] South Africa [that] we got brought up.'

Although Debbie was made a director of Bardeb Nominees in December 2006, she had no idea what being a director even meant.

QUESTION: Did you carry out any functions as a director?
DEBBIE: No.
QUESTION: When was the first time you became aware that you were a director?
DEBBIE: A couple of months ago when [Barry and I] were talking about it.

Though she authorised payments, she had no idea how that happened. For example, records in the company's books show Debbie Tannenbaum had paid Barry's friend Larry Brenner A$100 000. Can you explain that? she was asked.

'I have no idea,' she said. 'I didn't personally do it. My name is there, but I didn't.'

Though Debbie's name was all over the documents, she had not a clue how it worked.

'I've heard of Bardeb Trust. I don't know what it is, but I've heard the name,' she said.

Well, aren't you a beneficiary? the lawyers asked.

Debbie replied: 'I'm not sure … I don't know what a beneficiary is, but I think it [has] something to do with Bardeb.'

She let slip some details that provided intriguing insight into how Barry had complete control over her life. Debbie said that even during the good times, when they were living in Sydney, she would call Barry and ask: '"Can I go to the shops and do some grocery shopping or get some clothing?" And he'd say, "Yes you can", and I would go and spend.'

After the scheme imploded, however, Debbie would still seek permission to spend money, but then she would call and ask, '"Is there anything in the account? Can I go to the shops?" And he would say yes or no.'

Debbie tried to get a job and formed a company called Grass Cottage. 'When we first came to the Gold Coast, we were looking at any way of being able to bring in an income and I thought with fashion being my background, I could open up a little cottage store.'

But it never got off the ground. 'In my field of work, and at my age, it's not easy and also I've had to really concentrate on keeping the stability in the home for my children. It's been very, very traumatic for them as it has for myself.' They were still going through that trauma, she said.

The obvious question was, did Debbie know that her husband was running a massive illegal scheme? Why did she think all the bad things had begun to happen to her?

Perhaps it doesn't come as a surprise that Debbie had only a very flimsy grasp on what had happened. When she had asked Barry what was going on, he had just told her that 'something has happened with the business'.

'I don't really understand what the business did,' she said. 'I just know that he, Dean Rees, did something and then the blame fell on my husband because he owned the companies.'

Is that really all you know, asked the lawyers.

'I can remember a lot of change happening and a lot of devastation and a lot of tears and a lot of emotion … our lives changed in an [instant] – reporters outside, threatening phone calls, people arriving at our doorsteps threatening us.'

So what had Rees done, Debbie was asked.

'Mr Rees had taken the money or something. I don't really know. I just know that Mr Rees is not a very good person.'

Why would she think it was all Rees's fault?

She replied: 'Barry has always worked very hard and he has always had legitimate companies and when Dean Rees came along, everything went wrong.'

Debbie's testimony was heart-wrenching – mainly because she and her children clearly had no clue *why* they were being forced to scamper around a foreign country, moving houses every few months.

In Debbie's eyes, the Tannenbaums were victims of a scheming crook who had swindled the food out of their mouths. She had no idea what her husband had done, or why he had done what he did. When she found out, she was bewildered.

* * *

Towards the end of the first day's testimony, Barry Tannenbaum, under oath, must have felt his blood run cold when the lawyers turned the discussion in another direction.

QUESTION: Did you, while you were in South Africa, undertake any gambling at all?

TANNENBAUM: Not specifically. I mean, I did use to play a little bit, but nothing exhaustive.

QUESTION: Did you make payments from your accounts to gambling companies online?

TANNENBAUM: Sometimes, yes. I would play a little, but I can't recall exactly which company it could be.

The lawyers then handed him a forensic document they had been prepared by exhaustively collating all his bank accounts over the previous eight years. Barry appeared startled, flustered by the evidence. The document revealed that he, a man who said he did 'not specifically' gamble, had blown R62.5 million on gambling. Occasionally, he made some cash – in all, R36.7 million. But the bottom line was that R25.8 million had been flushed down the drain in late-night poker sessions while he was huddled over a computer in his house, hidden from his family.

QUESTION: That's a substantial amount of money. Do you accept that?

TANNENBAUM: That, it's – that is a substantial amount of money.

QUESTION: Yes. And do you have a recollection of playing or gambling with money in those types of amounts, those large amounts?

ANSWER: Not in that degree, I don't have a recollection, no.

South Africans have an uncomfortable relationship with gambling. Until democracy was instituted in 1994, gambling happened in the 'homelands', the quasi-independent states set up by the apartheid government to create the impression of separate development between white and black people. Only, the reality was that there was no 'development' whatsoever taking place in the dusty, godforsaken homelands, ruled over by puppet regimes ultimately answerable to the apartheid government.

In the 1980s, gambling took place in Bophuthatswana, a homeland in which casino magnate Sol Kerzner established Sun City, a gaudy, flashy casino complex modelled on the hotels of Las Vegas.

You might think that gambling is the preserve of the poor, but most people who visit casinos are in the top income band – people exactly like Barry Tannenbaum. In fact, 8 per cent of the country's adults, nearly three million people, go to casinos once a year to gamble. One in three of these, 976 000, gamble every month.[3]

When Barry begrudgingly admitted he made the occasional foray into a casino, he was being characteristically conservative with the truth. His gambling problem had begun long before the scheme started. At a time when he was supposedly earning R28 500 a month, back in 2001, his bank accounts show mountains of cash being splurged on gambling in frantic binges.

The truth was, Barry visited all the gambling joints: Montecasino, Emperors Palace, Grand West Casino in Cape Town, the Sundome. The earliest clue in his bank statements dates back to September 2000, when Barry's FNB credit card shows him running up some serious debt at the Sundome Casino, with its 1700 slot machines and fifty tables, run by Las Vegas chain MGM Grand.[4]

Poker was Barry's game of choice. 'That's what I enjoy the most, I suppose,' he said.

For a man who tried to present this as a casual activity, the details show otherwise. On 19 September 2000, Barry dropped R2 000 at the casino. He then repeated that two days later and again on 22 September, another R2 000 on 27 September and once again the following day. Two days later, for variety's sake, Barry headed to the tacky Carnival City on Johannesburg's industrial East Rand, a casino designed to look like a giant circus tent, and spent another R2 000.[5]

In October, he visited the Sundome Casino eight times, dropping another R16 000. This was more than half his salary at the time. Soon Barry began to open more bank accounts and split the gambling spending across them. He opened an account at Investec Private Bank, for example, and charged a large part of his gambling to that account.

From early 2002, Barry was spending thousands at a time on his Investec card at the cash desk of Caesars Palace, a casino next to O.R. Tambo International Airport and just fifteen minutes from Frankel's offices in Bedfordview.

Though there are periods when Barry's gambling activity seems to have become less frantic, every couple of months there were relapses, when he blew thousands at a time over several days. Take March 2003, for example. Using his

Investec card, Barry spent R16 000 at the Caesars Palace cash desk in eight separate visits. At the same time, he whacked another R20 000 onto his FNB card at Caesars that month.

QUESTION: Did you ever carry out any gambling at Caesars?
TANNENBAUM: Well, I sometimes used to meet with [suppliers] there and
    we would have dinner and possibly, yes, you know.

It's as if he can't say the word 'gamble'.

Barry continued in the same vein over the next few months, occasionally breaking the pattern by going to the ultra-kitsch Montecasino complex on the northern side of Johannesburg, designed in a faux-Tuscan style, complete with an artificial sky. The clumsy medieval Italian theme at Montecasino seems at odds with the occasional Vespa propped up against a wall, looking hopelessly out of place. It's where genuine culture would come to get murdered, had it a choice. It speaks volumes about the dearth of options in Joburg that this place won the title of best entertainment complex.

Not that this mattered to Barry, who would blow R2 000 at Montecasino's non-smoking casino, Salon Privé. He wasn't there to compare the gelato with what you'd get in Montepulciano or Siena, but rather to ride the seventy-eight tables of games like blackjack, poker, baccarat and roulette.

When asked about it later, he begrudgingly admitted, 'I have been there a few times, yes.'

* * *

Soon, however, Barry discovered the anonymity of online gambling, the sort of thing you can do at home while your wife is asleep.

First, he dabbled with the Piggs Peak online casino, a spin-off from the hotel and casino based in the tiny African country of Swaziland. Piggs Peak says it is 'renowned' for 'creating a number of instant online millionaires already'.

A lot like Barry then – theoretical money moving exceptionally fast. From July 2003, he began spending thousands at Piggs Peak in eleven separate transactions online, while still taking the occasional trip to Caesars Palace. In August, he spent R22 000 at Piggs Peak, R2 000 a pop.

By November 2004, he had graduated to Silver Sands, which bills itself as 'arguably South Africa's best and most popular online casino', having operated for fifteen years. It has everything: slots, poker, roulette, blackjack and pretty much anything you would get in the real gambling world. 'Silver Sands Casino allows players to play in rands and easily deposit and withdraw through credit cards and/or instant EFTs', the site explains encouragingly.

Too easily, it seems. The problem is that whereas Barry was previously only paying out fairly small amounts, R2000 at a time, now the size of the gambling debts began to swell.

From February to March 2004, for example, Barry's Standard Bank account shows nine transactions over the course of a month – the first for R15000 on 17 February to Silversandsonline.com. Two days later, another R37000 payment to the same casino, another R50000 on 25 February, another R15000 the next day, R22000 the day after, R10000 on 3 March, R15000 on 5 March, R40000 on 11 March and R30000 on 23 March.

Such a large chunk of cash dramatically raised the stakes. Little surprise that three months later, the first 'acknowledgement of debt' pops up, as Barry started taking money from investors.

Take February and March 2005, for example. Using an FNB gold credit card, Barry spent R88000 at Silversandsonline.com on gambling in fourteen transactions. Ironically, at the same time, the taxman gave him a R7439 credit on 15 February, as he declared a fraction of the money he was actually making.

On 3 August 2005 alone, there were nine debits for gambling, totalling R228735. Barry spent more on gambling on that single day than the average mineworker earns in a deep-level South African mine in a whole year.

As the Ponzi money began to sluice into his accounts, the gambling escalated. In the first three months of 2006, Barry's FNB card showed R145000 spent at Silversandsonline.com. And in the same three months, his Standard Bank cheque card showed an astonishing number of gambling transactions at Silver Sands totalling R509634 – more than the average salaried South African makes in a year. This total figure is made up of small and large amounts – from just over R6000 in some cases to R20200 in others.

Consider a particular week in January 2006 – Barry's Standard Bank account had been running pretty low, but on 17 January, Mervyn Serebro deposited R780000 and, the next day, Darryl Leigh transferred another R302000. That very day, Barry punched his credit-card details into the Silver Sands online casino ten times, ploughing a collective R140592 into gambling from the combined loot he had just taken from Leigh and Serebro.

From that point, there were fewer periods when Barry wasn't gambling, though some periods are more intense than others. In November 2006, for example, he spent R159000 at the same online casino.

QUESTION: Did you gamble through Piggs Peak?
TANNENBAUM: I think that must have been an online sort of situation there, yes.
QUESTION: Which [online gambling operations] did you do most of your gambling through?

TANNENBAUM: Basically some of the ones that you have said already. I think you mentioned Silver Sands and I think there was Piggs Peak.

* * *

Towards the end of the second day of testimony, the lawyers again raised the issue of how much Barry had spent on gambling.

QUESTION: Were you spending significant amounts of time each day gambling online?
TANNENBAUM: Yes. It was online on the computer.
QUESTION: But how long were you spending?
TANNENBAUM: Just generally in the evenings, at night, so a couple of hours.
QUESTION: How many hours?
TANNENBAUM: Two, three, four hours.

The lawyers raised the R228 735 spent on gambling on that one day, 3 August 2005.

QUESTION: Was that all something you were gambling online, for example, in one evening?
TANNENBAUM: Yes, it is.
QUESTION: Well, why did you gamble so much money? What was the motivation for it?
TANNENBAUM: I don't recall why. I mean, I don't know. I'm not sure.
QUESTION: Well, did you come home at night-time and say, well, I'm going to go spend two or three hours online gambling?
TANNENBAUM: No, it was just, I suppose, on the computer, and it's – you just get hooked on it, I suppose. I don't know. I'm not sure why.

Barry then rounded on the forensic investigators, saying he had no idea 'why they would break it down in those amounts, I don't know'. As if the breakdown of the amounts was somehow relevant, and not simply an objection meant to sidetrack the discussion. This was his character: reframe the discussion, move the debate away from his own motivations and actions, blame someone else.

He said he didn't 'recall the exact motivation at the time' for gambling so much cash, other than the hope of winning back money.

QUESTION: Is it some addiction you have to gambling?
TANNENBAUM: Not necessarily, no. As I said, I don't recall the exact reasoning why.

The lawyers took him laboriously through individual payments on his accounts, epic sums at a time, such as R150 000 blown in one transaction on 5 November

2005. Each time, Barry could provide no explanation. At one stage, he conceded he did it for 'entertainment'.

They then got to the nub of the issue: why Barry needed to construct a cross-border Ponzi scheme. His bank statements show that in 2005, Barry spent R10.2 million on gambling and won back R6.2 million – a net loss of R4 million. But Barry's declared income for 2005 came to only R137 130 – less than he would slap down on a single gambling deal, in some cases. Clearly, there was an immense disconnect.

QUESTION: So, where was your ability to fund those losses from gambling?
TANNENBAUM: I suppose it came out of my bank accounts and credit cards.
QUESTION: But credit cards have to be paid … what money did you use to pay for those losses?
TANNENBAUM: Well, some money that I earned out of the business, possibly from loans.
QUESTION: Loans to you?
TANNENBAUM: Yes.
QUESTION: Who loaned you the money or lent you the money?
TANNENBAUM: Friends.
QUESTION: Ok, can you identify who they are?
TANNENBAUM: Not specifically … At the time, I can't remember, but I had a few friends that used to loan me money from time to time.
QUESTION: Were they lending you the money … to enable you to spend it on private expenditure?
TANNENBAUM: Yes. It varied. Yes.
QUESTION: Did you have to pay interest?
TANNENBAUM: Yes.
QUESTION: Is that the best evidence you can give?
TANNENBAUM: Yes …
QUESTION: How could you repay the money if the money was lost on gambling?
TANNENBAUM: I don't know.

When pressed, Barry couldn't name one single investor offhand who lent him this cash. But it was ominously clear to him where the questions were leading.

QUESTION: Did you repay them?
TANNENBAUM: Some, yes.
QUESTION: And some not?
TANNENBAUM: Yes.

QUESTION: So who do you still owe money to?

TANNENBAUM: I'm not sure. I mean, this is quite some time back. You must have the lists there.

QUESTION: These are the investors, are they?

Tannenbaum: Yes.

This is the moment when Barry made the clear link, the intimation that his 'friends' were lending him millions to gamble. Right here, this was the smoking gun, his motivation, the essence of why he had started his Ponzi scheme. Corralled into a corner, he was forced to admit it.

QUESTION: So you used the investors' money to gamble?

TANNENBAUM: Not necessarily always, no. It depends if they were investors, or just loans.

Barry was squirming wildly, doing his best to avoid answering, failing dismally. The lawyers had him on the ropes and weren't about to let him down.

QUESTION: Isn't it really just the case that you know what I'm talking about when I'm talking about the investors, don't you? That you got the investors in and utilised the funds they provided for your private expenditure, including gambling? Isn't that the case?

TANNENBAUM: No, not necessarily.

QUESTION: Yes, but in some instances, you did.

TANNENBAUM: Possibly.

QUESTION: Is it 'possibly'? Are you unsure? It's the case, isn't it, that investors put money into your accounts and you utilised them for your private expenditure, including gambling? Isn't that right?

TANNENBAUM: Well, I think that – it depends how you look at it, I suppose.

Barry twisted and turned, but there was no way out. The lawyers kept pushing him.

QUESTION: You know, don't you, that during these years from 2004 to 2009 … when there was heavy gambling by you … that the only way you could fund this gambling was from … the money that investors put into your account, isn't it?

TANNENBAUM: Possibly so, yes.

But even that was not good enough for the lawyers.

QUESTION: Why don't you just say 'yes'? Why is there a reservation? Is it because you don't want to admit it?

TANNENBAUM: No, I mean, it's just difficult to pinpoint each and every transaction, I suppose, as to which money came from where.

But it was too late. He had been caught, and there was no turning back. He wheeled around, pretending not to know.

QUESTION: When you gambled, you sat at home at night on your computer, putting in money like R25 000, R100 000 and then R150 000, [and] you didn't think that I've been lent some money from a friend, [and] I've got that to utilise? Your thinking was that you had money in your account from investors?

TANNENBAUM: My thinking was that there was money available in my account, yes.

QUESTION: From the investors?

TANNENBAUM: From whatever, yes.

QUESTION: So you really didn't turn your mind then as to whether it was investors' money or private money?

TANNENBAUM: I don't recall thinking either/or … no.

QUESTION: So, if you'd gone online and gambled one night, and the only money … was from investors, you would have just used the investors' money?

TANNENBAUM: Yes.

On the third day of testimony, the lawyers came back to this, pummelling Tannenbaum.

QUESTION: [When you were gambling heavily], you couldn't have repaid the [investors] because you were using their money to gamble.

TANNENBAUM: Possibly not, it depends.

QUESTION: You couldn't have paid them back, if they wanted the money back … do you accept that?

TANNENBAUM: Possibly, yes.

QUESTION: No, it's correct, isn't it?

TANNENBAUM: Possibly.

QUESTION: It's correct, isn't it?

TANNENBAUM: Yes.

They were relentless, forcing Tannenbaum, the master weasel, to concede to the inevitable. 'Between 2004 and 2009,' they asked, 'you could not have repaid the lenders their loans plus interest?'

Tannenbaum replied: 'Well, I suppose not, no. Not [at] any given time.'

Having been forced to admit so much, Tannenbaum tried to wriggle out of the 'statutory declaration' he had signed under oath and given to Barwa in June 2009. He claimed that he had only signed it under duress.

QUESTION: Can you explain what was the 'duress'?
TANNENBAUM: I was personally afraid really that if I didn't sign it, I was not sure what the outcome would be.
QUESTION: [The lawyers] didn't force you to sign it, did they?
TANNENBAUM: Not physically, no.
QUESTION: But you signed it voluntarily, didn't you?
TANNENBAUM: Well, I felt I had no option, yes.

Though Barry had pinned the blame on Rees, even in his own unlikely version of events there was no escaping his own complicity. The lawyers asked him if he accepted the $30 million paid by Barwa into the Australian account of Barry's company Bartan was obtained using fabricated documents.

'Yes,' he said.

The lawyers then turned the screws and asked if all the money 'paid into your account from lenders' had been used to purchase raw materials.

'No, not necessarily,' he said.

* * *

That testimony over those three days in Brisbane was brutal for Barry. Squeezed into a corner, there was nothing he could do but give up the whole game. For example, in the email he sent to investors boasting about Eurochemicals' $50 million turnover, Barry admitted that the information was false. But this time, he blamed Leigh. 'The email was written in conjunction with Mr Leigh's assistance,' he said.

The lawyers shot back, putting it to him that he had no ability to repay the 'investors' because he wasn't making any money out of genuine transactions – plus he was gambling and using large chunks of the money for himself.

Barry was also forced to admit that Eurochemicals had two sets of financials – one with the real revenue of R11.7 million to show to the taxman, the other showing R432.8 million in revenue to show to investors. Why were there two sets of financials, he was asked.

'I do recall seeing this document,' said Barry. 'They were created by some-body else [who] at the time was doing a deal with a company called Och-Ziff in London, trying to create a facility with them, and the first time I saw those documents was when [they were] presented to Och-Ziff.'

'Who presented it [to Och-Ziff]?'

'There was Dean Rees and James Patterson and Gareth MacIntosh,' he said.

'Did you have an involvement in the preparation of the financials?'

'No,' said Barry.

So why didn't he tell Och-Ziff of the forgeries, he was asked.

'I left it in control of Dean Rees,' he said.

'Did you tell Mr Rees that he shouldn't be providing that?'

'Yes, and he said that it's all under control and for the purposes of the meet-ings.'

Every time Barry was asked a question, there was a lie waiting to be unmasked – even when it came down to ordinary documents, like an April 2007 application for a credit card at ANZ Bank. In the application, he declared his monthly salary as A$60 000, and said he had accounts with balances of around A$600 000. Under a sentence that read 'I acknowledge that all the information provided in this application form is true and correct', Barry signed his name.

QUESTION: Were you earning a monthly salary of A$60 000?

TANNENBAUM: No, I don't believe so.

QUESTION: Did you have any accounts opened in Australia with balances of A$600 000?

TANNENBAUM: No.

QUESTION: In the last sentence of [your loan application], you state that 'I acknowledge that all the information provided in this application form is true and correct' … is that not the case?

Tannenbaum admitted it was not true and correct. He also struggled to explain how a man with no resources was surviving day to day. Despite his claims, money was still coming in. In November 2009, Barry paid A$120 000 to a company called Sun Pacific Ventures, through his lawyer's trust account. He explained that Sun Pacific was 'a company that was set up by a colleague from America, and he was going to help me possibly get into some business, so that money was sent to that company in order to get a business going in terms of health products, just something for me to generate income. But sadly it didn't work out that way.'

This 'colleague's' name was Larry Brenner – a good friend of Barry's.

There was another A$50 000 paid to a company called Brand New Era, which, according to Barry, was going to 'assist some of the staff I had from Bartan group to possibly carry on a pharmaceutical business'. That plan also fell apart, so he claimed.

On 28 January 2010, there was a payment of A$95 303 made to Bartan. When asked where that came from, Tannenbaum said it was 'the proceeds from one of the properties from Sertan Investments'.

That Barry wasn't a whizz with cash is evident from the fact that in November 2009, he took out a second mortgage on the St Ives property for A$300 000. 'I needed the funds,' he explained. 'To pay for security at the house, to pay for the house, the bond at the house, the mortgage, to pay for various outstanding debts at the time.'

Sounds like Barry – take out an extra mortgage to finance the existing mortgage. How did he think he would be able to repay the second mortgage then? 'On sale,' he said. 'It was our intention to sell the house, because we had already started moving out of Sydney.'

This meant that when the St Ives house was sold for A$1.735 million, there wasn't a cent left over. In fact, there was a shortfall of A$27 000 between what Barry owed on the house and the price it fetched.

Although Barry dodged questions and specific details evaded him, he could nevertheless be mawkish and effusive in portraying his own hardship with remarkable clarity. For example, when asked how much he had got when he sold his furniture, he replied: 'Sadly, not much at all. A lot went to auction ... For example, I had a beautiful mahogany leather desk, sold for A$45, and I probably paid a hundred times more than that for that desk.'

* * *

Though Barry spent many hours gambling, his wife had no knowledge of it. When testifying, she was asked: 'Were you aware at all that your husband gambled?'

'Absolutely not, absolutely not ... as far as I know, he didn't gamble.'

When she was handed a folder containing every gambling transaction, she seemed confused, ambushed by the information.

'You never went to a casino?' she was asked.

'I've been to a casino institution called Sun City on a holiday with my children and some friends, but I don't gamble,' she said. 'We sat at the swimming pool.'

'So you didn't make any online payments then to any gambling institutions?'

'I wouldn't even know how to,' she replied. No one doubted her.

'Have you got any explanation as to where your husband would have had the ability to obtain sums in the order of R62 million to be able to pay online gambling enterprises?'

Debbie replied: 'I have no idea.'

Whether what was revealed over those three days in Brisbane has changed their relationship is unclear. After the first day, the registrar instructed Barry not to chat to Debbie about his evidence. 'Yes,' he said, 'I don't think she wants to talk about it, quite frankly.'

Some of the investors who were duped out of their money are astounded by the gambling, and struggle to believe that Barry, a devout Jew and family man, was doing something so sordid with so much of their money. Others believe it to be the perfect excuse to launder away dirty cash. 'Well, it's handy to have a gambling problem, isn't it,' says Ian Irvine-Fortescue. 'Who's to say where the money is, because I don't believe it's all disappeared, and he has nothing.'

But Barry's relatives aren't surprised by the gambling revelations, talking about long trips to the Carousel Casino, north of Pretoria, long before his days at Frankel, where Barry would throw down thousands at a time when he couldn't afford to.

'He's always denied the gambling,' says Derek Ziman. It turns out he was lying. In fact, he seems to fit the mould of the problem gambler perfectly – hiding away from his family; going on gambling binges for days; constructing a global Ponzi scheme to suck more cash from people to feed his habit.

Ziman seems to think that Barry 'just wasn't smart enough' to construct a global scam of this nature, simply to fuel a gambling habit.

And yet, the evidence says otherwise. The evidence shows that Barry gambled away investors' cash – R62 million of it – though he later got some of it back. While investors fretted and lost sleep over whether they would be repaid, Barry was on his computer playing Texas Hold'em, losing their shirts.

* * *

Barry's testimony was revelatory, not just because it unmasked his motive, but also for the insight it afforded into his character. Like many a sociopath, Barry always had someone else to blame for his misfortunes: his accountant, his lawyer, Dean Rees, Darryl Leigh, anyone he could think of.

For example, when his South African tax declaration for 2008 was raised, which said he had made R2 million in commission, Barry said, 'I wrote this letter under instruction from the accountant.'

'Did you derive any commission that year?' he was asked.

'No, I didn't,' he said.

'So why would you have then [signed it]?'

'Well, I'm not sure what his motivation was for me to do that,' he said. Again, blame someone else.

Barry admitted lying to the Australian Tax Office, but it was his accountant's fault, it seems. Bartan's tax return has a column for payments to 'associated persons', and it lists a payment to Barry for A$175 000 for consulting services and another A$75 000 for consulting fees for Debbie. 'But,' the lawyers asked him, 'your wife didn't provide any consulting services to Bartan, did she?'

'No, that was the advice of [the accountant],' said Barry.

Like a schoolboy caught behind the bicycle shed smoking a cigarette, someone else had made him do it.

It was reminiscent of Bernie Madoff. In his interview in *New York* magazine, Madoff said, 'I allowed myself to be talked into something, and that's my fault. I thought I could extricate myself after a short period of time. But I just couldn't.' Madoff explained that 'if you think I woke up one morning and said, "Well, listen, I need to be able to buy a boat and a plane, and this is what I'm going to do", that's wrong. I had more than enough money to support my lifestyle, and my family's lifestyle.'[6]

If Madoff felt sorry for anyone, it was himself. Describing how he secretly suffered, Madoff said: 'It was a nightmare for me. It was *only* a nightmare for me. It's horrible. When I say nightmare, imagine carrying this secret … Imagine going home every night not being able to tell your wife, living with this axe over your head, not telling your sons, my brother, seeing them every day in the business and not being able to confide in them.'

According to Madoff, even the regulators felt sorry for him.

* * *

At what stage did Barry decide to cross the line? When do you take that first step, after which you can't go back? And why do you take it?

For Madoff, it happened after the market crash of 1987. According to his interview in *New York* magazine, people panicked, and some clients bolted, which meant he had to unwind some long-term hedges on unfavourable terms, which cost him a large chunk of his cash.

'He had too much of other people's money, and not enough to invest in,' says journalist Stephen Fishman. 'That is when,' he says, 'the scheme began in earnest. Madoff started borrowing from his investors' capital to pay out those solid returns. The returns, false though they were, were their own advertisement.'[7]

What happened was that the sort of people who would have brushed off Madoff like so much lint off a dinner jacket a few years before were now queuing at his door.

'It feeds your ego. All of a sudden, these banks which wouldn't give you the time of day, they're willing to give you a billion dollars,' said Madoff. 'It wasn't like I needed the money. It was just that I thought it was a temporary thing, and all of a sudden, everybody is throwing billions of dollars at you. Saying, "Listen, if you can do this stuff for us, we'll be your clients forever."[8]

Madoff then stuck the money he was given by the banks into US treasury bonds – a conservative investment that only ever paid out close to 2 per cent a year – while producing fake statements showing returns of nearly eight times that.

For Tannenbaum, the most likely scenario is that as he began running up gambling bills, he dipped into whatever cash he could find. Quite how he hit on the idea of a furniture-investment scheme isn't clear, though it took him some time to fine-tune it into the drug-ingredients scam, perhaps a more obvious vehicle given his family's history at Adcock Ingram.

But it would have required him to sever his conscience from his day-to-day interactions with the people he was ripping off. At times, Tannenbaum seems divorced from reality: he was able to cause a disaster, then sit back and watch it as if from above, as if he had played no part in it and had no responsibility to respond to it. Whether it's a lack of smarts or some form of psychosis that allows him to do it is unclear.

Ziman believes it's the former: 'The bottom line for me is that two things are clear: first, Barry is not the bright fellow everyone thinks he is, and, secondly, Dean Rees is a smart operator.'

Rees responds: 'If I alone was supposed to figure out it was a scam, what about Sean Summers, Och-Ziff, Jeremy Ord, PwC and Investec? What about all these guys who also hadn't figured it out? The eloquence of the lie, the fortitude of the frauds from 2003, the brazenness of the promises to everyone (disclosed and undisclosed): it shows all the sophistication of a disarming person who got through everyone. It's a rare genome.'

Indeed, it is a useful conception to make out that Rees is a scheming Machiavelli who framed this poor simpleton. It seems unlikely. Barry may be no rocket scientist, but there is, at the very least, a level of cunning in the way he tricked people – first in the original scam, and then in the pharmaceutical scam – that hints that he was more intelligent than that.

And he had a degree of emotional savvy that allowed him to connect with investors and tap into their greed. Instant wealth is a potent pheromone.

When he gave judgment in the Miracle 2000 case against Sibusiso Radebe, Magistrate James van Wyk said that 'throughout the years, people have become bewitched and fascinated by promises of instant wealth, and it has become the duty of the court to protect people against their irresponsibility'.[9]

This, however, misconstrues the duty of the courts. Why should the courts be responsible for protecting people from their own stupidity? Especially considering that people often don't want that protection – and will often go out of their way to avoid being stopped.

In the Miracle 2000 case, for example, investors were told it was a scam, and there was no way to keep up the payments, but still they marched to the Union Buildings petitioning that Radebe be released.

In the Tannenbaum case, the victims were almost all well educated. Some even knew the basics of investment. Yet still they ploughed in their cash. As a result, they might end up carrying the losses – especially once the trustees are through levying large fees on the estate.

Some are contrite, some admit they were stupid and shrug it off, some pretend they didn't invest, while others have just spun around looking for anyone else to blame but themselves.

Tasha Rossen, Leigh's former girlfriend, says it was 'all pure undiluted greed; it showed the worst in me and others. No one coerced, forced or put a gun to my head.' She says she saw how money changed people, how money changed her. 'We lost ourselves in our desire for more and more money. Now we whitewash our own culpability and stupidity. Yes, we can blame Barry or Darryl or Dean. We may even hate them, but in the end, we can only blame ourselves.'

Which is all true. But then, it's not as if Barry doesn't deserve blame.

'Yes, I wish that Barry had been honourable,' she says, 'but like all great deceivers, he was kindness personified yet still ended up devastating many lives.'

The thing is, does Barry really not have their cash?

The view from the outside is that if Barry masterminded some huge con, he must have money stashed away somewhere, presumably well hidden. If you're going to put together a brilliant Ponzi scheme, you'd be daft not to.

But in Barry's case, it seems he just doesn't have much cash. Which may attest to the view that Barry isn't the sharpest knife in the drawer.

'I just don't think Barry has any cash,' Ziman says. 'There have been times in the court cases, where if he'd had any money squirrelled away, he would have come to me and said, "Look, Derek, this old mate of mine has found some money to help me through this", or some such explanation. But he never did.'

Some people have made fortunes from his scheme – Darryl Leigh made R114 million; Dean Rees is said to have made anything from R70 million to R600 million; while investors like Jawmend Rossi cashed in to the tune of R140 million. But Barry, apparently, never made this sort of cash.

Instead, it seems, he was just the guinea pig, scurrying furiously just to stand still on the wheel while, perhaps uniquely, being the only one who knew the whole truth of the entire scam.

This would explain why Barry packed for Australia almost as soon as the scheme started seriously hoovering cash. He would have known that the police would struggle to extradite him from Australia. And he wasn't wrong – as it stands now, the flailing NPA have not come close to lodging an extradition request, so it could be many years before he will see the inside of a jail cell.

The most plausible theory is that after Barry had dipped into funds that he shouldn't have to fuel his gambling, and ended up short, he invented a series of increasingly fanciful stories to paper over the holes. In the end, his stories had spun glossy brochures, suckered foreign investors and created agents who were able to charter multimillion-rand yachts on the Med. Yet Barry wasn't about taking the cash. Rather, he was about doing whatever he had to, just to keep the fairy tale intact.

'The easiest way to lose money is to give it away,' says Ziman. 'Look at people who win the lottery and end up penniless again. Not because they gambled it away, but because they gave it away. That was Barry.'

Notes

CHAPTER 1

1 Taken from author's notes of the meeting.
2 Author's interview with Howard Lowenthal.
3 Chris Gilmour, 'Success in succession', *Financial Mail*, 25 November 2005.
4 Jeremy Ord, communication with author.
5 National Treasury of South Africa, debt management report 2011/2012, p. 2.
6 United Nations HIV estimates based on 2011 data (http://www.unaids.org/en/ regionscountries/countries/southafrica/), accessed 21 August 2013.
7 Joanna Stephens, 'Dr Garlic and the battle for Aids policy in post-Apartheid South Africa', *The Monitor*, Fall 2007 (http://web .wm.edu/so/monitor/issues/13-1/1-stephens .pdf), accessed 21 August 2013.
8 Terry Leonard, 'S. Africa curbs Aids minister's influence', *Washington Post*, 9 September 2006 (http://www. washingtonpost.com/wp-dyn/content/ article/2006/09/09/AR2006090900774.html), accessed 21 August 2013.
9 Ibid.
10 Fran Blandy, 'Dr Beetroot hits back at media over Aids exhibition', *Mail & Guardian*, 16 August 2006 (http://mg.co.za/article/ 2006-08-16-dr-beetroot-hits-back-at -media-over-aids-exhibition), accessed 21 August 2013.
11 'Madoff pleads guilty, is jailed for $65 billion fraud', Reuters, 13 March 2009 (http://www.reuters.com/article/2009/03/ 13/us-madoff-idUSTRE52A5JK20090313), accessed 21 August 2013.
12 'SEC charges Bernard L Madoff for multi billion dollar Ponzi scheme', Securities and Exchange Commission press release, 11 December 2008 (http://www.sec.gov/ news/press/2008/2008-293.htm), accessed 21 August 2013.
13 'Evil Madoff gets 150 years in epic fraud', *Wall Street Journal*, 30 June 2009 (http:// online.wsj.com/article/SB124604151653862301 .html), accessed 21 August 2013.
14 Deon Basson, ''n Ope briewe aan minister Alec Erwin', *Volksblad*, 28 June 2002.
15 Rob Rose, 'Tigon duo face 3 160 charges of fraud', *Business Day*, 4 August 2005.
16 Ernest Mabuza, 'Tigon pair contest mediocre legal aid', *Business Day*, 5 October 2009.
17 De Bruyn v Minister for Justice and Customs, Australian Federal Court, 2004 FCAFC 334 (http://www1.chr.up.ac.za/ undp/other/docs/caselaw5.pdf), accessed 21 August 2013.
18 Author's interview with Wayne Gaddin.

CHAPTER 2

1 South African History Online, 'The First Anglo-Boer War 1880–1881' (http://www .sahistory.org.za/south-africa-1806-1899/ first-anglo-boer-war-1880-1881); SA Heritage Resources (www.sahra.org.za); 'Early Krugersdorp', a paper by Dr Janet du Plooy, which can be found on the website of the West Rand Heritage (http:// www.wrhc.co.za/documents/earlykruger .pdf), accessed 21 August 2013.
2 Ibid.
3 Ibid.
4 Dr Janet du Plooy, 'The West Rand during the Anglo-Boer War', from a presentation made to the Genealogical Society of South Africa, April 2004 (http://www.eggsa.org/ articles/Wesrand_ABO_E_duPlooy.htm), accessed 21 August 2013.
5 Ibid.
6 Finbarr O'Reilly, 'Hardship deepens for South Africa's poor whites', Reuters, 26 March 2010 (http://blogs.reuters.com/ photographers-blog/2010/03/26/hardship -deepens-for-south-africas-poor-whites/), accessed 21 August 2013.

7   Ibid.
8   Jewish Virtual Library
    (http://www.jewishvirtuallibrary.org/
    jsource/vjw/South_Africa.html), accessed
    21 August 2013.
9   Information based on interviews with
    Arnold Tannenbaum.
10 Arnold Tannenbaum, 'How the
    Tannenbaum brothers started Adcock
    Ingram', *SA Pharmaceutical Journal* 78 (8),
    2011 (http://www.sapj.co.za/index.php/
    SAPJ/article/view/1120/1467), accessed
    21 August 2013.
11 *Adcock Ingram: Celebrating 120 years*,
    Essential Publishing, 2010.
12 Arnold Tannenbaum, 'How the
    Tannenbaum brothers started Adcock
    Ingram'.
13 Ibid.
14 Blog forum, 'Who remembers Hillbrow
    the way it used to be?' (http://answers
    .yahoo.com/question/index?qid=
    20070624074756AAj13Xw), accessed
    21 August 2013.
15 *SA Jewish Report*, 4 February 2011
    (http://www.sajewishreport.co.za/pdf/
    2011/feb/4-february-2011.pdf), accessed
    21 August 2013.
16 Arnold Tannenbaum, 'How the
    Tannenbaum brothers started Adcock
    Ingram'.
17 *Adcock Ingram: Celebrating 120 years*.
18 Author's interview with Daryl Kronson.
19 See www.lronhubbard.org, accessed
    21 August 2013.
20 See www.lronhubbard.org/heritage-sites/
    joburg.html, accessed 21 August 2013.
21 Kotze Commission, report on commission
    into Scientology, 1973, letter from L. Ron
    Hubbard to Dr Hendrik Verwoerd,
    7 November 1960. Full report can be
    found at http://www.solitarytrees.net/
    pubs/kotze/html/03-05.htm#ref79, accessed
    21 August 2013.
22 Rob Rose, 'Manna from heaven', *Financial
    Mail*, 11 January 2008 (http://www.fm.co.za/
    fm/2008/01/11/religion), accessed 21 August
    2013.
23 Kotze Commission, report on commission
    into Scientology, p. 91.
24 Author's interview with Adcock CEO,
    Jonathan Louw.
25 *Moneyweb* profile of Jonathan Louw
    (http://www.moneyweb.co.za/moneyweb
    -wiki-profile/johnathan-louw-2), accessed
    21 August 2013.
26 Author's interview with Adcock CEO,
    Jonathan Louw.
27 Author's interview with Daryl Kronson.
28 Steve Fishman, 'The Madoff tapes', *New
    York* magazine, 27 February 2011 (http://
    nymag.com/news/features/berniemadoff
    -2011-3/), accessed 21 August 2013.
29 Kent Kiehl and Joshua Buckholtz, 'Inside
    the mind of a psychopath', *Scientific
    American Mind*, 19 August 2010 (http://
    www.scientificamerican.com/article.cfm?id
    =inside-the-mind-of-a-psychopath),
    accessed 21 August 2013.
30 Ibid.
31 Martha Stout, *The Sociopath Next Door*,
    New York: Broadway Books, 2006.

CHAPTER 3
1   Author's interview with David Shapiro.
2   Author's interview with Arnold
    Tannenbaum.
3   Author's interview with Daryl Kronson.
4   Author's interview with Norman
    Lowenthal.
5   Author's interview with Sharon Green.
6   Author's interview with John Hall.
7   Daniel Conway, 'Somewhere on the
    border of credibility: The cultural
    construction and contestation of "the
    border" in white South African society',
    in G. Baines and P. Vale (eds.), *Beyond the
    Border War*, Pretoria: University of South
    Africa Press, 2008.
8   Author's interview with Barry
    Tannenbaum's former schoolmate, name
    withheld at his request.
9   Author's interview with Ian Tasman.

CHAPTER 4
1   Janse van Rensburg v Steyn, Supreme
    Court of Appeal, case 66/10 of 2011.
2   Zelda Venter, 'Krion ring jailed', *Pretoria
    News*, 15 October 2010 (http://www.iol
    .co.za/news/crime-courts/krion-ring-jailed
    -1.686422?ot=inmsa.ArticlePrintPageLayout
    .ot), accessed 21 August 2013.
3   Ibid.
4   'Vaal still feeling Krion fallout', South

African Press Association, 6 October 2010 (http://m.news24.com/news24/SouthAfrica/News/Vaal-still-feeling-Krion-fallout-20101006), accessed 21 August 2013.

5 'Scams and other moneymaking schemes', *Readers Digest*, 1997, available at http://www.legalcity.net/Index.cfm?fuseaction=RIGHTS.article&Index=S&ArticleID=5235121&Page=1, accessed 21 August 2013.

6 Commissioner for Inland Revenue v Insolvent Estate JP Botha, Supreme Court of Appeal, Appellate Division, case 30/89.

7 Dominic Mahlangu and Elias Maluleke, 'Shady side of Miracle', *City Press*, 30 August 2000 (http://152.111.1.87/argief/berigte/citypress/2000/07/30/4/16.html), accessed 21 August 2013.

8 Detlev Krige, 'Fong Kong finance', report prepared to present to the London School of Economics, June 2009.

9 Ibid.

10 Peta Krost and Khanyisile Nkosi, 'R3m a day for Miracle kingpin', *Saturday Star*, 14 July 2000 (http://www.iol.co.za/news/south-africa/r3m-a-day-for-miracle-kingpin-1.43299#.UhLAz2bg7qo), accessed 21 August 2013.

11 Zanele Mngadi and Michelle Parkin, 'Miracle 2000 mastermind admits his guilt', *Independent Online*, 28 June 2001 (http://www.iol.co.za/news/south-africa/miracle-2000-mastermind-admits-his-guilt-1.68795#.UhLB-Wbg7qo), accessed 21 August 2013.

12 'Miracle 2000 boss evades jail term', South African Press Association, 3 August 2001 (http://www.iol.co.za/news/south-africa/miracle-2000-boss-evades-jail-term-1.69269#.UhLB02bg7qo), accessed 21 August 2013.

13 Matefu Mokoena, 'Radebe's party hangs in balance as he goes to jail', *City Press*, 15 December 2002 (http://152.111.1.87/argief/berigte/citypress/2002/12/15/6/6.html), accessed 21 August 2013.

14 *Jewish Chronicle*, 14 October 1898 (http://www.jewishencyclopedia.com/articles/4456-cohen-abner), accessed 21 August 2013.

15 'South Africa', *American Jewish Yearbook*, 1982, p. 270.

16 Author's interview with Rabbi Shlomo Wainer.

17 Barry Tannenbaum, banking records, 2006.

18 Rebecca Rosenthal, 'A new Torah comes to Umhlanga Rocks', 2 July 2006 (www.lubvitch.com, http://www.chabadnc.com/templates/articlecco_cdo/aid/402319/jewish/GRAND-OPENING-REPORT.htm), accessed 21 August 2013.

19 Ibid.

20 Ibid.

21 Author's interview with Mervyn Serebro.

22 Author's interview with Rabbi Shlomo Wainer.

23 'Shylocks and poor Israeli kids', *South African Jewish Report*, 3 July 2009, p. 10 (http://www.sajewishreport.co.za/pdf/2009/july/3-july-2009.pdf), accessed 21 August 2013.

24 Ibid.

25 Ibid.

26 See http://www.stormfront.org/forum/t613581/, accessed 20 January 2013.

27 Author's interview with Rabbi Mendel Lipskar.

28 Author's interview with David Shapiro.

29 John Perlman, 'Life, correction, prison life can be human', *Independent*, 20 July 1995 (http://www.independent.co.uk/life-style/life-correction-prison-life-can-be-human-1592257.html), accessed 21 August 2013.

30 Ibid.

31 Author's interview with David Shapiro.

32 Ibid.

33 Dan Goldberg, 'Another Madoff or wild allegations?', Jewish Telegraphic Agency, 21 June 2009 (http://www.jta org/2009/06/21/life-religion/features/another-madoff-or-wild-allegations), accessed 21 August 2013.

34 Author's interview with Cecil Zinn.

CHAPTER 5

1 André Damons, 'Ericsson-man brand dood ná "resies" in sportmotor', *Beeld*, 9 March 2009.

2 See http://www.wheels24.co.za/News/General_News/Supercar-dice-ends-in-tragedy-20090309, accessed 21 August 2013.

3 Affidavit by Johann van Loggerenberg, head of enforcement at SARS, 24 July 2009.

4 Author's interview with Tasha Rossen.

5 Affidavit by Piet Senekal, in possession of author, used in case of S v Leigh.

6 Affidavit by Janine Steynberg, South African Police Service captain, in the attachment case against Leigh, 30 July 2009.

7   Tann Leigh Properties, registration number 2006/150370/23.
8   Affidavit by Van Loggerenberg.
9   Ibid.
10 Affidavit by Christopher Leppan for the Reserve Bank, 12 June 2009.
11 Author's interview with Keith van der Spuy.
12 Author's interview with Sarah West.
13 Author's interview with Ian Irvine-Fortescue.
14 Author's interview with Tasha Rossen.
15 Telephone conversation between Darryl Leigh and author.
16 National Prosecuting Authority, draft request for mutual legal assistance.
17 Ken Romain, 'Larger than life: Donald Gordon and the Liberty Life story', in 'Sandton City: A property's history' (http://www.property24.com/articles/sandton-city-a-propertys-history/14670), accessed 21 August 2013.
18 Graham Norwood, 'Express route to selling luxury homes', *Observer*, 3 June 2001 (http://www.guardian.co.uk/money/2001/jun/03/observercashsection.theobserver7), accessed 21 August 2013.

CHAPTER 6

1   Author's interview with Estelle Wittenberg.
2   Nick O'Malley and Thomas Graham, 'Exposed: the Sydney man accused of $1.5bn scam', *Sydney Morning Herald*, 13 June 2009 (http://www.smh.com.au/national/exposed-the-sydney-man-accused-of-15-billion-scam-20090612-c640.html), accessed 21 August 2013.
3   Telephone discussion between Kevin Kramer and author.
4   Author's interview with Estelle Wittenberg.
5   Author's interview with Wayne Gaddin.
6   Email sent by Barry Tannenbaum.
7   Email response from Stephen Saad to questions from author.
8   Author's interview with Trevor Edwards.
9   Author's interview with Dr Jonathan Louw.
10 Author's interview with Robyn Daniel.
11 Telephone discussion between Tandy Houseman and author.
12 Author's interview with Robyn Daniel.
13 Author's interview with Daryl Kronson.
14 Author's interview with IAPA director David Grawitzky.

15 Ibid.
16 Draft request for mutual legal assistance, in possession of author.
17 Author's interview with Estelle Wittenberg.

INVESTOR PROFILE: SHERRY

1   Author's interview with anonymous investor.

CHAPTER 7

1   Dan Goldberg, 'Another Madoff or wild allegations?', Jewish Telegraphic Agency, 21 June 2009 (http://www.jta.org/2009/06/21/life-religion/features/another-madoff-or-wild-allegations), accessed 21 August 2013.
2   Ibid.
3   Author's interview with anonymous member of the Tannenbaum family.
4   Author's interview with Tasha Rossen, June 2013.
5   Dean Rees's affidavit, *Barwa v Rees*, in possession of author.
6   Ibid.
7   Pieter Senekal's affidavit in *ex parte* application of the National Director of Public Prosecutions, in application for preservation order, High Court of South Africa, North Gauteng (Pretoria).
8   Ibid.
9   Barbara Harrison, 'Gejubel oor Miracle 2000-baas nie trunk toe gaan', *Beeld*, 4 August 2001 (http://152.111.1.88/argief/berigte/beeld/2001/08/04/4/2.html), accessed April 2013.
10 Author's interview with Keith van der Spuy.
11 *Harris and others v Rees*, South Gauteng High Court, 25 June 2010, 09/32226.
12 Mark Gorrie's affidavit, used in *National Prosecuting Authority v Dean Rees*, in possession of author.
13 Information from http://www.burgessyachts.com/en/tommy-00006806.html, accessed 21 August 2013.
14 Email from Dean Rees to Moni Chin, 9 February 2009, in possession of author.
15 Martin Shipton, 'Former Peacocks chief Richard Kirk faces £3m claim from former wife', *Wales Online*, 12 June 2012 (http://www.walesonline.co.uk/news/wales-news/former-peacocks-chief-richard-kirk-2028942), accessed March 2013.
16 Ibid.

17 Richard Fletcher, 'UK bosses caught up in alleged \$1.2bn South African Ponzi fraud', *Telegraph*, 16 June 2009 (http://www.telegraph.co.uk/finance/newsbysector/banksandfinance/5553811/UK-bosses-caught-up-in-alleged-1.2bn-South-African-Ponzi-fraud.html), accessed March 2013.

18 Ibid.

19 'Sun and smiles over a glass of Chateau Ponzi', *Telegraph*, 20 June 2009 (http://www.telegraph.co.uk/finance/comment/citydiary/5586207/ready-Sun-and-smiles-over-a-glass-of-Chateau-Ponzi.html), accessed March 2013.

20 Mark Gorrie's affidavit.

21 Dean Rees's affidavit, *Barwa v Rees*, in possession of author.

22 Mark Gorrie's affidavit.

CHAPTER 8

1 Author's interview with Mervyn Serebro, February 2013.

2 'Shoprite snaps up OK for R1', *Mail & Guardian*, 4 November 1997 (http://mg.co.za/article/1997-11-04-shoprite-snaps-up-ok-for-), accessed 21 August 2013.

3 Author's interview with David Serebro, February 2013.

4 Author's interview with Mervyn Serebro, February 2013.

5 Author's interview with Gerald Nochumsohn, February 2013.

6 Author's interview with Clive Sergay, January 2013.

7 Author's interview with David Serebro, February 2013.

8 'Mervyn Serebro, schedule of investments 2007–2009', in possession of author.

9 Author's interview with Mervyn Serebro, February 2013.

10 Pieter Senekal's affidavit, used in *ex parte* application National Director of Public Prosecutions, North Gauteng High Court, signed 16 January 2013, in possession of author.

11 *Paredes-Taragon v Cobalt Capital*, South Gauteng High Court, 23 April 2012, 2009/44215.

12 Ibid., judgment by Judge Kathree-Setiloane.

13 Author's interview with John Storey, July 2013.

14 Pieter Senekal's affidavit.

15 Author's interview with Gerald Nochumsohn, February 2013.

INVESTOR PROFILE: SEAN SUMMERS

1 'Pick n Pay names new CEO', *Mail & Guardian*, 22 August 2006 (http://mg.co.za/article/2006-08-22-pick-n-pay-names-new-ceo), accessed 21 August 2013.

2 Adele Shevel, 'Custodian of the retail brand', *Sunday Times*, 27 August 2006.

3 Ibid.

4 'Important message from the CEO of Pick n Pay Sean Summers', Pick n Pay stock exchange announcement, 30 June 2003.

5 Malose Monama, 'PnP: no poison found', *City Press*, 3 August 2003 (http://www.news24.com/World/News/PnP-No-poison-found-20030803), accessed 21 August 2013.

6 'MFSA praises Pick n Pay', SA Press Association, 1 July 2003, (http://www.news24.com/SouthAfrica/News/MFSA-praises-Pick-n-Pay-20030701), accessed February 2013.

7 Sean Summers, personal communication with author.

8 Author's interview with Sean Summers, March 2013.

9 Ibid.

CHAPTER 9

1 Email, Barry Tannenbaum to Dean Rees, 12 November 2008, in possession of author.

2 Email, Barry Tannenbaum to Dean Rees, 7 November 2008, in possession of author.

3 Email, Dean Rees to Barry Tannenbaum, 20 October 2008, in possession of author.

4 Email, Dean Rees to Barry Tannenbaum, 12 November 2008, in possession of author.

5 Ibid.

6 Email, Barry Tannenbaum to Dean Rees, 12 November 2008, in possession of author.

7 Dean Rees's affidavit, in *Barwa Real Estate Company v Dean Rees*, High Court of Justice, United Kingdom Queen's Bench Division, 27 July 2009, case no 2009/847.

8 Concordia prospectus, in possession of author.

9 Frankel International GmbH, report by liquidator, Tamer Mohamed Khedr, 17 February 2010.

10 Letter sent by Concordia API Fund Limited to Barry Tannenbaum, by registered mail on 24 July 2009, in possession of author.

11 Funds under management as at 1 August 2013, according to Och-Ziff Capital Management Group's website (http://www.ozcap.com/our_firm/index), accessed August 2013.

12 Based on Forbes 2013 US billionaires list (http://www.forbes.com/profile/daniel-och/), accessed March 2013.

13 Christine Williamson, 'Strong character: Face to face with Daniel S. Och', *Pension & Investments* magazine, 19 October 2009 (http://www.pionline.com/article/20091019/FACETOFACE/310199990), accessed March 2013.

14 Kambiz Foroohar, 'Och-Ziff's 23% return lures investors even as shares falter', *Bloomberg Markets*, 2 August 2009 (http://www.bloomberg.com/news/2010-08-02/och-ziff-hedge-fund-s-23-return-lures-big-investors-even-as-shares-falter.html), accessed March 2013.

15 Email, Michael Tannenbaum to Barry Tannenbaum, 4 September 2008, in possession of author.

16 Email, Gareth MacIntosh, 25 January 2009.

17 Dean Rees's affidavit.

18 Email, Barry Tannenbaum to Dean Rees and James Patterson, 13 March 2009, 're: Barwa Order'.

19 Email, Barry Tannenbaum to Dean Rees and James Patterson, 14 March 2009, 'PHARMA-Q ORDER DOCS'.

20 Email, Barry Tannenbaum to Dean Rees, 17 March 2009, 'PHARMA-Q ORDER 28701-E'.

21 Court documents used in *Barwa Real Estate Company v Dean Rees*, High Court of Justice, United Kingdom Queen's Bench Division, 27 July 2009, case no 2009/847.

22 William Finnegan, 'The secret keeper', *New Yorker*, 19 October 2009 (http://www.newyorker.comreporting/2009/10/19/091019fa_fact_finnegan), accessed 21 August 2013.

23 James Doran, 'US investigators Kroll gave all-clear to alleged Ponzi pair', *Guardian*, 31 August 2009 (http://www.theguardian.com/business/2009/aug/31/pharmaceuticals-industry-southafrica), accessed 21 August 2013.

24 Kroll, personal communication with author.

25 PricewaterhouseCoopers, 'Report on the agreed-upon procedures in respect of the proposed funding arrangement with Euro Chemicals Pty Ltd', 5 September 2008, signed by Anton Esterhuizen.

26 Lawrence Jones, 'In the matter of Concordia API Fund Limited', 1 October 2008, in possession of author.

CHAPTER 10

1 Email, Sean Summers to Dean Rees, 12 September 2008, in possession of author.

2 Email, Dean Rees to Sean Summers, 12 September 2008, in possession of author.

3 Email, Barry Tannenbaum to Dean Rees, 20 October 2009, in possession of author.

4 Author's interview with John Storey, July 2013.

5 Email, Mark Gorrie to Barry Tannenbaum, 20 February 2009, in possession of author.

6 Email, Barry Tannenbaum to Mark Gorrie, 20 February 2009, in possession of author.

7 From David Croxon's affidavit in South Gauteng High Court, case no 09/23296, filed on 14 August 2009.

8 Email, Nick Pagden to Dean Rees and Patrick Ferreira, 5 March 2009, in possession of author.

9 Email, Nick Pagden to Dean Rees, 9 March 2009, in possession of author.

10 Email, Richard Goudvis to Dean Rees, 29 March 2009, in possession of author.

11 Emails between Tannenbaum, Rees and James Patterson, disclosed in *Barwa Real Estate Company v Dean Rees*, High Court of Justice, United Kingdom Queen's Bench Division, 27 July 2009, case no 2009/847.

12 Email, Dean Rees to Sean Summers, 27 March 2009, in possession of author.

13 Email, Dean Rees to Duncan Simpson-Craib, 27 March 2009, in possession of author.

14 Braam Viljoen, Merchant West, personal communication with author, June 2009.

15 Samantha Henkeman, South African Reserve Bank, personal communication with author.

16 Forged letter, supposedly from Aspen Pharmacare SA's Bert Marais to Barry Tannenbaum, 6 May 2009, in possession of author.

17 Bert Marais, Aspen Pharmacare, letter

'To whom it may concern, Re: Frankel Chemicals', 18 May 2009, in possession of author.

18 Pieter van der Sandt, Aspen Pharmacare, letter to Werksmans, 22 May 2009, in possession of author.

19 Ibid.

20 Telephone conversation with author, 2009.

21 Telephone discussion between author and Dr Jonathan Louw, 2013.

22 Ibid.

23 From David Croxon's affidavit in South Gauteng High Court, case no 09/23296, filed on 14 August 2009.

24 Suscito Investments, 'Re: Consolidation and update of your participation in the Investment Consortium', 27 April 2009, signed by Dean Rees.

25 Dean Rees, letter to investors, 'Re: Update on payment delays', 22 May 2009, in possession of author.

26 Email correspondence between Dean Rees and Barry Tannenbaum, May 2009, in possession of author.

27 Ibid.

CHAPTER 11

1 Email, Barry Tannenbaum to Dean Rees, 28 May 2009, in possession of author.

2 Dean Rees, personal communication with author, June 2009.

3 James Patterson, personal communication with author, June 2009.

4 Gareth MacIntosh, personal communication with author, June 2009.

5 Dean Rees, letter to investors, 29 May 2009, in possession of author.

6 Dean Rees's affidavit in Barwa litigation.

7 Ibid.

8 Ibid.

9 Ibid.

10 Dean Rees, letter to investors, 2 June 2009, in possession of author.

11 Julius Preddy's affidavit in South Gauteng High Court, case no. 09/30123, *Julius Preddy v Dean Rees*, 21 July 2009, in possession of author.

12 Telephone discussion between Barry Tannenbaum and author, June 2009.

13 Email, Barry Tannenbaum to author, June 2009.

14 Ibid.

15 Author's interview with Estelle Wittenberg.

16 Christopher Leppan's affidavit in South Gauteng High Court case, *Christopher Leppan v Barry Tannenbaum*, 4 June 2009.

17 Ibid.

18 Rob Rose, 'South Africa's Madoff?', *Financial Mail*, 10 June 2009.

19 Bruce Cameron, 'The R10bn betrayal', *Star* and *Independent*, 11 June 2009 (http://www.thepost.co.za/the-r10bn-betrayal-1.446062#.UiOFaGbg63U), accessed 21 August 2013.

20 Email, Nigel Croxon to Barry Tannenbaum, 5 June 2009.

21 Email, Barry Tannenbaum to Nigel Croxon, 6 June 2009.

22 Statement, Barry Tannenbaum, 12 June 2009, in possession of author.

23 Adriaan Basson and Ilham Rawoot, 'Agliotti, Selebi and the president's shoes', *Mail & Guardian*, 7 October 2009 (http://mg.co.za/article/2009-10-07-agliotti-selebi-and-the-presidents-shoes), accessed 21 August 2013.

24 Media statement, South African Revenue Service, 'Joint investigation into allegations of fraud and impropriety in investment structure', 14 June 2009 (http://www.sars.gov.za/AllDocs/Documents/MediaReleases/2009/SARS-MR-2009-029%20-%20Media%20release%20on%20JOINT%20INVESTIGATION%20INTO%20ALLEGATIONS%20OF%20FRAUD%20AND%20IMPROPRIETY%20-%2014%20June%202009.pdf), accessed 21 August 2013.

25 Nick O'Malley and Thomas Graham, 'Exposed: The Sydney man accused of $1.5 billion scam', *Sydney Morning Herald*, 13 June 2009 (http://www.smh.com.au/national/exposed-the-sydney-man-accused-of-15-billion-scam-20090612-c640.html), accessed 21 August 2013.

26 Renee Bonorchis, 'Tannenbaum says he's no Madoff as South Africans cry fraud', *Bloomberg News*, 21 June 2009 (http://www.bloomberg.com/appsnews?pid=newsarchive&sid=azH_yFjqupew), accessed 21 August 2013.

27 Statement, Barry Tannenbaum, 13 June 2009, in possession of author.

28 Dean Rees, personal communication with author.

INVESTOR PROFILE: PETER BEALE

1 *Health Professions Council of SA Bulletin*, December 2007 (http://www.hpcsa.co.za/downloads/press_releases/bulletin_02.pdf), accessed June 2013.

2 Dr Simon Huddart, 'Scatterlings of Africa – sabbatical 2008' (http://www.welshpaediatrics.org.uk/scatterlings-africa-sabbatical-2008), accessed June 2013.

3 Bhule Khumalo, 'Picture of child rape too horrific to publish', *Star*, 9 September 2002 (http://www.iol.co.za/news/south-africa/picture-of-child-rape-too-horrific-to-publish-1.92796#.UiyW8Wbg46U), accessed 21 August 2013.

4 Baldwin Ndaba and Caiphus Kgosana, 'Jubilation as sexual thug is sent to prison', *Star*, 16 June 2004 (http://www.iol.co.za/news/south-africa/jubilation-as-sexual-thug-is-sent-to-prison-1.215013#.UiyXgmbg46U), accessed 21 August 2013.

5 Author's interview with Professor Peter Beale.

CHAPTER 12

1 Statutory declaration, Barry Tannenbaum, signed 5 June 2009.

2 Ibid. Addendum to statutory declaration.

3 Twenty-two page statutory declaration of Barry Deon Tannenbaum, prepared by Barwa's lawyers but not signed by Tannenbaum.

4 Email, Dean Rees to Moni Chin, 9 February 2009, in possession of author.

5 Email, Moni Chin to Dean Rees, 9 February 2009, in possession of author.

6 Email, Volker Schultz to Barry Tannenbaum, 20 February 2009, in possession of author.

7 Unsigned statutory declaration.

8 Dean Rees's affidavit, submitted in United Kingdom High Court of Justice, Queen's Bench Division, case *Barwa Real Estate v Rees*, 847/2009.

9 Ibid.

10 Email, Dean Rees to Barry Tannenbaum, 31 March 2009, in possession of author.

11 Dean Rees, affidavit.

12 Ibid.

13 Email, Dean Rees to Chris Harris, 'My next deal', 26 March 2009.

14 Dean Rees, affidavit.

15 Finance Minister Pravin Gordhan, medium-term budget policy statement in Parliament's National Assembly, 26 October 2009, (http://www.pmg.org.za/hansard/20091027-medium-term-budget-policy-statement-adjustments-appropriation-bill-m), accessed 21 August 2013.

16 Dean Rees, affidavit.

17 Advocate Glynnis Breytenbach, National Prosecuting Authority letter to Bryan Biebuyck, Eversheds, 'Re: Dean Gillian Rees', 12 April 2010.

18 Renee Bonorchis, 'Tannenbaum says he's no Madoff as South Africans cry fraud'.

19 Transcript of hearing in United Kingdom High Court of Justice, Queen's Bench Division, case *Barwa Real Estate v Rees*, 847/2009.

20 Justice David Steele judgment, in United Kingdom High Court of Justice, Queen's Bench Division, case *Barwa Real Estate v Rees*, 847/2009.

21 Letter sent by Derek Ziman to A. Bellanto, QC, 'Our client: Mr Barry Tannenbaum', 3 September 2009, in possession of author.

22 Robert Tuttle, 'Barwa recovered 70% to 75% of money invested with Tannenbaum', *Bloomberg News*, 16 November 2009 (http://www.bloomberg.com/apps/news?pid=newsarchive&sid=aDIBvPxj3sHM), accessed 21 August 2013.

23 Emails submitted to court in United Kingdom High Court of Justice, Queen's Bench Division, case *Barwa Real Estate v Rees*, 847/2009.

24 Letter from Mohamed Randera to Routledge's B. Biebuyck, 'Barwa Real Estate Company QSC/Dean Rees', 30 November 2009, in possession of author.

25 Judge J.P. Horn, *Harris and others v Rees and others* (09/32226), South Gauteng High Court, 25 June 2010, (http://www.saflii.org.za/za/cases/ZAGPJHC/2010/51.html), accessed 21 August 2013.

26 Ibid.

27 Justice Ledwaba and Justice Van der Bijl, the *Law Society of the Northern Provinces v Dean Rees*, case 34483/2010, North Gauteng High Court, 6 October 2011.

28 Email, Barry Tannenbaum to Estelle Wittenberg, 13 July 2009, 'Names of Companies', in possession of author.

29 Email, Estelle Wittenberg to Barry
Tannenbaum, 13 July 2009, 'Re: Names of
Companies', in possession of author.
30 Email, Estelle Wittenberg to Barry
Tannenbaum, 14 July 2009, 'Re: Letter to
suppliers ... amendments', in possession of
author.
31 Letter from Barry Tannenbaum to Pier
Torti, Lusochimica SpA, 1 July 2009, in
possession of author.
32 Sertan Investments, profit and loss as of
30 June 2009, in possession of author.
33 Letter from Mervyn Serebro's lawyer,
Alistair McKeough, to Barry Tannenbaum's
lawyer, Derek Ziman, 14 September 2009,
'Sertan Unit Trust', in possession of
author.
34 Barry Tannenbaum, testimony to Federal
Court of Australia, Queensland Registry,
10 October 2012, transcript in possession
of author.
35 Ibid.

CHAPTER 13
1 Jeremy Ord, personal communication with
author.
2 Email, Jeremy Ord to Dean Rees, 25 March
2008, in possession of author.
3 Email, Jeremy Ord to Dean Rees, 25 August
2008, in possession of author.
4 David Fick, Entrepreneurship in Africa:
A Study of Success, Wesport: Quorum
Books, 2002.
5 From http://www.dimensiondata.com/
Global/AboutUs/Company-Highlights,
accessed June 2013.
6 Michael Bleby, 'Ord's wine farm may make
a little money, but that's not really the
point', Business Day, 8 September 2006.
7 Renee Bonorchis, 'Dimension Data
chairman Jeremy Ord gets $21.8 million
selling stock to NTT', Bloomberg News,
16 July 2010 (http://www.bloomberg.com/
news/2010-07-16/dimension-data-chairman
-jeremy-ord-gets-21-8-million-selling-stock
-to-ntt.html), accessed June 2013.
8 Transcripts of Tannenbaum estate inquiry,
in possession of author.
9 Bruce Watson, personal communication
with author.
10 KPMG investor spreadsheets 2009, in
possession of author.

11 Tony Beamish, 'Tannenbaum investors
received R3.1bn, says SARS', Moneyweb,
11 June 2013 (http://www.moneyweb.co.za/
moneyweb-south-africa/tannenbaum
-investors-received-r31bn-says-sars),
accessed June 2013.
12 'Insolvent estate Barry Deon Tannenbaum,
Enquiry Report 4 October 2010', Arnold
Sharp's testimony, in possession of author.
13 'Insolvent estate Barry Deon Tannenbaum,
Enquiry Report 12 May 2010', Michael
Mendelowitz's testimony, in possession
of author.
14 Ibid.
15 Office of Meir Levin, personal
communication with author.
16 Mannie Witz, personal communication
with author.
17 Michael Tannenbaum's response to Sunday
Times, 30 October 2009, in possession of
author.
18 'Strip king Lolly Jackson's round-about
life', Independent Newspapers, 9 May 2010
(http://www.iol.co.za/news/south-africa/
strip-king-lolly-jackson-s-round-about
-life-1.483248#.UiYxyGbg50s), accessed
June 2013.
19 Ibid.
20 Ibid.
21 Mannie Witz, personal communication
with author.
22 Ibid.
23 KPMG investor spreadsheets 2009, in
possession of author.
24 Mannie Witz, personal communication
with author.
25 Email correspondence between Barry
Tannenbaum and Mike Tannenbaum,
12 August 2009, 'Re: HAPPY BIRTHDAY',
in possession of author.
26 Ibid.
27 Ibid.
28 Ibid.
29 Michael Tannenbaum's response to Sunday
Times, 12 March 2010, in possession of
author.
30 Email, Barry Tannenbaum to Mike
Tannenbaum, 9 September 2009, 'Re:
HAPPY BIRTHDAY TO JUSTI', in
possession of author.
31 Mannie Witz, personal communication
with author.

32 Ian Fife, 'Dare to share', *Financial Mail*, 5 September 2008.

33 KPMG, investor spreadsheets 2009, in possession of author.

34 Lara Greenberg, 'Through Helping Hands, young adults walk the walk', *South African Jewish Report*, 25 May 2007 (http://www .sajewishreport.co.za/pdf/2007/may/ May-25-2007.pdf), accessed 21 August 2013.

35 Market capitalisation data sourced from www.etfsa.co.za, http://www.etfsa.co.za/ docs/perfsurvey/market_capitalisation2012 .pdf, accessed June 2013.

36 Biographical details on www.getthejob. co.za/about, accessed 21 August 2013.

37 Litsa Roussos, personal communication with author.

38 Litsa Roussos Twitter account (https:// twitter.com/litsaroussos), accessed July 2013.

39 Farida Parsad, personal communication with author.

40 KPMG, investor spreadsheets 2009, in possession of author.

41 See http://www.glomail.co.za/glomail _products_ez_cracker.asp, accessed September 2013.

42 See http://www.glomail.co.za/glomail _products_celltone.asp, and http://www .glomail.co.za/glomail_products_bobble _off.asp, accessed September 2013.

43 Bernard Hotz, lawyer for Alan Ber, personal communication with author.

44 'Insolvent estate Barry Deon Tannenbaum, Enquiry Report 30 June 2010', Duncan Simpson-Craib's testimony, in possession of author.

45 Tom Lawless, personal communication with author.

46 Statistics from http://www.jse.co.za/Markets/ Interest-Rate-Market/Interest-Rate -Market-history.aspx, accessed July 2013.

47 Moira Schneider and Dan Goldberg, 'Sydney Tycoon is another Madoff', *Jewish Chronicle*, 18 June 2009, http://www.thejc .com/news/world-news/15334/sydney -tycoon-another-madoff%E2%80%99.

48 Ibid.

49 Charles Kramer, personal communication with author.

50 Author interview with Leroy Tulip.

51 Allon Rock, personal communication with author.

52 'Cape to Cairo to London', press release, October 2011 (http://www.stephanwelzandco .co.za/Index.cfm?fuseaction=news.start&ID =7402896), accessed June 2013.

53 Biographical details on http://www. silverspirit.co.za/silver_spirit_team.html, accessed June 2013.

54 Biographical details on http://www.eaa.org .za/contact/contact_aug2010.pdf, accessed June 2013.

55 Daily report on http://www.silverspirit. co.za/daily_report.htm, accessed June 2013.

56 'Adventure: Across Africa in a Rolls Royce', 12 October 2009 (http://www. thesouthafrican.com/entertainment/ adventure-across-africa-in-a-rolls-royce. htm), accessed 21 August 2013.

57 Jeanette van Ginkel, personal communication with author.

58 See http://www.eaa.org.za/contact/ contact_aug2010.pdf, accessed June 2013.

59 'Insolvent estate Barry Deon Tannenbaum, Enquiry Report 4 October 2010', Jeanette van Ginkel's testimony, in possession of author.

60 Jeanette van Ginkel, personal communication with author.

INVESTOR PROFILE: KATE HOGGAN

1 Data from www.payscale.com, accessed September 2013 (http://www.payscale.com/ research/ZA/Country=South_Africa/Salary).

CHAPTER 14

1 Jerry Oppenheimer, *Madoff with the Money*, Hoboken: J. Wiley and Sons, 2009.

2 'Investigation of failure of the SEC to uncover Bernard Madoff's Ponzi scheme', Securities and Exchange Commission, report of investigation (http://www.sec .gov/news/studies/2009/oig-509-exec -summary.pdf), accessed 21 August 2013.

3 Ibid.

4 Ibid.

5 Ibid.

6 Ibid

7 Erin E. Arvedlund, 'Don't ask, don't tell: Bernie Madoff is so secretive, he even asks investors to keep mum', *Barron's* magazine, 7 May 2001 (http://online.barrons.com/ article/SB989019667829349012.html), accessed 21 August 2013.

8 'Investigation of failure of the SEC to uncover Bernard Madoff's Ponzi scheme'.

9 Pieter Senekal's affidavit, used in *ex parte* application National Director of Public Prosecutions, North Gauteng High Court, signed 16 January 2013, in possession of author.

10 Financial Services Board spokesman Russel Michaels, personal communication with author, 2009.

11 Author's interview with Bernard Agulhas, June 2013.

12 Ibid.

13 KPMG audit of the Tannenbaum scheme, details of bank account flows in possession of author.

14 Rob Rose, 'Mining giants circle Kebble's lost empire', *Business Day*, 12 March 2007.

15 Discussion with anonymous Investec employee.

16 Author's interview with P.J. Muller, May 2013.

17 Peta-Jane Muller, LinkedIn profile (http:// za.linkedin.com/pub/peta-jane-muller/11/ 456/7a0), accessed May 2013.

18 Kamini Moodley, personal communication with author, 2013.

19 *Investec Bank v Rees and another*, South Gauteng High Court, 5 March 2013, (12/24068, http://www.saflii.org/za/cases/ ZAGPJHC/2013/35.pdf), accessed 21 August 2013.

20 Ibid.

21 Investec response from Felicity Hudson, 'Questions regarding Barry Tannenbaum', sent to author on 27 June 2013.

22 Ibid.

23 KPMG audit of the Tannenbaum scheme.

24 Nick Pagden, report of testimony to inquiry of insolvent estate of Barry Tannenbaum, 1 June 2010, in possession of author.

25 Author's interview with Clive Douglas, July 2013.

26 KPMG audit of the Tannenbaum scheme.

27 Clive Douglas, report of testimony to inquiry of insolvent estate of Barry Tannenbaum, 4 May 2010, in possession of author.

28 Hopolang Selebalo, 'Let the investor beware: Lessons from Tannenbaum', Institute for Security Studies, 25 June 2009.

CHAPTER 15

1 Author's interviews with Howard and Norman Lowenthal.

2 Rob Rose, 'Court bid could frustrate liquidation of PSC fund', *Business Day*, 24 March 2003.

3 Rob Rose, 'Tigon duo face 3 160 fraud charges', *Business Day*, 4 August 2005.

4 Vernon Wessels, 'PSC fugitive Jack Milne breaks his silence', *Business Report*, 29 April 2003.

5 Rob Rose, 'Fury as Jack Milne packs for Christmas at home', *Business Day*, 13 December 2004.

6 Author's interview with Howard Lowenthal, January 2013.

7 Author's interview with David Shapiro.

8 David Smith, 'The Rand Club – where colonial fantasists are welcome', *Guardian*, 18 November 2010 (http://www .theguardian.com/world/2010/nov/18/ rand-club-johannesburg), accessed July 2013.

9 Sam Sole and Sally Evans, 'Enver Motala seeks absolution', *Mail & Guardian*, 2 March 2012 (http://mg.co.za/article/2012-03-02 -motala-seeks-absolution), accessed June 2013.

10 Ibid.

11 Author's interview with Stephen Harcourt-Cooke.

12 Renee Bonorchis, 'Tannenbaum-linked charitable donations may have to be returned', *Bloomberg News*, 26 August 2009 (http://www.bloomberg.com/apps/news?pid =newsarchive&sid=axD02jUZDxeg), accessed June 2013.

13 Ibid.

14 Details taken from websites: www. firechildren.org and www. joburgblindschool.org, accessed June 2013.

15 Ibid.

16 Renee Bonorchis, 'Tannenbaum-linked charitable donations may have to be returned'.

17 From www.joburgblindschool.org, accessed June 2013.

18 Author's interview with Howard Lowenthal, January 2013.

19 Alec Brooks, 'Response to questions for Brooks Brand' from author, 3 September 2013.

20 Author's interview with Howard Lowenthal.

21 *Gainsford et al representing estate of Barry Tannenbaum v Incentive Corporate Finance*, South Gauteng High Court, case no. 22571/10.

22 *Gainsford et al representing estate of Barry Tannenbaum v Jody Bloch*, South Gauteng High Court, case no. 46204/2010.

23 *Gainsford et al representing estate of Barry Tannenbaum v Leslie Sher*, South Gauteng High Court, case no. 48287/2010.

24 Author's interview with Mark Read.

25 Taken from KPMG's website (http://www .kpmg.com/ZA/en/about/ValuesCulture/ OurValues/Pages/default.aspx), accessed July 2013.

26 Author's interview with Tom Lawless.

27 Author's telephonic discussion with James Galloway.

28 David Gleason, 'Tannenbaum confusion deepens', *Business Day*, 10 August 2011 (http://www.bdlive.co.za/articles/2011/08/ 10/david-gleason-tannenbaum-confusion -deepens), accessed June 2013.

29 Carl Ballot, KPMG head of communications, email to author 'Questions for KPMG', 5 September 2013.

30 Carl Ballot, KPMG head of communications, email to author, 'Questions for KPMG', 6 September 2013.

31 'Pamodzi liquidators fired as safeguard', SA Press Association, 24 May 2011 (http:// www.thepost.co.za/pamodzi-liquidators -fired-as-safeguard-1.1073127#.Ug -fwmbg46U), accessed June 2013.

32 Ibid.

33 Carl Ballot, KPMG head of communications, email to author, 'Questions for KPMG', 6 September 2013.

34 Loyiso Sidimba, 'In search of the Bafokeng's lost millions', *Sunday Independent*, 5 May 2013.

35 Shirish Kalian, personal communication, 5 September 2013.

36 Molibinyane Makwakwa, SARS team leader, letter to investors dated 9 December 2009, in possession of author.

37 Elle-Sarah Rossato, SARS manager, 'Finalisation of audit letter' to Tannenbaum investor, 12 December 2012, in possession of author.

38 Carol Paton, 'Treasury assures on South Africa's welfare bubble', *Business Day*, 2 July 2013.

39 Author's interview with SARS head of inspections, Johann van Loggerenberg.

40 Ibid.

41 Chantelle Benjamin, 'Tycoon Dave King's R2.3 billion tax bill has finally landed him in court', *Sunday Times*, 1 May 2005.

42 Jana Marais, 'Why King agreed to pay R718 million for a new start', *Business Times*, 1 September 2013.

43 Author's interview with Johann van Loggerenberg.

INVESTOR PROFILE: JAWMEND ROSSI

1 Court documents in case of *Gainsford et al vs Jawmend Rossi*.

2 *Gainsford et al v Jawmend Rossi*, 'Defendants' plea as amended', South Gauteng High Court, case no. 27543/10, 25 March 2013.

3 *Gainsford et al v Jawmend Rossi*, 'Defendants' response to the plaintiff's request for further particulars', South Gauteng High Court, case no. 27543/10.

4 *Gainsford et al v Jawmend Rossi*, 'Plaintiff's reply to defendants', South Gauteng High Court, case no. 27543/10, 19 April 2013.

5 Judge Mathopo judgment in *Gainsford, Kalian, Matsepe v Jawmend Rossi Capital*, South Gauteng High Court, 12 February 2013.

CHAPTER 16

1 Jeanette Clark, 'R1.46bn proposed fine for construction industry', *Moneyweb*, 24 June 2013.

2 Lionel Faull and Sam Sole, 'Shock and ore: Dirt flies in Sishen battle', *Mail & Guardian*, 10 February 2012.

3 Rob Rose and Stephan Hoftstatter, 'NPA acts against top prosecutor', *Sunday Times*, 5 February 2012.

4 *Democratic Alliance v President of the Republic of South Africa*, Supreme Court of Appeal case no. 263/11, 1 December 2011 (http://www.saflii.org/za/cases/ZASCA/2011/ 241.html), accessed 21 August 2013.

5 Nelly Shamase, 'Fall from grace does not harm Jiba's climb in NPA', *Mail & Guardian*, 6 January 2012 (http://

amabhungane.co.za/article/2012-01-06-fall
-from-grace-does-not-harm-jibas-climb-in
-npa), accessed June 2013.

6   Charl du Plessis, 'NPA court action a
contradiction of Jiba's words – Breytenbach',
City Press, 29 May 2013 (http://www
.citypress.co.za/news/npa-court-action-a
-contradiction-of-jibas-word-
breytenbach/), accessed June 2013.

7   Zelda Venter, 'The men accused of sinking
Saambou', *Saturday Star*, 2 February 2008
(http://www.iol.co.za/news/south-africa/the
-men-accused-of-sinking-saambou
-1.387846#.Ui2b-Y0yYUM), accessed
July 2013.

8   Felicity Duncan, 'Saambou case thrown
out', *Moneyweb*, 7 May 2008 (http://www
.moneyweb.co.za/moneyweb-special-
investigations/saambou-case-thrown-out),
accessed July 2013.

9   Ibid.

10 'No jail time for Brown', *The Post*, 16 May
2013 (http://www.thepost.co.za/no-jail-time
-for-brown-1.1516809#.Ui2kpI0yYUM),
accessed May 2013.

11 Ibid.

12 Sasha Planting, 'Judge says state
mismanaged Fidentia case', *Moneyweb*,
6 May 2013 (http://www.moneyweb.co.za/
moneyweb-special-investigations/judge
-says-state-mismanaged-fidentia-case),
accessed May 2013.

13 Author's interview with Keith van der Spuy.

14 Author's interview with John Storey.

15 Draft document, 'Letter of Request for
Legal Assistance', 1 December 2011,
unsigned document given to author by
anonymous sources close to the
investigation.

16 Charl du Plessis, 'Single case for
Breytenbach since return to NPA, Labour
Court told', *City Press*, 2 June 2013 (http://
www.citypress.co.za/politics/single-case
-for-breytenbach-since-return-to-npa
-labour-court-told/), accessed June 2013.

CHAPTER 17

1   Deborah Tannenbaum, testimony to
Federal Court of Australia, Queensland
registry, 10 October 2012, transcript in
possession of author.

2   Nick O'Malley and Leesha McKenny, 'Run

to Paradise', *Sydney Morning Herald*,
29 January 2010 (http://www.smh.com.au/
national/the-diary/real-drama-is-on
-centre-court-20100128-n1sj.html),
accessed June 2013

3   Larry Schlesinger, 'What's happened to
alleged Ponzi scheme mastermind and
resident of Runaway Bay, Barry
Tannenbaum?', Freshly Worded, 24 June
2013 (https://freshlyworded.wordpress.com/
2013/06/24/whats-happened-to-alleged
-ponzi-scheme-mastermind-and-resident
-of-runaway-bay-barry-tannenbaum/),
accessed 25 July 2013.

4   From http://queenslandplaces.com.au/
node/740, accessed 25 July 2013.

5   Ibid.

6   Fiona Cameron, 'Grocon building
$850 million Gold Coast high rise', *The
Australian*, 22 March 2007 (http://www
.theaustralian.com.au/archive/business
-old/grocon-building-850m-gold-coast
-high-rise/story-e6frg9gx-1111113198970?from
=public_rss), accessed July 2013.

7   Deborah Tannenbaum, testimony to
Federal Court of Australia, Queensland
registry, 10 October 2012, transcript in
possession of author.

8   Ibid.

9   From www.allisee.net.au, accessed
August 2013.

10 Purchase agreement, 'purchase of lot
672/88 Royal Albert Crescent, Paradise
Point Queensland' from Deborah
Tannenbaum, in possession of author.

11 Deborah Tannenbaum, testimony to
Federal Court of Australia, Queensland
registry, 10 October 2012, transcript in
possession of author.

12 Judge J. Logan, judgment in the case of
*Gainsford, in the matter of Tannenbaum,
v Tannenbaum*, in the Federal Court of
Australia, Queensland district registry,
case no. 216/2012.

13 Draft document, 'Letter of Request for
Legal Assistance'.

14 Bartan Group, balance sheet as of June
2009, in possession of author.

15 Anneli Knight, 'MYOB founder's latest
venture no dinosaur', *Sydney Morning
Herald*, 17 December 2007 (http://www
.smh.com.au/small-business/myob

-founders-latest-venture-no-dinosaur-20090619-cq2m.html), accessed April 2013.

16 'Report as to affairs' of Bartan Group, filed to Australian Securities and Investments Commission by Trevor Pogroske, 6 April 2010, in possession of author.

17 'Schedule to practice note', form 564, on Bartan Group, compiled by Trevor Pogroske, 20 April 2010, in possession of author.

18 Ibid.

19 Email, Philip Stern, acting for Trevor Pogroske, to Alec Brooks, 1 September 2010, in possession of author.

20 Letter in possession of author, Derek Ziman to KGA Lawyers/Fragomen, attn: Ron Kessels, 14 September 2009.

21 Letter, Derek Ziman to Anthony Bellanto, in possession of author.

22 United Nations Office on Drugs and Crime, homicide statistics 2013 (http://www .unodc.org/unodc/en/data-and-analysis/ homicide.html), accessed July 2013.

23 Judge J. Logan, judgment in the case of *Gainsford, in the matter of Tannenbaum v Tannenbaum*, in the Federal Court of Australia, Queensland district registry, case no. 216/2012.

24 Author's interview with Derek Ziman, August 2013.

25 Author's interview with Hylton Tannenbaum.

26 Kenneth Freeling, affidavit submitted in United Kingdom High Court of Justice, Queen's Bench Division, case *Barwa Real Estate v Rees*, 847/2009.

27 Schedule prepared by Dean Rees for UK Justice Andrew Smith, 22 June 2009, in possession of author.

28 Dean Rees, affidavit submitted in United Kingdom High Court of Justice, Queen's Bench Division, case *Barwa Real Estate v Rees*, 847/2009.

29 'Settlement agreement' between Darryl Leigh and Gainsford, Kalian and Matsepe, made an order by the South Gauteng High Court on 17 August 2010, case no 27544/10, in possession of author.

30 Sharon Haarhoff, record of testimony to inquiry of estate of Barry Tannenbaum, 30 June 2010, in possession of author.

31 Author's interview with Sharon Haarhoff, September 2013.

32 Author's interview with Derek Ziman, August 2013.

33 'Factual findings report on the scheme conducted by Barry Tannenbaum and his assets and liabilities during the period 1 March 2004 to 5 June 2009', Stephen Harcourt-Cooke of Computer Forensic Services, in possession of author.

CHAPTER 18

1 Barry Tannenbaum, testimony to Federal Court of Australia, Queensland registry, 10 October 2012, transcript in possession of author.

2 Debbie Tannenbaum, testimony to Federal Court of Australia, Queensland registry, 10 October 2012, transcript in possession of author.

3 Eighty20 gambling report, http://www .eighty20.co.za/blog/2013/06/, accessed June 2013.

4 These, and the following bank records, are taken from bank statements from First National Bank, Standard Bank, Diners Club and other statements in the author's possession.

5 Barry Tannenbaum bank accounts, in possession of author.

6 Steve Fishman, 'The Madoff tapes', *New York* magazine, 27 February 2011 (http://nymag .com/news/features/berniemadoff-2011-3/), accessed February 2013.

7 Ibid.

8 Ibid.

9 Detlev Krige, 'Fong Kong finance', paper prepared for the London School of Economics, in possession of author.

Index